ONTEMPORARY LITERATURE
F THE WESTERN WORLD

VOLUME 4

RECENT AMERICAN LITERATURE

FTER 1930 BY DONALD HEINEY AND LENTHIEL H. DOWNS

companion to the literature of post-Depression America. Commentaries are cluded on the major works of each poet, novelist, and dramatist.

ward Albee
xwell Anderson
nes Baldwin
N. Behrman
ul Bellow
arl Buck
skine Caldwell
uman Capote
E. Cummings
S. Eliot
lph Ellison
mes T. Farrell
lliam Faulkner
Ernest Gaines
Lorraine Hansberry
Lillian Hellman
Ernest Hemingway
Langston Hughes
James Jones
Sidney Kingsley
Robert Lowell
Archibald MacLeish
Norman Mailer
Bernard Malamud
John P. Marquand
Carson McCullers
Arthur Miller
Henry Miller
Marianne Moore
Flannery O'Connor
Clifford Odets
John O'Hara
Elliot Paul
Ezra Pound
Theodore Roethke
J. D. Salinger
William Saroyan
Irwin Shaw
Robert Sherwood
Gertrude Stein
John Steinbeck
Wallace Stevens
William Styron
Robert Penn Warren
Eudora Welty
Nathanael West
Thornton Wilder
Tennessee Williams
William Carlos Williams
Thomas Wolfe
Herman Wouk
Richard Wright

RRON'S EDUCATIONAL SERIES, INC. $3.95

ESSENTIALS OF CONTEMPORARY LITERATURE OF THE WESTERN WORLD

VOLUME 4

Recent American Literature after 1930

BY

DONALD HEINEY
Professor of Comparative Literature
University of California, Irvine, California

LENTHIEL H. DOWNS
Professor of English
Denison University, Granville, Ohio

BARRON'S EDUCATIONAL SERIES, INC.
Woodbury, New York

All inquiries should be addressed to:
Barron's Educational Series, Inc.
113 Crossways Park Drive
Woodbury, New York 11797

Library of Congress Catalog Card No. 73-75772

Paper Edition
International Standard Book No. 0-8120-0450-7

PRINTED IN THE UNITED STATES OF AMERICA

TABLE OF CONTENTS

FOREWORD

The literature of the western world during the past hundred years has been remarkable for a number of reasons: its profusion, its diversity, its exciting experimentation, its successes and failures. Spengler may have been right in his prediction of the decline of the west, but literary creativity has burgeoned rather than declined since his thesis was enunciated some fifty years ago. Of course the profession has not all been good. Printing presses have worked overtime, and we may be in danger from the inundation of the mediocre and the banal, even of the trash which threatens cultural pollution. It has been estimated that an average of ten novels are published each day in the United States and Europe, and the figure is probably still on the rise. Now more than ever a guide is useful to keep head above paper. Prior to 1870 literature pretty much winnowed itself; it had to be reasonably good to be worth printing in the first place and time took care of whatever sneaked through on false merits. But the cries for relevance and the modern and technological progress have complicated our world. We cannot afford to let time do the job alone, because there are hidden voices that can speak to our condition now and we do not have that much time for waiting.

One of the most interesting facets of modern literature is the interrelatedness of its practitioners. It is impractical and too narrowly provincial to study English writers or American writers or French writers in isolation. It is even impossible. What do you do with a man like Samuel Beckett, ostensibly an Irishman for most of his life, who writes his most important works in French for the absurdist theatre in Paris and then translates them into English? Or Vladimir Nabokov, who might be claimed by Russian, English, German, French, or American literatures? (*Lolita* seems clearly American, if Humbert and Nabokov do not.) Or any of a dozen others?

Nationality just isn't that important any more. Movements cross borders without passport or visa: realism, naturalism, expressionism, Theatre of the Absurd—all of them. Therefore cross reference is a necessity, lest doors be closed rather than opened. Yet in these fluid times, when generic, historic, and national lines dissolve so easily, we must set up tentative boundaries even as we invite their crossing. Continental Europe, Britain, and America are recognizable in large outline as the areas of the Western World which have contributed most to the literature of our times, and with the sometimes admittedly arbitrary forcing of bedfellows we shall look at them in that order. The addition of new material to the first editions of *Contemporary Literature* and *Recent American Literature* has made advisable a reorganization into the following volumes: I, Continental European; II, British; III, Recent American (to 1930); IV, Recent American (post 1930). For a fuller understanding of movements, ideas, and innovative techniques, the reader of one volume is invited to refer to the others.

Although again somewhat arbitrarily, the discussion of contemporary criticism is reserved for the end of Volume III and Volume IV, not because there are no European or British critics but because literary criticism in our time has become rather surprisingly something of an American-Canadian industrial complex, with transatlantic voices as somewhat adjunct even when innovative. The big business of criticism, with its journals, Modern Language and College English Associations and Institutes, has carved out its empire even if it has not yet created a monopoly.

INTRODUCTION I

1. Approach to the Thirties

Literary periods are slippery concepts. When dates are established and cultural developments are outlined, predecessors and successors have a way of making them dissolve. One discovers that the Romantic Period in English literature so comfortably introduced as extending from 1800 to 1830 has a long Pre-Romantic development and that it really isn't over yet. The same thing is true of American literary history, perhaps more so. But if there is one date that seems to make a decisive cut in the continuity of twentieth century America, it is probably the stock market crash at the end of October 1929. By 1930 reassessment was forced on the American consciousness.

The Twenties have a character of their own, an individualized and particularized decade for which there has come to be felt considerable nostalgia among the older generation. Clear memories can hardly regard these years as the good old days (this was the era of prohibition and gangsters), but one of the blessings of the human condition is the tendency to forget unpleasantness and remember what one chooses to remember. Perhaps even the Sixties will become a happy recollection in the twenty-first century.

Three major designations arose in the Twenties to define the Twenties as a cultural phenomenon: the Jazz Age, the Lost Generation, and the Wasteland—all with significant literary associations. Of them all the Jazz Age, as represented best in F. Scott Fitzgerald's fiction, was most clearly cut off by the stock market collapse and the ensuing depression. It is the period of the Twenties alone. But the Lost Generation (as proclaimed in the double epigraph from *Ecclesiastes* and Gertrude Stein in the 1926 *The Sun Also Rises*—"You are all a lost generation."—Gertrude Stein in conversation) continued to be lost in the Thirties. The uprootedness and disillusionment of the post World War I fiction writers, many of whom had participated in that war and perhaps particularly of the Paris expatriate group including Hemingway, Elliot Paul, Henry Miller, and others, pursued them into the depression and beyond. The third term, the Wasteland, established by T. S. Eliot in his 1922 poem, had perhaps an even longer life; it has come to represent an age extending from the Twenties to 1945 and may indeed suggest the central features of the landscape of this larger period. The Wasteland poets, including Ezra Pound, Eliot himself, and possibly William Carlos Williams, Archibald MacLeish, and E. E. Cummings, although many of them had written distinctive poetry even before 1920 and certainly before 1930, continued to develop and sharpen both their verse and their ideas into the Thirties and Forties. The Wasteland runs into and disappears in the Age of Anxiety.

This is one reason for the inclusion of such American writers as Gertrude Stein, Ezra Pound, T. S. Eliot, Williams, Cummings, and Hemingway in the post-1930 volume rather than in the pre-1930 one. They had all certainly made a mark in the literary world before 1930, but they were ahead of their time and made a larger and deeper mark after that date. This is true even for Gertrude Stein who had only sixteen more years to live and who had begun her serious writing in the first decade of the twentieth century with *Things as They Are* (originally *Quod Erat Demonstrandum*) and *Three Lives* (1909). *Tender Buttons,* among her stylistically most radical work, appeared in 1914, and even *Four Saints in Three Acts* had been written and published in *transition* by 1929. But although she had been read and sought out by other writers like Sherwood Anderson and Hemingway, her initial impact on the public, even the most literate portion of it, probably did not come until the Thirties (and production of the Stein-Virgil Thomson opera, *Four Saints in Three Acts*) when people began to make fun of "A rose is a rose is a rose is a rose is" (often misquoting the lovely verse from *The World Is Round,* a book for children) and the phrase from *Four Saints,* "Pigeons on the grass, alas." Gertrude Stein was always avant-garde and probably still is. Although T. S. Eliot became the most important single literary influence on Hart Crane whose major creative period was over by 1930, again his greatest impact on a more general public had hardly begun. That half or third of his creative effort in verse drama did not get under way until the mid-Thirties.

It is in this fashion that American literature approaches the period which begins in 1930, trailing clouds of several impulses—some would say glory—as it comes. Realism and naturalism are by this time established as dominant modes, but the anti-realistic frames of reference like expressionism, surrealism, psychology, and religious ideology are also operative.

2. The Periods

Although the past half century is too close to us and too short a time to be broken up into neat chronological eras, each distinct in its literary character, and generic organization suggests itself as more practical, some things may be said about changing social environment and the temper of the times which increasingly, it seems, affect the character of the arts and literature in particular. Part of this is the cry for relevance and part, perhaps, the growing social conscience or at least consciousness of the writers involved.

From 1930 until 1945 the literature of the United States followed its bent in what might be called the Wasteland of the Depression Era. It almost coincides with the New Deal of Franklin Delano Roosevelt and, of course, merges into the new economic prosperity of the World War II years with scarcely a ripple. The magnitude of social changes during this period with a swing toward liberalism or radical socialism (depending on your political views) is still being evaluated and is quite remarkable for a generally conservative America. The year 1933, following Roosevelt's inauguration ("We have nothing to fear but fear itself."), brought about an end to prohibition (the beer trucks began to roll that fall); Joyce's *Ulysses* was finally admitted by the courts into the United States in Judge John M. Woolsey's memorable decision; and social programs were planned and initiated which stirred ardent support and violent antagonism. It is hard now to realize what the inception of the social security program elicited as response. The accusation of the drift toward the welfare state was among the mildest of the terms employed. (Yet even Republicans seem to be for it now, especially as they approach the age of sixty-five.)

But a new hope seemed to arise in the midst of our adversity (as if such reverses were good for us). Novelists responded in various ways to the need for reassessment of our values. Steinbeck perhaps most obviously supported the New Deal as a consistent independent liberal. *The Grapes of Wrath* (1939) is the most vivid of his fictional presentations of social problems—in this case the plight of migrant workers (which problem, as we can see on TV, has pursued us into the Seventies). He steered a course between communism and the American brand of laissez-faire capitalism which earned him the attacks of both sides. The poet E. E. Cummings followed quite independently a similar course, condemning both capitalism ("Poem, Or Beauty Hurts Mr. Vinal") and communism (*Eimi*) and opting for an independent individualism of the common man. Faulkner turned his attention to the moral problems of the American (not just Southern) way of life, becoming increasingly critical of mechanization and exploitation and ethical naiveté as destroying man's relationship to man and to nature. Hemingway, who came to the support of the lost cause against Spanish fascism in *For Whom the Bell Tolls* (1940), continued to uphold ritual and the rules of the game as a source of man's minimal salvation.

Some dramatists joined for a time the Works Progress Administration (better known as W. P. A.) sponsored Federal Theatre and its Living Newspaper experiments of the Thirties with such productions as *Triple-A Plowed Under* or *One Third of a Nation* (about housing problems, again an issue which is not without current relevance). Others associated themselves in various ways with political liberalism: Maxwell Anderson concerned with the Sacco-Vanzetti case, particularly in the successful *Winterset* (1935); Robert Sherwood (*The Petrified Forest,* 1934 and *Abe Lincoln in Illinois,* 1938), who became active in New Deal politics and wrote some of FDR's best speeches; Clifford Odets, who had been a Communist Party member briefly in 1934 and wrote the partisan proletarian drama, *Waiting for Lefty* (1935), but who resigned when pressured to write only propaganda. A number of American writers with leftist sympathies abandoned the cause when faced with disillusionment over Russia's accommodation with Nazi Germany in the dismemberment of Poland. Some, like Dos Passos, even turned to the right politically, anticipating the later about-face of such European writers as André Malraux and Ignazio Silone.

American poetry in this period divided itself, leaving out the comfortable middle, into those who went along with the liberal Cummings in his criticism of American society, like Archibald MacLeish in *Frescoes for Mr. Rockefeller's City* (1933), who later became Librarian of Congress under the New Deal, and those who withdrew to religious and conservative positions like T. S. Eliot in England who moved through *Ash Wednesday* (1930) and *Murder in the Cathedral* (1935) to *Four Quartets* (1943). Pound in Italy became even more rightist without becoming religious and even more corrosive in his attacks on American capitalism than any of the leftist sympathizers. This was a vigorous period, alive to social issues and existential choices, and was over before it could realize its end shortly after the dropping of the atomic bombs in 1945.

It was W. H. Auden, the British poet who spent most of the war years in America, who gave the most often used name to the following fifteen years (1945–1960). *The Age of Anxiety* (a Baroque Eclogue—see Volume II) was published in 1947, its setting a New York City bar where four characters come together in a chance meeting during the Second World War. Their hang-ups, their neuroses, their existential anxieties, become the focus of the worries of the post World War II world (dreaming on World War III).

This war, in spite of general prosperity, did not lead into a Jazz Age (even Rock music, in some ways a derivative of jazz, produced quite different effects). The American public did not enter the war in 1941 with the same naive idealism they had shown in 1917, and as a result they were less affected by a post-war disillusionment. They were affected eventually, however, by post-war fears, by living with the threat of the bomb after it became generally available, by scientific "progress" which soon made the atom bomb the H-bomb and annihilation a daily possibility. There was also an almost imperceptible sliding into the Korean War or Police Action, which made peace time curiously resemble the war years. In America, however, there was a political swing to the right, from McCarthyism (U.S. Senator 1946–57—Joe, not Eugene) and anti-intellectualism which swept the nation during his career to the victory of moderate Republicanism under Eisenhower. The growth of the military-industrial complex against which President Eisenhower issued his warnings at the close of his administration in 1960 assured economic prosperity at the cost of some of our previous social gains and freedoms.

Literature experienced something of a closing-in, a withdrawal, during this period. Of course writers of the stature of Faulkner and Hemingway and T. S. Eliot (happily expatriated in England) continued to produce major work and developed what came to be seen as a mythological symbolism in their total structure. All three were awarded the Nobel prize for literature during this time. But the younger generation for the most part were content to imitate the past. In fiction and poetry both, the age of technical innovation was over; only in drama did new things get tried like the "memory" play of Tennessee Williams and new combinations of realism and expressionism in his plays and those of Arthur Miller. (Albee comes late in the Fifties, to be sure, but seems to belong to the next age.) Wallace Stevens emerged to a place of honor during these years, but he had been writing his poetry steadily since 1916 and only put the capstone on his career in this period. Eudora Welty was almost the only fiction writer to develop an original and distinctive style between 1945 and 1960 and to arrive at major stature.

There was a certain imitative quality, a technical sterility, to the age as a whole; it seemed that all the new things had been invented, and the new generation of writers was forced to turn somewhat monotonously to rewriting the books, poems, and plays of the Twenties. Here and there a Tennessee Williams or a Eudora Welty showed genuine originality, but in general the post-1945 period was a time of assimilation and synthesis. American writers, having discovered their true national idiom in an earlier time, now set about perfecting and refining the literary techniques invented by the generations before them.

Whether or not the decade of the "Shattering Sixties" will extend itself to the fifteen-year limit in 1975 cannot yet be known, but there is some probability of such a period and the adjective does not now seem too strong. An era of moderate Democratic leadership following moderate Republicanism was begun with the election of John F. Kennedy (men of letters were honored in his decision to have Robert Frost participate in the inaugural ceremony—see Volume III); although problems were not minimized and attention was directed at winning the race to the moon by 1970, the nation nevertheless staggered under the Cuban crises and internal social and racial unrest. The formation of the Peace Corps was hailed by some as a positive step forward, and civil rights legislation of a new order was initiated. But the American image and soul received their most shattering blows with the triple assassinations of President Kennedy in November 1963 and Martin Luther King in April 1968 and Senator Robert Kennedy in June 1968. In spite of investigations and reports, clouds of doubt and distrust still hang over many American minds concerning forces behind the assassinations.

The widely acclaimed "return to religion" of the previous decade melted in the sixties except for the revivalist manifestations of certain groups, including what are now called "Jesus freaks." Drugs and Zen Buddhism and gurus seem to be taking over the scene, displacing to some degree more traditional American religion. Institutional Christianity—even the Roman Catholic establishment—has been repeatedly subjected to seismic shocks. The advent of such rock musicals as *Jesus Christ—Superstar* and other treatments like *Godspell* in 1971 may confuse rather than clarify this issue. But optimists see the basic idealism of American youth reemerging in love and "flower power" as they do their own thing.

Americans had criticized as immoral two wars before the nineteen-sixties: the Mexican War of the 1840's and the Spanish-American War of 1898, but at least they were "declared" wars. The American involvement in Vietnam and southeast Asia has eaten away at the moral fiber of the American people for more than a decade. It has also engulfed our economy with spiraling, almost runaway, inflation; we are apparently spending ourselves bankrupt as the Communists once predicted and hoped. The attempt to make the war in Vietnam a crusade against communism never really worked; Mr. McIntyre's voice seems tired and attenuated and nobody listens. The extent of drug addiction in the American armed forces in Asia is beginning to frighten everyone, including the army. The deterioration of law, order, and morals that Shakespeare viewed in *Troilus and Cressida* as a result of the Greek-Trojan conflict where neither side could find a good reason for fighting (Helen wasn't worth it) has become our own. Whatever one's position—and the Sixties have polarized America into two divisive factions with more bitterness against each other than ever before—the shame and loss of face of the assassinations and the Vietnam "war" have deeply disturbed the American conscience and consciousness. Everyone campaigned in the 1968 elections to end the war in Vietnam. For a time President Nixon's Vietnamization and timed withdrawal seemed to offer a way out. But time drags on and in 1971 so did the war. "Bring us together" appears ironic in retrospect. The aftermath of the war is likely to run on some years after its official end, the war that had no official beginning.

It has seemed to many in 1973 that the phrase "Peace with Honor" is somewhat inconsistent at the conclusion of a war that was never honorable enough to warrant a declaration. But the use of language in a political context may have become progressively debased since George Orwell's essay on "Politics and the English Language" first appeared in 1946 and called attention to it. Even conservative critics have referred to the Vietnam conflict as the Oriental torture of the thousand cuts. The wounds, economic, social, and moral, may require a long time for healing. The division over the amnesty question is one example of it. How Americans can ever again refer to Oriental face-saving presents a strange problem and could require totally new and devious dexterities. But the peace is a kind of victory, and should perhaps be celebrated very quietly, almost silently, thankfully, prayerfully. The most significant and hopeful American development of the early Seventies may be seen in the approach to working arrangements with (de facto recognition of and possible peaceful coexistence with) the very large part of the world represented by Communist China and the Soviet Union. This could become the most positive forward step of the Nixon era.

Other major problems have emerged in the Sixties. The confidence gap between the people and the government (which has come to be seen as Establishment) is probably greater than ever. Suddenly in terms of ecology, the Wasteland that Eliot had visualized as metaphor in 1922 is literally all around us, filled with garbage, bad water, and bad air; there seems to be little choice, either clean it up or die. Our cities have deteriorated at an alarming rate: urban renewal is imperative. Overpopulation may present a similar crisis. Campus riots and drug use; social, economic, and judicial inequalities (the depressed poor, white, black, and red, rising in protest); systems that must change in order to cope—for all these, solutions must be found. To minimize the shocks and turmoil of this period of American life is to stick one's head in the sand. To underestimate the resilience, idealism, and energies of the American people addressing themselves to their real problems would be equally foolish.

Literature in this period has responded in an often chaotic way to the new situation. Protest singers have engrafted their lyrics based on current issues from Vietnam to black power to ecology onto folk music or pseudo-folk music with electric guitar and microphone, sometimes with great success, particularly in terms of record sales. There may be a new folk poetry of street and bar; it has already influenced many of the younger of our young poets, Ferlinghetti for instance. Concrete poetry, which is sometimes discussed, seems more concrete than poetry and headed for a dead end. In fiction the new life-style of the road made some literary sense in Jack Kerouac (1922–69), the best of his group with such books of the late Fifties as *On the Road, The Dharma Bums,* and *Dr. Sax,* finally being reprinted in the early Seventies. Kerouac, his close friend Allen Ginsberg, and their followers have come to be known as the "beat" generation, an invention by Kerouac, instead of the earlier Lost Generation and loosely corresponding to the British group of Angry Young Men; but they have not yet produced the indubitable classics of the other two and with fading interest seem unlikely to do so. The word "beat" has been interpreted as "worn down" or "beatific," but the former is more easily discernible.

Black writers are writing and getting published, almost too easily now; but some have literary talents of merit. From Richard Wright and Langston Hughes to James Baldwin, Ralph Ellison, Lorraine Hansberry, and Ernest Gaines, they are making the scene. A host of Jewish fiction writers have emerged in the Fifties and achieved eminence in the Sixties, sometimes conscious or self-conscious of their racial minority but often also of the human plight. Of the best among them Bernard Malamud and Saul Bellow have made major contributions to the American novel. Ralph Ellison made a profound statement to a group of college English teachers assembled in 1970. He said that all American literature is a literature of minorities, and he meant to include Emerson, Thoreau, Poe, and Whitman as much as anybody. There is no cultural and ethnic majority, not even the WASP, silent or vocal; there is only a possible coalition of minorities.

Drama has been making some of the most interesting responses of all to the problems and turmoil of the new era (off off Broadway, for instance), from the absurdist-based theatre of Edward Albee and the newly dramatic problem plays of Lorraine Hansberry to the sharpened satire of Jean-Claude Van Itallie in *America Hurrah!* and Sam Shepard. A view of where we are involves a view of where we are going, and more will be offered in the section on Preview. At this point it might suffice to call attention to Charles A. Reich's book, *The Greening of America* (1970), which deals precisely with the sum of the problems of American society in the Sixties but sees hopeful answers in the attitudes and life-style of the young (most of them Yale students for his examples). It has been called everything from pure applesauce, simplistic, misleading, presumptuous to challenging, provocative, and a first-rate piece of creative thinking. The truth probably lies midway, but hope does spring eternal not only in the American dream but in the American nightmare as well. Is it too much to believe that this new period of adversity will call forth literary responses of the quality of the Thirties? One thing seems certain. To be ultimately persuasive the new literature will have to be "written" rather than thrown together. George Steiner has pointed out the "inescapable monotony of pornographic writing," and much recently published material has either leaned in this direction or fallen backward in it. Nor have uncritical reviewers been lacking to praise it. Literary chaos must be ordered in some fashion before it can compel assent.

3. Review and the Problems

In reviewing the literature of our times, particularly of the past decade, one is faced with major problems of selection and evaluation. Never has so much issued from the presses, an inundation of material of which probably ninety percent is of ephemeral interest at best. We are threatened with cultural pollution from the mediocre, the banal, and just plain trash, as much as we are by air and water pollution. The arts certainly need to reflect contemporary society and events, but they must not expect to take the place of newscasts. The release of the Lieutenant Calley song in a country-western recording right after the trial publicity is an excellent example of trash making money on timing. Occasional literature used to be literary or at least literate; now it's most often just occasional. Some aesthetic distance is essential.

"Happenings" in the theatre are mostly so improvisational and multi-media as to lack any form of permanence of art. The Living Theatre of Julian Beck and Judith Malina, for instance, which started off in the Fifties with some reasonably interesting productions of old plays and even made something of Jack Gelber's *The Connection* in 1959 and Kenneth H. Brown's *The Brig* in 1963, has degenerated into what may be living (loosely defined) but is hardly theatre. Form and order enclosing some content must be there for definition and for evaluation.

Black literature must be given some consideration but not special consideration. In these days when almost every anthology is being reedited to include black literature, the pendulum has swung pretty far to include the most, presumably to balance earlier neglect. Objectivity and immunity to criticism are impossible to attain, but to be condescending is not likely to be helpful. There is as much trash being published by black writers as by white writers in proportionate numbers. It should be obvious that a poem, a novel, a play is not good because it has been written by a black, nor is it bad for that reason. One must attempt to let it stand beside other works in its genre and take its chances in a critical wind. This results, like any middle of the road humanistic course, in equal charges of favoritism or tokenism. But charges, potential or actual, must not deter one from right action.

Another discernible literary phenomenon of the Sixties is the group of writers who have produced what is called Black Humor. This is not the humor of black writers, although it has on occasion been misunderstood that way. Basically, black humor is not all that new. It is grim, dark if not black, rather savage, satire, employing the grotesque in a completely unrealistic or fantastic picture of reality. Its shock value is strong. In 1950 André Breton (see Volume I) edited an *Anthology of Black Humor* (*l'Humour Noir*) to which he contributed a 1939 essay of explanation, "Paratonnerre," quoting Baudelaire on the disengagement of the comic from "emanation, explosion." Black humor, he tells us, is delimited by many things, stupidity, skeptical irony, but above all it is the enemy of sentimentality (which always has a "blue" background) and it possesses a certain fantasy. His anthology begins with selections from Jonathan Swift and the Marquis de Sade, includes Nietzsche, Apollinaire, and Kafka. Americans have always had great trouble with satire, even Sinclair Lewis; since it depends for effect upon exaggeration, how is one to exaggerate that which in American life is already exaggerated?

Perhaps this is why Bruce Jay Friedman in his 1965 *Black Humor* anthology has such trouble with definition. He talks about the fading line between fantasy and reality in the modern world, an almost invisible line—"if you are alive today, and stick your head out of doors now and then, you know that there is a nervousness, a tempo, a near-hysterical new beat in the air, a punishing isolation and loneliness of a strange, frenzied new kind." He finds it in the prose style of Joe Heller and Gogol and Isaac Babel, too. Mr. Friedman continues, "It confirms your belief that a new, Jack Rubyesque [John F. Kennedy's murderer's murderer] chord of absurdity has been struck in the land, that there is a new mutative style of behavior afoot, one that can only be dealt with by a new, one-foot-in-the-asylum style of fiction." He calls this the surprise-proof generation. What could possibly surprise Americans? The role of the satirist has been usurped by the news media. "The novelist-satirist, with no real territory of his own to roam, has had to discover new land, invent a new currency, a new set of filters, has had to sail into darker waters somewhere out beyond satire and I think this is what is meant by black humor."

Among the fourteen writers included in Friedman's anthology are Louis Ferdinand Céline (*Journey to the End of Night*, originally *Voyage au bout de la nuit*, 1932), one of the most interesting of twentieth century French black humorists, Vladimir Nabokov (see Volume I), Thomas Pynchon, Joseph Heller, Edward Albee, and John Barth (*The Sot-Weed Factor*, 1960). The most striking and unexplained omission among American novelists is Kurt Vonnegut.

At the center of this group of American black humorists appear Joseph Heller with *Catch-22* (1961) and Kurt Vonnegut, Jr., somewhat too prolific with a series of novels including *Mother Night* (1961), *Cat's Cradle* (1963), and *God Bless You, Mr. Rosewater* (1965). Besides the grotesque, heavy satire, and sensationalism of such fiction is a tendency to incorporate "science fiction" into the satiric genre. But in comparative terms Lawrence Durrell (see Volume II) seems to do this kind of thing much better in *Tunc* and *Nunquam*. *Catch-22* is probably easier to see in the film release of 1970 than it is to read, all the way through. Both Heller and Vonnegut, the best of their kind, may be seen as too diffuse and ultimately rather tiresome. But they have been much in vogue with the young. Benjamin DeMott in a 1971 review of Vonnegut's work refers to this enthusiasm as the appeal to "Youthcult," a neat neologism. And the genre, if it may be called that, of black humor fiction has a great potential for the future writer who can use the rapier of a Swift instead of wielding the machete of Heller and Vonnegut, who can find the compression and precision as well as incision of a Voltaire's *Candide*.

The movement of the last half dozen years which has come to be known as the Counter-Culture is really not as new as it might like to think. Nor is it as much of a threat to culture itself as some of its militant spokesmen suppose. Of course there may be forces under the counter which *are* destructive and it is not recommended that the Michelangelo Pietà or the great paintings of western civilization or its architectural monuments be left unguarded (music and literature are more difficult to destroy). But coexistence and cross-fertilization between culture and sub-culture have a long history. Folk literature and sophisticated literature have always existed side by side, beast fables and folk ballads beside the courtly romance and epic. And when culture tends to become too effete, it can borrow life, strength, and vitality from the imagination of the common people. In twentieth century America, for example, we have had comic strips and later comic books as well as a native popular music. Almost never has the appreciation of jazz been inconsistent with an appreciation of Beethoven or Bach. Nobody really cares when *Don Quixote* is caricatured in a comic book version or popularized and simplified in *Man of La Mancha,* which can be admired by very good Cervantists. Free interaction is healthy and necessary for growth. Soul food may indeed join Keats' midnight snack in *The Eve of St. Agnes* or Proust's asparagus and madeleines, even if its classic statement has not yet appeared. There is no necessary antagonism between culture and counter-culture, although there appear to be squabbles and name-calling.

And so, finally, choices must be made. One question may be held to predominate: Will this writer be read twenty years from now? And twenty is only a provisional number of years, an initial weeding. The answers involve risk, but that's the name of the game. Anyone can play.

4. Preview

To borrow an analogy from Ibsen's *Hedda Gabler,* back near the beginnings of modern literature, every George Tesman who is good with scissors and paste would like on occasion to be an Eilert Lövborg and write imaginatively about the future. Leave Brabant and the Middle Ages and look at the cultural developments to come. As Eilert says, "We may not know anything about the future, but there are one or two things to be said about it, all the same."

There appears to be a shift in the making in the novel. The confessional, autobiographical novel (now sometimes referred to as "energized biography," a rather horrendous term) is still a popular form; but the non-fiction novel (see the discussion of Truman

Capote's *In Cold Blood*) and "history as novel" (distinguished presumably from the historical novel—one is referred to William Styron's *Nat Turner*) have entered the arena too. Greater attention may well be paid to such works as *The Sea Around Us* (1951), *The Edge of the Sea* (1955), and *Silent Spring* (1962) by Rachel Carson (1907–1964) and *African Genesis* (1961) by Robert Ardrey (born 1908), in which excellently written non-fiction borders on if not crosses over into the area of fantasy. Further exploration on the border between fiction and non-fiction may be expected. The new anti-novel (developed in France as the *Nouveau Roman*—see Volume I) seems unlikely to take root in America, despite some critics' trying to seize on Vladimir Nabokov by virtue of his one-time professorship and residence at Cornell University as an American.

The Theatre of the Absurd has reached its limits of reduction and there is no place to go further on that dead end, although American variations may continue to play on the theme. As a theatre colleague has remarked, what we need now is poetry and nobility in drama, and we may get them, although the hero will probably look more like Sidney Brustein than like Sir Thomas More or Thomas à Becket.

Some poetry is going to be more oral (and aural), designed to be spoken, sung, or chanted; and this bardic poetry will continue to deal with social issues and to be highly emotional. Cerebration has probably temporarily run its course in poetry. Certainly we are going to get more satire in all genres. The return of satire is welcome and overdue from *That Was the Week That Was* to Heller to Van Itallie's *America Hurrah!* and Sam Shepard and Laugh-In. This is true in spite of often gauche productions like *MacBird*. Black humor may well be refined in the theatre as well as in fiction, even in poetry, and sharpened and controlled by a master writer (perhaps someone like Günter Grass—see Volume I) yet to appear.

Irving Howe (born 1920) in "The City in Literature" (*Commentary*, May 1971) and earlier in "The Culture of Modernism" has announced the end of "modernism" in literature, although not without some equivocation. In the earlier essay he writes, "In the past hundred years we have had a special kind of literature. We call it modern and distinguish it from the merely contemporary;

for where the contemporary refers to time, the modern refers to sensibility and style. . . . Modernist literature seems now to be coming to an end." He says that the modernist is difficult, inaccessible, works with unfamiliar forms, chooses subjects that disturb and threaten the audience (little chance of that fading for some time to come), and provokes critics to such responses as "unwholesome" and "decadent." It is not the hostility of the early years but the patronage of the later ones, robbing modernism of the dignity of opposition, that threatens it. What awaits modernism is "publicity and sensation, the kind of savage parody which may indeed be the only fate worse than death."

In the later essay, which Mr. Howe also used as an address for the Ohio English Association in April 1971, after distinguishing two views of the city, one the sacred City of God coupled with the secular Aristotelian view that "Men come together in the city in order to live, they remain there in order to live the good life," the other the typically modernist view of the city as inimical, threatening, the city of Dickens, Gogol, T. S. Eliot, Bellow, Joyce, Kafka—"pesthole, madhouse, prison," he comes to his conclusion: "Modernism is no longer threatened, nor in question. Its achievements are solid and lasting, its influence incalculable." It is becoming historical like Romanticism, taking its "place in the development of Western culture," presenting itself to our ironic evaluation. Though the city remain "The pesthole and madhouse, the prison and setting of spiritual void," we can no longer be satisfied with this perception alone. Taking a cue from James Joyce, "literary modernism itself," who portrayed the city with such severity but who also surmounted its nihilism with the theme in Leopold Bloom that "casual kindness overcomes unconscionable power," we must make a radical struggle for the City of the Just—a different version of urban renewal. He quotes Lewis Mumford that "the city in its higher aspects . . . is a place designed to offer the widest facilities for significant conversation."

Without entering into the city-country opposition of allegiances and with noting only that Mr. Howe covers too much ground with some simplistic or non-existent transitions, nevertheless there is a sense in which "modernism" has run its course—not to die but to be transmuted. Another name will be found for the last hundred years, because "modern" we shall want to take with us. We have not suddenly dropped the negative, critical view, but we do not have to rely on Joyce alone for a more positive spirit, for Molly Bloom's "Yes" (see Volume II), manifested either in the rural but certainly not pastoral northeast corner of Mississippi (Eudora Welty) or in New York City itself (Saul Bellow).

Pessimism will no doubt continue to permeate our fiction as well as poetry and drama, but the American spirit now seems able to wrest affirmation out of despair. The two great novels of the 1969–70 season show this. *Losing Battles* may be the order of the day, but the lost cause is the one that doesn't tarnish. And as long as family and hope and love remain or can be reborn we may endure, to use Faulkner's term, and go on talking. The human voice persists, a truer vision, one feels, than Beckett's. And *Mr. Sammler's Planet* may be a poor, worn-out earth, repellent and nauseating at times, but like Mr. Sammler most of us will choose it rather than emigrate to the moon or the planets of outer space.

II

AMERICAN FICTION IN THE MID-TWENTIETH CENTURY (1930–1970)

5. Realists and Naturalists before and into World War II

The writers included in this section certainly represent something of a mixed bag in relation to realism and naturalism. Those who are included in Volume III, like Dreiser, Upton Sinclair, and Dos Passos, may represent American naturalism better than any similar group from this section, although not one of them goes to the extremes of Henry Miller. For a discussion of the European influences and the distinctions between realism and naturalism the reader is referred back to the previous volume.

At this point we might do well to examine the relationships between present company and the larger movements as well as interpersonal contacts. Gertrude Stein in her early writing, certainly in *Three Lives* (1909), can be identified as a realist. Of the novella from that volume called *Melanctha,* "the first long serious literary treatment of Negro life in the United States," Richard Wright went on to say in 1945, "As I read it my ears were opened for the first time to the magic of the spoken word. I began to hear the speech of my grandmother, who spoke a deep, pure Negro dialect and with whom I had lived for many years." When he read this story aloud to a group of semi-literate Negro stockyard workers in Chicago, "They understood every word. Enthralled, they slapped their thighs, howled, laughed, stomped, and interrupted me constantly to comment upon the characters." Her realism here is not only the realism of speech patterns and rhythm but also the kind of psychological realism to be found in Henry James—perhaps more accurately the kind to be found in his brother William James with whom Gertrude Stein had studied psychology while a student at Radcliffe. Her psychology then was an American kind (not Freudian), generally behavioristic with an admixture of Gestalt, "description and explanation of states of consciousness." The Baltimore world of *Three Lives* is as realistic as anything in our literature. But the Gertrude Stein of the cubistic "painting with words" is more likely to impress a reader as the most extreme anti-realism in a surrealistic vein that could be encountered. Therefore it must be noted that Miss Stein makes her impact in two quite different and often opposed literary styles.

Although Elliot Paul, after serving in France during World War I, remained there to work until 1931 joining *transition,* a journal which published such expatriate writers as Gertrude Stein, Hemingway, and James Joyce, and although usually associated with naturalism as a writer, he was among those who fastidiously avoid shocking detail. Henry Miller, on the other hand, who arrived in Europe late but spent most of the Thirties in Paris, deliberately sought out shocking detail and pushed the naturalistic flair for the sordid about as far as it could go. Marquand, after the First World War, returned home to America and wrote in the realistic tradition of Henry James and Edith Wharton with shades of satire added to his realism.

Hemingway, who may be classified either as realist or naturalist and perhaps falls somewhere between, learned more about writing from Gertrude Stein than he ever cared subsequently to admit. The opening paragraphs of *A Farewell to Arms* clearly have the Steinian mark. Hemingway, if a naturalist, is a notable exception in certain ways: not only is he devoid of scientific or sociological pretensions, but he is a highly personal writer with a careful and conscientious devotion to style (again thanks to Gertrude), an author whose main concern is to communicate the essential quality of personal experience rather than to portray a cross-section of a social milieu. It was Sherwood Anderson who had gained Hemingway an entrée to Gertrude Stein by writing a warm letter of introduction in 1921. He also sought advice on his manuscripts from Ezra Pound who was much in Paris during the Twenties.

Lastly Thomas Wolfe may be the most difficult of all the writers in the group to classify with any feeling of assurance. The mass of details and almost excessive documentation from experience suggest naturalism. But he is also certainly a regionalist, although he has more than one region. First there is the North Carolina of Asheville and Chapel Hill which fills *Look Homeward, Angel.* But he becomes equally at home and something of an urban regionalist in New York City and Brooklyn in particular in *You Can't Go Home Again.* The intense subjectivity of Wolfe and his exuberance of style make him also a romantic writer if anybody in the twentieth century is one. Trying to put writers in categories is generally frustrating and eventually unsatisfactory; it is one way, however, with such reservations of looking at them one at a time.

Gertrude Stein (1874–1946)

With the possible exception of James Joyce, Gertrude Stein has been heaped with more accusations of charlatanry than any other modern author; Sinclair Lewis openly accused her of "conducting a racket." The most conventional of her books must be considered eccentric, and certain things like the drama *Four Saints in Three Acts* seem downright incomprehensible to some. Nevertheless Miss Stein has had an incalculably important influence on younger authors, and her influence on Hemingway alone would mark her as an important literary personage. It appears that quite independently and originally she conceived certain devices of style and syntax which were taken up by a whole school of young American naturalists in the Twenties, and which have continued to filter their way into American literature until there is scarcely a modern writer who can be said to have totally escaped them. Her importance as time passes may lie in such influences rather than in her work itself, as fascinating as this may be to specialists and connoisseurs of the curious. It was Gertrude Stein above all who shattered the forms of conventional grammar and syntax, who demonstrated the possibilities of free association and the abandonment of conventional word-values in literary experimentation. Although she was the trail-breaker, she did not always do these things as well as her imitators, who could concentrate on refining the technique she had created out of nothing. As she herself said (of Picasso): "When you make a thing, it is so complicated making it that it is bound to be ugly, but those that do it after you don't have to worry about making it and then can make it pretty, and so everybody can like it when the others make it." It is relatively easy to be a good writer; it is hard to be a genuinely original one.

As an instance of her originality, Miss Stein was the first American author to try to transcribe banal daily speech, almost exactly as it occurs in life, into literature. As a student of psychology she learned that the human brain does not always operate on a sequential and logical level, that an ordinary conversation is full of repetitions and divergences. In *Three Lives* and in *The Autobiography of Alice B. Toklas* she attempted to utilize this natural conversation in prose narrative. But she went further; her psychological training under William James had given her an interest in internal mental activity, especially in the process of associative thought. She began to create something like automatic writing, a prose in which the imagination created word-pictures without the intervention of the intellectual or logical part of the brain. The mind, she felt, gives to words a special significance which is independent of their dictionary meaning; words provoke emotions and recollections through their sound and their associations as well as through their denotational content. In short, Miss Stein applied the findings of modern psychology on mental activity to the word theories of the Symbolists, and incorporated the resulting technique into narrative derived from her own literary materials. She was also strongly influenced at this point by the cubist painters, laying words together for color values and structural effects. The most radical of her word-experiments are contained in *Tender Buttons* (1914) and *Four Saints in Three Acts* (1934); in both these works the literal or denotational content of the language is virtually nil. In her "sensible" works (*Three Lives* and the various autobiographical books) as well as in her more radical experiments she uses a language rich in adverbs and participles and rhythmic to the point of undulation (parts of Faulkner's *Light in August* are very similar). The phrases, devoid of metaphor and simile, are strung together with "and" (a technique imitated by Hemingway); whole paragraphs are built around a single statement, phrased and rephrased until it becomes imbedded in the reader's consciousness. The lesson of this technique is clearly apparent in the styles of Hemingway and Dos Passos; Miss Stein was not entirely wrong when she proclaimed that she had taught Ernest Hemingway to write.

Life: Gertrude Stein was born in 1874 in Allegheny, Pennsylvania of German-American parents. Her childhood was spent in Vienna, in Paris, and in San Francisco; she attended schools both in Europe and in California. As an undergraduate at Radcliffe (1893–97) she came under the influence of two great teachers, Hugo Münsterberg and William James, and resolved to make psychology her life work. Her quick intelligence and excellent memory soon manifested themselves; James at one time remarked that she was the best woman student he had ever encountered. Her first published work was a paper, done in collaboration with Leon M. Solomons, entitled "Normal Motor Automatism," in the *Psychological Review* in 1896. It is likely that this paper, or the studies it reflected, determined the nature of her entire literary career; it was a study of automatic writing in normal subjects, and the examples quoted as well as the language itself foreshadow in an uncanny way the style of Miss Stein's later literary work.

Without finishing her degree at Radcliffe she went on to Johns Hopkins University with the idea of taking a medical degree. She studied medicine four years and again left without a degree; returning briefly to San Francisco, she abandoned America definitely for France in 1903. The date is an important one; it marks the founding of the Paris-expatriate cénacle of American authors which was later to include Hemingway, Pound, Elliot Paul, and others. If Miss Stein was not the most important of these expatriates she was at least the first, and she consciously conceived of herself as the spiritual godmother of the group. Soon after (1907) she was joined by her friend Alice B. Toklas, who was to serve as her lifetime companion. The two young American women took up residence on the Left Bank, eventually settling at 27, rue de Fleurus, an address that was to become the headquarters of avant-garde literary and artistic activity. Miss Stein entertained Matisse when he was still virtually unknown; she became the intimate of Picasso, Braque, and "Le Douanier" Rousseau, and acquired a fine collection of their paintings when they were still relatively inexpensive; a famous portrait of her by Picasso (now in New York's Metropolitan Museum) dates from this period. She also took under her wing a whole covey of young American expatriates of whom the most important were Sherwood Anderson and Hemingway. She eventually broke with most of these people or they broke with her, usually because they became famous in their own right and escaped from her influence; she was inclined to run her salon with a firm and sometimes tyrannical hand. She had strong opinions about virtually everything, and had little patience with those who disagreed with her. Nevertheless her insight into literary talent and into social tendencies was remarkably sound; it was she who coined the term "a lost generation" which was so aptly applied to the intellectual youth of the Twenties.

In 1934 Miss Stein briefly returned to America for the presentation of her play *Four Saints in Three Acts,* and was escorted on a lecture tour by Thornton Wilder. She soon returned to France; in her twenty years of foreign residence she had become a permanent expatriate. In spite of this she remained an American to the end of her days; her French was passable, but she continued to speak flowing, idiomatic, and colorful English in her daily life and wrote always in American English. During the occupation of 1940–45 she and Miss Toklas retired to a villa in Culoz, in the Rhone Valley, where she was treated politely by the Germans although she was known to be an American. In 1945 she was working on a play, *Yes Is for a Very Young Man,* and she published an account of her occupation experiences as *Wars I Have Seen*; and the following year appeared *Brewsie and Willie,* an amusing but perceptive sketch of the American GI's in Europe. She died in France the same year.

Her deathbed words have been recorded as "What is the answer?" Pause. "Well, then, what is the question?"

Chief Works: *Three Lives* (novellas, 1909) contains a trio of matching stories, each an analysis of the life and character of a girl of the servant class in Bridgepoint, which is probably fictional for Baltimore, Maryland (*not* Bridgeport, Connecticut, as the Modern Library edition would lead you to believe). "It was an early spring day in the South." (page 27) "The street door opened straight into the parlor, as is the way in the small houses of the south." (page 59) The brownstone houses are the houses of Baltimore, and that's where Miss Gertrude and Miss Mathilda lived and where they took off from for Europe. The book was undoubtedly suggested by Flaubert's *Trois Contes* (*Three Tales*), which Gertrude Stein had just been translating in Paris; indeed two of the stories, about Anna and Lena, are identical in structure and psychological treatment to the most famous of Flaubert's tales, *A Simple Heart*. "The Good Anna" describes a German housekeeper who watches jealously over her mistress, Miss Mathilda, surrogate for Miss Gertrude and like her in many ways, and protects her from what she considers to be undesirable influences in her environment. Anna has no life of her own; she lives entirely for Miss Mathilda, her widow-friend, Mrs. Lehntman, and her decrepit spaniel Baby, as she had for her former employers, Miss Mary Wadsmith and Dr. Shonjen, when she was younger. Her entire existence is vicarious; she is indignant at the persecution of her friends and scornful over their own moral lapses, as well as those of the dogs of her neighborhood. Their romances are the only passion in her life, and their afflictions her only tragedy. She dies at the end of the story, and her last thoughts are for her friends.

"Melanctha," the longest and most original of the three tales, concerns an impulsive, easy-going, and emotional young Negro girl whose life is blighted by her inability to understand men. In addition to a series of petty flirtations with various white and Negro men, she has two serious affairs: a long and bitter psychological struggle with the Negro Doctor Jefferson Campbell, who is too rational for her elemental emotions, and a fierce encounter with Jem Richards, a gambler who seeks to use her only as an instrument of his pleasure. Rose Johnson, a married friend, ostensibly tries to help, but actually patronizes her because she has not found a steady man as she, Rose, has. Melanctha is a moody creature entirely dominated by her emotions, which invariably lead her into the melancholy her name suggests. She goes into a decline and finds out that she has consumption. "They sent her where she would be taken care of, a home for poor consumptives, and there Melanctha stayed until she died." This novella has been greatly admired by Richard Wright, who has called it "the first long serious literary treatment of Negro life in the United States." He recalls his first reading of the story, "I began to hear the speech of my grandmother, who spoke a deep, pure Negro dialect. . . . All of my life I had been only half hearing, but Miss Stein's struggling words made the speech of the people around me vivid."

The last tale, "The Gentle Lena," is very short; its heroine is a German immigrant girl who comes to Bridgepoint and finds a place as a maid, is ill-treated by a succession of cooks and mistresses, and eventually drifts into a marriage with Herman Kreder, a young German tailor. Dully following the path destiny and her superiors have mapped out for her, she provides Herman with three children and dies bearing the fourth. Lena's main quality is her bovine complacency, which allows her to be dominated by the selfish and tyrannical people about her.

Three Lives is undoubtedly Miss Stein's most important work, her one book which seems most likely to assume a permanent place in American literature. This is due chiefly to its accurate and convincing characterizations; it is one of her few works of fiction to create believable and colorful people. More conventional in style than most of her work, it also contains some of her best dialogue: the natural, repetitive, flowing conversation which is her chief gift to other writers such as Hemingway and Anderson.

Tender Buttons (1914) was Miss Stein's first radically experimental work. It was originally printed in a small limited edition, and exerted little influence until it was reprinted in 1928, except on a few writers like Sherwood Anderson who paid it high tribute in an introduction he wrote for Gertrude Stein's *Geography and Plays* in 1922. He and his brother had been excited by reading it in Chicago some years previously. At the time she wrote this book Miss

Stein was developing an interest in the problem of detaching words entirely from their dictionary meanings; she sought to use them merely as associative projectiles to strike the reader's brain. The book consists of three sections. "Objects" consists of aphoristic definitions of physical substances ranging from "a piece of coffee" to a piano; images of free association are used to provide a wandering, diffuse, but oddly pleasing surrealistic effect. "Food," the second section, contains similar associative definitions of meat and vegetables, stressing their visual and olfactory impact. "Rooms" presents longer and somewhat more abstract discussions of subjective experience, especially physical sensation. The technique of *Tender Buttons* has been compared to that of the cubist abstractions Miss Stein's friends Picasso, Braque, and Juan Gris were then painting. Since the work was read in its limited edition by several of Miss Stein's acquaintances who later became writers, its influence is probably greater than its publication figures would indicate.

The Autobiography of Alice B. Toklas (memoirs, 1933) is actually a journal of Miss Stein's own life, playfully written in the person of her companion Miss Toklas. This device makes it possible to comment impersonally on her own character, to praise (often with tongue in cheek) her own wit and genius, and in short to serve as her own Boswell. The character of Miss Toklas is clearly defined through her "own" remarks: she is more naive, but less spiteful, than Miss Stein. The narrative begins with Miss Stein's childhood in Pennsylvania and continues through her youth to the period of the apartment in the Rue de Fleurus. There are fascinating accounts of Picasso, Matisse, Rousseau, and others, as well as shrewdly perceptive remarks on literary figures of the day.

Four Saints in Three Acts ("opera libretto," 1934) is one of Miss Stein's most controversial works. The opera was successfully performed on several occasions; the premiere took place with an all-Negro cast in Hartford, Connecticut in 1934. Music for the libretto was written by Virgil Thomson. Earlier versions of the work, without music, had appeared in 1929 and 1932. Remounted in 1952 by ANTA, the performance included Leontyne Price as Saint Teresa and was taken to Europe to represent American artistic accomplishment. The recording of *Four Saints in Three Acts* makes delightful listening in the fun and games department.

Miss Stein's libretto for the opera is an exercise in surrealistic imagination, with little denotational meaning and no plot whatsoever. She calls it a series of landscapes. Actually there are at least fifteen saints, excluding those in the chorus, and four announced acts (five if the prologue is included—the author has fun playing havoc with theatre conventions, mixing up numbered scenes). The most important real saint is Saint Teresa of Avila (who becomes a split personality); the next most important real saint is Saint Ignatius; following in importance are the fictional Saints Chavez, Settlement, Plan. The theme has something to do with the relationship between sainthood and childhood, which is not meaningless. If for nothing else, the libretto is remarkable for containing what is probably Miss Stein's most often quoted line: "Pigeons on the grass alas."

The relative success of this work as compared with *Tender Buttons* and other experiments is probably due to the fact that its audiences, diverted by the music and the spectacle, did not object to the apparent lack of meaning of the text. Accompanied by music, the evocative but relatively senseless lines achieved a curiously pleasing and hypnotic effect. This is no criticism of Miss Stein's talent, since it was precisely her intent to divest literature of its logical content and to present it as a form of quasi-sensual pleasure.

Wars I Have Seen (autobiography, 1945) returns to the more comprehensible style of *The Autobiography of Alice B. Toklas*; the presentation is more straightforward, however, since Miss Stein in the earlier book was limited by her playful imitation of Miss Toklas' way of speaking. *Wars I Have Seen* contains some of her most conventional writing, and some of her best. The book is mainly concerned with the period 1940–45, the period of the German Occupation which Miss Stein and Miss Toklas spent in the Rhone Valley, although numerous observations on the First World War and other wars of history are included. Interesting pictures are presented of the life of the French countryside under the Occupation, the activities of the Resistance in the Rhone Valley as seen through the eyes of Miss Stein, and the change in the attitude of the German troops as their victory turned to defeat. The final section, "The Coming of the Americans," contains a vivid and moving account of the last days of the Occupation, one of the few passages in which Miss Stein stirs up any genuine excitement in her reader. The passage also reveals the extent of her warm and nostalgic love for America and Americans. As she explains in her account of the Liberation, she is fortunate in having two countries to be proud of, France and America; and this book reveals the extent of her love for both.

Yes Is for a Very Young Man (play, 1945), produced for the first time at the Pasadena Playhouse, March 13, 1946, had originally been called *In Savoy*. It is about a French family divided during the war, as our American families were divided during our Civil War and even our Revolutionary War. Gertrude, in the Pasadena program notes said about her mother's Civil War stories, "I loved these stories and then when I was in France during the occupation, knowing intimately all the people around me, I was struck with the resemblance to the stories my mother used to tell me, the divided families, the bitterness, the quarrels and sometimes the denunciations, and yet the natural necessity of their all continuing to live their daily life together, because after all that was all the life they had, besides they were after all the same family or their neighbors, and in the country neighbors are neighbors." The family is Denise, married to Henry, and she wants him to cooperate with the Germans so they can live better. But Henry's younger brother, Ferdinand, an idealist and patriotic Frenchman and the friend of Constance, the American, and for whom the word "Yes" is an affirmation of resistance, refuses his cooperation. Achille, the brother of Denise, joins Marshall Pétain's army. Ferdinand has to go to Germany to work in the factories, but gets back home and decides to disappear, Maquis-fashion. Just before the American liberation the father of Ferdinand and Henry is killed by the Germans, and Henry gets revenge with the Maquis. Achille finds himself in difficulty trying to get back in the regular army. There have been several effective university and experimental theatre productions of this play, which is somewhere between the straightforward and experimental Stein.

Harold Rosenberg in a January 30, 1971 article in the *New Yorker* on the collection of paintings made by the four Steins in Paris early in the century, Gertrude, her brothers Leo and Michael, and Michael's wife Sarah, and shown at the Museum of Modern Art —a hundred Picassos, more than eighty Matisses, plus Gris, Cézanne, Renoir, Manet—reports Gertrude as saying: "America is my country and Paris is my home town." And it was true.

Elliot Paul (1891–1958)

Although he expected his reputation to be made on his novels, Elliot Paul will be remembered chiefly for his two autobiographical accounts of expatriate life in Europe and his part in founding the important avant-garde review *transition. The Life and Death of a Spanish Town* and *The Last Time I Saw Paris* are important documents in American literary history, whatever their intrinsic merit may be: they sum up, perhaps better than any other two books, the nostalgia for Europe that led so many American intellectuals and writers to abandon their country in the period between the two wars. They bear comparison with similar books of Hemingway, for instance, *The Sun Also Rises,* but there is an important difference: where Hemingway is concerned mainly with his own reactions to Europe and with studies of other American expatriates, Paul tries to get at the essence of European culture, especially the culture of the humble classes, the working people among whom he chose to live. That Hemingway is capable of this is shown by *For Whom the Bell Tolls.* Yet this is after all an adventure story; it makes no serious attempt to give a comprehensive picture of the Spanish people. Paul is a better naturalist; his goal is to portray an accurate cross-section of the life of a people. But if his intention is sociological, his style is journalistic; in spite of his personal connection with Eugène Jolas, Stein, Joyce, and other experimentalists he is relatively unconcerned with problems of literary technique. His intention is simply to get the idea across. "When you write rapidly you write in your own style," he said in an interview with Robert Van Gelder. "There is no good in trying for style by rewriting, by torturing sentences. You knock the life out of it and probably out of your ideas." Because of his journalistic background he often seems to be writing for an aüdience which needs everything explained to it and would be shocked by candid references to sex. When he mentions France's chief Catholic poetic dramatist of the twentieth century he feels obliged to explain, "Paul Claudel, a French writer, was sent to Washington as an ambassador." His accounts of the life of the flesh in the Rue de la Huchette are discreet, even prudish, when compared with *The Sun Also Rises* or Miller's *Tropic of Cancer*. It is for such reasons that *The Last Time I Saw Paris* became a best-seller, while *Tropic of Cancer* had not yet been admitted into the United States—and was not to be until the Sixties, after which time anything goes.

Paul began his literary career during his Paris period with three novels all more or less in the same style, impressionistic, consciously bohemian and anti-bourgeois in attitude, and rather immature in treatment: *Indelible* (1922), *Impromptu* (1923), and *Imperturbe* (1924). A group of novels in his middle period (*ca.* 1930) shows a more naturalistic technique, often attempting a cross-section of a community in the same way as *The Last Time I Saw Paris*: *Low Run Tide* (1929), the story of the decline of a New England fishing village, is typical of these. After the Second World War he devoted himself chiefly to an autobiography in several volumes under the general title of *Items on the Grand Account*; the volumes including *Linden on the Saugus Branch* (1947), *A Ghost Town on the Yellowstone* (1948), and *My Old Kentucky Home* (1949). He has also written a number of mystery stories of a satirical tendency.

Life: Elliot Harold Paul was born in 1891 in Malden, Massachusetts. After a few months at the University of Maine he went west to work at a number of odd jobs, then joined the Army Signal Corps to serve in France during the First World War. He stayed in France when the war was over, making his living writing for the Associated Press and for the Paris editions of the *Chicago Tribune* and the *New York Herald*. He soon became a familiar figure in the American expatriate circle: bearded, vigorous, a talented musician and a master of idiomatic French, popular with working-class Frenchmen and with the humble inhabitants of the Rue de la Huchette, just off the Boulevard Saint-Michel in the Latin Quarter. In 1927 he joined the French critic Eugène Jolas in founding the review *transition*, which became the most important center of expatriate writing in Paris during the Thirties and published authors of such stature as Gertrude Stein, Hemingway, Hart Crane, James

Joyce, and W. C. Williams. In 1931 Paul went to live at Santa Eulalia, on the island of Ibiza in the Balearic Islands. In 1936 he managed to escape from Santa Eulalia just before the arrival of Fascist troops. In 1939 he returned to the United States, where he made his headquarters thereafter. He was married twice, the second time to Flora Thompson Brown, who appears along with Paul's son in *Life and Death of a Spanish Town.* Paul died in 1958.

Chief Works: *Life and Death of a Spanish Town* (autobiography, 1937) is two books in one: it is an account of Paul's life with his family in the Balearic town of Santa Eulalia del Rio on the island of Ibiza between 1931 and 1936, and it is a study of Spanish culture in general as exemplified in the life of this small town, especially in its reactions to the political events of 1931–36 and the outbreak of the Spanish Civil War. The term autobiography is not a very accurate one to apply to this book, since Paul is not writing about himself but about the town and its inhabitants; yet "journalism" does not adequately describe it either, since its approach is entirely subjective and literary. The first half of the book is a humorous but sympathetic study of folk-manners: the noble indolence of the Spanish temperament, the eternal conflict between Left (the fishermen, the town artisans, the intellectuals) and Right (the priests, the landowners, the Guardia Civil), and the contrast between the calm serenity of the Spanish town and the neurotic "go-getter" pace of life in America. The second half of the book, describing the events leading up to the Civil War and the outbreak of violence in Santa Eulalia, is markedly different in style; it is terse, dramatic, and militantly partisan in its bias for the Loyalist cause. The account of the shelling of the town by a Loyalist gunboat and the consequent evacuation of the town (Chapters 19–20) is a well-written and dramatic piece of narrative, as is the story of the final escape of Paul and his family from the island in a German destroyer. Although the style of this book is generally straightforward and conventional, there are occasional passages demonstrating the influence of Gertrude Stein and the *transition* writers, for instance this from Chapter 19, suggesting the Hemingway of *Big Two-Hearted River*: "When the pieces were well browned, I put a little bacon into the hot center, let the grease fry out, then added a cupful of

Marques de Argentera (*tinto*) and let simmer slowly. Slowly bubbling, with especial care, for I wanted so badly to pay strict attention and watch slow bubbling, smelling tones of bacon and the sea and the wine from sunny slopes and thinking after all that it was a simple dish to make since worthy pig the sea had been working on the octopus for at least a dozen years and the sun had conjured vines from the earth and grapes that gave wine of an inimitable flavor." Passages such as these have an unmistakable quality of American expatriate writing of the Twenties.

The Last Time I Saw Paris (autobiography, 1942) covers the periods both before and after the events of *Life and Death of a Spanish Town,* roughly 1920–31 and 1937–39. During most of this period Paul lived in the Hôtel du Caveau in the Rue de la Huchette. *The Last Time I Saw Paris* is a detailed portrait of this short street, its shops and hotels, and its inhabitants. There are several dozen main characters, none of whom dominates the narrative; structurally the book is merely a documentary study of a typical Paris quarter. The treatment, however, is personal and informal. There are occasional lyric passages similar to the one quoted above from *Life and Death of a Spanish Town,* but on the whole the style is intended to appeal to the general American reading audience. The best parts of the book are the conversations with the young Hyacinthe Goujon, a sensitive, spirited, and dissatisfied girl whom Paul treats as a kind of symbol of the French temperament. Yet Paul is curiously reticent about personal confessions; his more intimate relations with the inhabitants of the street are only hinted, and the events described, although occasionally Rabelaisian, are nothing that an American student could not write home to his mother. Yet the book is a valuable document of the attitude of the typical American expatriate toward Paris in the Twenties and Thirties. It is interesting to compare it with the genteel admiration shown by Henry James for France (e.g., in *The Ambassadors*) or with the fervent francophilia of Edith Wharton (e.g., *A Son at the Front*). Paul is severely critical of some aspects of French culture: government corruption, technical inefficiency, the insolence and incompetence of public servants. "Never in the history of France has the ordinary citizen received good service of any kind." Yet in the end, knowing France better, he admires it more truly than did either James or Mrs. Wharton, who knew and admired its "civilization" rather than its daily life. *The Last Time I Saw Paris* is good reading for an understanding of the American expatriate movement in the period between the two wars.

Henry Miller (born 1891)

It is difficult to assess the importance of an American writer whose two most important books were not published in the United States until his creative period was essentially over in the Sixties, who is surrounded by a fervent and evidently maladjusted band of disciples, and who obviously owes much of the limited popularity he enjoys to the sensational aspect of his work. On the one hand it would be a mistake to take Miller on his own valuation, or that of his followers; on the other hand it is impossible to dismiss him as a mere pornographic exhibitionist. Probably his main importance in American literature is analogous to that of Scott Fitzgerald: he epitomizes and records a certain social phenomenon peculiar to his generation, in his case the revolt of the American expatriates in Paris against the puritanism, the sterility, and the "respectability" of their homeland. In a sense he is not really a novelist at all. Most of his so-called fiction is actually autobiography, although there is evidently a certain amount of exaggeration and hyperbolic drumbeating in it. It resembles the "fictionalized autobiography" of Elliot Paul except that where Paul remains an observer, chiefly interested in the lives of the people around him, Miller is interested primarily, perhaps exclusively, in himself. A certain amount of pose is involved; Miller obviously fancies himself as a rebellious and satanic hero who is as physically irresistible to women as he is obnoxious to the bourgeois. His fiction is unabashedly frank; if his two *Tropic* books are not pornography (and the American Customs authorities on several occasions decided that they are) they sometimes skirt it dangerously. Like D. H. Lawrence, he stands for the complete destruction of sexual and other taboos which stand in the way of the fulfillment of the individual; but unlike Lawrence he is often led by this credo into a preoccupation with the abnormal and degraded aspects of sexuality. But all these comments, while true, have nothing to do with his literary quality; they are remarks that might as easily be made about Cellini or Rousseau, both writers of autobiography with whom Miller shows an affinity of personality.

Upon actual inspection Miller's work is often energetic and talented, if not competent. Most of its faults are due to his own pose of genius: he is impulsive and careless in style, and often merely suggests through involved circumlocution what a better writer would have worked to express in concise and lucid form. His merits are those that go with his faults: energy, spontaneity, Rabelaisian humor, colorful if somewhat grotesque characterizations, a freshness of metaphor and dialogue. The best parts of his novels are the autobiographical passages, the pictures he draws of his own character in the process of formation. The sketches of male cronies, for example the confused and naive expatriate Fillmore in *Tropic of Cancer,* are also often superb. The characterizations of women are usually inferior; Miller is not interested in the more subtle or human aspects of female temperament.

An important aspect of Miller's work is the influence he has exerted on little-magazine and avant-garde writing in America. Numerous reviews (e.g., *The Tiger's Eye*) have been founded by his disciples or imitators, and whole bookstores have been devoted to his work, especially in the San Francisco-Berkeley area. His influence in Europe has also been important; in avant-garde literary circles in France, for example, he has often been considered one of the most prominent American writers of the century. With the admission of *Tropic of Capricorn* and *Tropic of Cancer* to the United States, his reputation may at last be given a fair contest in his own country, although it may also be a little late for the effect that could have been produced ten or twenty years earlier.

Life: Henry Miller was born in 1891 in New York of German-American parents; he spoke German himself until he began to go to school. During his boyhood he was a model juvenile delinquent; he quit City College in disgust, drifted from job to job, and by his own admission swindled his father out of a fund for his further education to spend the money on a female companion twice his age. Around the time of the First World War he dabbled with Communism; he met Emma Goldman in San Diego, but was unable to apply himself to the aims of the Party any more than he could concentrate on any other extended project. For five years beginning in 1920 he held one of the few steady jobs of his career: employment manager for a New York utilities company. This experience he incorporated almost verbatim into *Tropic of Capricorn.* His first book, *Clipped Wings,* was written in 1923; it was a study of twelve eccentric messengers, based on his telegraph company experience. He visited Europe briefly in 1928 and returned for a nine-year sojourn in 1930. In Paris he joined a group of avant-garde literary expatriates whose informal chief he soon became; he wrote his two most important novels during this period under conditions of extreme poverty and dissipation. In the late Thirties he was persuaded by his friend, Lawrence Durrell, to take a trip to Greece, which resulted in one of his best books, *The Colossus of Maroussi* (1941) about his travels. The outbreak of the war forced his return to America; a vitriolic essay on American culture, *The Air-Conditioned Nightmare,* appeared in 1945. He settled in Big Sur, on a desolate stretch of California coast between 1941 and 1960. Here he worked on a fictionalized autobiography, *The Rosy Crucifixion,* appearing in the volumes, *Sexus, Plexus,* and *Nexus* (1949–1960). After travel in Europe, Miller moved to Southern California, writing his first play, *Just Wild About Harry,* 1963. Correspondence with Lawrence Durrell and Anaïs Nin has appeared, but mostly these days he receives visitors from among his devotees. His two chief novels which remain The *Tropics* were printed in France and were not published in America because of their alleged obscenity until *Tropic of Cancer* was brought out in 1961, climaxed by the most publicized obscenity trials since *Ulysses* in 1933 and *Lady Chatterley's Lover* in between. *Tropic of Capricorn* followed in 1962 and *Black Spring* in 1963. Miller is an exaggerated symbol, perhaps the epitome, of the literary generation of the Twenties in revolt against American Puritanism. He has remained in California for the last thirty years where a considerable colony of writers, artists, and eccentrics has gathered around him. Occasionally a poet like Ferlinghetti will find the title of a book in his writings.

Chief Novels: *Tropic of Cancer* (autobiographical novel, 1931) is based on the author's experience as an expatriate in Paris, where he lived in poverty in the St. Germain quarter in the midst of a frantic circus of eccentrics: his roommate Boris, the half-mad Van Norden, and many others, including a monotonous succession of women each irresistibly attracted to the hero. The better parts of the book are the chapters where Miller momentarily departs from the cataloguing of his amatory escapades and turns to the study of character: the description of the eccentric Hindu Nanantatee, or the disconnected episode in which the hero, desperate for money, travels to Dijon to take a job as lycée instructor and is bored to the brink of lunacy. Also justly famous is the passage near the end of the novel in which the hero encounters his friend Fillmore, who has married a French girl and settled down to respectable boredom. Fillmore, at the end of the encounter, has gone off in a drunken haze to return to America, and the hero has calmly pocketed the money Fillmore has given him to provide for his abandoned wife.

Tropic of Capricorn (autobiographical novel, 1939), although written subsequently, concerns an earlier period in Miller's life. It begins with a discussion of his family background and takes him through the interlude of his steady job, through his intellectual awakening and the discovery of his own personality, to the point in his life where he determined to abandon America and turn to a literary vocation in Europe. A more evenly written book, it lacks the blatant obscenity of *Tropic of Cancer* but lacks its shrewdly-drawn character sketches as well. The character of Miller's father is notable, however, and the description of the daily routine in a telegraph office is a little masterpiece of its kind. Most of *Tropic of Capricorn* is laid in New York City and Brooklyn.

Two non-fiction works of Miller deserve brief mention. *The Colossus of Maroussi; or The Spirit of Greece* (1941) is an unusual and highly subjective travel book, a favorite among Miller's inner circle of admirers; and *The Air-Conditioned Nightmare* (1945) is a caustic summary of American culture, based on Miller's reactions upon his return to America from his long exile in France. This second book, along with Philip Wylie's *Generation of Vipers* (1943), is one of the most violent rejections of American materialism and puritanism to appear in the first half of the twentieth century. It lacks Mencken's wit and Sinclair Lewis' social insight, however, and it is interesting chiefly for the light it sheds on Miller's personality and attitude.

In the post-1945 period two shorter works by Miller appeared in America in popular editions. *Nights of Love and Laughter* (1955) collects short pieces written between 1939 and 1947. The two most interesting of these are "The Alcoholic Veteran With the Washboard Cranium," a long monologue by a somewhat confused iconoclast whom Miller evidently met in a bar, and "Via Dieppe-Newhaven," an autobiographical account of an incident in which Miller, attempting to visit England during his stay in Europe, was barred from the country by the British authorities as a vagrant and an undesirable. A short excerpt from *The Colossus of Maroussi* is also included. *A Devil in Paradise* (1956) is an autobiographical novel laid in Big Sur; it is devoted chiefly to a character sketch of Conrad Moricand, an eccentric Swiss astrologer whom Miller brought to America out of charity and who proceeded to tyrannize over the household through his hypochondria, his egocentricity, and his elaborate and pathological fastidiousness. This short novel, which begins in the brash style of the *Tropic* books, succeeds in the end in drawing a vivid and poignant characterization; the reader is brought powerfully to share the mixture of aversion and pity which Miller feels for the grotesque figure of Moricand.

John P. Marquand (1893–1960)

Even more than Scott Fitzgerald, Marquand is the heir of the literary tradition of Henry James and Edith Wharton. He is conservative in his social attitude, yet he is satirical in his treatment of the very aristocrats he admires; he is a modernist in the sense that he recognizes the obsolescence of the tradition of New England gentility, yet in literary technique he is conventional, even old-fashioned. He has little sympathy with the more radical literary experiments of his age; he rejects the characters of Steinbeck and Hemingway and Fitzgerald because to him they seem freakish, because "they were never like anyone I knew." Like Edith Wharton, he seems slightly shocked by the manners of the new age; he recognizes the existence of sexual license, profanity, and other vulgar realities of the post-World War I age, but he cannot bring himself to take them for granted as a Faulkner or a Hemingway does.

Like Howells and James, Marquand is basically a novelist of manners in the New England literary tradition. If he differs from these two, it is because he lived a half-century later under new conditions and among a new race of people. His typical hero is a New England gentleman of distinguished family who finds himself somewhat incongruously living in the twentieth century and tries to make the best of it. On the one hand his hero feels like a stranger amid the vulgar and crass materialism and the casual morality of the twentieth century, and on the other hand he rebels, as a twentieth-century man, against the rigid conventions of his traditional background, which he instinctively resents as obsolete. His continually recurring themes are the conflict between conformity and individualism and the waste of human power in creative individuals who are forced to live according to the standards set by earlier generations. Around this framework he builds novels of careful and profusely detailed precision. If he is a realist (and this is the most satisfactory way to classify him) it is in his thorough and studied mastery of his subject-matter, in the care with which he studies his upper-class milieu and transcribes its every detail faithfully into his fiction. In style Marquand is competent but unremarkable; his dialogue is slightly more terse and "modern" than that of Henry James, but is basically in the Jamesian tradition. He is fond of the flashback as a structural device and uses it extensively, especially in *Point of No Return*, where virtually the entire story is told in flashbacks. In *The Late George Apley* he uses an even more venerable form: the "papers" left behind by a great man, used by a biographer to construct an official picture of his life. It resembles both Howells' *The Rise of Silas Lapham* and Thomas Mann's *Doktor Faustus* (1947) in its construction and in its retrospective point of view. Marquand, who began as a popular magazine writer, learned conventional writing thoroughly, and he seldom departs from popular style, form, and construction even in his more pretentious works.

Life: John Phillips Marquand was born in Wilmington, Delaware in 1893; his mother's family was from traditional New England, and his maternal grandfather was a brother of Margaret Fuller. During his boyhood he lived at Rye, N.Y. and at Newburyport, Massachusetts. In 1907 the financial slump greatly reduced the wealth of his family, and he was obliged to work his way through Harvard, which he did in three years. He worked as a journalist, served in the army in the Mexican campaign of 1916 and in the First World War, and tried advertising for a while, but presently quit and determined to make his living by writing. His first fiction, a romantic historical novel entitled *The Unspeakable Gentleman,* appeared in *The Ladies' Home Journal* in 1922. From that time until 1937 he wrote popular fiction, chiefly magazine stories of the formula variety; the period is also the era of the famous Mr. Moto stories, adventurous romances built around the figure of a Japanese secret agent (e.g., *Thank You, Mr. Moto,* 1936). His first novel of literary importance was *The Late George Apley* in 1937; it proved to be a popular as well as a critical success, and since then he turned out similar novels steadily but slowly, at the rate of approximately one every two years. Meanwhile he continued to write formula fiction; the Mr. Moto books continued until the international events of 1941 made the theme unsuitable for light literature. In addition to *The Late George Apley,* his most important novels are *Wickford Point* (1939), *H. M. Pulham, Esq.* (1941), *So Little Time* (1943), *Repent in Haste* (1945), *B. F.'s Daughter* (1946), *Point of No Return* (1949), *Melville Goodwin, U.S.A.* (1951), and *Sincerely, Willis Wayde* (1955). Mr. Marquand was married twice, the second time in 1937, and had five children. After publishing *Women and Thomas Harrow* in 1958 and having written some twenty-six novels, the Pulitzer Prize-winning John P. Marquand died in his sleep in July 1960, apparently from a heart attack.

Chief Novels: *The Late George Apley* (1937) is presented as the biography of an eminent Bostonian who is born in 1866 and dies in 1933, ostensibly written by the staid, conventional, respectful, and somewhat obtuse Horatio Willing. Thus the satire is double-edged; the reader sees the pedanticism and conventionality of Willing as well as the futility of the life of George Apley. Apley, born at the height of the era of Boston gentility, is thoroughly at home in the world of his youth. When he goes to Harvard, however, he falls in love with an "unsuitable" girl, Mary Monahan, and his family is forced to break up the affair and pack him off on a sea voyage. He conforms; he accepts the conventions of his family and society, works at an acceptable profession, and marries Catharine Bosworth, a fiancée selected by his family. As he lives into the twentieth century, however, Apley sees the traditions by which his family lived crumbling about him. His son marries a divorced woman and his daughter goes off with the kind of an "unsuitable" mate he was denied in college, he is confused by the "immoral" new novels and angered by prohibition, and he is finally struck down by the market crash of 1929, which leaves his personal fortune relatively untouched but destroys his faith in the established economic order. Before he dies in 1933 he begins to perceive the mistake of his life: that he tried to live it according to the standards of a previous generation. This novel, Marquand's most intricate technical accomplishment, was awarded a Pulitzer Prize in 1938.

Wickford Point (novel, 1939) is the study of a slick popular writer named Jim Calder. In many respects his career parallels Marquand's: he is born about the same time of a respectable but not wealthy family, goes to Harvard, serves in the World War, and makes his living by writing formula fiction. The difference is that Jim Calder never writes a novel as good as *George Apley* or *Wickford Point*; as he himself eventually realizes, he lacks the true creativity needed to be a great writer. The title refers to the estate of the Brills, Calder's conventional and snobbish relations; much of the novel concerns the life of the Brills, especially the marital crises and confusion of the attractive and popular Bella. *Wickford Point* is a triumph of technical competence. The story is told almost entirely through flashbacks; its approach to its material is discreetly satirical, and the portraits of Calder and Bella are especially perceptive and convincing.

H. M. Pulham, Esq. (novel, 1941) is similar to *George Apley*; the main difference is that the action focuses more on the hero's personal love-life and less on his family and public affairs. Pulham, like Apley, abandons an earlier love under pressure from his family and instead marries a "suitable" girl. Twenty years later he meets his earlier sweetheart again, and decides to throw up everything and run away with her. At the last moment, however, his conventional character asserts itself, and he returns to his wife to live out a monotonous and respectable life. His conflict is paralleled by a similar one in the life of his wife Kay; she too considers running away with an old lover, but changes her mind and stays with Pulham.

Point of No Return (novel, 1949) established a well-known American metaphor. Charley Gray, a successful and rising banker, stops in the middle of his career and wonders whether it has been worth while. He decides, however, that it is too late for him to seek a more creative or spiritual way of life; he has passed the "point of no return" in his journey toward conventional success, and can only live out his life in the career he has chosen.

Sincerely, Willis Wayde (novel, 1955) is Marquand's most cutting and satirical portrait of an American business-man. The hero resembles Lewis' Babbitt more than he does anything else in Marquand's work; he has an infinite capacity for hypocritical rationalizing and sentimental self-deception. His life is devoted to a consecrated and solemn struggle for success; he does push-ups every morning, reads Dr. Eliot's Five-Foot Shelf of Harvard Classics as other people take medicine, and continues to make "business contacts" through his honeymoon. Yet in the end the reader is brought to sympathize with him, just as he is with Lewis' Babbitt; Wayde is after all "sincere," as the title implies, even in his materialism and his go-getter ideals, and in the end he is a victim of the standards around him more than of his own weakness. The final scene, in which his wife tucks him into bed with a kiss and a Nembutal, is masterful.

Ernest Hemingway (1899–1961)

The publicity directed on Hemingway's colorful and adventurous life has often tended to obscure the fact that he is primarily a creative artist whose business it is to write. Although he is free from the pretensions of the aesthetic cultists, he approaches the craft of writing with a careful and conscientious devotion. He once remarked that his job as a writer was to "put down what I see and what I feel in the best and simplest way I can tell it." In spite of his occasional stylistic experiments and his rare excursions into politics, this has remained his ideal.

In the early Twenties Hemingway, a left-bank expatriate, contributed poetry to avant-garde reviews. He soon turned to the short story and the novel, but he retained an almost poetic interest in economy of language and in precision and brilliance of imagery. From the beginning he bore one of the marks of a great author: his style was original and unmistakable. A single paragraph of his prose is easily identifiable; he prints upon each sentence the mark of his temperament and style. Hemingway at his best establishes a characteristic mood, a literary ambience which is entirely personal and inimitable, as much as his disciples may try to imitate it.

An extremely subjective author, Hemingway is not interested in writing from sheer imagination or in making use of documentary materials in the traditional naturalistic manner. He writes only about those aspects of life he has encountered personally, although these are many: warfare, big-game hunting, sport fishing, bull-fighting, skiing, and life in the expatriate society of Paris. Conversely, there is very little he has done that he has not written about. In Africa in 1933–34 he was stricken with dysentery and had to be flown out to Nairobi for treatment. Many writers would consider this incident only an unfortunate interruption in a vacation, but out of the experience Hemingway wrote the superb story "The Snows of Kilimanjaro." Each of the locales of his life—Michigan, Wyoming, Paris, Italy, Spain, Switzerland, Africa, and Cuba—has had a novel or a cycle of stories written about it, and most of Hemingway's friends find themselves sooner or later converted to characters in his fiction. Like Joyce and Proust, Hemingway is a writer who uses the material of his own life to construct a transformed and artistically heightened fiction.

Because of the subjective nature of his approach to fiction, Hemingway's male characters are usually more believable than his women. His heroes themselves are lifelike in proportion as they are projections of his own personality. With a few exceptions, as with the Cohn of *The Sun Also Rises* and most of the bull-fighters of his fiction, his central characters are merely Hemingway as he pictures himself or as he would like to be. His work is autobiographical not only in the incidents related but in the attitudes and reactions of his characters to their situations. His female characters seem to be seen through masculine eyes; he is not a master of feminine psychology. The best of his women, e.g., the Pilar of *For Whom the*

Bell Tolls, have a certain masculine quality about them. His love-heroines, e.g., Catherine in *A Farewell to Arms* and Maria in *For Whom the Bell Tolls,* are passive and erotic embodiments of male desire; they are devoid of intellectual individuality and seem to have little existence apart from their lovers.

The sensations which interest Hemingway, and therefore the experiences he relates in his fiction, are generally on the physical level. He is interested in sensation *per se:* the sensation of drinking wine chilled in a Spanish mountain stream, of passing one's fingers through the hair of a girl whose head has recently been sheared, or of being blown up by a trench-mortar shell in Italy. He dwells over these sensations and analyzes them with an intensity which would be Proustian if it were not so terse. Even the finer sensations in Hemingway—love or political loyalty—seem to be essentially physical reactions; the hero feels them with his body rather than his mind, and generally manages to make a response to them through some sort of bodily reaction. This is not to say that Hemingway views life from a bestial standpoint; on the contrary his sensations are extremely refined, and he is sometimes given to an immature and romantic sentimentality about them. His mind operates exclusively on the level of concrete image and is wary of dead abstraction. He is anxious to communicate to the reader "how it was," to recreate the exact physical sensations that he, or his heroes, felt under certain conditions. This is the most successful aspect of his technique. After reading Hemingway the reader is left with a strong impression of "how it was" to shoot lions in Kenya, to take part in the retreat from Caporetto, or to live in Paris in the early nineteen-twenties.

Hemingway derived his style from two chief sources: his early experience as a newspaperman and his encounter with Gertrude Stein and other avant-garde writers in Paris in the Twenties, including Ezra Pound. As a journalist on the *Kansas City Star* he learned to write succinctly, to avoid superfluous adjectives and adverbs, and to pack the maximum content into the minimum space. In Paris he fell under the spell of Gertrude Stein's undulant prose, with its consecutive phrases connected by "ands" in an almost Biblical manner, its understatement, and its trick of repeating an image or an idea until it has become imbedded in the reader's mind. During the Thirties he gradually weaned himself from this style, but his most characteristic works are written under the influence of Stein. In *For Whom the Bell Tolls* he returned to this style to create the best book of his later period. It has been rightly remarked that this style has ruined more budding authors than any other influence since Sterne, but it is still true that when Hemingway utilizes it he achieves a distinctive, powerful, and entirely personal idiom.

Actually the most typical Hemingway novels—*The Sun Also Rises, A Farewell to Arms,* and *For Whom the Bell Tolls*—are written in two styles in alternation. First there is the highly condensed description and narration, written in the flowing chain of images suggestive of free verse; the opening page of *A Farewell to Arms* and the fishing scenes in *The Sun Also Rises* are typical. The second style is the terse dialogue, almost bare of comment and full of conversational blind alleys and *non sequiturs,* which Hemingway's detractors find it so easy to parody. The dialogue style appears at its best in the conversations of the hero of *A Farewell to Arms* with his Italian comrades and in numerous short stories of the type of *The Short Happy Life of Francis Macomber.* It is through the alternation of these two styles that Hemingway avoids the monotony which has been the downfall of his imitators.

There are many scenes of violence, pain and tragedy in Hemingway, yet the total effect is seldom offensive. He relates the most violent of incidents in a totally matter-of-fact and objective manner. He never comments, and he never degenerates into pathos. His scenes of violence are effective through the facts related and not through appeals to sentimentality. His concept of character is "hard" —i.e., his heroes are laconic and cynical, and not given to gushing —yet we perceive that under their hardness they have the same impulses and emotions as the rest of mankind.

Although Hemingway is primarily interested in conveying experiences to the reader, his work is not devoid of ideas. The ideas, however, are latent and conveyed through physical sensation; Hemingway is anything but a philosophical novelist. Yet beneath the surface of his work is an integrated and consistent philosophy. The chief concepts in his work may be listed as follows:

(1) Like Dreiser, Hemingway is an advocate of NATURAL ACTION, although the two writers differ greatly in their concepts of

nature. To Hemingway natural action consists chiefly in pursuing the impulses of the body, with the emphasis on the finer and more noble impulses. He is a hedonist in the classic sense, yet he is no mere seeker after sensation; perversions of bodily desires, including excesses, over-refinements, and artificially stimulated tastes, are opposed to natural action. Contrary to popular opinion, he is no believer in chest-pounding masculinity or in brute force. Cohn, who resorts to fisticuffs in *The Sun Also Rises,* is presented as wrong in doing so. A man who admires force for its own sake may well come to admire fascism, and Hemingway dislikes fascism precisely because it is dispensed by "legally constituted bullies." His attitude is often disparagingly called "adolescent," but it should be noted that the code of boyhood includes censure of bullies and an idealistic respect for fair play.

Natural action to Hemingway therefore implies, not mere bestial hedonism, but a healthy and intelligent exercise of one's sensual appetites. Prostitution, drunkenness, and brawling play a large part in his work; yet examination will show that the decent characters reject this way of life, or at least find little satisfaction in it. It would be too much to claim that Hemingway is a moralist, but at least he is no disciple of vice.

(2) Hemingway is a believer in RITUAL—naturally not the ritual of church or lodge, but the unspoken rituals which men have handed down, sometimes unconsciously, for generations. He views bull-fighting as a ritualistic form of art involving bloodshed and death rather than as a mere excuse for sadism. Hunting too has its ritual; there are rules which the hunter must observe, and even the hunted seem to accept the ritual as natural. Nick Adams is careful to throw back fish under the legal game size; not only the game laws but the ritual of fishing demand that no life be wasted unnecessarily. Francis Macomber, wounding a lion which then escapes into the bush, proposes to abandon it; but the hunter Wilson insists that the beast must not be left to suffer. The pair therefore risk their lives to put their erstwhile victim out of its pain. There is a similar ritual in warfare; Hemingway finds fascism particularly repugnant in that it does not observe this traditional code. It is by shooting civilians and bombing from the air that the fascists in *For Whom the Bell Tolls* reveal their ignorance of the code of warfare.

(3) Hemingway finds a sort of mystical experience, a quasi-metaphysical quality, in PAIN, VIOLENCE, AND DEATH; in his work he utilizes this mystique as an element of tragic catharsis. He is ostensibly a pacifist and is constantly depicting the brutality and senselessness of war, but there is no doubt that he himself and his heroes live at the highest pitch in the midst of armed combat. War is a vast and intricate game, the most gripping of all games since it is the most dangerous; even one's opponents, provided they observe the rituals and play the game according to the rules, are to be respected. Hemingway is closer to the attitude of the professional officer than he is to the fervor of the civilian patriot.

A similar mystique is involved in hunting, one of the dominant interests in Hemingway's life. To him hunting is not so much a means of killing an animal as a contest between animal and man. Francis Macomber finds a deep spiritual satisfaction in hunting he has never found anywhere else in life; he is regenerated by the experience and develops character visibly. The animal in death, provided it has been fairly stalked and cleanly killed, Hemingway finds one of the most beautiful of sights. He distinguishes, however, between the natural and beautiful in the animal world—the lion, the kudu, and the buffalo—and the ugly and "monstrous," including the baboon and the hyena. It would be too much to argue that the animals derive an equal satisfaction from the hunt; yet the quarry often seems to be aware of the rules of the game and quite conscious that it is engaged in a gripping ritualistic contest with man.

Finally, sex and death each have their mystiques. In sexual experience Hemingway's characters often reach a height of understanding they cannot achieve on a purely intellectual basis; this is particularly true of the Frederick-Catherine affair in *A Farewell to Arms* and of the love of Robert and Maria in *For Whom the Bell Tolls.* In *The Sun Also Rises* Hemingway shows the dangers of obsessed sexuality in Cohn and Mike, and Jake is warped because this satisfaction has been denied him. Sexual activity is one of the normal functions; if it is denied, or if it is overemphasized, it becomes abnormal and unsavory. The mystique of death is connected with the sensation of the imminence of death. Those who have constant contact with death—soldiers, bull-fighters, and the seriously ill—

see more clearly than other people; they are wiser and surer in their grip on reality. It is only the nearness of death which brings to Harry (*The Snows of Kilimanjaro*) a lucid insight into his own nature and his relations with others.

(4) Hemingway is by no means devoid of RELIGION, as the above discussion implies, although his concept of supernatural forces is not the conventional religious one. His position is practically that of a pantheist. Nature in its unspoiled state is hardly amiable or friendly, but there is a sublimity about it lacking in urban culture; at least it is clean and free from hypocrisy. Often, as in *The Sun Also Rises,* a clean and inspiring landscape is contrasted with the bitter, quarrelsome, and ugly people who inhabit it. Such "sublime" landscape Hemingway usually associates with mountain regions, with snow, and with clear, cold weather. The perverted "human" landscape is that of the plains, dripping with rain and soiled with the mud of warfare or disaster. This might be considered a kind of private mythology in Hemingway's work. The symbolic contrast between mountain and plain occurs in *The Sun Also Rises, A Farewell to Arms,* and *For Whom the Bell Tolls*; its most striking use is in *The Snows of Kilimanjaro,* where the hero's flight from the warm, damp plain to the snow-capped mountain symbolizes his escape from a sordid life into the purity of death. This demonstrates the religious element in Hemingway's cult of natural action and purity; Kilimanjaro is simultaneously a high snow-covered mountain, a token of purity, and a symbol of the death into which the hero passes at the end of the story. The contact with nature, whether in the Swiss Alps or in the lake country of northern Michigan, brings out the best in Hemingway's characters and exalts them spiritually in the way religious experience does for other people. In *A Farewell to Arms* the landscape of the Abruzzi is specifically associated with the priest who is the only truly religious character in the novel.

In 1970 a posthumous novel "discovered" among his papers was published as *Islands in the Stream.* One wonders about it, especially at ten dollars a copy, and why it took nine years to find it. Reviewers, including Edmund Wilson, find it very uneven, some passages of almost unconscious self-parody. It will be meaningful to the Hemingway aficionado but can hardly add much to the established reputation.

Life: Ernest Hemingway was born in 1899 in a prosperous Chicago suburb. His father, Dr. E. C. Hemingway, was a prominent Chicago physician and sportsman. Hemingway has written a number of tributes to his father in short stories, chiefly those laid in Michigan in which the hero is named Nick Adams. After finishing the public schools and traveling in France, Hemingway took a job on the *Kansas City Star.* Although he held this position only a few months, the journalistic training he acquired at this formative age marked his style for the rest of his career.

In 1917–18 he went to Italy to serve as an ambulance driver on the Austrian front, where he acquired some of the experiences he was to fictionalize in *A Farewell to Arms.* He was severely wounded in the summer of 1918; he was left with numerous scars, and his knee was patched with a platinum cap he was to retain the rest of his life. Returning to America, he married and went to work for the *Toronto Star.* In 1921 he returned to Europe and settled in Paris, where he joined the American expatriates who were forming a literary and artistic circle centering in the Saint-Germain quarter. Here he formed close attachments with Gertrude Stein, Sherwood Anderson, and Ezra Pound; this period had an important influence on his later style. *Three Stories and Ten Poems,* his first book-length publication, appeared in 1923. *The Torrents of Spring* (1926) marks his emancipation from Anderson and others who had previously influenced him; it is a farcical parody of Anderson's style mixed with burlesque on Gertrude Stein, Henry James, Ford Madox Ford, and James Joyce. From 1924 on he traveled widely, seldom remaining in the same place for more than a few months. His literary output continued at a steady rate. His base during much of this time was Key West, Florida, which attracted him through a combination of solitude and sport fishing. In 1933–34 he traveled to Africa on a hunting expedition and emerged with the material for *Green Hills of Africa* (1935) and several of his best stories. *To Have and Have Not* (novel, 1937) was generally considered inferior to his earlier work; it was written in the lull following the African trip. In 1936–37 he made two trips to Spain to cover the

Civil War, and out of the experience wrote the drama *The Fifth Column*, a number of stories, and the novel *For Whom the Bell Tolls*. In this period he engaged in considerable political activity on behalf of the Spanish Loyalists; the Civil War brought to the surface the anti-fascist sentiments he had been developing ever since his travels in Italy in the early Twenties. During the Second World War he served as a war correspondent in Europe; although technically a civilian, he actually took an active part in the campaign in France as an irregular raider. *Across the River and Into the Trees* (1950) made use of these war experiences.

Hemingway contracted, in all, four marriages, three of which ended in divorce. From his 1921 marriage with Hadley Richardson a son, John, was born, and his second marriage with Pauline Pfeiffer (1927) produced two more: Patrick and Gregory. His third wife (1940) was the journalist Martha Gelhorn, and the fourth, whom he met as a war correspondent in England in 1944, Mary Welsh. After the war Hemingway made his home in Cuba, where he divided his time between fishing and writing. A novella, *The Old Man and the Sea*, laid in Cuba and utilizing his fishing experience, appeared in 1952. In 1954 Hemingway was awarded the Nobel Prize for Literature; *The Old Man and the Sea* was specifically mentioned in the Swedish Academy's citation.

Hemingway had been many times injured, grave physical wounds besides the metaphysical "mystic wound," from the war injuries in Italy at eighteen—over two hundred shrapnel fragments, to brain concussions, including a skull fracture, three serious automobile accidents, two airplane accidents within two days in the African jungle with severe internal injury (on this occasion several obituaries appeared which Ernest read later with great pleasure), and miscellaneous war-time wounds. After leaving Castro's Cuba he made a brief trip back to Spain for the bullfights and, seriously ill, returned to the United States to live near Sun Valley, Idaho; twice hospitalized at the Mayo Clinic, he underwent electroshock treatments for deep depression and anxiety. On July 2, 1961, he blew off most of his head with a favorite shotgun. In spite of some attempts to suggest accident while cleaning the gun, his suicide echoes that of his father in 1928 with a civil war pistol, and the incident of an early Nick Adams story, "Indian Camp," the first in the book,

In Our Time: " 'Why did he kill himself, Daddy?' 'I don't know, Nick. He couldn't stand things, I guess.' " Hemingway had been haunted by the idea of suicide for some time.

Chief Works: *The Sun Also Rises* (novel, 1926) is a story of a set of expatriates in Paris who make a hectic trip over the Pyrenees to Pamplona for the bull-fights. The party includes Jake Barnes, an American who has fought in Italy and has been made impotent by a war wound; Bill Gorton, Jake's friend and fishing companion; Lady Brett Ashley, an English woman of breeding who is gradually degenerating into a nymphomaniac and adventuress; Michael (Mike) Campbell, who is waiting for Brett's divorce to become final so he can marry her; and Robert Cohn, a Jewish novelist who is obsessed with a racial inferiority complex and who is slighted and snubbed by the other characters. The early chapters are laid in Paris; Hemingway captures the mood of expatriate life so successfully that it seems unfortunate he did not treat such settings at greater length. After the trip to Spain there are jewel-perfect descriptions of tramping and fishing in the Spanish mountains; this section also contains classic accounts of the details of the bull-fight festival in a provincial Spanish town. While Jake and Bill are enjoying the countryside, however, Brett, Mike, and Cohn are involved in a sordid erotic triangle. Brett dallies with Michael and even goes off with Cohn for a few days, but does not fall in love until she meets Pedro Romero, a young matador. This affair brings the little group, and Romero along with them, almost to the brink of disaster. Finally Brett, in an act of generous renunciation, abandons Romero rather than wreck his career. Cohn, a skilled boxer, takes out his resentment on Jake, Mike, and Romero; Brett decides to marry Mike after all, and Jake, Bill, and Cohn are left in their original state of cynicism.

Although this novel seems negative and pessimistic upon superficial reading, its latent content offers a positive philosophy. Bill and Jake, the "natural" pair, are men of character; they contrast sharply with Mike and Cohn, who are continually bickering over Brett. Mike, Cohn, and Brett are the real representatives of the "lost generation" referred to in the novel's epigraph. Bill and Jake are at their finest when they are out in the sunshine fishing and drinking wine in the Pyrenees; Mike and Cohn are at their most typical in a hotel-room brawl or a tavern orgy. Bill and Jake are occasionally drawn into this environment temporarily, but they feel little kinship with it. They admire Romero because he is a man of tradition (or ritual) and therefore a man of character; he stands up to a beating by the larger Cohn without flinching. The idea that Bill and Jake, for all their superficial cynicism, are "religious" characters is pointed up by contrast with Brett, who feels an instinctive uneasiness in the presence of religion. She is symbolically denied entrance to a church at one point, and confesses her moral vacuum to Jake on another occasion. When she sacrifices her own happiness to Romero's career, an act of renunciation which the reader feels compensates for her previous sins, she remarks, "It's sort of what we have instead of God."

But Jake, the decent part of mankind in its struggle with the "lost generation," has been deprived of his virility by the war; he feels unable to take more than a passive rôle in the events of the plot. Idealism and sensitivity have been killed in the war, and now the "lost generation"—Mike and Cohn—comes to the surface. *The Sun Also Rises* is therefore more than a portrait of the postwar generation; it is a study of the forces which went to make up this generation and which drove its natural and latent idealism temporarily below the surface.

A Farewell to Arms (novel, 1929) is largely autobiographical in its external details. Its hero is Frederick Henry, an American lieutenant in the Italian ambulance corps during the First World War. Henry meets Catherine Barkley, an English nurse, and enters into an affair with her which at first he considers merely casual. When he is wounded by a mortar shell, however, he is thrown together with Catherine in a hospital, and the romance becomes more serious. Catherine is portrayed as a deeply feminine woman who has the ability to "make a home"—i.e., to create an atmosphere of stability and serenity—wherever she pauses, be it in a hospital room or in a sordid hotel. She is temperamentally monogamous; her intense love for Frederick has a deep maternal permanence about it. Under her care he begins to regain his health and to find a new meaning in life. During the period of his convalescence there are several interesting conversations with doctors, nurses, and fellow-patients;

Henry's dialogues with the eccentric major of his outfit are particularly notable. Rinaldi, an Italian army doctor, is a minor classic among Hemingway's characters.

The turning-point of the novel is the retreat from Caporetto, a debacle in which the Italian army is completely disorganized and in which Henry narrowly escapes being shot as a deserter. At length he regains Catherine; they flee to the high mountains of Switzerland, where they find happiness for a time. But Catherine dies in childbirth and Henry is left disillusioned and cynical. The structure of *A Farewell to Arms* is that of the classic tragedy; the cathartic ending is carefully prepared by foreshadowing and mood. Catherine dies not so much because of the war as through the tragic fate which has determined that she and Frederick shall not succeed in their love; the novel has been compared to *Romeo and Juliet* with its "star-crossed lovers." The symbolic contrast between the plain (war, misery, corruption) and the mountain (happiness, purity, love) extends throughout the novel.

To Have and Have Not (novel, 1937) is generally considered an inferior work, although as one of Hemingway's full-length novels it is a book of some importance. Its hero Harry Morgan, cynical, defiant, and independent, is the owner of a Key West sport-fishing boat. As the novel opens Morgan, trusting no one and living shrewdly through his own wiles, is making his living by crossing to Havana with the boat and chartering it to wealthy American sport-fishermen. When one of these sportsmen cheats him out of his charter-fee he is left destitute, and is forced to accept a job smuggling Chinese to Florida. He accepts the money for this job and then cynically puts his passengers ashore again in Cuba, although he is forced to murder a man to accomplish this. In the second part of the novel, several months later, he is shot while running liquor from Cuba in his boat; the boat is confiscated and Harry loses his arm. In the third section, having recovered from his wounds and his amputation, he is propositioned by a band of Cuban revolutionaries—actually little more than gangsters—who want him to smuggle them back into their country. This job is more complicated; it involves stealing his boat back from the officials who have seized it. He manages to steal the boat and get away with the Cubans, only to realize when they murder his mate that they have no intention of paying for their passage and will probably murder him when they get within sight of Cuba. With great ingenuity and courage he manages to catch the Cubans off guard and kill them with their own weapons, but he is mortally wounded in doing so. When he is found by the Coast Guard he has just enough strength to speak the message it has taken him all his life to learn: "No matter how a man alone ain't got no . . . chance." Thus the ethical theme of this novel anticipates that of *For Whom the Bell Tolls*: that man cannot stand alone, that only in union with other men can he find the strength to stand up to evil. Harry, cynical, confused, and lacking in moral conscience, is nevertheless no villain; he is simply not very wise, and learns his wisdom when it is too late. A sub-plot involves a satire on retired business-men, professors, would-be writers, and other members of the leisure class commonly found in resorts like Key West.

For Whom the Bell Tolls (novel, 1940) came out of Hemingway's experiences in the Spanish Civil War. The hero, Robert Jordan, is an American teacher who has come to Spain to fight for the Loyalists out of idealism. The early chapters describe his trip into the mountains north of Segovia and his contact with a secret guerrilla band he is to lead on an important mission: the destruction of a bridge on the highway leading out of the canyon into Segovia. The guerrilla band includes Pablo, its brooding and cowardly leader; Pilar, his courageous and colorful wife; and Maria, daughter of a government official, who has been mistreated by the Fascists before her rescue by the guerrillas. Jordan and Maria fall in love and become intimate; they hope to marry and go to America eventually, but they also realize that in their present situation they must seize every moment of pleasure while they can. For her part Pilar has no illusions; she has read Jordan's fate in his hand and knows he is soon to die.

As plans are laid to blow up the bridge a neighboring guerrilla squad is searched out and massacred by Fascist troops aided by a plane, but there is nothing Pablo's band can do to help. In another scene Jordan makes his way through enemy lines to the Loyalist army; he is struck with the contrast between the devotion and bravery of the guerrilla bands and the confusion and corruption of the army in the plain. He now knows that the battle will be lost, but he returns to his mission. Finally, as a Fascist column comes down the canyon to finish off the battle around Segovia, the band attacks the bridge, drives off the guards, and drops the steel structure into the river with a few well-placed charges. The plans must be revised at the last minute, however, because of Pablo's treachery, and as a result Jordan is fatally wounded. The others offer to attempt to carry him off, but he insists on remaining with a machine-gun in a spot where he can ambush and mow down the pursuing column before he is killed.

On the factual level an adventure novel, *For Whom the Bell Tolls* is in a deeper sense a study of war and the reactions it provokes in men and women. Men are carried away by the partisan slogans of war, but women, wiser, see that life is more important than parties. Jordan the idealist is willing to give his life for his cause, but Maria's first loyalty is to her lover. Pablo is a third type: a moral coward, he becomes a defeatist and seeks to avoid personal danger. In doing so he endangers the whole group, imperils the project of blowing up the bridge, and even causes the death of Jordan. Pablo is wrong; but both Jordan and Maria are right in their way. Pilar stands somewhere between these extremes: a courageous and fervent patriot, she nevertheless understands the importance of individual human happiness.

Across the River and Into the Trees (novel, 1950) came out of Hemingway's Second World War experiences as *For Whom the Bell Tolls* came out of the Spanish Civil War. There, however, the similarity ends. The basic difference is that *Across the River* takes place after the war is over, and thus the combat incidents which interested Hemingway and would doubtless have interested his reader are merely mentioned in passing. In many respects the novel is autobiographical. The hero, the American colonel Richard Cantwell, is Hemingway's age, and he is credited with most of Hemingway's exploits in the Italian army in the First World War. In a sense Cantwell represents what Hemingway would have become had he chosen to become a professional soldier rather than a writer after the war, a choice he might well have made.

The scene is laid in Venice, where the fifty-year-old Cantwell loses himself in an affair with Renata, a "nearly nineteen" year old countess. Most of the novel is devoted to conversations with Renata and others; Hemingway uses the novel as an outlet for a motley set of personal ideas including his opinions of Second World War generals, theories of strategy, remarks on American politics, and innuendoes about his former wives. Young (in his *Ernest Hemingway,* N.Y., 1952) sums up the difficulty well when he remarks that Hemingway seems to be writing the novel under the impression he is being interviewed. "T/5 Jackson, Renata, and others act as straight men, setting up implausible questions so that Cantwell can pontificate." There are better passages: the hunting scenes, especially the opening chapter describing duck-shooting in Venice in winter, and the Colonel's description of America to Renata (Chapter XXXVII). In the end Cantwell dies of a heart attack in his car, shortly after he reminds his driver of the dying words of Stonewall Jackson: "Let us cross over the river and rest in the shade of the trees." In spite of such occasional fine passages, however, *Across the River* has been considered the weakest of Hemingway's full-length works, and often reads like an unconsciously funny parody of his own style (seen even more clearly in *Islands in the Stream*). But minority opinions on the value of *Across the River* have been expressed, by C. Hugh Holman, for example, and the novel may be in for ultimate upgrading.

The Old Man and the Sea (novella, 1952) is sometimes considered to be a short novel. In fact Carlos Baker, official biographer, says categorically it is "neither a short story nor a novella." But it is not a novel either, because it doesn't feel like one. The story is simplicity itself; so are the characters; and a novel has some kind of complexity. The old man, Santiago, is a Cuban fisherman down on his luck who, after eighty-four days without a fish, makes preparations to go out again, helped and encouraged by the boy, Manolin, who can no longer go with him because his father has ordered him to fish with another luckier boat. These two, Santiago and Manolin, share the faith. Alone Santiago hooks a giant marlin in the Gulf Stream. For three days and three nights the voyage lasts. The marlin pulls him far out to sea—too far out—during a two-day struggle until the old man brings the fish alongside, harpoons it with all his strength, and lashes it to the skiff. During the return to harbor sharks attack; the old man kills them with oar, knife, and broken tiller, fighting them until they have eaten all but the skeleton, head, and tail of the great fish, which he tows home, half-dead with exhaustion, achieving a kind of victory in defeat, as the boy rejoins him to minister to his needs.

There are recurrent images in Santiago's mind—Joe DiMaggio and the Yankees, a dream of lions on the coast of Africa, symbols of Christian and early Biblical literature, the stigmata, the sea, the face of the waters, and man given dominion over the fish of the sea, the brotherhood of life. Critical opinion is widely divergent between those who view *The Old Man and the Sea* as a *Moby Dick* with infinite meaning and those who feel that here Hemingway was imitating instead of creating the style that made him famous. There is possibly an unintentional self-parody, but the novella seems to be able to stand, after the shouting has died away, beside Faulkner's *The Bear,* Melville's *Billy Budd* and two or three other great American works of fiction of this intermediate but independent genre.

Most of the dialogue in this story is purportedly taking place in Spanish, which Hemingway "translates" literally to produce a curiously elegant and lyrical effect. The device is sometimes comic, as when Santiago and the boy discuss American big-league baseball in their poetic Spanish. But the more common result is a kind of Biblical dignity which is exactly suited to the subject of the book. The style is seen as well in the Spanish conversations in *For Whom the Bell Tolls* and in some of the bull-fighting stories (e.g., "The Capital of the World") as well as in some stories in which the dialogue takes place in Italian. In another sense *The Old Man and the Sea* belongs with Hemingway's hunting stories: it expresses the theme of the "kinship between hunter and hunted" in the sense of beauty and pity that the old man feels as he struggles with the fish. It has been pointed out that Santiago is established as a saintly, even Christlike figure through the scars on his hands as well as by his name and the austerity of his life; in a sense *The Old Man and the Sea* is a religious story. It is perhaps this aspect of the novella which inspired the Swedish Academy to cite it specifically in awarding Hemingway the 1954 Nobel Prize.

Stories: Hemingway has published in all five volumes of stories, including a definitive volume, *The Fifth Column and the First Forty-Nine Stories* (1938), which includes all his shorter fiction published up to that time. This material may be roughly divided into three groups according to subject matter: (1) stories laid in America, including the Nick Adams fiction of the Michigan wilderness and the American stories of boxing and crime; (2) stories of Americans in Europe, including experiences of the First World War in the Italian army; and (3) African hunting stories.

Of the first group, "The Killers" (1927) is the best known. It is, in fact, Hemingway's most successful story in the popular sense; it was made into a successful motion picture and is often anthologized. The scene is laid in Michigan, the locale of Hemingway's own boyhood. The action is seen through the eyes of the boy Nick Adams, who remains a spectator instead of a central character, although in the end it is his emotional reaction to the situation which chiefly interests the author. Two Chicago hoodlums, Al and Max, come to an unnamed small town to murder Ole Andreson, a Scandinavian prizefighter who has gotten on the wrong side of the gangsters either by throwing a fight or failing to throw a fight, probably the latter. They order dinner in a lunch-room, where a dialogue takes place with George, the counter-man, Sam, the negro cook, and Nick himself, who works there. This dialogue is one of the best examples of the terse and hardboiled style which Hemingway has made famous. When the two gangsters depart, Nick, young and idealistic, feels that something must be done to save the doomed Ole. He goes to Ole's rooming-house to warn him, but Ole is tired of running away from his avengers and has decided to accept death: "After a while I'll make up my mind to go out." But Nick cannot share his resigned cynicism; he is too young and too optimistic. The story implies that this experience marks a turning point in his life, his first contact with evil and his resolution to struggle against it no matter what the cost. This story, short and superficially simple, is actually a minor masterpiece; its dialogue has been polished to perfection, and the ethical statement implied is typical of the best Hemingway.

"Big Two-Hearted River" (1925) is a long two-part story of Nick Adams' adventures tramping and fishing in upper Michigan; it contains the best statement of Hemingway's love for the outdoors as well as some masterfully detailed accounts of the technique of fishing and camping.

The Nick Adams stories as a group, when arranged chronologically, form a most impressive work by Hemingway, which will certainly be included among his most significant and enduring writing. Some critics would call it his best. But they have to be culled from at least three separate volumes, *In Our Time* (1925), *Men Without Women* (1927), and *Winner Take Nothing* (1933). They include "Indian Camp," "The Doctor and the Doctor's Wife," "The End of Something," "The Three-Day Blow," "The Battler," "Big Two-Hearted River," "The Killers," "Fathers and Sons," "Ten Indians," "Now I Lay Me," "Cross Country Snow," and other first person stories and fragments where "Nick" as the earliest autobiographical character created by Hemingway can logically be assumed. A fairly successful Hollywood film has already been put together from these sources. Nick Adams, first as a boy, then as a young man, lives through experiences with his doctor-father mostly in upper Michigan, later in World War I in Italy where Nick makes a famous "separate peace" with the enemy, then the returned young man suffering from shell-shock back in Michigan trying to recover his equilibrium on a fishing trip on Big Two-Hearted River and the continued search for sanity in a post-war world. Nick is an honest, likable, outdoors-type young man with a lot of nerve, but also very sensitive and very nervous. Once understood, he very easily slips into other Hemingway heroes like Jake Barnes, Frederick Henry, and Robert Jordan. The Nick Adams stories, if printed separately, would make a collection comparable to *Winesburg, Ohio* and *The Dubliners.*

"In Another Country" (1927) is typical of the European stories. Outwardly simple, it contains some of Hemingway's most finished dialogue as well as his best examples of laconic irony. The material is drawn from Hemingway's own experience in a Milan hospital following his wounding on the Austrian front in 1918. The story consists almost entirely of conversations between the narrator, a wounded American officer, and an Italian major, before the war a great fencer, whose hand has been hopelessly crippled. The major takes a liking to the narrator and tries to teach him Italian, but grows angry when the American reveals that he "hopes to be" married. The reason is presently revealed: the major's wife has died, and he is unable to resign himself. This revelation breaks down the courageous reserve and self-control he has shown toward his war mutilation. He cries, but he still carries himself "straight and soldierly." The major personifies Hemingway's ideal of heroism, which here seems a fine and splendid one; the major has great physical courage and self-control, but is inwardly sensitive. The true hero is not a brute, nor is he a reckless fanatic; he is a man of emotional sensitivity who controls his instinctive weakness through sheer force of character.

"The Snows of Kilimanjaro" (1936) is one of several stories based on Hemingway's hunting expedition to Africa in 1933–34. Its experimental construction and style make it one of his most radical pieces of fiction from the technical point of view; it is essentially an exercise in stream-of-consciousness. The style alternates between the sparse dialogue and action of *The Sun Also Rises* and flashbacks, set in italics, recalling the hero's past career. These retrospective vignettes resemble Gertrude Stein more than anything else Hemingway has written; their thought is disconnected, their syntax undulating, and their imagery evocative. The story concerns Harry, a cynical and unhappy American writer who is wounded in a hunting accident in a remote district of Africa. In long dialogues with his wife, a former society girl he has married for her money and has grown to hate, he tortures her with reminders of his impending death. His resentment toward her comes from the fact that he has become forced to lead her way of life in order not to lose the money that goes with her; he has grown so used to this level of spending that he knows he can never get along without it. This is the problem of the "sell-out" of the writer, which greatly interested Hemingway at this time; *cf.* similar discussions in *Green Hills of Africa.*

At last Harry dies of gangrene; but at the moment of his death he has a dream in which a friend's airplane carries him off to the "great, high, and unbelievably white" peak of Kilimanjaro, whose supernatural quality has been established early in the story. To Harry in his hallucination the mountain symbolizes purity and escape: escape from the mean, bickering life he has led with his wife, escape from the commercialism into which his writing has degenerated, and, on a physical level, escape from the hot damp plain upon which he lies dying. Again, as in Hemingway's novels, snow, cold, and purity are equated with the finer nature in man and with all that is sublime in the physical world.

Julian, the friend mentioned in the story, is based on the character of Scott Fitzgerald. Several other actual persons are included under altered names.

"The Short Happy Life of Francis Macomber" (1936), also based on the 1933–34 African trip, is written in a more conventional style. An American couple, Francis and Margot Macomber, arrive in Nairobi and hire a professional hunter named Wilson to take them on a game expedition. Macomber is a rather spineless character; his wife despises him and makes no effort to conceal her affairs with other men. Macomber hopes the solitude of the safari will bring them together again. But on his first day of hunting he disgraces himself and loses his chance to win his wife's esteem; he wounds a lion, follows it into the bush, but bolts in terror when the lion charges. Margot now snubs him totally and begins to throw herself at Wilson. The latter is not particularly attracted to her, but as a professional hunter he has learned to accommodate himself to his clients' whims; he accepts her overtures. Macomber knows of the affair, but in his disgrace he is too weak to make any objection. At this point Margot hates Francis, Francis hates Wilson, and Wilson is beginning to despise them both. But the next day, hunting buffalo, Macomber suddenly finds his courage in the excitement of the chase. In the course of a half hour (his "short happy life") he develops character and enthusiasm for life; both Wilson and Margot sense the transformation. Wilson congratulates him on his entry into manhood, but Margot, who realizes she can no longer control him as she has, is inwardly furious. Macomber presently goes with Wilson into the underbrush after a wounded buffalo, and as the two fire at the charging animal a bullet from Margot's gun kills Macomber from behind. When Wilson accuses her of murdering her husband she collapses in tears; but the implication is that she killed him rather than concede to his newly-won status as a man of character and courage.

Thomas Wolfe (1900–1938)

An orderly and established civilization is always wary of Titans. Literary critics especially are inclined to condemn sheer, wild, and uncontrolled force and to admire control and technical perfection; for instance, Willa Cather, restrained, competent, a perfectionist in style, has generally been received more favorably by academic critics than Wolfe, who seems to defy standards of good writing. Wolfe is an author of incredible energy, power, creativity, and ego; he exhibits all the outward marks of genius. He has been criticized with justice for his naïveté, for his egocentricity, and especially for his blundering and inchoate style. It is true he shows certain technical and personal limitations, but he surmounts them well enough with the sheer force of his creativity to be assured of a place as one of the great authors of the twentieth century.

Everything Wolfe wrote was personal and subjective; he had little interest in environments other than his own. His novels are constructed entirely out of the persons and things he encountered during his own lifetime: his home town of Asheville, his family, the town characters of his boyhood, the University of North Carolina, Harvard, and New York City. But although Wolfe writes in great detail about all these things, he is really interested only in one thing: himself. If he was sure of any one fact it was that he himself was a genius. His two principal autobiographical heroes, Eugene Gant and George Webber, are marked men who are somehow different from the rest of humanity; they have monstrous bodies, they eat, drink, fight, weep, and make love on a gigantic scale, and they rage furiously at the banality and indifference which surround them. When Eugene Gant or George Webber receives a rejection slip (an accident which happens frequently to all authors) it is a tragedy of cosmic proportions; all other human calamity palls beside it. When George Webber deserts his mistress the world is shaken to its foundations, and the thunder and lightning continue for a hundred pages. Wolfe conceived his heroes on a gigantic scale which he thought only proper to the subject, but he lacked the insight to see his own emotions in their proper proportions.

The major theme of Wolfe's books is the "cult of genius," the genius, of course, being Wolfe himself. The genius as a type is marked from his birth as different from other children; he is moody, unpredictable, spasmodically violent, and unhappy. He is misunderstood by his fellow men, who persecute him because they unconsciously sense his superiority. He is forever doomed to loneliness; his stature isolates him like an elephant among monkeys. He loves mankind in the abstract, but shrinks from contact with it at close quarters; the bestiality, the materialism, and the shallowness of ordinary men fill him with horror. He creates his tremendous masterpieces, all the time wracked by torment, and then dies, murdered by a complacent and unfeeling society. The remarkable thing is that Wolfe actually lived this legend in many respects; if he errs it is chiefly in overestimating the enmity of ordinary mankind toward the genius.

If Wolfe's novels have any structure at all it is due to the efforts of his editors, Maxwell Perkins and later Edward C. Aswell. Wolfe himself was incapable of limiting the flow of words that streamed from his brain onto paper; it was a sort of compulsion. When the manuscript of *Look Homeward, Angel* was first presented to the publisher it was twice as long as *War and Peace,* or about twelve times as long as the ordinary novel. His editors were forced to attack this material with scissors and pencil and somehow cut it down to publishable length, inserting transitional links where necessary. Wolfe evidently wished to record everything that had happened to him; he had to be persuaded to delete incidents which were intensely interesting to him but which had no organic connection to the novel.

In style Wolfe is inconsistent, awkward, and frequently inchoate. Some of his best passages are written in bare naturalistic narration. Other scenes are strongly influenced by Joyce; these are usually less successful, since Wolfe lacked Joyce's sensitivity for word values. The worst of his prose is to be found in the dithyrambic passages where he pulls out all the stops and loses himself in a tumult of adjectives; often these chapters degenerate into sheer nonsense. The same thing is true of his dialogue; it is best when it is simplest, and becomes mawkish as his characters grow passionate and lyrical. In his moments of greatest violence Wolfe's vocabulary fails him, and he retreats into such nebulosities as "inexpressible," "indescribable," "unspeakable," "inconceivable," "transcendent," "inexorable," and "ineffable." He himself was aware of some of his faults; in "The Story of a Novel" he cites his addiction to adjectives, his Whitmanesque "chants" which blunder on for pages in rhythmic but meaningless rhetoric, his long and tedious catalogues of things seen, of dimensions, textures, hues, architectural details, and countrysides, his fascination with the mere magnitude of experience, with "Amount and Number," his excessively explicit narrative, which could never leave anything to be inferred. He learned something from the critical reception of his first two novels, and became slightly more precise and objective in *The Web and the Rock* and *You Can't Go Home Again*. Yet the two later books lack the splendid energy of the Eugene Gant novels. In struggling for restraint Wolfe may have crippled the one irreplaceable gift he had: his titanic exuberance and creativity. His talent was essentially a romantic one. Of *Look Homeward, Angel* he says, "I really cannot say the book was written. It was something that took hold of me and possessed me, and before I was done with it . . . it seemed to me that it had done for me. It was exactly as if this great black storm cloud I have spoken of had opened up and, mid flashes of lightning, was pouring from its depth a torrential and ungovernable flood." This statement reflects a certain amount of pose, but it nevertheless summarizes Wolfe's own attitude toward the creative process. It is basically a romantic attitude, the theory of "possession" or divine inspiration which Coleridge claims inspired him to write "Kubla Khan," or something of that sort.

Such a theory of art, naturally, is not conducive to economy and precision. When Wolfe began to write the sequel to *Look Homeward, Angel,* which he planned as a novel of two hundred thousand words, it grew into a Frankenstein monster which filled several wooden packing cases. The opening scene alone was longer than the average novel. Since no public could ever be induced to read such a novel, Wolfe and his editor were obliged to cut it drastically, although Wolfe complained, "My soul recoiled before the carnage of so many lovely things cut out upon which my heart was set." Finally, taking advantage of Wolfe's absence on a trip to Chicago, the editor sent it to the presses; the result was *Of Time and the River,* which many critics complained was unselective and unwieldy, although it contained only a tenth of what Wolfe had originally planned for it. Such was Wolfe's obsessive, almost pathological compulsion to write, to express everything he had thought and everything that had happened to him in order to assure it the immortality of the printed page.

After the sheer force of the language itself, the quality that remains in the mind of Wolfe's reader is the color and vividness of his characterizations. It is perhaps not accurate to say that Wolfe has a "skill in characterization"; his most convincing characters are drawn from life itself. Yet he is not without creative imagination in this respect; when the Eugene Gant books were criticized for their subjectivity he went out of his way in *The Web and the Rock* to create believable characters out of whole cloth. The best of these is the athlete Nebraska Crane, a completely fictitious invention, who is nevertheless a striking and convincing character. It seems, therefore, that Wolfe's skill in characterization is a genuine one; it is merely that the people who interested him, and therefore the ones about whom he wanted to write, were those who had stimulated his imagination through intimate personal contact in real life. Luckily Wolfe came from a colorful family and encountered many fascinating people during his life. Yet the success of his novels is not due only to this; a lesser author might have made dull novels even out of such material. It is interesting to compare the account of the affair between Monk Webber and Esther Jack in *The Web and the Rock* with the novel *The Journey Down* by Aline Bernstein, the real-life model for Mrs. Jack, in which she depicts the same relationships from a different point of view and in a different literary technique. *The Journey Down* is not a bad novel, but the comparison will demonstrate the difference between talent and genius. Bernard DeVoto titled a famous essay on Wolfe "Genius Is Not Enough"; yet a novel can succeed on mere genius where it could not succeed on talent or skill alone.

Whatever his stature as a novelist, Wolfe is not a thinker. He has been hailed as a Whitmanesque champion of democracy, but he was equally influenced by the cranky and anti-democratic racism of Mencken, whom he greatly admired; there is anti-Semitism in his work, as well as hostility to negroes, half-breeds, Southern Europeans, and non-Anglo-Saxons generally. He is capable of referring to "the great Boob Public" in one paragraph and waxing eloquent over "all the poor blind fumbling Creatures that inhabit this earth" in the next. He has likewise been typified as a regionalist. This label is somewhat more valid, since all his novels begin with the same characters living in the same narrow and circumscribed rural region of North Carolina. But Wolfe does not share the Cult of the Land of the Southern agrarians; he despises everything that is mundane and mean, the agricultural life included. He is a regionalist only because he wrote entirely about himself, and because he passed the formative years of his life in Asheville, North Carolina. He was as little at home there as he was later in New York or Paris, but he nevertheless felt a genuine affection for the region of his youth. Like most Titans, he is inconsistent; he belongs with Rabelais and Whitman rather than with Flaubert or Henry James. Wolfe is probably not the greatest novelist America has produced, but he is certainly among the most gigantic of America's literary personalities.

Life: Wolfe was born in 1900 in Asheville, North Carolina, a mountain town near the Tennessee border. His father, William O. Wolfe, was a stonecutter and tombstone sculptor who had come to North Carolina in his youth; his mother Julia kept a boarding house, and the family also included a brother Ben. The main events of his early life, concealed only by a few transparent name-changes, are to be found in *Look Homeward, Angel.* Thomas, precocious and well-read, was sent to the University of North Carolina at fifteen. He enjoyed a normal collegiate career, edited the student paper and magazine, and tentatively began writing plays; he graduated in 1920. Through the efforts of his mother he was enabled to continue his studies at Harvard, where he participated in George Pierce Baker's famous "47 Workshop" in playwriting and wrote a drama which was almost accepted by the Theatre Guild. Upon receiving his M.A. from Harvard he joined the English faculty of New York University, where he taught intermittently for six years. Legend has it that his scribbled comments on freshman themes were often longer than the themes themselves. During his N.Y.U. days he made two trips to Europe; on the second trip he began writing the material which was later to be organized into *Look Homeward, Angel.*

The main part of the book was written in America, chiefly in New York and Brooklyn. He made a third trip to Europe in 1928–29, and shortly after his return submitted the enormous manuscript to Scribner's. Maxwell Perkins, the Scribner's editor assigned to the book, began to cut the great mass down and organize it, and with the help of Wolfe produced a publishable manuscript. When *Look Homeward, Angel* was published later the same year it caused a tremendous stir. The respectable society of Asheville rose up in arms; one lady wrote Wolfe that although she disapproved of lynching she would not lift a hand to prevent his "big overgroan karkus" being dragged across the public square to the nearest tree. Numerous lawsuits were instigated, although most of them were later dropped. Critical reception to the book was mixed, although preponderately favorable. Wolfe deeply resented the comments of some critics that the style of the novel was awkward and formless; he castigated professional critics and academicians warmly in his later novels.

The second section of the Gant material was published in 1935 under the title *Of Time and the River.* By this time Wolfe had resigned his teaching position and was living on his royalties in Brooklyn. Shortly after the publication of this novel he left again for Europe, where he began the second, more objective cycle of autobiographical material in which the hero is named George Webber. He had finished an enormous mass of this material by 1938; but in July of that year he was stricken with a tenacious case of pneumonia while on a western trip. Complications ensued, and Wolfe died of a cerebral infection in September of 1938. His remains were brought back to Asheville on Pullman car K-19, the car on which the fictional Eugene Gant had first departed from Altamont. Soon after his death the publishers began working on the huge unfinished manuscript he had left; out of it they constructed *The Web and the Rock* (1939) and *You Can't Go Home Again* (1940). A set of "leftovers" formed *The Hills Beyond* (1941).

The Novels: *Look Homeward, Angel* (1929) is Wolfe's most famous book and his most typical one; both his merits and his failings are here seen in their sharpest form. The novel is entirely autobiographical: Eugene Gant, the hero, is Wolfe himself, his parents are converted to W. O. and Eliza Gant, his brother Ben remains Ben, Asheville becomes Altamont, and the University of North Carolina (sometimes called Chapel Hill) becomes the State University at Pulpit Hill. Eugene is depicted, however, as a member of a large family: there are two sisters, Daisy and Helen, and three brothers, the dissolute Steve, Luke, and the quiet and bitter Ben. Eugene's early childhood is relatively happy, but his later years are marred by continual family strife. The moody and unstable father leaves the household intermittently and finally abandons his family for good; Eliza, driven by an obsession for property and security, opens a boarding-house. At the age of fifteen Eugene goes off to the University, where he is introduced to the world of ideas and begins to recognize his vocation for the first time. His brother Ben dies; the scene of his death from pneumonia, surrounded by the wrangling of the family and the self-pitying maundering of the father, is the height of the novel and a masterpiece of effective narration. After the death of Ben, Eugene, alienated from his saddened mother, realizes he must break with his family and plunge out into the world on his own.

Of Time and the River (1935) continues the story of Eugene Gant. He studies playwriting at Harvard under Professor Thatcher (George Pierce Baker), "tears the entrails" from two thousand books a year, and spends thousands of good hours brooding over a waitress with whom he has fallen in love. At Harvard he meets Francis Starwick, an affected and precious young littérateur; Eugene is impressed with Francis' sophistication and elegance, and they become friends. After his graduation Eugene goes to New York to teach English; later he and Francis go off on an escapade to Paris. Romantic complications occur, and then Eugene discovers that his idol Starwick is a homosexual. Disillusioned, he abandons him to wander over Europe alone until his money runs out. The novel also contains an account of the father's reconciliation with Eliza and his pathetic death.

The Web and the Rock (1939) is a fresh start; Wolfe begins attacking his autobiographical material all over again. The hero, George Webber, called "Monk" because of his extraordinary proportions, is a child of divorced parents; he goes to live with his Uncle Mark and Aunt Maw in the town of Libya Hill (still Asheville). There are many anecdotes of the Joyner clan, to which Mark and Aunt Maw belong. George's friend and protector is the half-Indian Nebraska Crane, athlete, adventurer, and later baseball star. Crane is one of the few entirely fictional characters in Wolfe's work. A notable incidental scene is the rampage and death of Dick Prosser, a pious Negro who goes berserk and is finally killed by a posse, who put his corpse on exhibition in a store window. The story continues with George's college days at Pine Rock College; his hero is the popular social leader Jim Randolph. After a brief interlude in New York with Jim and others, Monk goes to Europe; on the return trip he meets Mrs. Esther Jack (based on the character of Wolfe's friend Aline Bernstein), a Jewish costume designer, wealthy, attractive, understanding, yet maddening to Monk in her suave *savoir-faire* and her sophisticated society attachments, even in her self-assured Jewishness. Monk's affair with Esther occupies the rest of the novel. At last, emotionally exhausted and creatively empty, he blames the loss of his vitality on Esther and abandons her to go back to Europe.

In *You Can't Go Home Again* (1940) Monk comes back from Europe and renews his intimacy with Esther. His novel is accepted, and his relations with the editor Foxhall Edwards (Maxwell Perkins) are described. Aunt Maw dies; he returns to Libya Hill for the funeral but finds the town modernized and altered. He feels awkward and out of place, and realizes "you can't go home again"; the happiness of youth cannot be recaptured by returning to its geographical setting. Back in New York he goes to a lavish and abandoned party at Esther's, during which a fire breaks out and kills two elevator boys. This fact is kept secret from the revelers. It is this party which makes it clear to Monk that he is not of Esther's world; he breaks with her definitely. Monk's existence in Brooklyn during the Depression years is next described at great length. Later he goes to London, where he meets Lloyd McHarg (Sinclair Lewis), who praises and encourages him. The novel closes with an analysis of his break with Foxhall Edwards.

Although the tendency has been to view the Monk Webber novels merely as another version, or as a continuation, of the Eugene Gant sequence, there are essential differences. The background of the hero, in the first place, is not identical; for instance Monk is raised not by his mother but by an aunt, whose clan is described in some detail. More important, the literary approach of the second pair of novels is different; the Monk Webber material is more objective, and Wolfe makes a deliberate effort to stand farther off from his hero. In great measure he succeeds; Monk, although a less "titanic" character than Eugene, is better rounded and perhaps more believable. His faults and the instances of his "wrongness" are often frankly described; in his relations with Esther Jack, for example, he often seems wrongheaded and irrational and Mrs. Jack calm and reasonable. Yet this attempt at objectivity often weakens Wolfe's power; many passages in the Webber books are pedestrian, and the magnificent (although exasperating) ebullience of the Gant books is lacking. Muller convincingly argues in his volume on Wolfe that his death was perhaps not the great literary loss it seemed; he had written all he knew in *Look Homeward, Angel* and *Of Time and the River,* repeated himself less effectively in the second two novels, and would have found himself at a loss for something to express if he had gone on writing. Two novels of genius, however, are enough to demand of an author, and Wolfe's place of honor in American literature is assured.

6. Regionalism and Rural Naturalism before and after Mid-Century

Regionalism as a term has been applied to different literary techniques and schools. In American literature it has been used most often to describe folklore, "local color" writing, and the agrarians. The region is most frequently a rural one, and in the twentieth century a new school of fiction in rural settings has appeared connected with the dominant modes of naturalism. Whatever label may be used to describe this movement, it is a significant and important one, and one which reflects a definite attitude of contemporary authors toward modern civilization.

The naturalistic movement, properly speaking, represented an attempt to create a literature for an age of science and industrialism. It thus tended to emphasize the more typically modern aspects of society: the factory, the city, the proletariat, suburban life, and the world of commerce. Its locales are generally urban or suburban, and its characters are persons who are in one way or another involved in the world of capitalism. When coupled with strong feelings of attachment for place, for the city where the author has his living roots, the result is an urban regionalism which will be discussed later. In the twentieth century a wing of the naturalistic movement, however, has turned in the opposite direction: toward the land, the farm, and the peasant. This school represents in part a reaction to industrialism, and even to civilization itself. Essentially these authors are critical of mechanization and the decline of the traditional values of family and small-town community and man's intimacy with nature.

The movement itself takes two principal forms. Regionalism (of the country variety) may be defined as a form of pastoral literature laid in rural settings and making extensive use of local customs, language, and characteristics, but in which the chief interest lies in the personality and psychological motivation of the rural characters involved. Earlier American authors of this persuasion like Hamlin Garland, Ellen Glasgow, and Willa Cather are discussed in Volume III. Faulkner, Welty, Ernest Gaines, and to some extent Robert Penn Warren, are the major writers in this section who fall primarily in the same category. In some respects these authors, especially Cather, Faulkner, Welty, Warren, and Gaines, are psychological and artistic rather than "agricultural" in their approach to the novel, but their settings are strongly influenced by regional characteristics.

Rural Naturalism, or agrarian literature, on the other hand, is economic and technical in its approach; it is the rural equivalent of the city novel of industrialism. The practical problems of farming are related in great detail; the rural population is shown struggling against nature and the land rather than against each other. Naturally the two tendencies sometimes overlap; Steinbeck's *Of Mice and Men* treats of human conflict as well as the struggle for life. The agrarian novel, however, does tend to show the peasant or farmer as a creature whose main problem lies in wresting a living from the land. Rölvaag (Volume III) and Steinbeck are its chief modern American advocates.

Certain other authors, notably Pearl Buck and Saroyan, are not ordinarily considered regionalists in the strict sense. Their affinity with this group lies in their preoccupation with a limited locale and people—China and the Chinese for Pearl Buck, and the San Joaquin Valley and the Armenian-Americans of the Fresno region for Saroyan. Both these authors have written books about other things and other people, yet their names are mainly associated with their "regionalistic" books, and their fame rests on this part of their work. Other authors who might have been included here, for instance Thomas Wolfe, have been classified elsewhere because it seemed that the psychological or personal element in their work outweighed the importance of the regional element.

The one section of America which has produced the greatest wealth of regional literature is the South. A number of reasons for this could be cited: the South, isolated from the rest of the nation socially and psychologically as a result of the Civil War, has retained a regional culture to a larger extent than any other section of the nation, and in addition its ante-bellum past has provided it with a kind of nostalgic tradition to maintain. Moreover, the antagonism which the South has nurtured for a hundred years against the North, Northern industrialism, Northern commerce, and Northern culture in general has provided it with an emotional focus, however negative, for literary adaptation; in other words the modern Southern writer, in addition to having something to be "for," also has something to be "against," and his work gains a certain emotional sharpness thereby. Finally, the social problems caused by the legal emancipation of the Negro have provided a fertile ground for psychological and social conflict in fiction. It is difficult to imagine how an author like Faulkner would have written had he not lived amid the hatreds, the cruelties, the injustices, and the heroic acts of idealism caused by the Negro problem in the South. This is certainly true for Ernest Gaines as well.

The variety of regions represented in this section should be noted. Between them Faulkner and Welty divide the state of Mississippi, Faulkner's portion being the northwest corner, an enlarged Yoknapatawpha County reaching to Memphis, Tennessee. Robert Penn Warren is Kentuckian but extends his fictional interests to somewhat broader areas of the South. Caldwell represents Georgia, although Carson McCullers and Flannery O'Connor, included under other rubrics, also work this territory. Thomas Wolfe, had he been included here, would have spoken for North Carolina; New Orleans-born Truman Capote for Alabama; and William Styron for the post-Ellen Glasgow Virginia. Ernest Gaines, across the river from Faulkner and Welty, gives us the flavor of French Louisiana, the bayou plantation country north and south of Baton Rouge. Saroyan and Steinbeck between them handle California, the San Joaquin and Salinas Valleys.

The evident reason for the vigor and size of the regionalistic movement in recent American literature is a social one: a reaction against the slick and efficient modernism which has come to dominate American life in the first half of the century. A primitive people do not write pastoral literature; from Hesiod and Virgil to Cather and Welty pastoralism reflects the nostalgia of the city-dweller for the country. America in the twentieth century is the most "civilized" (in the material sense) culture the world has ever seen; it is therefore in some respects the most artificial, the most removed from the elemental realities of life, growth, and death. It is typical of the American writer of the twentieth century to reject this shining, mechanical, but monotonous world of the suburbs, the office, and the factory. Sinclair Lewis rejects it through satirizing it; Hemingway abandons it for Europe, Africa, Cuba, and adventure; and others retreat from it into a world of fantasy. The regionalist escapes in another way: by returning to the country, the farm, the primitive, the inefficient, the elemental. Saroyan's whimsically indolent Armenians are as far from the Chamber of Commerce view of the "American way of life" as are the grotesque Georgia sharecroppers of Caldwell or the decadent Southern aristocrats of Faulkner. The retreat into the past is parallel: Willa Cather writes of the frontier, of American history, of seventeenth-century Quebec, and in doing so tacitly rejects twentieth-century America. Faulkner is also much preoccupied with history and the past. Paradoxically, this rejection of urban American culture has produced some of America's best and best-known writers, the rural naturalists who are considered in Europe the "American school"—Faulkner, Caldwell, Saroyan, Steinbeck, and Welty.

Pearl Buck (1892–1973)

It seems at first unsatisfactory to regard Pearl Buck as a regionalist, yet her main contribution to literature has been the presentation to American readers of a region which is virtually her homeland. Reared in China by missionary parents, she spoke Chinese before she spoke English. Her first published stories were laid in Chinese settings. Since then she has produced books, both fiction and non-fiction, on many different subjects from the problem of the American career woman to the raising of mentally retarded children; yet her main interest has remained China, and she is known to the general public as well as to academic criticism chiefly as the interpreter of Chinese culture to America. When she was awarded the Nobel Prize in 1938—only the third American at that time to be accorded this high honor—the citation specifically referred to her "rich and truly epic descriptions of peasant life in China" as well as her "biographical masterpieces," presumably the fictionalized portraits of her missionary parents. It is worth noting that the two types of works mentioned, along with her own autobiography, comprise all her Chinese stories and tacitly exclude her works which treat only American characters in American settings.

The sense in which Mrs. Buck is not a regionalist is in her treatment, in her approach to the subject. She is not interested in local color; indeed her very choice of Chinese settings seems to have been little more than an accident of environment. Under other conditions she might easily have written books about Peruvians, Eskimos, or the sharecroppers of the American South. Her interest lies entirely in what is general, universal, and human in the Chinese people: the struggle of men to wrest a living from the soil, the intricate tensions of family relationships, the human reactions to violence and disaster, the effects of success and prosperity on the humble and hardworking, and the contrast between decadent aristocracy and crude but vigorous yeomanry. Yet she is not primarily interested in social processes or social relationships; her method is internal, analytical, and primarily concerned with the individual. The reader lives intimately with her fictional characters; they are not sentimentalized or glamorized, neither are they rendered brutal by an excessively naturalistic treatment.

The fact that Mrs. Buck's characters are foreigners, speaking an intricate foreign language which is almost impossible to translate adequately into English, involves her in certain stylistic difficulties. Under the conditions it is almost impossible, for example, to write natural dialogue; few American readers understand, or are interested in, the way Chinese really talk, and to make them talk like Americans (in slang, for instance) would be ludicrous. She approaches the problem by having them speak distinguished if somewhat stilted English, attempting through diction and syntax to recreate the peculiar dignity of the Chinese language as she knows it. The effect has often been described as "Biblical," and it is likely that she has consciously or unconsciously modeled the style on the

English Bible. Many sentences begin with "Now" or "And," and occasional archaisms in construction and vocabulary heighten the effect. A flowing, dignified, almost epic quality results: "When the child was a month old Wang Lung's son, its father, gave the birth feasts, and to it he invited guests from the town and his wife's father and mother, and all the great of the town." In surmounting her problem Mrs. Buck has created a style with an unusual advantage. Since it is, so to speak, "translated from the Chinese," it is devoid of American idioms and slang, and thus is easily translatable into other languages. It is easy to see how the Swedish Academy committee, examining candidates for the Nobel Prize, might find a Swedish translation of *The Good Earth* more impressive than a Swedish version of Hemingway, Wolfe, or Faulkner, who would tend to lose their peculiar stylistic merit in translation. The effect of translated dialogue is not unlike that which Hemingway achieves with his Spanish characters. It legitimatizes a certain poetic highlighting of prosaic speech without violating basic realism.

Life: Pearl Buck, *née* Sydenstricker, was born in 1892 in Hillsboro, West Virginia, where her missionary parents had returned on a brief furlough. She traveled to China with them while still an infant, and for all practical purposes was reared solely in China. Growing up in Chinkiang, a city on the Yangtse River, she learned Chinese folklore and Buddhist and Taoist magic from a nurse. Even as a child she manifested a natural story-telling facility, and her juvenile stories were published in the *Shanghai Mercury* when she was still a girl. She received her formal education at a boarding school in Shanghai and at Randolph Macon Woman's College at Lynchburg, Virginia, where she was elected class president and wrote for a student paper. Returning to China, she found her mother seriously ill and spent two years nursing her; meanwhile she married Dr. John Lossing Buck, an "agricultural missionary." When her mother recovered, the family followed Dr. Buck to his work in a town in North China; they remained there for five years, then moved to Nanking, where Mrs. Buck taught English at the University of Nanking. In March 1927 the city was looted by Nationalist troops; the Bucks' house was burned and the family narrowly escaped death. The catastrophe also destroyed the manuscript of Mrs. Buck's first novel; by this time she was writing steadily, and had published in *The Atlantic Monthly* and other American magazines. Her first novel, *East Wind: West Wind,* appeared in 1930. In 1931 she wrote *The Good Earth* in three months; the novel was an immediate success, and she was awarded a Pulitzer Prize the following year. Although none of her subsequent books were considered to come up to the standard of this masterpiece, her work has generally been favorably regarded by critics. In 1933 she published a translation of one of China's most famous modern novels, *All Men Are Brothers*; her own *House of Earth* trilogy, the continuation of *The Good Earth,* was completed in 1935. The same year she was awarded the Howells Medal by the American Academy of Arts and Letters, and in 1938 she was awarded the Nobel Prize for Literature, a remarkable achievement when it is remembered that *The Good Earth* had appeared only seven years before. Beginning in 1938 she wrote several novels with American settings, of which *The Proud Heart* is best known. Around 1941 she began to return to her Chinese material. In recent years her work has been extremely versatile; she has published children's books, essays in defense or support of China and its people, an autobiography, and several collections of short stories. Mrs. Buck lived more or less permanently in the United States since 1934. Divorced in 1934, she was married again in 1935 to Richard J. Walsh, president of a publishing firm and editor of the magazine *Asia.* She died in Vermont in March, 1973.

Chief Works: *The Good Earth* (novel, 1931) describes the lives of Wang Lung, a hard-working Chinese peasant, and his wife O-lan, passionately attached to the soil and struggling to raise themselves from the poverty of their class. The novel begins with the marriage of Wang Lung to O-lan, a slave girl from the formerly aristocratic but declining House of Hwang. The two work together through hardship, famine, flood, and sickness to wrest a living from their land and to increase their holdings, and eventually they achieve prosperity as the decadent Hwang clan declines. Three sons and two daughters are born to the marriage; Wang Lung, now wealthy, takes a concubine, the beautiful young Lotus, but O-lan serves him and her children patiently until her death. A sub-plot describes a family of shiftless relatives who come to live with Wang Lung; one year during the great flood Wang Lung's farm is miraculously spared by pillaging robbers, and he learns that his uncle is secretly allied to the robber band. Wang Lung cleverly succeeds in inducing the opium habit in this troublesome uncle and his wife, and they become too involved in their dreams to bother him further. After O-lan dies and his sons begin to marry, Wang Lung begins to enter into the decline of his life. He lives almost alone on his land, attended only by a single daughter and by his slave, the young Pear Blossom. As the novel ends he exhorts his sons never to relinquish the land he will bequeath them upon his death, but they are already secretly planning to sell the land and use the proceeds for various projects of their own. Lacking Wang Lung's dogged attachment to the soil, they belong to a new generation of "wreckers and builders"; one son is a revolutionary, and the other two are modern and practical in attitude. Thus the course of Wang Lung's career parallels the development of modern China and the emergence of progressive and revolutionary elements in her peasantry.

The Good Earth is the first volume of a trilogy titled in its entirety *The House of Earth*. The second volume, *Sons* (1932) follows the career of the three sons described in the earlier novel; they become respectively a merchant, a rich man, and a "good" war lord. The novel is said to be based on the traditional Chinese theme of the benevolent war lord, a kind of Robin Hood who robs the rich to aid the poor. *A House Divided* (1935) continues the story through the era of the Kuomintang and the agrarian reform. Yuan, a grandson of Wang Lung, is educated in America and returns to his country to aid his people in modernizing their agricultural system.

The Exile (novel, 1936) is a fictionalized biography of Mrs. Buck's mother, in which her father appears as a secondary character. The pendant to this novel is found in *Fighting Angel* (1936) another fictionalized biography in which the same marriage is seen from the point of view of the father. These two novels are probably Mrs. Buck's most important works after *The Good Earth*, and were specifically referred to by the Nobel committee in their award citation.

Dragon Seed (novel, 1941) marks Mrs. Buck's return to the Chinese setting after several American novels. The scene is the Sino-Japanese war; the plot follows the fortunes of Ling Tan and his family through this national catastrophe. The remarkable scenes of the looting of Nanking are drawn from Mrs. Buck's personal experience. A sequel, *The Promise* (1943), depicts the Japanese conquest of Burma; the chief character, Lao San, is a son of Ling Tan who fights the Japanese in the army of Chiang Kai-shek. These later novels are particularly interesting as social and historical documents, and for the picture they present of Mrs. Buck's own experiences, but they are not considered the equal of *The Good Earth* in literary quality.

William Faulkner (1897–1962)

The awarding of the Nobel Prize to Faulkner in 1950 brought home to the American public the fact that in Europe he was considered at that time the foremost living American author; today many American critics are inclined to agree in this judgment. The distinction is one his work properly deserves. Close to thirty book-length critical studies of Faulkner have appeared in the sixties, which indicates something of his stature and the growing recognition of it. He is sometimes considered an agrarian naturalist in the manner of Erskine Caldwell; actually he is more meaningful and profound, as well as more artistically original, than any of the American naturalists with the possible but not necessary exception of Hemingway. His novels are generally laid in rural settings, but the problems they treat are psychological and moral rather than physical. His great subject on the surface is the decline of the South: its economic sterility, its moral disintegration, and its struggle to resist the progressive and materialistic civilization of the North. But by implication and enlargement there must be the same struggle to preserve "the old verities" wherever they are threatened. The protagonists of his novels are the decayed aristocrats of the "Sartoris" type; whether their names are Sartoris, Compson, McCaslin, or Stevens, they are old Southern families past the peak of their prosperity and riddled with moral decay, yet still finer than their antagonists, the "Snopes" clan—the efficient, materialistic carpetbaggers, merchants, and entrepreneurs—who are gradually superseding them. In each of Faulkner's novels the Sartoris characters struggle valiantly but futilely against the encroachment of the Snopeses. In *The Sound and the Fury* the Compson family struggles against a Snopes in their own midst: their brother Jason. In *Sartoris* the Sartoris and Compson clans are confronted by the Snopeses themselves; and these latter are seen at the height of their triumph in *The Hamlet, The Town,* and *The Mansion.* Even in *Sanctuary,* the least profound and the most sensational of Faulkner's novels, the "Sartoris" Temple Drake is defeated physically and symbolically by the perverted "Snopes" Popeye. A third class of characters are the Negroes, often more heroic and admired than either Sartoris or Snopes, perhaps best represented by Dilsey in *The Sound and the Fury,* who endured, but also by Lucas Beauchamp of *The Bear* and *Intruder in the Dust,* Nancy Mannigoe of *Requiem for a Nun,* and Uncle Parsham Hood of *The Reivers.* Faulkner's mission is to preside over the spiritual death of the old South and to study the forces which are preparing its new awakening.

Faulkner is a highly individual author, and therefore difficult to classify. His earlier Yoknapatawpha County material (*Sartoris* and the early stories) is naturalistic regionalism, slightly influenced by the style of Sherwood Anderson and demonstrating as well a personal lyrical quality which was to become more prominent in his later work. Beginning with *The Sound and the Fury* (1929) his work may be more aptly described as "symbolic naturalism," and his style a radical form of stream-of-consciousness utilizing difficult and highly original experiments in chronology and point-of-view. The trend away from realism continues throughout his career. The beginning of *Absalom, Absalom!* is the best example of expressionism in American fiction. Because of his interest in stream-of-consciousness techniques Faulkner may also be considered a kind of psychological novelist. In both *The Sound and the Fury* and *Light in August* the action centers around the events of a single day, but previous and subsequent incidents are filled in through recollections of the characters and through adroit and complex flashbacks, in either case seen internally, through the often semi-conscious reactions of the characters involved. The interest of the author is not so much in the incidents themselves as in the complicated mental reactions of the characters to the incidents (like Quentin's answer to Shreve McCannon's question at the end of *Absalom, Absalom,* "Why do you hate the South?"—"I don't hate it. *I don't. I don't! I don't hate it!*")—reactions often so thoroughly non-verbal that new narrative techniques must be devised to communicate them. Here Faulkner resembles Proust and Joyce more than he does the American naturalists Farrell, Dreiser, or Hemingway, and comes closer to their stature too.

From another point of view Faulkner is a regionalist, although his region is an imaginary one based on reality: "Yoknapatawpha County," including its county seat of Jefferson. Since Jefferson is described as seventy-five miles south of Memphis on the Illinois Central Railroad, it can easily be identified as Oxford, Mississippi, where Faulkner has passed most of his life; but at the same time Yoknapatawpha County is a fictional region (William Faulkner, Sole Owner and Proprietor) only loosely related to the real Mississippi county of Lafayette. But when Faulkner departs from Yoknapatawpha territory (as in the early novel, *Soldiers' Pay,* and in *The Fable,* 1954) his fiction loses a measure of its grass-roots strength and significance. Unlike Wolfe, Faulkner has not faithfully and painstakingly recorded the history of his own family. Certain incidents, like the murder of old Colonel Sartoris, are drawn from family traditions, but in the main Faulkner's characters are the product of his own imagination. For this reason Faulkner is able to create characters of a greater diversity than Wolfe: the gangster Popeye, the spinster Miss Burden, the rebellious young Temple Drake, and the brooding Harvard student Quentin Compson are equally forceful, real, and meaningful.

Faulkner, like Hemingway, is greatly concerned with erotic passions, with cruelty, and with the connection between the two. Where Hemingway's cult of violence is uninhibited, almost innocent, Faulkner's is twisted, melancholy, and guilty; his mood resembles that of Baudelaire or Poe. His characters are seldom moved by normal urges: Quentin Compson (*The Sound and the Fury*) is in love with his sister, Popeye (*Sanctuary*) is impotent, the idiot Ike Snopes (*The Hamlet*) is in love with a cow, and Joe Christmas (*Light in August*) becomes the paramour of a spinster a generation older than he is. Except in the case of *Sanctuary,* however, Faulkner does not relate these horrors for mere shock effect; he is interested in aberration as a symbol of Southern decline, and as such treats it with the superb objectivity of a true artist.

Many of Faulkner's characters, although diverse, tend to fall into a set of clearly defined groups. There are rebellious and nymphomaniacal young girls of aristocratic families (Caddy Compson, or at least her daughter, Temple Drake); there are naive country girls, easily exploited by town slickers (Dewey Dell, Lena Grove); there are moody younger sons, reckless and rebellious but proud of their family backgrounds (Quentin Compson, Bayard Sartoris). But although Faulkner sometimes recreates the same characters, he seldom repeats his stories; with a tremendous inventiveness he finds a new situation, plot, or structure for each novel.

There is little overt political content in Faulkner's work. It is apparent, however, that he is not an easy liberal in the ordinary sense. His sympathies are with the aristocratic and highly principled Sartorises, as decadent as they may be, and against the parvenu Snopeses. He shows little interest in humanitarianism or socialistic planning, especially in his earlier works, and has even been wrongly accused of condescension toward Negroes. A Sartoris would any day rather go hunting with a Negro than with a Snopes. His later work, however, shows evidence of a more openly liberal attitude: in *Intruder in the Dust* (1948) he offers a positive solution to the Negro problem, although one which may not be acceptable to Northern liberals, and since then he has frequently condemned racism, violence, and the activities of "White Supremacy" groups in the South. During the controversy over school desegregation in the South in 1954–56 Faulkner at first took a liberal stand endorsing the Supreme Court decision and then, in a *Life* editorial, attacked the extremism of Northern pressure groups like the NAACP and warned the North to "go slow" now that it had won an important victory in principle. Actually Faulkner is no social thinker and is out of place in a political controversy. His approach to the Negro problem is purely aesthetic, psychological, and physiological—although underneath, it is also always moral; he describes both Sartorises and Negroes as they appear to him without idealizing them for didactic purposes. It should be pointed out again that one of the most frequently recurring characters in his work is the strong-willed, courageous, and loyal Negro woman whose character is superior to that of the whites around her (Dilsey in *The Sound and the Fury,* Nancy in *Requiem for a Nun*). His strongest condemnation of slavery is perhaps that found in the long version of *The Bear,* where he develops at some length the idea that the fertile land of the South has been eternally cursed by this unnatural domination of man over land and man over man and by the sexual and psychological evils that have come out of it. It should not be imagined that because Faulkner uses the word *nigger* and sometimes shows Negroes as lazy and incompetent like other people that he is a white supremacist. He is an artist, and where this particular problem is concerned he faithfully records the events and attitudes of the culture he is describing. Rightly understood Faulkner's compassion and comprehension of responsibility for racial problems are outstanding not only in the works mentioned just above but also in *Absalom, Absalom* and *The Reivers.*

Although Faulkner's best work is ostensibly concerned with the American South, as deeply rooted in place as Joyce is in Dublin, the problems of the South, people's relationship to the land, the moral wrong of possession, people's relationship to people, the vulgarization of a materialistic age with the loss of old courtesies and values, are the problems of the nation as a whole and the problems of the twentieth century world—which Europeans are likely to call Americanization. With a sharp focus on Yoknapatawpha County, the picture is the world's universal image. Otherwise the early European enthusiasm for Faulkner would be incredible. Faulkner always used a double frame of reference in his fiction (which helps to universalize it) although with considerable sublety. First is the Bible itself, appropriate to Bible-belt South. Casual references to scriptures are meaningful to the people of his stories, Absalom, the affair of Noah's sons used so centrally in *The Bear,* the nativity, the passion. And the dominant denominations of the South are all there too—Baptists, Methodists, Presbyterians, Episcopalians. There is also as a second frame the classical inheritance of the South—the modified Greek columns, the Grecian urn, Clytemnestra, the sense of Greek tragedy. This southern combination of the two is convincing and effective.

Where Faulkner's style is most difficult and the narrative line most complex, he demands the active participation of the reader in the creative process. As Quentin tries to get at the truth of the past in *Absalom, Absalom* by a compulsive telling and retelling of the story, bringing in new historical sources including interviews and letters, finally bringing Canadian Shreve into the telling or reconstruction as well, so is the reader drawn in. The demands are great—you may have to puzzle out an impossible sentence or go back to pick up a lost thread, but the rewards are great. Among other prose writers who make similar demands are Joyce in *Ulysses* and *Finnegans Wake,* Proust, Kafka, Gertrude Stein. Poets do it more often, like Eliot and Pound. As has been said of some of their work: it doesn't have to be difficult to be good, but it helps. Perhaps one other element in Faulkner's fiction should be noted, its capacity for comic vision, as in *The Hamlet, The Town,* and *The Mansion.* It is Joycean in size but thoroughly indigenous and American. His last novel, *The Reivers,* published shortly before his death, is hugely comic, analogous in kind to the last gift of Thomas Mann, *The Confessions of Felix Krull, Confidence Man.* Here the "reivers," or thieves, or con men are three in number. The 1970 film release with Steve McQueen as Boon Hogganbeck catches the spirit of the Faulkner novel very well. The exuberance and love of life manifested by that beautiful early automobile, the Winton Flyer, the wild trip to Memphis, and the horse race are equivalent to affirmation. Like Molly Bloom we have to say, "Yes."

Life: William Faulkner (the family's name is more traditionally spelled Falkner) was born in New Albany, Mississippi in 1897. His family was a distinguished one; its founder, Col. William C. Falkner, was a Civil War hero and a novelist in his own right. To Faulkner his great-grandfather is a symbol, the epitome of the gallant aristocracy the war had destroyed. He recreates him in his fiction as Colonel Sartoris, a distinguished figure in the post-war gentry of Yoknapatawpha County. Faulkner's father, Murray C. Falkner, was for many years treasurer of the State University at Oxford (later the University of Mississippi); during the writer's lifetime the family, like the fictional Sartoris clan, was aristocratic and financially secure but no longer wealthy. Faulkner himself, exaggerating somewhat, describes its status as that of "genteel poverty." His education was incomplete; he quit school at the eleventh grade, but finished a year's work at the University after the war. His war experiences played an important part in the formation of his character and his fiction. Too short in stature for the Army Air Corps, he enlisted as a cadet in the Canadian branch of the Royal Flying Corps in 1918. He was trained as a pilot in Toronto but the war ended before he was commissioned. A legend that he was wounded in combat is unfounded; actually he was injured in a flying escapade while celebrating the Armistice in 1918. His disappointment at missing the experience of combat was a great one; the theme appears in several of his early stories and recurs years later in *The Fable.*

Faulkner began to write soon after the war; he thought at first he wanted to be a poet, and wrote fiction only to support himself while he wrote poetry. The poetry, although it showed talent, was not remarkable. He enrolled in the University, failed an English course, and restlessly went on writing. He was greatly aided during this period of his life by a friend, Phil Stone, an Oxford lawyer who gave him advice, encouragement, and financial assistance. On Stone's advice he went briefly to New York, where he worked in a bookstore and turned out a large number of stories. His first published work, a volume of poems entitled *The Marble Faun,* appeared in 1924. The following year he went to New Orleans, where he met Sherwood Anderson, by this time already an established author. Under Anderson's influence he wrote *Soldiers' Pay,* his first novel; Anderson persuaded a publisher to print it, and Faulkner was launched as an author. From 1925 to 1929, however, he was forced to continue working part-time at odd jobs, including furnace-tending at the University of Mississippi. After a brief trip to Europe in 1925 he went on writing novels; *Mosquitoes* (1927) and even, to a certain extent, *Sartoris* (1929) were pot-boilers which he wrote in the hope of winning financial independence so he could write something more significant. The strategy was a mistake. Stone now persuaded him to try to write the best book he could, regardless of its marketability. The result was *The Sound and the Fury* (1929), a rewriting of a novel he had earlier abandoned. The novel was a critical success, although not a financial one. On the strength of it, however, he married Estelle Oldham

(1929) and gave up his old jobs to devote himself to full-time writing. *Sanctuary* (1931), which he allegedly wrote solely to make money, achieved its end; it created a sensation, became a popular success, and brought its author financial independence. From that time his reputation has constantly grown, although in 1946, immediately before interest in his work was revived by Malcolm Cowley's publication of *The Portable Faulkner,* there was a brief period when all of his nineteen volumes were out of print.

In 1933 Faulkner made the first of several expeditions to Hollywood to work as a screenwriter. For the most part, however, he preferred to remain in Oxford, where he lived simply and took little part in literary or intellectual activities until he became resident writer at the University of Virginia at Charlottesville in 1957. He had one child, a daughter who often traveled with him. He was awarded the 1949 Nobel Prize for Literature in 1950 and delivered a brief speech of acceptance before the Swedish Academy which has become a classic in our time. Often reprinted it contains important clues to Faulkner's work: "Our tragedy today is a general and universal fear so long sustained by now that we can even bear it. There are no longer problems of the spirit. There is only the question: When will I be blown up? Because of this, the young man or woman writing today has forgotten the problems of the human heart in conflict with itself which alone can make good writing. . . . He must learn them again. He must teach himself that the basest of all things is to be afraid, and, teaching himself that, forget it forever, leaving no room in his workshop for anything but the old verities and truths of the heart. . .—love and honor and pity and pride and compassion and sacrifice." It concludes with the vision that man will endure and prevail. Since 1950 criticism of his work has been extensive and generally sympathetic. In June of 1962 William Faulkner was thrown from a horse; three weeks later he died from a heart attack on July 6 in Oxford, Mississippi.

Chief Novels: *The Sound and the Fury* (novel, 1929) marks Faulkner's first radical departure from the traditional form of the novel; it is also his most complicated book technically, and one of his most successful artistically. The title is from *Macbeth,* V:5: ". . . a tale told by an idiot, full of sound and fury, signifying nothing." The structure is extremely complex. The story is divided into four sections, each related through the mind of a different character, and there are countless flashbacks and switches in chronology. The "central time" of the action is 1928, but parts of all four sections take place in 1910. The main characters are Jason and Caroline Compson, heads of the aristocratic but declining Compson clan of Jefferson; Candace (Caddy), their daughter; her daughter named Quentin for her brother; Benjamin (Benjy), an idiot son; Quentin, the idealistic thinker of the family; Jason, a third son, materialistic and selfish; Dilsey, a self-effacing and intelligent old Negro servant; and Luster, the fourteen-year-old Negro companion and bodyguard of Benjy. The kernel of the plot is as follows: Caddy is seduced by the worthless Dalton Ames and later married off to an opportunistic Northerner, who abandons her. Quentin, who only half-realizes he is in love with his sister, is filled with shame at her betrayal and finally drowns himself in Cambridge as a sort of expiation. Benjy is at first happy playing in his pasture, but the land is sold to pay Quentin's tuition at Harvard (symbol of the selling-out of the Southern land-holding class to the North). Later his brother Jason obtains legal guardianship over Benjy and has him sterilized (symbol of the extinction of Southern aristocracy at the hands of materialists); in the end Benjy is put into a state institution. His niece Quentin finally tricks and gets the better of Jason. Since the mother is self-centered and helpless, Dilsey presides over the disintegration of the family with loving patience and resignation. This novel makes extensive use of stream-of-consciousness narration, free association, and diffuse location in time. The narrative section filtered through the consciousness of Benjy is, literally, a tale told by an idiot and one of the most compelling, imaginative *tours de force* by any modern artist.

As I Lay Dying (novel, 1930) relates the death of Addie Bundren, a farmer's wife in Yoknapatawpha County, and the efforts of her family to carry out her dying wish to be buried in the family plot in Jefferson. As in *The Sound and the Fury,* the story is seen through the eyes of various characters in succession, in this case Addie herself, Addie's husband Anse, her daughter Dewey Dell, and her sons Cash, Darl, Jewel, and Vardaman. As Addie dies she supervises Cash in the construction of her coffin; the doggedly precise Cash explains carefully in his section just why he built the coffin as he did. The family are burdened with a staggering set of obstacles in their efforts to carry Addie's body to Jefferson. A flood wipes out a bridge, the mules are almost drowned in the river, Cash's leg is broken in a wagon accident, Darl, losing his wits, sets fire to a barn and is packed off to the insane asylum, and Dewey Dell, seeking a "remedy" for her illegitimate pregnancy, is seduced by a cynical town druggist's helper. As the journey proceeds it assumes the proportions of a saga. When the mother is finally buried, Anse buys himself a set of store teeth and suddenly marries "a duck-shaped woman with pop eyes" he encounters in the town. His obligation to his dead wife is fulfilled, and he now looks only to the future. Addie Bundren's funeral journey is an epic one, suggesting the exodus from Egypt, crossing the river Jordan, or the trip of the dead across the river Styx.

Sanctuary (novel, 1931) is the most lurid of Faulkner's novels in content, although relatively conventional in technique. This unbeatable combination made it an enormous popular success; it was later made into a motion picture upon which Faulkner collaborated. The heroine is an intelligent but rebellious and neurotic young college girl, Temple Drake. She flees on an escapade with Gowan Stevens, the characterless young nephew of the lawyer Gavin Stevens, who later reappears in *Intruder in the Dust*. Through Gowan's drunkenness the car is wrecked, and he leads Temple to a lonely farmhouse where she falls into the hands of a gang of moonshiners. The leader of this band is the strange and perverted social misfit Popeye, himself impotent, who derives a vicarious satisfaction from Temple's violation at the hands of Alabama Red, another member of the gang. Gowan, beaten, disappears, and Temple subsequently undergoes various exotic and painful adventures including a confinement in a Memphis brothel whose madam is at first proud to gain the patronage of the important Popeye but later shocked by his depravity. Alabama Red is killed by Popeye in the act of making an unscheduled visit to Temple, who eventually escapes. Meanwhile Goodwin, another of the bootleggers, has been arrested for a murder actually committed by Popeye. He is defended by Horace Benbow, a lawyer who wishes to expiate his selfish and conventional life by fighting for this unpopular cause. Benbow attempts to use Temple's evidence to save his client, but she has been so unbalanced by her experience that she only prejudices the jury against Goodwin. Goodwin is lynched by a mob, Benbow barely escapes, and Temple goes off to Paris to forget her three months' nightmare. Popeye, the evil focus of the whole drama, escapes to Florida and is later hanged for a murder he did not commit. Faulkner at one time declared that he wrote *Sanctuary* solely to create a sensation and make money. It did both these things; it is not, however, as bad a novel as Faulkner's statement, or a summary of its plot, would suggest. Temple's character is vividly established, and the plot achieves more suspense and general interest than it does in much of Faulkner's work. There is also an underlying symbolism—the rape of the South at the hands of an impotent North (Popeye)—but the theme is not of any importance in the basic structure of the book and means little to the ordinary reader. An important sequel to *Sanctuary* is found in *Requiem for a Nun.*

Light in August (novel, 1932) opens as a country girl, Lena Grove, comes to Jefferson on foot seeking Lucas Burch, the father of the child she is about to bear. When she reaches the town, however, her destiny becomes involved with that of Joe Christmas, a young sawmill worker with a touch of Negro blood. Christmas, an orphan, has been raised to manhood by a dour Scotch farmer; a bitter experience with a small-town harlot has made him antisocial and brooding. His wanderings throughout the South have at last led him to Jefferson, where he becomes the protégé of a mysterious spinster named Burden, daughter of carpetbaggers who settled in the town after the Civil War. He lives in a cabin on Miss Burden's land and eventually becomes her lover. When Lucas Burch, fleeing Lena, arrives in town Christmas utilizes him as a partner in his secret bootlegging enterprises, which involve high-jacking liquor from trucks and selling it to the town loafers by the bottle.

All this is background; the key action of the novel takes place on the day Lena arrives in town. On the morning of this day Miss

Burden, brooding over her imminent old age, attempts to kill Christmas and herself with an obsolete Confederate pistol; the weapon misfires, and Christmas, emotionally overwrought, kills her with a razor. Burch, drunk, sets fire to the house, is caught, and arrested for the murder; he escapes by putting the blame on Christmas. When Lena gives birth to her child Burch flees, hopping the first train he can get and leaving Byron Bunch, a good man who has already taken care of Lena, to look after her. At the end of the story Byron and Lena take up the journey, crossing over into Tennessee, just as Lena at the beginning leaves Alabama, coming to Jefferson in Mississippi. In the meantime Christmas has been captured in a nearby town and brought back to the Jefferson jail. When he escapes he is tracked to the house of the Rev. Hightower, a disgraced minister, and brutally slain by Percy Grimm, a conceited young national guardsman. *Light in August* is structurally similar to Joyce's *Ulysses*: it focuses on the events of a single day and describes the reactions of various characters to these events. There are also passages, especially of transition, that sound much like Gertrude Stein. This novel with three separate story strands, centering on Lena, Joe Christmas, and the Reverend Hightower, is skillfully put together with a sense of the variety and multiplicity of life itself. It is one of three or four candidates for the position of Faulkner's greatest achievement.

Absalom, Absalom! (novel, 1936) is one of Faulkner's most intricate and difficult novels. Its plot centers around the career of the Mississippi planter Thomas Sutpen, who dies in 1869; but the story is seen through the eyes of young Quentin Compson in 1910. The mysterious and demonic Sutpen comes to Jefferson when it is still a frontier community. He buys a hundred-square-mile section of land ("Sutpen's Hundred"), imports a French architect to build a mansion, and brings in a wagon-load of slaves. After he has finished furnishing the house in expensive taste, he consolidates his position in the community by marrying Ellen Coldfield, daughter of a leading citizen of Jefferson. Although he is considered strange and unfriendly, he grows immensely rich; he invites his neighbors to lavish dinners and entertains them with wrestling matches between his slaves. His wife bears him a son, Henry, and a daughter, Judith. Both of these children have strange qualities; Judith takes an unnatural pleasure in the ferocious combats of her father's slaves. Henry goes off to the University and there meets Charles Bon; by coincidence Charles is Henry's half-brother. Thomas Sutpen has been married before to a West Indian woman, but has abandoned her after discovery of her Negro blood. Now this ghost of his first marriage returns to haunt him; Charles meets his half-sister Judith and falls in love with her. At this point the source of Sutpen's wealth is revealed; it came from the dowry of the first wife he has abandoned. He refuses to recognize Charles as his son.

The war intervenes. Then, as Charles is about to marry Judith, he is mysteriously killed by Henry Sutpen. Henry flees and drops out of sight for many years. Meanwhile Thomas Sutpen returns from the war to find his wife dead, and develops an obsessive desire to perpetuate his line. Since Charles is dead, Henry a fugitive, and Judith vowed to spinsterhood, he plans another marriage with Rosa Coldfield, one of the narrators of the novel, if she can produce a son first. Rosa flees from him in indignation, and in 1867 Sutpen, still seeking an heir, enters into a liaison with Milly Jones, granddaughter of the loafer and sometimes tenant farmer Wash Jones. In 1869 Milly bears a child, and Wash kills Sutpen in a rage. Henry returns to Jefferson, is hidden at Sutpen's Hundred by Clytemnestra, a Sutpen daughter by a Negro slave, and both die in the 1910 burning of the mansion to the ground. The last Sutpen survivor is Charles Bon's grandson (with two additional influxes of Negro blood), Jim Bond, who disappears from Sutpen's Hundred in 1910, whereabouts unknown. He is the disinherited inheritor of mixed blood who may conquer the western hemisphere in time.

The structure and style of this novel are complex; the story is related from diverse points of view, always in retrospect, and the language of presentation is purposely chaotic. The major part of the narrative is related by Quentin Compson to his Harvard roommate Shreve McCannon. Quentin himself acquires the story only obliquely; he hears part of it from his father, part from Rosa Coldfield, and part of it from family documents and letters. The rise, triumph, and decline of the Sutpen clan is symbolic; it represents the history of the Southern landowning class from 1830 to 1910. Thomas Sutpen, at first creative, vigorous, and ruthless, eventually becomes old, degenerate, and obsessive. In his "innocence" or naiveté he was always asking what went wrong in his "design" of founding a dynasty—his flaw and Henry's and the South's was to fear miscegenation more than incest, to fail to recognize the Negro as human being, to miss the primary concepts of right and wrong. The character of Quentin, who also appears in *The Sound and the Fury*, is brilliantly drawn through his relations with the Canadian Shreve McCannon and people back home like Miss Rosa. His intensity in seeking the truth whatever it might be and in continuing to love the South in spite of its shame makes this one of Faulkner's greatest novels.

The Hamlet (novel, 1940) is an integrated set of sketches, some of them first published as magazine stories, centering around the crossroads village of Frenchman's Bend in Yoknapatawpha County. The dominant theme is the emergence and rise to power of the Snopes clan in the eighteen-nineties, and the central character in Flem Snopes, the most efficient and ruthless of his clan.

The novel is divided into four sections. In the first, titled "Flem," the hamlet of Frenchman's Bend with its ruined antebellum mansion is dominated by the Varner family, who own the local store and control the region's economy. The Snopes clan soon arrive and begin to work their way into the community. Flem, one of several sons of old Ab Snopes, goes to work for the Varners as clerk in their store, and through his uncanny and intelligent perspicacity soon makes himself an essential part of the business. He saves his money and presently buys the local blacksmith shop as an investment; he has begun the first of his "capitalistic" enterprises. The section also introduces V. K. Ratliff, a shrewd but friendly itinerant peddler who serves as an observer and commentator in the novel. A comic interlude relates how Ab Snopes sells the trader Pat Stamper a horse which is later sold back to him, dyed a different color and "fattened" by being blown up with a bicycle pump. This is the only time a Snopes fails to get the upper hand on a deal.

The second section, "Eula," relates the history of Will Varner's daughter Eula, whose phenomenal sexual charms attract half the men in the region before she is twelve. When one of her swains gets her with child, Flem quietly makes a deal with Varner to marry her, thus acquiring the most desirable woman in the county and simultaneously assuring his penetration into the Varner family.

"The Long Summer," the third section, contains two main incidents. In an ironically related idyll, Ike, an idiot offspring of the Snopes clan, becomes romantic over a cow and finally "elopes" with it. Meanwhile Mink Snopes and the farmer Jack Houston quarrel over a bull which wanders into Houston's pasture, and Mink murders Houston from ambush. He hides the body in a hollow tree, and he and his cousin turn to squabbling over the money Houston was carrying when he died. Earlier in the section the Snopes clan agree to cure Ike of his infatuation by killing his cow and feeding him a steak from it.

In "The Peasants," the final section, Flem Snopes achieves two crowning triumphs. Returning from Texas with his bride, he brings along a herd of wild horses in charge of a Texan hostler. The Texan sells the beasts to the local farmers and then vanishes, whereupon the horses break out of their corral and disappear into the countryside. When the farmers remonstrate with Flem he claims he has nothing to do with the horses. Later he carefully drops hints that treasure is buried on the grounds of the old mansion, which he now owns. By "salting" the ground with coins he manages to trick the astute Ratliff and two other men into buying the place for an exorbitant price. The money from these and other successful ventures in his pocket, he then moves on to Jefferson and greater triumphs, leaving the village ruined and demoralized.

The Hamlet, employing the "tall tale" tradition of the American frontier, shifts between folk idiom and courtly romantic language; parts of it are virtually parody. Ike's romance with the cow (which seems somehow more genuine than the other love stories: Houston's marriage, Mink Snopes' marriage, Eula's affair and subsequent loveless marriage to Flem) is lyrical Wordsworth; and the various horse-dealing incidents are related in the tradition of American folk humor that suggests Mark Twain or Bret Harte. Behind this grotesque comedy, however, lies a serious pattern: the rise of the brash Snopes clan and its victory over the traditional Varners, who are squeezed dry and cast aside like a lemon before the novel is over. Thus *The Hamlet* shows the beginning of the process of the commercialization and vulgarization of the South, the climax of which is shown in other novels, principally those that round it out as a trilogy: *The Town* and *The Mansion,* where Flem Snopes moves his base of operations from Frenchman's Bend twenty miles into Jefferson itself. The clan qualities of the Snopeses, the shrewd and ruthless aggressiveness which earn them their success, are clearly shown in this first novel of the trilogy. The character of V. K. Ratliff, almost as shrewd, but sympathetic, witty, sometimes caustic, as the sewing machine agent who wanders through much of Faulkner's fiction, is superbly presented here.

The Bear (novella, 1942) is a difficult, complex story about the growing up to manhood of a boy, Isaac McCaslin, usually called Ike but more often He because the story is filtered through his consciousness and through his conscience. Portions of the novella were published separately as short stories, but the total work is the masterpiece. Structured in five sections, the chief interlocutor for the boy is his cousin, Carothers McCaslin Edmonds, who is usually called McCaslin, which adds to the confusion, but that's the way it is, especially in the South where family names and given names seem often inbred. But the story is Ike's story. He is sometimes ten, sometimes thirteen, sometimes sixteen, sometimes eighteen, sometimes twenty-one, even seven, eight, and nine, but not in that order; the ages are significant, however, in the coming of age of Isaac. Most important are the initiation rites in the hunting of Old Ben, the bear, killed when Ike was sixteen; his education in woodcraft at the hands of his chief mentor, Sam Fathers, half-Indian, half-Negro, and a secondary tutor with a drop of Indian blood, Boon Hogganbeck, which takes place between ten and sixteen; and his probing into the past, including his father's and grandfather's papers and ledgers, and later, after arguing with cousin McCaslin, repudiating his inheritance at the age of twenty-one.

Section I slips back into the ten to thirteen period. At ten he had made his first trip to the camp in the woods to join in the hunt for Old Ben, a semi-legendary crippled bear who roamed the forests near Jefferson. From the time his memory begins Isaac has heard tales of the giant bear to whom bullets are "so many peas blown through a tube by a boy"; now he joins the annual hunting party including his cousin, Major de Spain, General

Compson, and Tennie's Jim, another cousin though Negro and apparently brother to the Lucas Beauchamp of *Intruder in the Dust*. Of course Sam Fathers and Boon were there too. Under Sam's tutelage he becomes, year by year, a skilled hunter and tracker; he learns endurance, humility, and courage and that no one owns or should own or exploit nature, the land; the year he is eleven he sets out alone to find the bear. At first he has no luck; then, guided by a suggestion from Sam, he leaves behind him the paraphernalia of civilization (the gun, his watch, his compass) and goes into the forest alone. Thus meeting the wilderness on equal terms, he finds Old Ben; the two confront each other silently in the depths of the forest, and then Old Ben goes his way.

In Part II the boy has killed his first deer and had his face marked with the hot blood. At his second sighting of Old Ben, this time armed, he does not fire but throws down his gun instead, rushing to save his small dog, a fyce, which is dashing itself suicidally on the bear. Later he understands why he didn't shoot, as Cousin McCaslin quotes to him from Keats' "Ode on a Grecian Urn." Sam Fathers hadn't shot either, but talks about the dog they need to find for the final confrontation. It turns out to be a wild mongrel named "Lion" that Sam and Boon train to run Old Ben. In Part III Lion corners Old Ben and is mortally wounded as the giant bear is killed by Boon Hogganbeck's knife. Immediately afterwards Sam Fathers, who has been Ike's spiritual father as well as teacher, goes into a rapid decline; and his burial on a platform, Chickasaw fashion, brings this part of the story to a close, although memories continue to push into the conscious thoughts of Isaac long after.

Section IV, the most recalcitrant for the average reader, is a long dialogue between Isaac on his twenty-first birthday and Cousin Cass (McCaslin Edmonds) of the bear hunts. This would be in 1888, but events before and after tend to intrude in Ike's mind. One other minor difficulty is the frequent "and he" at the end of a paragraph and the words that he speaks in the next paragraph, which does suggest rapidity and the cutting off of the previous speaker. Isaac refuses his inheritance for two major reasons. First the land doesn't really belong to anybody ("it was never old Ikkemotubbe's to sell to Grandfather") and he refers to the

Book and dispossession from Eden to prove it. Secondly he has been profoundly disturbed by what he has found out gradually about his Grandfather, old Lucius Quintus Carothers McCaslin, who in addition to his legitimate children, Theophilus ("Uncle Buck" and Ike's father), Amodeus ("Uncle Buddy"), and Mary (the mother of Cousin Cass) had fathered on Negro slaves another progeny, the daughter Tomasina by Eunice (a slave purchased in New Orleans in 1807 for $650) and then by his own daughter, Terrel or "Turl," before whose birth Eunice had drowned herself in the creek and to whom old McCaslin left a thousand dollar legacy to be paid at the child's coming of age. Isaac thinks: "So I reckon that was cheaper than saying My son to a nigger. . . . But there must have been love . . . ; not just an afternoon's or a night's spittoon." He says to his cousin, "Don't you see? This whole land, the whole South, is cursed, and all of us who derive from it, whom it ever suckled, white and black both, lie under the curse?" In an intricate flashahead, Isaac is confronted by Lucas Beauchamp in 1895 when Lucas is twenty-one, "Where's the rest of that money old Carothers left? I wants it. All of it." Lucas, like "Tennie's Jim," was a son of "Turl" and an inheritor.

Section V takes Isaac back to the camp in the woods one more time before the lumber company moved in; the implications are that he is eighteen in this part of the story. He remembers Old Ben and Sam Fathers, "who had been his spirit's father if any had," and meets there Boon Hogganbeck, who has his own trauma and violently breaks his gun into pieces. Both lament the passing of the woods and the wilderness.

Intruder in the Dust (novel, 1948) presents a more optimistic analysis of the problem of the South than any of Faulkner's earlier works. The plot, centering around a lynching story, is banal and has often been treated by lesser authors; the interest of the novel lies in its memorable characterizations and in its implied socio-political ideas.

The action opens as Lucas Beauchamp, an eccentric old Jefferson Negro, is accused of the murder of a white man, Vinson Gowrie. Feeling among the "white trash" runs high, not only because Lucas is seized near the body with a pistol in his hand, but because he has a long reputation as a "high-nosed nigger" who has refused to accept the inferiority of his race. A lynching seems certain. The affair causes a vague feeling of guilt in the boy Charley Mallison; years before he fell in a creek and was taken to Lucas' place to dry out, and the Negro's intelligent friendliness on that occasion has remained in his mind ever since. Charley's uncle, the lawyer Gavin Stevens, agrees to take Lucas' case, but Lucas will tell the attorney nothing. It is to the boy that he confides his innocence; he asserts to Charley that if Vinson's corpse is dug up it will be found not to have been shot with Lucas' pistol. In the middle of the night Charley, his friend Aleck Sander, and the courageous spinster Miss Eunice Habersham go to the cemetery and exhume the body; to their surprise it is not Vinson, but the loafer and petty criminal Jake Montgomery. Meanwhile, as the mob from Vinson's home district, Ward Four, clusters around the jail, Miss Habersham guards the prisoner with the weapon of her feminine dignity, and the sheriff and Stevens go back to dig the corpse up again. This time the grave is empty. Both corpses are found buried in the riverbed, and Vinson's relatives are persuaded that Lucas could not have committed the crime. The solution to the mystery gradually comes out. Crawford Gowrie, partner of his brother Vinson in a lumber business, has been stealing lumber from the shed at night. Detected by Lucas, he has killed his brother and thrown the evidence toward Lucas in order to silence the Negro. Later he has been forced to kill Montgomery to cover his tracks. Lucas, freed, is used as a decoy to capture Crawford, who commits suicide in jail.

It is the lawyer Gavin Stevens in this novel who serves as the spokesman of Faulkner's own ideas. Stevens' conversations with the sheriff and with his nephew Charley constitute a comprehensive statement on the Negro problem in the South as it stands today. It is the men of good will—Stevens, the sheriff, Charley, the Negro Lucas, and their kind—who must set about fighting lynching and discrimination with courage. But the job must be done by the South itself. Intervention of the North, through "Yankee" legislation, will turn both the men of good will and the ignorant Snopeses and crackers against the North; they will unite in a fanatic defense of Southern independence, and the Negro's lot will be worse than before. If the South is allowed to handle the problem itself progress will be slow, as all true progress is; the Civil War adequately demonstrated that no mere Constitutional Amendment has the power to free the Negro. The South, led by its young and educated, must progress in its own way; and Faulkner in this novel shows a constructive and optimistic picture of how this may be done.

If *Absalom, Absalom* seems most in the tradition of Hawthorne and Charles Brockden Brown, *Intruder in the Dust* suggests some interesting parallels with Mark Twain. The relationship between Lucas Beauchamp and young Charles Mallison—the boy's slow learning to accept the old Negro as human equal—recalls Nigger Jim and Huck Finn. And certain bizarre incidents in one novel suggest those of the other. Charley and Lucas are chiefly what the novel is about.

Requiem for a Nun (novel, 1950) is a sequel to *Sanctuary*; it follows the life of Temple Drake eight years after the action of the earlier novel. Ostensibly a novel, *Requiem for a Nun* is cast in dramatic form and is in fact virtually a play; it has been produced on the stage with little adaptation. It is like the dialogued novels of Galdos which go back to the 1499 Spanish *Celestina* for their form. The incidents of the story become apparent only through gradual revealment. Temple, it develops, has married Gowan Stevens, the college boy whose drunken accident eight years before threw her into the hands of the perverted Popeye. Two children have been born from the marriage. Shortly before the novel opens, one of them, a girl six months old, has been murdered by Nancy Mannigoe, a Negro servant. Nancy has been condemned to hang for the crime, but for some undisclosed reason Temple feels an obsession to save her. She is aided by Gavin Stevens, the cultured and intelligent lawyer who had earlier appeared in *Intruder in the Dust* and a number of Faulkner's stories. Gavin, who is Gowan's uncle, nevertheless defends Nancy at her trial for murdering his own nephew's child. In a scene in the office of the Governor of Mississippi and in a flashback to the time of the crime, the true facts are revealed. During her ordeal in the Memphis brothel Temple had become infatuated with Alabama Red, a member of Popeye's gang, who was killed by Popeye when he was surprised trying to climb into her room. Certain shameless letters she had written to him had come into the possession of his brother Pete. When Pete comes to her to attempt to blackmail her with the letters, she sees in him the sexual image of the dead Red, and is ready to allow herself to be "kidnaped" by him. Nancy, a prostitute and dope addict who is nevertheless a religious and inwardly decent person and who is determined to prevent Temple's surrender to evil, finally smothers the baby to prevent her mistress from going off with Pete; she hopes through her execution for this crime to obtain expiation for her life of vice. Gowan, the young husband, learns the full details of the sordid history when he hides in the Governor's office as Temple tells the story. The Governor refuses to grant a reprieve, and Nancy dies forgiven by Temple and secure in her inward religious faith. But there is no such solace for Temple, who has to face a life in which both she and her husband know every detail of her own vicious past.

Temple, who is not basically an evil person in *Sanctuary,* is here seen corrupted and destroyed by the evil that was done to her by Popeye and his confederates. Evil begets more evil, and the chain is broken only by the unselfish sacrifice of Nancy. Gowan is also involved in the moral tangle; he began the whole chain of evil through his drunken escapade, and now he finds himself punished through the death of his child and the corruption of his wife. Although Gavin Stevens is the spokesman of Faulkner's ideas in *Intruder in the Dust,* here he seems less important; it is the strong, courageous, and selfless Nancy, a sinner yet a true Christian martyr, who provides the positive message of the novel. Even Temple is impressed by her unshakeable religious faith at the end, although she realizes it is something that she herself could never attain. This novel demonstrates the idealistic and religious tendency as it appears in Faulkner's later work.

Requiem for a Nun is also interesting from a structural point of view. The middle section of the novel is written as a drama with lines of dialogue alternated with stage directions. This section includes the flashback scene in which Temple is prevented from fleeing with Pete by Nancy's murder of her child. Preceding this is a long expository chapter written in the style of *Absalom, Absalom!* and the other prewar novels in which the history of the Jefferson courthouse is described in detail from the time of its construction around 1830. Following the central dramatic section is another chapter relating the history of the jail in which Nancy is confined, and the novel then ends with a short scene in drama form depicting the final interview between Temple and Nancy shortly before the Negro woman is executed. Thus *Requiem for a Nun* is a more pretentious book technically than *Sanctuary,* as well as a more sincere work of art. Yet its unusual form, lacking in action and devoted mainly to remembered incident, cripples its interest; in the end it is a less gripping narrative than *Sanctuary.* The two "historical essays" included are valuable sources of information about the history of the fictional Yoknapatawpha County.

The Fable (1954) is radically different from anything else Faulkner has written, and was long awaited as the climactic achievement of his career. Upon its publication in 1954 it was revealed to be a long and technically difficult parable of humanity and war, the most idealistic of Faulkner's novels but in some way the most unsatisfactory. The plot is so complicated as to defy synopsis. The setting is the First World War, and the story is built around the actual incident of the "false armistice" of May, 1918, and the folk-legend of the appearance of a Christ-like figure in the trenches who came to bring peace to the battle-weary armies. In Faulkner's novel the Christ-figure is an anonymous French corporal whose career clearly parallels that of the Passion: he has twelve disciples, one of whom, his friend Polchek, betrays him and later commits suicide; two women who follow him are named Marthe and Marya (Mary); he is executed between two criminals, his body is taken by his women to a farm where it is blown up (i.e., the Ascension) by a chance shell, and he is later chosen by a series of coincidences as the Unknown Soldier whose remains are interred at the foot of the Arch of Triumph. Behind his story lies the mysterious organization known as *Les Amis Myriades et Anonymes à la France de Tout le Monde* with its saint-like leader, the American Negro Reverend Tobe Sutterfield. A long digression, adapted from Southern folklore, tells the story of an English horse trainer and two Negroes who travel around the South winning horse races with a stolen thoroughbred. Another important sub-plot concerns the French division commander General Gragnon, whose career is ruined when an entire regiment, under the influence of the Christ-like corporal, mutinies when it is ordered to attack and thus precipitates the false armistice. The most interesting narrative passages of the novel, however, are those dealing with a young British aviator (called only "David"), eager to get into combat, who arrives in France just in time for the mutiny and the false armistice. His sole combat sortie is a weird mission to escort a German general behind the Allied lines to confer with the Allied high command over the crisis caused by the mutiny (i.e., the militarists, the generals, band together regardless of nationality against the "men of good will" when a dangerous pacifistic movement arises). David, who does not understand the significance of the mission, gradually becomes aware of a vast and mysterious plan contrived to effect the meeting: the guns in his own plane have been loaded with blank ammunition, and both the German and Allied anti-aircraft guns have secretly been provided with dud shells so that the planes may cross the lines unscathed. Later in the novel David, fearing he has joined the war too late to take part in combat, falls into despair and presumably commits suicide.

In many ways *The Fable* is the weakest of Faulkner's major works; its various plots are poorly coordinated, much space is given to incidents which are not relevant to the central theme, and the whole novel suffers from a kind of vague and maundering spuriousness. Much of the difficulty is due to the fact that Faulkner has abandoned his Mississippi material, where he is thoroughly at home, to deal with Europe, which he visited only once, and the First World War, which he saw only from America and Canada. In support of this view it might be argued that the best parts of the book are those closest to Faulkner's own experience: the story of the stolen horse, a tale something like those related in *The Hamlet,* and the parts dealing with flying, drawn from Faulkner's own service as a Canadian air cadet. The main ideas of the novel are expressed in a long dialogue between the corporal and the Allied commander-in-chief (pp. 342ff). The passage is evidently modeled on the famous "Grand Inquisitor" chapter from Dostoyevsky's *The Brothers Karamazov*; the general, like the Grand Inquisitor, argues that mankind must be cynically manipulated for its own good, and the corporal, like Dostoyevsky's Christ, holds fast to his faith in man's essential goodness and wisdom.

The Town (novel, 1957), the second of the Snopes trilogy, has three narrators: Gavin Stevens, who is romantically in love with Eula Varner Snopes; his nephew, Charles Mallison, also a romantic but twenty-four years younger, with a different and more detached perspective; and V. K. Ratliff, the sewing-machine salesman originally called V. K. Surratt in *Sartoris*, not a romantic, probably a cynic, and whose name we learn in this novel is Vladimir Kyrilytch—which is why he uses only his initials. Flem has moved his base of operations into Jefferson; Eula, the sex goddess often referred to as Helen, Semiramis, Isolde, or Lilith, takes as her lover, Manfred de Spain, son of the Major of *The Bear* (her husband we find out has always been impotent), and produces a daughter, Linda. Stevens and Ratlif both fight against the encroachment of Flem but without success. The rivalry between Gavin and de Spain for Eula's attentions is Rabelaisian comedy at its best, and Gavin is almost constantly the butt of the author's jokes. Gradually, after almost eighteen years of the Eula-Manfred liaison, discreet of course, Gavin shifts his concern to Eula's daughter, transferring his romantic dreams to his aspirations for her. The size of the somewhat Dogpatch-like mythic exploits of a Snopes in Frenchman's Bend seems to be restricted and diminished in the town. Flem learns painfully what you can steal and not steal with profit in his new environment but he does get to be vice-president of the Sartoris bank before he becomes completely concerned with acquiring respectability as well as money. He closes down Montgomery Ward Snopes' dirty-picture exhibition and eases other relatives out of Jefferson. His wickedness becomes human and meaner when he manipulates the affections and destiny of his supposed daughter Linda. To prevent her open disgrace when Flem holds all the cards, Eula commits suicide and Flem has carved on the stone: Eula Varner Snopes, 1889–1927, A Virtuous Wife Is a Crown to Her Husband. If *The Town* strikes some critics as a lesser accomplishment than *The Hamlet* it is nevertheless a fitting bridge to *The Mansion* and contains some comic episodes that it would be too bad to miss.

The Mansion (novel, 1959) is what Cleanth Brooks calls Faulkner's Revenger's Tragedy; Mink, Linda, and Flem give their names to the three sections. Flem has achieved his ultimate victory in converting the house formerly belonging to the de Spain family into a mansion, symbol of wealth and respectability. He stays there alone, fearing only the return of Linda Snopes Kohl (widowed by 1937) and Mink Snopes, cousin, serving a life term in the Parchman penitentiary for Houston's murder and manipulated into an attempted escape in women's clothing by Flem himself. Flem breaks the law of the clan by refusing his aid to Mink. The same characters of the preceding novel view the action (from 1908 through 1946, which brings to its most recent period the epic of Yoknapatawpha County which Faulkner begins in the early 1800's with Ikkemotubbe, Chickasaw chief): Lawyer Gavin Stevens, a grown-up, somewhat pert Chick Mallison, and V. K. Ratliff. But it takes a Snopes to get a Snopes, and the real achievement of this novel is the creation of Mink Snopes, a minimal epic hero but none the less heroic. As Faulkner himself says, contradictions and discrepancies with the Mink presented earlier in *The Hamlet* there are but it's because the author has learned to know the human heart and his characters better in thirty-four years. Mink, the meanest of the Snopes' clan, is the only one with a sense of honor—that is, "who can feel resentment and lash out against it" even if it hurts himself. This Flem is too much of a weasel with too much self-interest to do.

With a review of the murder of Houston we find out that Mink acted from this sense of honor, and it prepares us for his vengeance against Flem. It is Linda, returned to her father's home in 1937 after losing husband and hearing in Spain and now a card-carrying Communist, and returned again in 1945 after a war-time welding job in Pascagoula, who arranged for Mink's release from the penitentiary at Parchman—with the aid of Gavin as lawyer. Mink, against incredible odds, makes his way to Memphis, buys a ten-dollar pistol and three bullets, continues on his way to Jefferson, and shoots Flem with a second try in the mansion. Linda smilingly presides and gets her measure of revenge too. Now Mink can rest on the earth and is given a kind of apotheosis.

The Reivers (novel, 1962), a more or less genial name for scoundrels or thieves in the picaresque tradition, are three in number: Lucius Priest, eleven years old; Boon Hogganbeck, whom we know from *The Bear*; and Ned McCaslin, Negro kin of the Priest-McCaslin family. Lucius is innocent at the beginning of the story which is about his growing toward knowledge and manhood; Boon is a kind of innocent too; but Ned already knows a great deal about the ways of the world. The events of the story take place in 1905, as remembered by Lucius in his sixties, which gives a soft golden light to the action but never makes it soft-headed or soft-hearted. It starts in Jefferson with the purchase of the first automobile, a Winton Flyer, by Grandfather Priest; Boon drives. When the father, mother, and grandfather have to go to a family funeral in Bay St. Louis, Lucius, Boon, and Ned (who stows away and claims his right to go as "kin") take off on a wild trip to Memphis. The roads are terrible, Hell Creek bottom almost impassable, but they arrive and Boon puts up with Lucius at Miss Reba's brothel, later in the country at Parsham for some fantastic horse-racing (Ned has traded the Winton Flyer for a horse and they have to win the race to get back the car). A theme which runs throughout the education of Lucius Priest is what makes a gentleman, which makes this novel, as Mr. Brooks has pointed out, a sort of latter-day Elizabethan "courtesy book." The boy constantly tries to preserve a code of conduct being violated by his elders, to be a man, to protect the good name of a woman, even Everbe, a prostitute at Miss Reba's who is Boon's "girl." For this he takes a knife-wound on the hand in fighting with her nasty young relative, Otis; but it accomplishes Everbe's reform, the "honest whore" who will become again a good woman, and eventually Boon's wife. Lucius learns a great deal from Uncle Parsham Hood, patriarch, pillar of the church, gentleman, a natural aristocrat, with whom he stays during the horse-racing episode. Butch, the deputy-sheriff, is the only out-and-out villain (perhaps Otis is too); even Miss Reba displays understanding and sympathy. Our world is a mixture of good and evil, and the boy learns just how intermingled they are. His own idea of the unforgivable sin is breaking one's word or telling a lie; and this is what worries him most when he gets back home to face his family. He is willing to accept the punishment of his father and the razor strop, indeed yearns for it as atonement; but both father and son feel that a whipping is not enough—Lucius has stepped over the threshold from boyhood to manhood. The impasse is resolved by the grandfather who comes into the cellar to take over the job. "This is what you would have done to me twenty years ago," the father says, and Grandfather Priest answers, "Maybe I have more sense now."

His grandfather explains to Lucius that his punishment will come in living with and redeeming what he has done. The boy protests that he can't forget, he can't live with his guilt as a burden for the rest of his life. But the answer is, "Yes you can. You will. A gentleman always does. A gentleman can live through anything. He faces anything. A gentleman accepts the responsibility of his actions and bears the burden of their consequences, even when he did not himself instigate them but only acquiesced to them, didn't say No though he knew he should." Lucius has learned his final lesson, and Faulkner has given us his last insight. There is no falling-off of power in this last novel; its structure is as controlled as *The Sound and the Fury,* but its tone is lighter, more cheerful, more genial, and the comic vision is good-humored rather than satanic.

Stories: "A Rose for Emily" (1931) is an allegory of decadence built around the life of a simple Jefferson spinster, Miss Emily Grierson. The events, however, are related by indirection and seen only from the point of view of public rumor; thus the structure and chronology are more complicated than the story would seem to demand. The basic plot, disclosed by gradual revelation, is as follows: after the death of her father the unmarried Miss Emily lives alone in an old house with a single Negro servant. Stricken by her father's death, she seldom goes out. Then a construction company comes to lay sidewalks in Jefferson, and Miss Emily falls in love with Homer Barron, a strong and vigorous Yankee foreman. The affair continues for some time; then, presumably, Homer loses interest in what for him has been merely a passing diversion. But for Miss Emily her passion for Homer is the center of her life; she poisons him, preferring to retain him dead rather than allow him to escape alive. For thirty years she keeps the corpse in a tightly sealed upstairs bedroom, never going out, refusing to pay her taxes, considered a little crazy but still respected by the town. Then she dies; the Negro man steals unobtrusively away, and her secret is revealed. On the pillow next to Homer's decayed body the townspeople find "a long strand of iron-gray hair."

The most obvious interpretation of this story is that it depicts the "seduction" of the aristocratic South (Miss Emily) by a vigorous and enterprising North (Homer). The North for all its vigor is corrupted by its selfish and materialistic exploitation of the South; then the South, having destroyed its seducer, lives on to the end proudly cherishing the shreds of its traditional aristocratic dignity.

"Barn Burning" (publ. 1939) is a popular Faulkner story frequently anthologized. The hero, the boy Colonel Sartoris Snopes, is the son of a ne'er-do-well sharecropper, Abner Snopes, who nevertheless admired his old Civil War commander Colonel Sartoris enough to name his son after him. Thus the boy's character is symbolically a battleground in which the qualities of Snopes and Sartoris struggle for supremacy. As the story opens the Snopeses are driven out of a town where the father has burned a barn out of revenge. They move to another part of the county, and the father hires out to work a farm on shares from Major de Spain, the wealthy and aristocratic landowner who appears in several other Faulkner stories. But the father, sullen and arrogant, starts off on the wrong foot by soiling an elegant imported rug in de Spain's house, is forced ignominiously by the Major to clean the rug, and resolves again on the only kind of revenge he knows: barn-burning. The boy, seeing now that his father's irrational criminality is destroying the family, is torn with an inner conflict: is his first loyalty to his father or to the abstract concept of justice? He decides for justice, goes to Major de Spain and warns him, and the Major kills his father in the act of burning the barn. The boy is left in "grief and despair," but Faulkner holds out hope for tomorrow; a Snopes has made a choice for human dignity, and thus it is seen that decency and idealism appear spontaneously even in the most degraded of human clans. The last paragraph is significant: the season is spring and the boy "did not look back"—there is promise for the Snopeses, and for the South, in the future.

John Steinbeck (1902–1968)

Steinbeck is a model example of the modern American nostalgia for the primitive, the counter-reaction to the triumphant urbanization of American culture which took place in the first half of the twentieth century. He stands at the opposite extreme from the Horatio Alger myth, for he admires everything that is not a material success: the have-nots, the misfits, the racial minorities unjustly deprived of their civil and economic rights, the simple, the poor, and the oppressed. His rural heroes, illiterate and sometimes weak-minded, are nevertheless essentially noble; far from realistically described, they are actually poetized rustics in the traditional romantic manner. It is true that Steinbeck is a naturalist, and that his novels are based on first-hand research, carefully documented, and essentially faithful to the facts. But everything is transformed: the creative process simplifies character, idealizes qualities, and casts over the whole a web of significance so that what might have been mere documentary reporting becomes a form of art comparable to the Greek tragedy or the Homeric epic.

Steinbeck is a regionalist as well as a naturalist; his region is the Salinas Valley in central California and the nearby Monterey coast, a rather exotic enclave in American civilization populated with Mexican farmworkers, Italian fishermen, and assorted artists, bohemians, and eccentrics. In addition to Steinbeck both Henry Miller and Robinson Jeffers have made literary use of this region. But neither Jeffers nor Miller has found in the Monterey country the wealth of native material that Steinbeck extracts from it. Whether he describes the country faithfully is, in the end, a question of secondary importance; his Monterey and Salinas counties are as much imaginary realms as the Yoknapatawpha County of Faulkner. Here live his poetic Mexicans, his sentimental cannery workers, his eccentric and colorful fishermen; here his rural tragedies unfold in the atmosphere of the naturalistic novel mingled with that of the Greek pastoral. Like Willa Cather, Steinbeck is fascinated with the foreign elements in the American population; and like most regionalists he believes the elemental life of the country infinitely superior to that of the city. When his characters are established securely on the land they are hard-working and good-hearted, if somewhat inclined to drink and argumentation. When their agricultural activities are dislocated—when the Joads are driven from Oklahoma, or when a seductive woman intrudes her way into the agrarian dream of Lennie and George in *Of Mice and Men*—tragedy and bitterness result.

Steinbeck, like many naturalists, presents scenes of great cruelty and passion in his novels. *The Grapes of Wrath*, upon its appearance in 1939, excited a torrent of puritanical indignation almost equal to that which greeted Dreiser's *Sister Carrie.* Steinbeck is not interested in mere frankness for shock effect, however. His characters use profanity because they know no other way of speaking; it is a sort of tic or mannerism with them. This is the reason profanity is so frequent in the speech of illiterate people; foul language is as conventional in some groups as polite formulae are in cultured society. Actually Steinbeck's characters are seldom deliberately cruel, and are more likely to be gentle. When they commit crimes it is usually through accident (*The Grapes of Wrath*) or out of sheer stupidity (*Of Mice and Men*), and they generally regret such acts as soon as they realize their full implications.

In politics Steinbeck during the Thirties was a consistent independent liberal. Some of his novels are mere allegory or folklore, devoid of any social content (*The Wayward Bus, The Pearl, Of Mice and Men*). *The Grapes of Wrath* is compassionate toward the plight of migrant Oakies, but offers little as a solution but the organized philanthropy of the New Deal. *In Dubious Battle* is a strike story which ostensibly glorifies the left-wing labor movement, but violence is tacitly condemned, and official Communism found the "line" of the novel unacceptable. During the Second World War Steinbeck wrote outright war propaganda in *Bombs Away* (1942) and something very close to it in *The Moon Is Down* (1942). Steinbeck is generally sympathetic to the proletariat and to the rural laborer. He has not, however, adhered consistently to the platform of any one party or movement.

Steinbeck is more conscious of style than most naturalists; there is a certain poctic quality to his prose. Several of his novels represent attempts to create a synthetic folklore, utilizing the traditional stylistic devices of the folk-tale. He makes strong use of rhythm and repetition: Lennie's theme of "George . . . are we gonna have rabbits, George?" is woven into *Of Mice and Men* like the recurring motif of a sonata. His descriptions of nature are terse but highly charged with imagery. Sometimes he feels the same tenderness toward the sea or the hills that he does toward his rural folk-heroes. Occasionally, especially in *Of Mice and Men,* he consciously creates the classic tragedy; the catastrophe of George and Lennie proceeds inevitably out of their tragic flaws in the same manner as the catastrophe of Agamemnon. The figures are drawn on a smaller scale, it is true, but it is precisely Steinbeck's point that humble and illiterate people may have their tragedies too.

Steinbeck's fiction technique is "dramatic" in another sense: it is based largely on dialogue, connected together with brief descriptive passages, and is almost barren of formal exposition. The situation of the characters and their previous history are explained through conversation rather than through explicit exposition by the author, just as they must be on the stage. For this reason Steinbeck's novels and stories are easily dramatized; several of them have been converted into successful plays and films. At least two of them, *The Moon Is Down* and *Burning Bright,* were deliberately written as "dramatic stories" which can be converted into dramas with a minimum of adaptation; they consist entirely of dialogue interspersed with brief passages of action which are really nothing but stage directions. The others among his novels which are most dramatic in style are *Of Mice and Men, In Dubious Battle, The Grapes of Wrath,* and *The Pearl.* The group of his works which are not easily convertible into dramas includes especially the semi-humorous Monterey stories: *Tortilla Flat, Cannery Row,* and *Sweet Thursday.* Here there is much exposition, usually ironic or whimsical, written from the abstract point of view of public opinion or rumor in the Monterey community.

Steinbeck's work is diverse not only in style but in quality. His styles may be roughly classified under four headings: (1) naturalistic tragedies (*Of Mice and Men, The Grapes of Wrath, In Dubious Battle,* etc.), (2) the whimsical Monterey idylls (*Tortilla Flat,* etc.), (3) pastorals (*The Red Pony* and similar lyrical-sentimental works) and (4) miscellaneous adventure stories laid outside the Salinas-Monterey region (*The Moon Is Down, Bombs Away,* etc.). Of these, groups (1) and (3) are superior in quality, although *In Dubious Battle* is not usually considered the literary equal of the others. The stories in group (2) are considered well done but of lesser importance; Steinbeck is here writing for a popular audience and seeking frankly to amuse. Group (4) is consistently inferior; the two works cited are little more than propaganda, and Steinbeck's lack of intimate personal contact with his material produces a quality of abstraction that destroys their effectiveness. A fifth group of minor works might be cited: the symbolic parables, including *Burning Bright* (1950) and *The Pearl* (1948). Steinbeck, the artist of primitives, is no primitive himself; he is a competent professional writer who is always conscious of formal literary technique and of literary history, and who can write in a diversity of styles to suit his material.

Life: Steinbeck was born at Salinas, California, in 1902 of educated middle-class parents. He was educated in the Salinas high school and at Stanford University, although he did not finish his degree. His principal interest in college was biology, a preoccupation he has retained throughout his life. As a young man Steinbeck worked on newspapers and held a variety of odd jobs; he began writing during a winter as a caretaker in a snowbound Lake Tahoe resort. His first three books were unsuccessful, but *Tortilla Flat* (1935) won him considerable recognition. *Of Mice and Men* (1937) was even more successful; and *The Grapes of Wrath* (1939) created a storm of controversy which made him a famous figure overnight. Except for a period of war reporting and for numerous fishing and scientific expeditions, he remained for some years in Monterey or in nearby Los Gatos, where he continued to turn out stories drawn from the life of the region: *The Wayward Bus* (1947), *The Pearl* (1948), and *East of Eden* (1953). When he left his home area and moved to New York City, his literary work suffered a decline.

When John Ernst Steinbeck was given the Nobel Prize in 1962, the award was not universally acclaimed by critics, many of whom felt either that it had come too late or that his work was not of the same quality as that of Lewis, O'Neill, Faulkner, or Hemingway, previous American recipients. Nobody said much about Pearl Buck. He was clearly past the height of his powers, although the Swedish Committee of the Academy professed to admire *The Winter of Our Discontent* (1961), a 311 page allegory, set on Long Island, unaccustomed territory for Steinbeck. In 1962, perhaps feeling that he had lost close touch with his nation, Steinbeck undertook a cross-country trip in a camper with his poodle Charley. *Travels With Charley* (1962) sold well but remains "a somewhat bloodless travelogue" for the sixties. John Steinbeck died at the end of

1968 of heart disease in Manhattan. At his best he had written with cinematic clarity, and the late show reruns of *Grapes of Wrath* with Henry Fonda and *East of Eden* with James Dean with an occasional rereading of *The Red Pony* and *Of Mice and Men* may remain America's best memory of him.

Chief Works: *Tortilla Flat* (novel, 1935) is actually a set of connected incidents rather than a single integrated narrative; it has the structure of *Pickwick Papers* or of Daudet's *Tartarin* stories. The setting is the uphill Mexican district of Monterey, California, called Tortilla Flat, populated by the colorful Mexican-Americans Steinbeck calls *paisanos*. The chief characters of the narrative are Danny, prodigious drinker of wine and free-hand battler; his friends Pilon, Pablo, Big Joe Portagee, and Jesus Maria Corcoran; the beggar Pirate; the wine-merchant Torrelli; and a number of sentimentally promiscuous ladies. Danny comes back from the First World War to find himself an heir and a property-owner; an uncle has died leaving him two houses in Tortilla Flat. Danny moves into one of the houses and rents the other to Pilon, who moves into it with all his friends and presently burns it down. Thenceforth all of them live with Danny in his house, and when they discover that Pirate possesses a hoard of hidden coins they invite him to move in with them too, along with his five dogs. A fantastic and slipshod household is established. The six men and five dogs live by occasional odd jobs, by begging handouts from restaurants and by adroit thefts from their neighbors. In spite of their basic amorality, however, and their many and colorful sins, they win the reader's sympathy through their naive and innocent charm. The chief incidents are a farcical hunt for buried treasure (VIII), Danny's gift of a motorless vacuum cleaner to a lady-friend whose house is not wired for electricity (IX), the poignant incident of the Mexican soldier whose baby dies in spite of the ministrations of the Tortilla Flat inhabitants (X), Pirate's gift of a golden candlestick to the Church (XII), Danny's madness, caused by brooding over the responsibility of his possessions (XV), and the gloriously destructive party at which Danny is cured of his melancholy (XVI). In the last chapter (XVII) Danny destroys himself heroically and magnificently by leaping into a ravine, and the novel closes with a description of his funeral and the dispersal of his friends, who solemnly burn the house before they go as a tribute to Danny.

This novel, the book which made Steinbeck famous, is the most successful of the three works of its type. In style it is a kind of mock epic; Steinbeck pokes fun at the epic tradition on the first page, and there is a thread of ludicrous heroism running through the narrative. The dialogues are sentimental; the style of lyrical "translation" from the Spanish in which the familiar second person (thee-thou) is rendered literally lends a kind of spurious poetic quality to the conversations. The characterizations are romantic, although ironic, and little distinction is drawn between the characters of Danny and his friends. *Tortilla Flat* is far from realism; its characters are exotic to begin with, they are seen entirely from the outside, they are romanticized and poetized, and the novel in the end is almost a fantasy. Yet this is the source of its charm: it lacks the sordid realism of Steinbeck's more serious work, but it creates its own mythical world of great interest and fascination.

In Dubious Battle (novel, 1936) is a strike story, Steinbeck's bitterest and most partisan narrative, and at the same time one of his most powerful novels. Jim Nolan, a young employee of a San Francisco store, is beaten by the police while innocently watching a radical demonstration and as a result is fired from his job; bitter, he joins the Communist Party. He is introduced to Mac, an organizer, who is to be his mentor in Party work. Mac, hard-bitten, cynical, and realistic, is militant Marxism personified; he welcomes trouble and bloodshed because they will provoke the class hatred he can manipulate for Party purposes, and he cynically finds ways to use the deaths of Party comrades for propaganda purposes. The central action of the novel is a strike among itinerant apple-pickers ("fruit tramps") in the fictional Torgas Valley. Before the Party cell comes from San Francisco to organize them, the pickers have little class consciousness and passively accept their cut in wages. Mac and his comrades succeed in persuading them to strike, but brutal violence and destruction are involved: a man is killed during a riot over the arrival of strikebreakers, the lunchwagon of a Party sympathizer is burned and he is beaten, several men including Jim are shot in a battle with the strikebreakers, and Anderson, a farmer who has agreed to let the striking pickers camp on his land, is ruined financially when vigilantes burn his barn containing his entire apple crop. Mac secretly encourages this violence, since he knows it will build up the hatred needed to solidify the working class in the Valley as well as in the rest of the country. The strike is a failure; the pickers are reduced to starvation, some of them are shot, and as the novel ends Jim Dolan is killed by vigilantes who ambush him through a ruse. But Mac's purposes have been served; his main interest has not been in the plight of the Torgas Valley pickers but in the Party's long-term plans for revolution, which are best served when workers are martyred and a strong class feeling is stirred up. A doctor, Burton, serves as a philosophical commentator and spokesman for the intellectual class in the novel, and thus perhaps serves as Steinbeck's mouthpiece. The attitude of the author, however, is ambiguous; *In Dubious Battle* is at first glance a piece of Party propaganda, yet the Party tactics are often seen to be foolish, irrational, and gratuitously destructive. Communist criticism did not approve of the novel, probably because it shows so many human weaknesses and passions in consecrated Party workers; and it is likely that this cool reception helped to turn Steinbeck away from Communism toward other and more moderate forms of liberalism. The style of *In Dubious Battle* is violent, coarse, and forceful; the climactic ending, in which Mac, carried away by anger, harangues the crowd in an effort to use Jim's murder for propaganda purposes, is especially well done.

Of Mice and Men (novel, later drama, 1937) is a folk tragedy laid in the setting of a California ranch. To the ranch come George Milton, an impractical but intelligent and hard-working laborer, and Lennie Small, his strong, half-witted, and gentle companion. The pair have formed a sort of tacit partnership: George protects Lennie from the pitfalls of a clever and unscrupulous society, and Lennie puts his enormous strength at George's disposal. The pair meet Candy, a decrepit old man who has managed to save a few dollars through the years, and the three enter into a sentimental partnership to retire and buy a little ranch of their own. Candy is to furnish the money, George the brains, and Lennie the brute strength. Their dream occupies their entire attention; they can talk of nothing else. Soon it becomes a kind of drug which makes their hard life bearable. Lennie, however, comes to disaster in a moment when George is not there to protect him. Curley, the conceited young ranch owner's son, has married a flirtatious young woman who is a continual source of trouble on the ranch. The wife, bored, dabbles with Lennie; she is fascinated by his strength and tries her seductive tricks on him. Lennie, bewildered, crushes her like an egg without knowing what he is doing. He is aware he has done something wrong, and, afraid George will punish him, he stumbles away in flight. George, however, tracks him down and finds him before the posse reaches him, and kills him with a revolver as he lulls him with tales of their dream ranch.

The Red Pony (novella, 1938) has been published in several forms: a short version as a story in 1937, the complete novella, comprising four sections which are virtually individual stories, as part of *The Long Valley* in 1938, and a revised version with added material published as a separate volume in 1945. The four connected stories relate the youth and coming to maturity of Jody Tiflin, a boy on a California ranch. In "The Gift" Jody's father gives him a red pony, and under the tutelage of the wise and experienced ranch hand Billy Buck he learns how to ride it, feed it, and take care of it. But the pony takes cold and dies; in the magnificent closing scene of the story Jody, hysterical with sorrow and anger, beats off the buzzards which are attacking the corpse with his bare hands. In "The Great Mountains" an old *paisano* named Gitano (i.e., Gypsy) comes to the ranch to ask for work, claiming he was born on the land and that it once belonged to his family. Jody associates the old Mexican with the mountains to the west of the valley, an unknown wilderness which represents for him the primeval and the mysterious. But time has passed Gitano by; he is old and good for nothing, and Jody's father will not hire him. At the end of the story Gitano disappears, taking with him a worthless old horse named Easter which the father was keeping only out of kindness. Horse and man ride away into the western mountains, and there Gitano presumably kills Easter and himself with a sword handed down as an heirloom of his family. Thus "The Great Mountains" allegorizes the passing of the old Spanish order in California. "The Promise" takes up again the theme of Jody's desire to own a horse. This time the father promises him a colt to be born of the mare Nellie; Jody is to take the responsibility for the colt from the time of its conception, and thus the whole cycle of life will be made clear to him. When the colt is finally born there are difficulties, and the mare must be destroyed to save it. Jody has his colt, but he has learned that only through passion, cruelty, pain, and blood can new life come to birth. "The Leader of the People," the final section of *The Red Pony,* completes Jody's "education." A visitor comes to the ranch: his mother's father, an old plains scout who brought a wagon train to California in pioneer times. Scorned by the father as garrulous and foolish, the grandfather seems to Jody wonderful and heroic, a semi-mythical figure out of a past age. He tells of buffalo hunts and Indian attacks, and Jody can respond only with a description of his mouse hunts in the woodpile. The man wryly comments on the irony of the comparision: "Have the people of this generation come down to hunting mice?" The visit ends sadly when the grandfather overhears an insulting remark the father makes about him. The old plainsman realizes he is superfluous, that his time has passed. "There's a line of old men along the shore hating the ocean because it stopped them." With the disappearance of the frontier a new race of farmers has arisen, and there is no place for pioneers. This realization completes the coming to maturity of Jody, who has observed the life cycle in men and animals on the ranch and now perceives its operation in generations of human society. *The Red Pony* is one of Steinbeck's most successful works artistically; its style is faultless throughout, the mood is maintained without sentimentality, and the underlying motif is developed simply and unobtrusively. The novella also lacks the profanity and coarseness which offends some readers in works like *The Grapes of Wrath,* and the relations of the boy with his mother and father and with his friend Billy Buck are related with great tact and insight.

The Grapes of Wrath (novel, 1939) is the story of itinerant farmers—the "Oakies" of the Depression period—who are driven from the Oklahoma dust-bowl to seek a new prosperity. The Joad family are lured to California by leaflets promising easy and well-paying jobs; they load themselves and their possessions into a decrepit automobile and strike out for the west. The family, headed by Tom Joad, includes the lusty and indecent Grampa, the suffering and religious Granma, the hard-working and tenacious Ma, the children Noah and Connie, and Connie's wife Rose of Sharon. At the end of their hectic trip, during which Granma dies and is buried without formality, their arrival in the San Joaquin Valley is a bitter disappointment. Jobs are ill-paying and hard to get, and the Oakies who crowd into the valley by the thousands are worse off than they were in the dust bowl. Violence, passion, and labor strife break out; Tom Joad is involved in a murder and after a while becomes a fanatic labor agitator. The most famous scene of the novel is the final one in which Rose of Sharon, her newborn baby dead, nourishes a dying man with her own milk; it is this scene which moralistic critics have found most objectionable.

Although the subject matter and dialogue of this novel are occasionally shocking, the total effect on most readers is moving and sympathetic. *The Grapes of Wrath,* which won Steinbeck a Pulitzer Prize in 1940, is generally considered his most important work; it is certainly his most controversial. Much of the sensation it caused was due to its subject matter, but apart from its lurid content it is still a remarkable book. In some respects it is Steinbeck's most naturalistic novel; its style is objective, it is highly detailed, and it shrinks from no banal or loathsome detail. It has, however, an underlying symbolic current which distinguishes it from American naturalism of the type of Dreiser; here it resembles Norris and Sinclair, although it is superior to anything these two authors have done. The implied political attitude is similar to that in *In Dubious Battle*; the conclusion is that only through organization can the itinerant fruit-tramps and other workers better their condition. If the attitude is generally leftwing, however, the book is not communistic; actually it stands closer to the social liberalism of the New Deal. The political aspects, however, are not here the main point of the novel as they were in *In Dubious Battle*; the interest is centered on the characterizations of the Oakies, the epic quality of the incidents, and the underlying symbolic motifs which break to the surface in such scenes as Rose of Sharon's feeding of the old man.

Cannery Row (novel, 1944) returns to the locale of *Tortilla Flat* but portrays different characters, this time chiefly Anglo-Saxon. As in the earlier book, however, the construction is episodic, consisting of little more than a set of interconnected short stories. The chief characters are the carefree and alcoholic Mack; his friends Hazel, Eddie the bartender, Hughie, and Jones; and the biologist Doc, who operates a small marine laboratory. Mack and his friends move into a house owned by Lee Chong, a Chinese storekeeper, and engage in a series of Rabelaisian adventures similar to those in *Tortilla Flat*. The climax of the novel is a surprise party which the denizens of Cannery Row throw for Doc, their friend and benefactor. This novel has the advantage over *Tortilla Flat* that it has at least one well-rounded and convincing character: Doc, unassuming and at home with the bums and harlots of Cannery Row, yet a sensitive person who enjoys poetry, fine wine, and Gregorian chants. The same locale and characters appear again in a sequel, *Sweet Thursday* (1954). Neither of these books should be considered among Steinbeck's major works, yet they are charmingly successful examples of their own genre of literature.

East of Eden (novel, 1953) was Steinbeck's first major novel since *The Grapes of Wrath* and evidently represents an attempt to create a work of important literary and mythical significance. The theme is the conflict between good and evil as symbolized in the Biblical story of Cain and Abel, here recast in the setting of the Salinas Valley. Actually the novel relates two recurrences of the Cain-Abel situation in successive generations. Adam Trask (Abel) is the favorite son of his father, a Connecticut farmer; because of this he incurs the jealousy of his brother Charles (Cain). Charles, who basically loves his brother in spite of his contempt for and jealousy of him, fights him, but the matter ends inconclusively. Then, when Adam marries and has twin sons, the myth is reenacted on a ranch in the Salinas Valley. Caleb (Cain) worships his father and is jealous of Aaron, who without caring or deserving it wins Adam's preference. Finally, in his rage, he finds a way to get even with his brother. Aaron venerates the memory of his mother, whom he imagines dead. The truth about her is that she had been a prostitute before she met Adam, and after the birth of her sons has returned to her old profession. Finding that she is still alive and now madam of a Salinas house, Caleb vindictively takes Aaron to see her. Shattered, Aaron flees and in irrational despair joins the army. When word comes that he has been killed Adam has a stroke; Cal feels the full weight of his own guilt. The old Chinese servant Lee serves as a philosophical commentator on this drama; he exhorts Adam to forgive Cal. But Adam leaves his son with only a single enigmatic word: *Timshel.* This Hebrew allusion is interpreted by Lee and others to mean "Thou *mayest* rule over sin"; abandoning his son to evil, he nevertheless leaves him the possibility of redemption through his personal effort if he wishes to accept good. Thus *East of Eden* treats mankind's most basic enigma: the presence of evil in the universe, and the cause of man's curse in the eyes of God. Steinbeck's interpretation is in the end an optimistic one; mankind is abandoned by God in its struggle with evil, yet God, through Adam the father of humanity, holds out hope of rehabilitation through the gift of free will. Two other perhaps greater treatments of the Cain-Abel story in the twentieth century are worth considering for comparative purposes: Unamuno's *Abel Sanchez* (see Volume I) and Joyce's *Finnegans Wake* (see Volume II).

Erskine Caldwell (born 1903)

Although Caldwell is a prolific writer who produced almost thirty volumes between 1930 and 1950, his reputation continues to rest on two novels: *Tobacco Road* (1932) and *God's Little Acre* (1933). To these may be added a group of stories which come roughly from the same period and are in the same style. Yet, although he is known to the general public chiefly as the author of *Tobacco Road,* there is some justification for viewing him as a writer whose main talent lies in the genre of the short story. There is, in fact, a kind of episodic quality even in his novels, a quality which suggests that they were formed in his mind as story situations which he later welded together into a novel. As for his stories, they fall into two general groups: the comedies, many of them laid in Maine or in other parts of America out of the South, and the naturalistic Georgia stories in the manner of *Tobacco Road.* The comedies demonstrate his versatility as well as his literary sophistication; they dispel the myth that he is a primitive and somewhat naive Southern naturalist who "writes about what he knows" and owes his success mainly to the shocking content of his material. Actually he is far less primitive than, for example, Faulkner; he is an educated person and a man of the world, a competent professional author who can write in many styles and on many subjects. If he wrote his most successful fiction about the Georgia back-country where he grew up, it is because he saw the literary possibilities of the material and used it skillfully and effectively.

Nevertheless, from the standpoint of literary history Caldwell is mainly important as a Southern writer, and in his treatment of Southern materials he is a typical modern regionalist. He is concerned chiefly with the manners of the back-country Georgia farmer both black and white, and he describes these people and their land always in the implied contrast to the city. In other words his task is to reveal the country to the city reader; he writes for urban audiences with urban tastes and sensibilities, and the shock many readers feel from his writing is derived from the sharp contrast to their own urban environment. Ellen Glasgow and Willa Cather attempt to show us the universal and human in the lives of country dwellers; Erskine Caldwell shows us the grotesque, the strange, and the exotic. If naturalism means the presentation of the most brutal facts of human existence with utter candor, then Caldwell the Southern regionalist is a naturalist par excellence. The characters of his Georgia stories—share croppers, white trash, back-country pig farmers—demonstrate few human attributes; they resemble animals grotesquely clad in human form. In books such as *Tobacco Road* Caldwell has committed most of the literary crimes wrongly attributed to Faulkner. He presents pornography for its own sake, he is fond of shocking his audiences into attention, and he creates human beings devoid of any sense of decency. There is no doubt, however, that he is sincere in his desire to present the less savory aspects of Southern rural life as he sees them, and to produce eventual amelioration through the tactic of exposé. Flannery O'Connor in some ways carries on this "tradition" of the Southern Gothic or Georgian grotesque, but adds the city to the country and religion to the successive shocks.

The technique of Caldwell's sharecropper idylls is simple. He assembles a group of laconic and degenerate rustics, attributes to them a set of flesh-creeping and depressing antics, and relates the whole in the flattest manner possible without comment or emotion. This bald manner has won him a reputation as a cool and objective social observer; actually his insouciance is a studied literary attitude. "Atrocities related laconically"—this formula has won him fame, money, and even a measure of praise by critics. Caldwell has achieved a reputation as the leading, and most typical, journalist of Southern degradation.

Life: Erskine Caldwell was born in Coweta County, Georgia, in 1903, the son of a Presbyterian minister who traveled frequently as he was transferred from church to church throughout the South. His schooling was sporadic, and it was from his mother that he received most of his early learning. Later he attended a succession of colleges: Erskine College in South Carolina, the University of Virgina, the University of Pennsylvania, and another session at Virginia. He began writing as early as 1928; his first published works were two novelettes, *The Bastard* and *Poor Fool,* in 1929 and 1930 respectively. His first real success came with *Tobacco Road* (1932), which not only rose to the best-seller lists as a novel but went on in a dramatized version by Jack Kirkland to achieve one of the longest runs in the history of the American theatre. In 1933 his story "Country Full of Swedes" appeared in the *Yale Review* and won the *Yale Review* Fiction Award for the following year. Mr. Caldwell has been married three times: the first time to Helen Lannigan in 1925, a marriage which produced two sons and a daughter; to the photographer Margaret Bourke-White in 1939; and in 1942 to June Johnson, by whom he has another son. A 1941 trip to Russia with Margaret Bourke-White resulted in a number of books on the U.S.S.R., including the non-fiction *All-Out on the Road to Smolensk* (1942) and the novel *All Night Long* (1942).

Caldwell has continued to write and publish prolifically in the Fifties and Sixties, turning more and more toward travel, memoirs, and the problems of creative writing for his subject matter. Among these books are *Call It Experience* (1951), *When You Think of Me* (1959), *Wordsmanship* (1961), *Close to Home* (1962), *Deep South* (1968), and *Summertime Island* (1968). It is likely, however, that *Tobacco Road* and *God's Little Acre,* often reprinted in paperback and hard cover editions, will remain his best-known works.

Chief Works: *Tobacco Road* (novel, later drama, 1932) describes the life, times, and eventual decline of the Georgia sharecropper Jeeter Lester and his family. The plot actually consists of a set of episodes; the novel is really a set of integrated short stories. An in-law, Lov Benson, married to the twelve-year-old Pearl Lester, visits Jeeter and is clumsily robbed while Jeeter's daughter Ellie May serves as decoy. Jeeter's sister, the widow-preacher Bessie Rice, entices his son Dude to marry her by displaying a new automobile, which Dude later wrecks, killing his grandmother. Jeeter's only effort to farm his land consists of an attempt to borrow money for improvements; when this is not successful no one really cares when a fire burns up both house and Lester family.

God's Little Acre (novel, 1933) is a similar story laid in the hill country of Georgia. A mountaineer, Ty Ty Walden, wastes his life digging for gold on his land. His family is every bit as grotesque as Jeeter Lester's. It includes the promiscuous daughter Darling Jill and her sister Rosamund, whose husband Will betrays her with Griselda Walden and later dies in a labor riot. These family calamities grieve Ty Ty only briefly; he is more interested in his prospecting. The characterizations in this novel are slightly more subtle and three-dimensional than they are in *Tobacco Road.*

Stories: Most of Caldwell's stories are included in *Jackpot* (1940); a shorter collection is *Stories By Erskine Caldwell,* New York (1944). "Country Full of Swedes" (1933), originally published in the *Yale Review,* is typical of his light and gusty comedies, most of them written during his stay in Maine (1926–31). The story is related by a hired hand on the Maine farm of Jim Frost, who warns of the carnage and destruction likely when the Swedes, driven out of the sawmill towns by hard times, descend on their countryside. Stan, the narrator, is skeptical, but when the Swedes arrive their antics convince him. A small boy begins the destruction by climbing a tree after a cat; his father chops the tree down, and presently the Frost farm is virtually wrecked. But when Stan proposes revenge, Frost in terror pleads, "Good God . . . don't go making them mad." Henry Seidel Canby describes this story as "nothing but a symbol of the disturbing rush of vitality over the unvital, like a comber over a sterile beach."

"My Old Man's Baling Machine" is an eccentric-relative story that might well have been written by Saroyan. The hero's father is tricked by a traveling salesman into buying a paper-baling machine which he hopes will make him rich; he then proceeds to stuff every piece of paper into it that he can lay his hands on, including his wife's love-letters. Caldwell has written several other stories about this family, including "The Night My Old Man Came Home" and "Handsome Brown and the Goats."

"Saturday Afternoon" (1935) belongs to a markedly different group of stories: brutal tales of Negro-white relationships in the cotton country of Georgia. It is a lynching story, but an unusual one in construction; it relates the incident solely from the point of view of the town loafers, who feel no particular emotion at all toward the victim, a harmless "good" Negro named Will Maxie, but who participate in the killing out of sheer boredom of life in the Georgia village. The central character is the fat and sleepy butcher Tom Denny, whose friends wake him up from his afternoon nap so he won't miss the lynching. In spite of its apparent callousness, this story is one of the most effective anti-lynching pieces ever to be written by a Southern author.

"Kneel to the Rising Sun" (1935) is similar in mood. The cowed and stupid white sharecropper Lonnie is so subservient to his landlord Arch Gunnard that he scarcely protests when his own father, out prowling for garbage in the middle of the night, is eaten by Gunnard's sleek pigs. A courageous Negro, Clem Henry, stands up to Gunnard and is consequently lynched by a mob; but Lonnie, feeling vaguely that something is wrong, lacks the character to oppose them. This story shows Caldwell at his most typical; his faults (sensationalism, grotesque exaggeration) as well as his merits (a powerful plot, a total and dispassionate objectivity) are here seen in their purest form.

Robert Penn Warren (born 1905)

Warren is a self-declared leader of the organized Southern agrarian movement, a group which set out to create a new Southern literature and to attack the conservatism and sentimentality of the "highcaste Brahmins of the Old South." He was the youngest member of the "Fugitive Group" of Nashville poets and critics, and he is the only member of that cénacle to achieve any prominence as a novelist. His success has been both a critical and a popular one; he has gained numerous awards including a Pulitzer Prize (1947), and Malcolm Cowley, one of his warmest advocates, has referred to him as "more richly endowed than any other American novelist born in the present century." He is also an important literary critic, the co-author with Cleanth Brooks of *Understanding Poetry* and a leader of the New Criticism (see entry elsewhere). Finally, he is a poet. His poems, chiefly on Southern themes, are well suited to stand beside those of John Crowe Ransom and others of the Southern school, and are marked by a coolness and detachment lacking in the more impassioned Southern poets.

Sensitive and intellectual in temperament, Warren writes poetry of great subtlety and precision. This is perhaps not surprising considering his background. What is surprising is that his fiction, while perceptive in the same way his poetry is, is nevertheless hard and naturalistic in the manner of Steinbeck, Hemingway, or Faulkner. While he does not totally resemble any one of these authors, he shares their laconic vernacular dialogue, their use of coarse or shocking detail, their apparent callous irony for literary effect. It is this hard quality of his style that saves his basically romantic plots from sentimentality. A lesser writer might have made a mawkish and sentimental historical novel out of the material of *World Enough and Time*; Warren treats it with the detached irony of modern naturalism, and the result is a first-rate novel.

As a regionalist Warren writes almost entirely about Kentucky, his home state, spilling over into Tennessee, which he knows well from his Vanderbilt experience in Nashville, and, of course, ranging into Louisiana in *All the King's Men.* He has remarked, in the course of advising younger authors, that in Kentucky courthouses alone is buried enough material for a whole generation of writers. Yet he is more than a regionalist in the superficial sense of the word; he is concerned with more than mere local color or fictionalization of local history. On the surface his approach to Southern material might be described as sociological or political. Two of his three chief novels treat political themes, and even in *World Enough and Time* the contrast in ethics of various social classes is constantly implied. He also has "philosophical pretensions," although this is not to imply that his philosophy is unsound; it is simply that his philosophical comment often seems superimposed, superfluous, organically unconnected to his central plot. This difficulty is particularly apparent in *All the King's Men,* where the effort of the narrator Jack Burden to work out his personal philosophy often slows down the unfolding of the central plot. If his philosophical dissertations are not effective, however, his moral analyses are. The realer is made vividly aware of the moral implications of Willie Stark's career, and of the moral dilemma confronting Burden, through the unfolding of the action itself. The same is true of *Night Rider,* which is essentially a study in Percy Munn's personal moral problems and their final resolution through tragic expiation. In spite of the regionalistic preoccupations which dominate his work, Warren's novels are essentially studies in moral conflict laid in the richly suitable setting of the South.

An often cited flaw in Warren's fiction is his inability to limit his canvas. Like Faulkner and Wolfe, he is a writer of prolific imagination; he continually conceives scenes, characters, and situations which seem to run away with him and divert his attention from the central theme of his novel. The best example of this is the story of Judge Irwin in *All the King's Men,* which was intended as a "chapter in the longer story of the Boss" but which grows so large it almost dominates the novel. *Night Rider,* with its simpler structure and more limited cast, is superior in this respect; and *World Enough and Time,* in spite of its technical complexity, is Warren's most tightly organized novel.

As a poet Warren produces work of high quality but of rather limited originality. He resembles the other Fugitive Group and *Southern Review* poets in subject matter and even in form, but he is the most objective of the school; even his poems involving Negro-white conflicts are effective through their calm detachment rather than through their emotion. His poetry shows the effect of his highly developed critical faculty, yet his training as a critic has not inhibited his creativity. There is a quality in his verse that corresponds to the Faulkner-like naturalism of his fiction; he is closer to the earth than most other Southern poets. "Its strength no less than its fecundity," Untermeyer remarks of his poetry, "rises from Kentucky soil."

Life: Robert Penn Warren was born in Guthrie, Kentucky in

1905, in the section of Todd County which served as the setting for *Night Rider*. As a student at Vanderbilt University he became a member of the "Fugitive Group," a cénacle of young Southern writers who rallied around the bimonthly literary review *The Fugitive*. He later took a master's degree at the University of California and a B.Litt, as a Rhodes Scholar, at Oxford. He has spent most of his career as a university teacher, serving on the faculties of Southwestern College, Vanderbilt University, Louisiana State University, and the University of Minnesota. His first important published book was a biography, *John Brown: the Making of a Martyr*, in 1939. Mr. Warren was one of the founders of the *Southern Review* and served as editor of this important quarterly until its demise in 1942, when he became associated with the *Kenyon Review* as advisory editor. In 1947 *All the King's Men*, which had won the Southern Authors' Award in 1946, was awarded a Pulitzer Prize.

Warren continues to be productive in all his chosen fields of activity. As a teacher he has moved to Yale University. *Promises* (1957) won the Pulitzer Prize, the Edna St. Vincent Millay Prize, and the National Book Award for poetry. The much discussed novel, *The Cave*, appeared in 1959 and *Flood* in 1964. *Audubon, A Vision* (1969) is poetry based on incidents from the life of the naturalist. Mr. Warren lives in Connecticut with his wife, Eleanor Clark, and their two children.

Chief Novels: *Night Rider* (1939) is based on an actual outbreak of violence between Kentucky farmers and tobacco companies in the early years of the twentieth century. The protagonist, Percy Munn, is a lawyer who has been educated out of the South and who returns to his home county to take the part of the farmers in the struggle. Moderate and reasonable by nature, disliking violence, Munn is a "good man" who is at first loath to become involved in the affair, but his innate idealism persuades him that his loyalty is due to the farmer class from which he sprang. He joins an Association formed by farmers and politicians to force the companies to raise their prices, and soon finds himself involved with unsavory companions: the brash and vulgar grower Bill Christian and the unctuous and self-satisfied Senator Tolliver. The Association leaders also include Captain Todd, "a kindly, bearded man, a veteran of the Civil War," and the cynical but courageous Dr. MacDonald. Meanwhile Munn has voluntarily defended and procured an acquittal in a murder case for a local poor-white, Bunk Trevelyan, who thus becomes his admirer and defender. The Association goes about its work of persuading farmers to join together and refuse to sell their tobacco except at an agreed price, but the movement is a failure; selfish growers hold out and sell at the high prices caused by the shortage, and others betray their companions by selling secretly after they have signed with the Association. Senator Tolliver, selfish and opportunistic, abandons his friends and joins forces with the companies. Finally the hard core of the Association members band together in another organization, this time a secret one to send "night riders" out to destroy the tobacco of recalcitrant growers. Munn, drawn into this plot half against his will, soon finds himself deep in crime and violence. When Trevelyan, by this time a member of the night riders, betrays them, Munn is forced to murder him; other violence in which he is involved includes the burning of tobacco company warehouses. Finally he is a fugitive, accused of murder; he seeks out Senator Tolliver to kill him, but at the last moment, weary of violence, he relents. The novel ends as he is killed by a posse.

The point of the plot is that Munn, a man of integrity drawn into the struggle out of principle, is the one who is made to suffer from its consequences precisely because of his high character; except for MacDonald the others abandon him one by one, and in the end he is the scapegoat. An interwoven sub-plot describes his relations with his cold and hostile wife May and his affair with Sukie Christian, daughter of "Old Bill." Although the central interest of the novel lies in Munn's inner moral struggle, the descriptions of violence and death, related with magnificent detachment, contribute to the high quality of the work.

All the King's Men (1946) describes the career of Willie Stark, a Louisiana dictator and demagogue, as seen through the eyes of Jack Burden, a newspaperman who becomes one of his assistants. Stark's career is roughly based on that of Huey Long, although the parallel is confined to the public part of Long's career; the family relationships and the inner psychological tensions of Willie's organization are Warren's inventions. Willie Stark begins as a naive country lawyer who sincerely wants to better the lot of the "hicks" and "rednecks" from whose ranks he sprang; he is taken in hand by two people, Burden and the wisecracking "secretary" Sadie Burke, and with his natural talent for demagoguery he soon becomes a powerful figure. As the novel opens he is already governor, and Burden, a trained researcher, is engaged in digging up material on enemies Stark hopes to slander and blackmail. Meanwhile Stark's family life deteriorates; his wife Lucy, a country school-teacher, is repelled by his new coarseness and arrogance and leaves him, and his son Tom, spoiled and self-satisfied, is continually in trouble. The remaining important characters of the novel are Anne Stanton, daughter of an old Southern family, whom Burden loves but who eventually becomes Stark's mistress; Adam Stanton, her brother and Burden's friend, an eminent surgeon who accepts a position as director of a medical center Stark is building; and Judge Irwin, who has befriended Burden in his boyhood but is later betrayed by Burden because he has become Stark's enemy. The plot, becoming successively more involved, ends in a series of catastrophes: Irwin commits suicide and Burden learns that the man he has destroyed was actually his father; Tom, playing football while out of training through dissipation, breaks his neck and dies; and finally Adam, discovering his sister's relations with Stark, kills him and is in turn killed by Stark's bodyguard. As the novel ends Burden, disillusioned and cynical, nevertheless sets out with Anne to build a new life out of the wreckage of the old.

This novel is more than a mere fictionalized portrait of a dictator; it is an intricate network of moral conflicts and psychological relations in which each character exerts an influence on the others. The central character is Burden, cynical and detached yet retaining a basic decency. Stark himself is sometimes genuinely concerned for the people who worship him as an idol, sometimes callous and brutal. Adam Stanton, consecrated, idealistic, somewhat resembles the hero of Lewis' *Arrowsmith*; Anne, who serves merely as a focus for Burden's love and disillusionment, is less well motivated but still a convincing character. The minor characters—Sadie, the politician Tiny Duffy, the perverted chauffeur-gunman Sugar-Boy—are vivid and well-drawn. *All the King's Men,* winner of several literary awards including a Pulitzer Prize, is probably Warren's most important work.

World Enough and Time (1950) is a novel of passionate psychological and moral conflict in a historical Kentucky setting. Jeremiah Beaumont, a young lawyer in Kentucky in the eighteen-twenties, falls in love with Rachel Jordan, but she consents to marry him only on condition that he kill Colonel Cassius Fort, Beaumont's friend and spiritual father, who has earlier seduced her. He does so, but is afterwards tormented by agonies of conscience and philosophical doubt before he is finally executed for the murder. This novel is based on an actual incident, the so-called "Kentucky Tragedy" of 1824–25, in which Jeroboam O. Beauchamp was encouraged by his bride Ann Cook to murder Solomon P. Sharp. The case has served as the subject of several other literary works including Chivers' *Conrad and Eudora* (drama, 1834), Charlotte Barnes' *Octavia Bragaldi* (drama, 1837), Poe's *Politian* (drama, 1837), Hoffman's *Greyslaer* (novel and drama, 1840), and Simms' *Beauchampe* (novel, 1842).

The Cave (novel, 1959) tells the kind of story you might read about in the papers, the kind of real incident that Stendhal used as a basis for *The Red and the Black*, and Robert Penn Warren uses a similar kind of artistry to transfer it to fiction. In a small town in Tennessee, Johntown, between Knoxville and Nashville, a young hillbilly, Jason Harrick, gets trapped in a cave. We never meet him, except in the memories of other characters, but his predicament and tragedy affect the lives of several townspeople, a varied assortment. Among them are the parents of the doomed man, John T. or Old Jack and his wife Celia Hornby Harrick (former teacher of the third grade), his younger brother Monty, the local banker Timothy Bingham and his awful wife Matilda with their sixteen-year old daughter Jo-Lca, a thrice-failed Greek restaurant owner Nick Papadoupalous and his whining wife, and the local Baptist preacher Mac Sumpter with his son Isaac ("Ikey"), who as a shrewd and unscrupulous college boy exploits the situation expertly, laying the foundations for a fortune and a public relations career. In the lives of most of them, the entrapment forces a crisis, the result of which is a greater self-knowledge and awareness of others.

Upon its appearance the novel received a storm of critical attention, running the gamut from "the best novel by our best novelist" to "lack of economy" and "thin message out of Bible-slapping farce."

Some readers may find the language as rough as a corncob (realistic, earthy), but it is honest and appropriate to the "hillbillies" who speak it or think it. The sexual sensations are neither gratuitous nor white-washed. The characterizations are excellent, varied, and convincing. There are fine satirical thrusts at the mass media's publicizing of the suffering and heartbreak of those concerned with rescue operations, but the satire is controlled and not allowed to interfere with the novel's main purposes: to tell a good full-bodied story and to present some simply realized, through experience, philosophical ideas about living and dying. Symbolism and allegory are there but not insistent.

The epigraph from Plato's *Republic* should have clued readers and critics in to Warren's deeper meanings: "You have shown me a strange image, and they are strange prisoners. . . . Like ourselves, I replied; and they see only their own shadows, or the shadows of one another, which the fire throws on the opposite wall of the cave. . . ." This is a good novel and a dangerous one, for the critical reader is likely to see only his own shadows and get from its content what he puts in it. The "cave" may be four things: a cavern much like Mammoth Cave which can become a tourist attraction, Plato's cave, the womb, or the tomb (even the Freudian death-wish) to which we all want and do not want to return under ground (where the seasons and temperature do not vary, where there is peace). Human relationships are examined with care and understanding. The man-wife complex is probed, but the father-son connection is probed even more deeply. There is an Abraham-Isaac, God and sacrifice, parallel in the story of Mac Sumpter and his son Isaac, which is particularly meaningful—Isaac may very well be the main character to be trapped by the cavern, his fall and failure in his success being the most tragic human outcome of the narrative. But the relationship of Jack Harrick, particularly to his son Jasper, and the new relationship to Monty, are of significance too. The "touch" between one human being and others is made important. Lying and truth and guilt are seen in varying lights; to be human, to have lived, is to compound guilt. Old Harrick, as he nears death from cancer but still seeks his identity, has a near Lear-like vision in his wheelchair: "I am an old nigh-illiterate, broke-down blacksmith, sitting here in the middle of the night, and my boy is dead. . . . Are all men like me?" It is Mr. Bingham who sees the value of fiction, of the imagination, over the reality: "The picture, he guessed, was more outside some of the trouble of life."

Perhaps what can be safely said at this point in time is that *The Cave* is a major novel by one of our major novelists.

Flood (novel, 1964) was subtitled by its author "a romance of our time." The story begins with the coming of two men to a small Tennessee town in April 1960. Brad Tolliver, successful screen writer and long-absent native son, and Yasha Jones, famous director who is a stranger to the region, arrive with the purpose of creating a great film about the town, Fiddlersburg, which will soon disappear under the waters held back by a newly constructed massive dam downstream (another Tennessee Valley Authority project, one assumes). Brad's history is here, including the scandal that destroyed his first marriage and suspended the lives of Calvin and Maggie Fiddler. To Yasha the town is only a spur to his imagination. But they both become involved in the last days of Fiddlersburg.

In general a critical coolness met this book because of a confusing complexity of time jumps and construction more like a clever piece of engineering. But "engineering" may not be inappropriate to the subject matter, and Warren as usual packs narrative interest into tight places. By an unknown writer this would appear as a good novel, but it is not probably among Warren's best.

Poetry: Warren's most important verse until recently was contained in the volumes *XXXVI Poems* (1936), *Eleven Poems on the Same Theme* (1942), and *Selected Poems* (1944). Typical of his early work is the well-known "Pondy Woods" (1929), an account of a Negro lynching related in calm, reflective, but nevertheless moving verse. "Pro Sua Vita" and "Letter of a Mother," both from *XXXVI Poems,* are tributes to a mother-figure, the first on the occasion of her death, which suggests comments on the futility and irony of human birth, and the second expressing a vague womb-nostalgia, meditating over "The mother flesh that cannot summon back/ The tired child it would again possess."

From "The Ballad of Billie Potts" (1943), a small masterpiece of narrative poetry with naturalistic diction (Little Billie was "A clabber-headed bastard with snot in his nose"), to *Audubon, A Vision* (1969), a more mature, astringent masterpiece, Warren's poetry has developed and deepened its channels. *Audubon* is a series of poems, individual but related and seven in number, suggested by episodes from the life and passages from the writings of John James (Jean Jacques) Audubon (1785–1851). In this book we get Warren's version of the poetic sequence, developed by Theodore Roethke, and Robert Lowell in *Life Studies* (1960) and claimed by "projectivists" as a goal, "that single real contribution to the art of the longer poem by the modern age." The subject matter (and treatment, too) might well have been suggested by Eudora Welty's short story, "A Still Moment" (from *The Wide Net,* 1943); at least there are interesting parallels: the Lost Dauphin legend, the same white heron. The media differ: Welty's poetic prose, "In that quiet moment a solitary snowy heron flew down not far away and began to feed beside the marsh water"; Warren's sharp verse image, "And the large bird,/ Long neck outthrust, wings crooked to scull air, moved/ In a slow calligraphy, crank, flat, and black against/ The color of God's blood spilt, as though/ Pulled by a string." And then: "Moccasins set in hoar frost, eyes fixed on the bird,/ Thought: 'On that sky it is black.'/ Thought: 'In my mind it is white.'/ Thinking: '*Ardea occidentalis,* heron, the great one.' " What emerges is a story of deep delight, intellectually and emotionally moving, told with an "Ancient-Mariner" talent; the gory and the ethereal, the grim and the contented, beautiful and predatory birds, coincide. This is a poetic epitaph for Audubon and an "apologia for the endlessly seeking, destroying and atoning destiny of all artists, of man himself."

William Saroyan (born 1908)

William Saroyan began as an unknown and penniless writer in the Depression period, and his early books are his best: bitter, but poetically bitter, a naive and sentimental bitterness that is far from the harsh cynicism of a Dos Passos or a Farrell. He portrayed the lives of unfortunates, of human wrecks, of the meek and humble of the earth. He became a success doing this, and even made some money, but in achieving success he unfortunately left behind the people and the world his temperament best fitted him to write about. Like Wolfe, he is essentially an autobiographical writer, preoccupied with his own childhood and his own people. When he moved out of this milieu into the world of Broadway and Hollywood something essential in his work was no longer there. His best books are, and will remain, *The Daring Young Man on the Flying Trapeze, My Name Is Aram,* and the dramas written in the period around 1939: *My Heart's in the Highlands, The Time of Your Life,* and *Love's Old Sweet Song.* All these early works are concerned in one way or another with the lives of unsuccessful and humble people in the San Joaquin Valley of central California, especially the town of Fresno and its environs; they are sincere, spontaneous, youthful, and fresh. The later books are too often either sentimental (*The Human Comedy*) or insincere and studied, often with a view toward commercial success (*The Assyrians*).

The chief quality which strikes the reader in Saroyan's early works is their spontaneity, their naive but convincing warmth. Many stories have been written about young artists starving in garrets, but few have achieved the poignant and ironic understatement of the title story of *The Daring Young Man on the Flying Trapeze,* whose hero finds a penny in the street and thinks, "In the evening I shall polish it until it glows like a sun and I shall study the words." Yet, although parts of this story are masterfully written, Saroyan seems to have an almost pathological aversion to style. He has devoted a number of essays and prefaces to attacks on academic critics, on theories of literature, on rules of all kinds. He argues that a young writer should study not books but life, that he should write according to the "jump-into-the-river-and-start-to-swim-immediately" technique, that is, without any technique at all except the consciousness of what he wants to say. This attitude links him with the school of "automatic writers" of the twentieth century, especially with Gertrude Stein. His finished work does not greatly resemble Miss Stein's but it does often resemble Hemingway's. In "Seventy Thousand Assyrians" his hero goes to a barber college for a fifteen-cent haircut and thinks. "Outside, as Hemingway would say, haircuts are four bits." In spite of such satire, numerous Hemingway-like passages can be found in all his work up to approximately 1939; for all his condemnation of books and imitative writing, it is obvious that Saroyan is very well read in modern American literature and that the new techniques have had an obvious influence on his writing.

In spite of his Armenian background Saroyan is one of the most "American" of twentieth-century writers. His scenes are laid in the most American of locales—the bar-and-grill, the grocery store, the small-town neighborhood—and his style, especially his dialogue, is colloquial and unerringly faithful to the American idiom. In addition he has a tremendous, almost Whitman-like emotional attachment to America, a sentimental patriotism that becomes more prominent as his work progresses. The bitterness toward Depression America in *The Daring Young Man* (1934) is replaced in *The Human Comedy* (1943) by a sentimental affection for the homeland, an affection which is not at all contradicted by his continuing antagonism toward bourgeois materialism and other upper-middle-class aspects of American life. Saroyan's America is in a sense his private invention, yet it corresponds to an important element in the real America; and he has remained faithful to this image throughout his career. It is this element, the depiction of a sentimental, poetic, and anti-materialistic American undercurrent, that has made his work so popular abroad, especially in Europe; in France and Italy, for example, Saroyan is often considered one of the most important American authors of the century. Saroyan stands in the line of literary evolution represented by Thoreau, Whitman, and Mark Twain and continuing through Stein, Anderson, and other naturalists of the Twenties; it is a literary tradition hostile to form, concerned in its subject matter with the lives and tragedies of the humble, and spontaneous and highly subjective in style.

Out of this sentimental kinship with the humble and weak has come Saroyan's philosophy, or what passes for philosophy in his work: that there is a kind of success in failure, that the meek are blessed, and that the poor in spirit are compensated by a world of fantasy far more rewarding than the glittering and streamlined world of material success. To the "American Dream" with its promise of bourgeois luxury to be obtained through hard work, diligence, prudence, and thrift he opposes the "Cult of Failure," the sentimental admiration for the imprudent, the impulsive, and the poetic. Saroyan, at least in his early work, never portrays a character who is both successful and admirable; on the contrary he portrays many characters who are warm, lovable, and sympathetic precisely because they are impractical failures.

This attitude toward character is probably connected to Saroyan's Armenian background. As a member of a racial minority he felt himself, as a boy, to be an outsider in American culture, and this led him to a kinship with all the excluded, with the "proletariat" in its technical sense as "those who are in a society but not of it" (Toynbee). A list of the people Saroyan admires includes precisely all those elements tacitly excluded by the Chamber-of-Commerce patriot in talking about "the American way of life": the unemployed, barflies, Japanese, Assyrians, petty juvenile delinquents, prostitutes, vagabonds, itinerant Negroes, Greeks, drunken telegraphers, and miscellaneous job-drifters. Above all Saroyan admires his own people, the Armenians, persecuted for centuries, lacking a nation of their own, lacking even the acumen and diligence of the homeless Jews, lacking everything except the dignity of their history and their impractical and sentimental inner poetry. If Saroyan is a regionalist his region is not only a geographical area: it is also a people, the Armenians of California and all those who are kin to them through their inner goodness and their failure in the material world.

Life: Saroyan's early life is roughly that described in *My Name Is Aram,* which does not, however, fill in all the details. He was born in Fresno, California in 1908; his father, who died when he was two, had been a Presbyterian minister but later became a grape-rancher. After the death of the father the mother was obliged to send her children to an Alameda orphanage until William was seven; when the family was reunited in Fresno, Saroyan attended public schools, read avidly, and worked as a telegraph messenger. From the age of seventeen he was on his own, drifting from one odd job to another and finally settling down temporarily as manager of a Postal Telegraph branch in San Francisco. His first published stories appeared in 1934, and the same year he made the O'Brien volume of *The Best Short Stories* and published his own first volume: *The Daring Young Man on the Flying Trapeze.* The book was an immediate success; Saroyan paid off his debts, worked briefly in Hollywood, then returned to his writing. Since 1935 he has lived mainly in San Francisco and Fresno, with brief sojourns in New York City. *My Name Is Aram,* his second major book, consisted of pieces originally published in magazines, including *The Atlantic Monthly, The New Yorker,* and *Story.* Form 1939 to 1941 he concerned himself chiefly with the drama; he directed or co-directed several of his own plays, including *My Heart's in the Highlands,* in New York, and turned down a Pulitzer Prize (1940) for *The Time of Your Life* because he felt a bourgeois society had no right to patronize "sincere" art. The Second World War affected him deeply, making him more socially conscious and intensifying his sentimental patriotism; out of this experience came *The Human Comedy,* a more idealistic work than anything he had previously published. Since the war his output has been prolific but has generally been considered inferior; the pieces of *The Assyrian and Other Stories* (1950), probably his best work after 1945, were written according to his own statement "in the hope of being sold to magazines for big money because a writer's got to live," a far cry from the bitter declaration of literary independence he expressed in *The Daring Young Man.*

The Cave Dwellers, a play, was published in 1958. More recently books with essay-like titles have appeared. *I Used to Believe I Had Forever, Now I'm Not So Sure* (1968) is a collection of stories, plays, essays, and poems. Saroyan's 1970 publication was entitled *Days of Life and Death and Escape to the Moon.* The plays, *My Heart's in the Highlands, The Time of Your Life,* and *The Beautiful People,* which John Gassner felt to reveal the "vivacity of affirmations, even sentimentalities," may well come to be his most memorable work.

Chief Works: *The Daring Young Man on the Flying Trapeze* (stories, 1934) contains Saroyan's most typical work and some of his best. The title story is the most important one in the volume; it is a simple impressionistic account of the death by starvation of an unpublished writer, related in a subjective but restrained style with faint overtones of irony. Paradoxically, although this story is the most "Saroyan-like" of anything Saroyan has written, it is also the most imitative of his works; the opening section particularly shows the mark of Joyce, Eliot, and the poignant silent comedies of Chaplin. Of the twenty-five other stories in the volume, typical examples deserve brief mention. "Seventy Thousand Assyrians" begins as a sketch of a barber in a San Francisco barber college and gradually turns into an essay on writing and a statement of literary creed. The style of the narrative sections often suggests the early Hemingway. "Love, Death, Sacrifice, and So Forth" is a satire on the typical Hollywood film, funnier yet more penetrating than most of its kind. "1, 2, 3, 4, 5, 6, 7, 8" is another starving-young-man story, also involving an attack on the mass-production society similar to that in Chaplin's *Modern Times*; and "And Man" is a sketch of the struggle between the sensitive boy and an insensitive society, personified in a school principal who straps the boy for taking walks in the country on school days. This last story treats themes later to be taken up in *My Name Is Aram* in a lighter and more whimsical style.

My Name Is Aram (stories, 1940) is virtually a novel; the stories are all about the same characters and contain a common thread of development. The book is frankly autobiographical; although Saroyan makes the conventional statement that the book is not about "any persons living or dead" he candidly adds, "neither is any person in this book a creation of fiction." The central figures are the members of the Garoghlanian family, Armenian farmers and vineyard workers in the San Joaquin Valley; the book is narrated in the first person by Aram Garoghlanian, a boy who has slightly more detachment and gravity than the puckish relatives who surround him and can thus view them with a certain objectivity. The best pieces of the book are the first story, "The Beautiful White Horse," involving the narrator's cousin Mourad who has a very flexible concept of what constitutes stealing and therefore sees nothing wrong with borrowing a neighbor's horse for six months to take early-morning rides; "The Journey to Hanford," about a "sad uncle" who has a constitutional apathy toward work; and "The Pomegranate Trees," about another uncle, Melik, who spends thousands of dollars trying to make the desert bloom into pomegranates and succeeds in producing only cactuses and sage brush. The conversation in the last-named piece between Aram and Melik over horned-toads is one of the most idiotic and yet most charming dialogues in modern literature. Most of the remaining stories are concerned with Aram's struggle against organized education ("One of Our Future Poets," "A Nice Old-Fashioned Romance") or with other anecdotes about eccentric uncles and cousins. *My Name Is Aram,* free from the bitterness of *The Daring Young Man* yet more sincere, straightforward, and unpretentious than Saroyan's later work, is probably his best book.

The Human Comedy (novel, 1943) is actually a set of sketches only slightly more unified than those of *My Name Is Aram;* as a novel it is episodic and lacks any single strong plot-line. Saroyan temporarily abandons his Armenians, although one or two appear as minor characters; the main characters are the Macauley family of Ithaca, California (actually Fresno), and a number of other residents of the town. Homer Macauley, the central figure, is a boy of high-school age who works, as Saroyan did, as a telegraph messenger; his friends in the telegraph office include the hard-boiled but basically kind manager Mr. Spangler and the alcoholic old telegrapher William Grogan, who dies at the end of a heart attack. The era is the period of the Second World War; Homer's brother Marcus is away in the army. The family also includes the four-year-old Ulysses and the sister Bess; the father has died some years before. Homer, as a telegraph messenger, has to deliver many messages telling mothers of the death of their soldier sons; he is depressed by this but at the same time matured through acquisition of a tragic view of life. The climax of the novel (and the shock which causes old Mr. Grogan's death) is the arrival of a telegram announcing that Marcus has been killed; Homer and his mother, both hardened to tragedy by the events of their lives, accept the news stoically and with resignation. Other notable scenes are the fascination of Ulysses with a friendly Negro who waves to him from a train (Chapter 1) and the interlude of the three lonely but madcap soldiers who treat two Ithaca girls to a movie (Chapters 17–20). This novel, which contains much good writing, is unfortunately marred by the excessive sentimentality with which Saroyan treats the war, soldiers, and patriotic matters generally. It is nevertheless his sole attempt at an integrated novel and one of his most important works. Parts of the story were made into a motion picture in 1944; Saroyan was originally offered a contract to collaborate on its production, but quarreled with the studio and quit before the picture was finished.

Dramas: Saroyan's most important dramas are contained in the volume *Three Plays* (1940); another book by the same title but dated 1941 contains three plays of lesser importance. The three dramas in the 1940 volume were all produced in New York by the Group Theatre, an outgrowth of the Theatre Guild, in 1939–40, and are similar in style and attitude. "My Heart's in the Highlands" (1939) is based on a 1936 Saroyan story and has also been published as a one-act play. In its longer form it is still intended to be played without intermission, but has assumed the scope of a three-act drama. Ben Alexander, an unsuccessful poet, lives in Fresno with his son Johnny; the two keep alive mainly by persuading Mr. Kosak, the local grocer, to give them food on credit. When Jasper MacGregor, an itinerant bugler, happens by they invite him to stay as a guest in the house, and his bugle-music is so beautiful that the neighbors crowd in to give them gifts of food. Mr. MacGregor, the romanticist whose "heart's in the Highlands," eventually proves to be a fugitive from an old folks' home, and is taken away by his keepers; meanwhile the owner of the house, who has not been paid for some time, rents it to somebody else, and father and son are thrown out into the world. The play ends as Johnny remarks, "I'm not mentioning any names, Pa, but something's wrong somewhere." The moral of the play is evidently that landlords should allow unsuccessful poets to live in their houses rent-free, in the same spirit in which Mr. Kosak has given them groceries. Whatever the dubious social implications of this theory, the play is a charming and poignant one, succeeding in spite of its lack of structure and its general obscurity. The *Three Plays* volume of 1940 includes an amusing set of criticisms of "My Heart's in the Highlands" taken from New York newspapers and magazines, showing the mixture of exasperation and bafflement with which critics greeted Saroyan's first important drama.

"The Time of Your Life" (1939), the second of the *Three Plays*, is a five-act drama, heavier and more involved than "My Heart's in the Highlands." The scene is a San Francisco bar, a "waterfront honky-tonk" presided over by the calm and philosophical bartender Nick. The other chief characters are the pure-hearted prostitute Kitty; the "loafer" Joe and his half-witted assistant and errand-boy Tom; Arab, an "Eastern philosopher and harmonica-player"; Krupp, a thoughtful waterfront cop who is ashamed of roughing up strikers; McCarthy, an intelligent and socially conscious longshoreman; Blick, a vulgar and obnoxious vice-squad detective; and Kit Carson, an old desert rat and Indian fighter. The plot is confused but basically consistent. The thick-headed Tom falls in love with Kitty and resolves to rescue her from her life of sin; Blick tries to make trouble for everyone in the bar and especially for Kitty, and is removed from the scene through an ingenious and undetectable murder by Kit Carson, whom everyone had previously taken for a garrulous and slightly crazy old idiot. The moral is that of most of Saroyan's work: that the little and confused people of the world, even in their vices, are more admirable than the big, the powerful, the organized, and the puritanical.

"Love's Old Sweet Song" (1940), the third drama of the volume, is a farcical love story set in Bakersfield, California in the back yard of "a beautiful unmarried small-town woman" named Ann Hamilton. The Greek boy Georgie Americanos, a telegraph messenger, serves as observer and commentator on the action. Through a joke Ann is sent a telegram announcing that Barnaby Gaul, a passer-by who barely met her when she was sixteen, is coming from Boston to ask for her hand in marriage; when an itinerant medicine man, Dr. Greatheart, happens by she takes him for her lover and he willingly accepts the part. Meanwhile the Yearling family, a large clan of migratory workers from Oklahoma, arrive and camp in Ann's back yard; Saroyan has a great deal of fun satirizing Steinbeck (in the person of Richard Oliver, an "unpublished novelist") and other writers who sentimentalize the plight of the "Oakies" while shrewdly using them for literary material. ("I don't know how I'm going to be able to write this and give it social significance," worries Oliver after the Yearling brothers give him a thorough thrashing.) Finally, after Dr. Greatheart, alias Barnaby Gaul, reveals that he is actually "Jim Doherty," Ann agrees to marry him, heedless of the fact that the Yearlings have burned down her house. An interlude in Act III of this three-act comedy depicts the lives of Georgie's father Stylianos and his grandfather Pericles, typical Saroyan eccentrics in the manner of *My Name Is Aram.*

The dramas of the 1941 *Three Plays* include "The Beautiful People," "Sweeney in the Trees," and "Across the Board on Tomorrow Morning," similar in style but inferior in quality to the three plays described above. *Razzle-Dazzle* (1942) collects a number of short plays, most of which are semi-dramatic sketches rather than genuine playable theatre dramas.

Eudora Welty (born 1909)

It seems by now clear that Eudora Welty has arrived at the position once held by Edith Wharton and later by Willa Cather, that of America's foremost living woman writer of fiction. Although she began her literary career as a short-story writer, and the term itself is not quite adequate—short fictions as applied to Borges and Lagerkvist might be better, and proved herself so consummate an artist in this genre that many critics concluded that her talent was restricted to this limited scope, she has since proved them wrong. Katherine Ann Porter, in the 1941 preface to *A Curtain of Green,* remarked, "It is quite possible she can never write a novel, and there is no reason why she should." But with *The Robber Bridegroom* in 1942, called by critics novel, short novel, or novella, and dedicated to Katherine Ann Porter, Miss Welty had made her start. In *Delta Wedding* and again in *The Ponder Heart* she produced one exquisitely finished novel and an equally effective novella which not only showed a complete mastery of the forms but demonstrated that her mature talent needed this wider scope to display its full power. *Losing Battles* in 1970 won the war as a full-scale novel of major significance. Parallels with *Ulysses* are suggestive and not far-fetched; although its subject matter and technique are worlds apart from Joyce and quite original, its view of the human condition is equally well-grounded and affirmative—Stephen Dedalus and Leopold Bloom lose their battles too, but the last word is Yes.

Miss Welty is a writer with few pretensions, and with no grandiose literary ambitions at all. Like Ellen Glasgow, she is a southern writer (and like Miss Porter and Carson McCullers and Flannery O'Connor), a kind of regionalist, and an intensely feminine writer who views human situations with an insightful feminine sensitivity; but there the resemblance ends. Miss Glasgow's stated purpose was to paint a complete panorama of Virginia life from the Civil War times to the present; Eudora Welty has no other mission than to tell stories about the land and people she knew best. For Katherine Ann Porter land and people meant Texas; for Carson McCullers and Flannery O'Connor they meant Georgia. Miss Welty does share Mississippi with Faulkner, but they carve out their respective regions without serious trespass on each other's preserves, geographical or imaginative. Her land is the Natchez Trace area, cutting a broad swath from northeastern Mississippi (the Alabama-Tennessee corner) southwest to Natchez on the Mississippi river, including the Yazoo Delta region and particularly that part of the trace which runs past Jackson, Miss Welty's home. Faulkner's Yoknapatawpha County lies north and west, some two hundred miles from Jackson up toward Memphis. To an outsider this region seems similar, even identical, to the Oxford district of Faulkner; yet it is typical of the South that Miss Welty's Delta inhabitants view northern Mississippi as a strange and distant land and its denizens virtually foreigners, and vice versa. The "low-born" Troy in *Delta Wedding* from the hill country in northern Mississippi is treated as an outlander by the self-satisfied and provincial Delta aristocrats of the Fairchild family. And Cleo of the Delta is similarly viewed by the Beechams in *Losing Battles*.

With few exceptions, Miss Welty's best work is laid in this region and among its people, yet she is not a Southern regionalist in every sense. She does not treat the social and psychological implications of the Negro problem to any extent at all when compared with Faulkner; she has no plan for the regeneration of the South like Ellen Glasgow, and she is not particularly interested in the problem of the Southerner who emigrates into Northern culture. Moreover she has none of the sentimental traditionalism and patriotism of Ransom and the Fugitive poets. Whether she has captured the "real" South or not, she has created a fictional world of great charm, a world caught in the grip of an indolent and often ludicrous decadence, yet poetic, gallant, and above all vivid. We are emotionally moved by Faulkner, shocked into attention by Erskine Caldwell, and amused by Eudora Welty. Yet she is more than a humorist; in some respects her fiction gives us as good an insight into southern society, even into the "problem of the South," as that of the other two authors. Eudora Welty is concerned mainly with whatever people she has closely observed as individuals rather than classes. But when she shows us vulgar townspeople (as in "Petrified Man") she does so from the implied point of view of finer southern ideals; and her eccentric and slightly mentally deficient country clans (*The Ponder Heart*) are nevertheless imbued with a proud and highly disciplined sense of family tradition. Her Fairchilds (*Delta Wedding*) are like Faulkner's Compsons acting comedy instead of tragedy; both families share the same ingrown clan feeling and the same nostalgic consciousness of proud tradition amid the vestiges of decaying wealth.

Yet there are other distinctive differences between Eudora Welty and the southern writers whose names may be associated with hers, even one as important as Faulkner. First, although Eudora was born in Jackson, Mississippi which has always been her home, her parents had come from other areas, her mother, Mary Chestina Andrews Welty, from West Virginia, and her father, Christian Webb Welty, from Ohio; they had moved to Jackson shortly after their marriage in 1904, immigrants from the North. She once humorously conceded that she had "suffered" as a child only through her "father's being from Ohio, a Yankee." She could seriously see the advantages of her parentage in giving her perspective; there were no ancestors of the landed aristocratic South to create the blinders of emotional bias. So she has enjoyed the attachment to her own land of birth and the detachment of being somewhat outside. There are also the perspectives of temperament, ironic distance, and the artistic techniques of drawing back to frame a picture (see her story, "A Memory") whether painting or photograph and of using her ear in much the same fashion as her eye, to register the speech patterns and rhythms that she could pick up like a tape recorder. She has only "to see and record, to listen and write 'by ear,'" which was true of Joyce and his Dublin world too. But obviously there is more to great art than that, selection and arrangement among other things. The lack of southern ancestry may account for the absence in the Welty fiction of any preoccupation with the Civil War. She deals with frontier tall-tales, although freely mixed with European folk material, but the Civil War just isn't there, except for one isolated story, "The Burning," where it is almost incidental. Faulkner, on the other hand, is, like his characters, obsessed by it and emotionally involved as in *Light in August* and *Absalom, Absalom*; the Civil War for him is a great wound and the scar tissue binds together the years before and the years after.

But it is above all as a stylist that Miss Welty is superb. Her writing is careful, delicately whimsical even when she is relating farcical incidents, and unerring in diction and image. Her dialogues are as subtle and as colorful as those of any modern writer; on the one hand they are precise examples of Southern vernacular, and on the other hand they have a particular Eudora Welty flavor which is instantly recognizable and which no other Southern writer has achieved. Her narrative style is highly compressed; two or three ideas may be interwoven into a single sentence, and yet the result is not intricate or difficult in the way of Joyce. Miss Welty began to write for magazine publication, and even in her later works there is a great clarity and unpretentiousness about her style.

Robert Daniel has distinguished four types of settings in her work, as follows: 1) historical tales of the Natchez Trace ("First Love," "A Still Moment," and other stories in *The Wide Net*); 2) tales of the countryside, usually the Delta region of Mississippi, including *Delta Wedding*, the novellas, and the best of her stories; 3) the middle-class town stories, like "Asphodel" and "Petrified Man"; and 4) tales of the metropolis, including such as "Flowers for Marjorie" and "Music from Spain," both from *The Golden Apples*. To these four categories must be added the stories of European setting contained in *The Bride of the Innisfallen* and now the region of Northeastern Mississippi which is the setting for *Losing Battles*. For each of these settings Miss Welty has a different style and treatment; she is a conscious and versatile artist who writes skillfully to create a given effect, and her work shows a remarkable diversity: she spreads a wide net, indeed. Yet it is in the tales of the Delta, including the early novels and stories like "Why I Live at the P. O.," and in *Losing Battles* that Eudora Welty is at her finest, and it is through these stories that her position as a major writer is assured.

Life: If asked about herself, Miss Welty replies, "Except for what's personal, there is really so little to tell, and that little lacking in excitement and drama in the way of the world." In spite of "the modesty, simplicity, and privacy of the life and public manner," according to an early biographer, it adds up. Eudora Alice Welty was born in Jackson, Mississippi in 1909, her father reasonably comfortable as president of an insurance company, and grew up with two brothers. After high school she attended Mississippi State College for Women (1925–27) and earned her B.A. at the University of Wisconsin (1929). After further study at the Columbia University School of Business, she held a number of odd jobs in advertising and radio, and with the W. P. A. as Junior Publicity Agent, taking photographs and writing copy, but always working on the serious and exploratory writing of short stories on the side. Her father had died on her return to Jackson in 1931; always a "family" woman, she continued to live closely with her mother and brothers until their passing. Her earliest publication of stories in the mid-thirties was in *Manuscript* and then in the *Southern Review,* soon thereafter in *Atlantic Monthly* and *Harper's Bazaar.* Writing to a friend, "When I think of Ford Madox Ford! You remember how you gave him my name and how he tried his best to find a publisher for my book of stories all that last year of his life . . . ," Miss Welty recalls the ease rather than the difficulties of her acceptance; in 1940 Diarmuid Russell (son of the Irish poet AE) became her literary agent and her friend; in 1941 the first collection of her stories, *A Curtain of Green,* appeared.

According to the introduction to that volume, "she loves music, listens to a great deal of it, all kinds; grows flowers very successfully, and remarks that she is 'underfoot locally,' meaning that she has a normal amount of social life." Publication has continued at a steady pace but not too fast to allow time for careful writing: *The Robber Bridegroom* in 1942; a second collection of short stories, *The Wide Net,* the next year; *Delta Wedding* in 1946; and a very special collection of related stories titled *The Golden Apples* in 1949. *The Ponder Heart* as a short novel appeared in the *New*

Yorker in December 1953, the following year in book form, and a dramatization for Broadway by Jerome Chodorov and Joseph Fields in 1956. Eudora Welty remembers with amusement that she was allowed a walk-on part for one performance. Recognition came almost as steadily: two O. Henry Prizes in 1942 and 1943, an award from the American Academy of Arts and Letters in 1944, and the Howells Medal for fiction in 1955. This was the year she published another story collection, *The Bride of the Innisfallen*, partly the result of a trip to Europe. Now she was being included in significant anthologies of short stories by Jarvis Thurston and by Robert Penn Warren in *Understanding Fiction.*

By the 1960's Miss Welty was in demand as lecturer and resident writer at American universities. In 1962 she was the William Allan Nelson Professor at Smith College and in 1964 the first Harriet Ewens Beck writer-in-residence at Denison University, returning in 1967. On such occasions she gave generously of herself, consulting with student writers and reading her stories with a dry, detached but amused, and expressive voice that caught and projected character intonations beautifully. The Caedmon recording company has made available her reading of "A Worn Path," "A Memory," and "Why I Live at the P. O."; other stories should be recorded for the sake of posterity. Where would we be without the Dylan Thomas records? In 1964 she published a book for children, *The Shoe Bird*; and in 1970 almost universally enthusiastic reviews greeted *Losing Battles.* Miss Welty, often described as a quiet, tall, plain, gray-haired lady with blue eyes and a shy smile, reminds those who have seen and talked with both of Eleanor Roosevelt—the same grace and graciousness (old-fashioned terms as they are) and warmth but underneath a strength and independence like steel. She too has a Ponder heart but not a Ponder head.

Chief Works: Out of the volumes of short stories, *A Curtain of Green* (1941) and *The Wide Net* (1943) one ought to select some for special comment, either as they contribute to the author's created fictional world or as they represent particular techniques or concepts developed further in her longer fiction. The title stories in each book and "Livvie" from *The Wide Net* are masterpieces in themselves, but the place to start is with the brief autobiographical story-sketch called "A Memory." In it a girl, lying on a sandy beach after a lake swim, frames pictures with her fingers as she does for her painting lessons and dreams up a love affair with a boy she hardly knows. Into the picture suddenly comes a family-group of vulgar bathers, noisy and not pretty to look at. The girl feels "a peak of horror" when the fat woman stands, pulls down the front of her bathing suit to let out lumps of mashed and folded sand, "as though her breasts themselves had turned to sand, as though they were of no importance at all and she did not care." This, the "epiphany" of a brutal mystery that beyond the chaos human beings have neither dignity nor identity, must be squared with the dream vision, still vulnerable, "solitary and unprotected."

"Petrified Man" initially seems like satire. Yet further reflection makes one understand why it is so difficult to write satire in America, to exaggerate that which is already exaggerated. Leota and her friends, the beauty shop itself, are probably a careful and realistic presentation. Of course there is some slanting. Mrs. Pike could have been given a less symbolic name. The story, typical of Miss Welty's comedies of lower-middle-class town life, is seen obliquely as related by Leota, a beauty-shop operator, to her customer, Mrs. Fletcher. The plot concerns Mrs. Pike, an almost incredibly vulgar friend of Leota's, who leaves her three-year old son, Billy Boy, in the shop and who unmasks a side-show petrified man as a fugitive from justice who is wanted for raping "four women in California, all in the month of August." The real point of the story lies not in the plot but in the fascinatingly vulgar beauty shop conversations, the preoccupation of the female characters with sex ("He's turning to stone. How'd you like to be married to a guy like that?"), and the general confused and earthy quality of Leota's narrative. The theme has been called "woman's inhumanity to man," and there is something chilling about what has happened to Fred, Leota's husband, Mr. Pike, and especially Mr. Fletcher. Billy Boy, the only male not yet completely dominated, kicks Leota and Mrs. Fletcher at the end of the story and breaks away from them. Here the comic spirit is Swiftian and "frightens us out of laughter into dismay."

"Why I Live at the P. O." foreshadows the style of *The Ponder Heart* in that it too is a monologue related in a typical Welty-flavored Southern vernacular by a woman who reveals her character as she talks. "Sister," the narrator, is jealous of her sister Stella-Rondo, who has gone off to marry an itinerant photographer and now returns with a two-year old girl, Shirley T., who, she declares, is adopted. Sister, jealous, quarrels with her, and the whole family, including Uncle Rondo and the severe grandfather, Papa-Daddy, takes Stella-Rondo's side. Finally Sister hauls away her possessions and moves into the post office in China Grove which belongs to her by virtue of the fact that Papa-Daddy has had her made postmistress through his political influence of this next to the smallest postal facility in the state of Mississippi. This is Bergsonian comedy at its best in the rigidity of Sister's character and her automatic, repetitive reactions to any situation. Other stories have a less comic flavor and penetrate the brutal mysteries.

The Robber Bridegroom (novella, 1942) is a fairy tale of the American frontier set along the historic Natchez Trace. It tells how a young maiden, bestowed by her father unknowingly upon a murderous bandit, eventually succeeded in capturing him by her courage and her wits. The three main characters are all in some sense "double"; Clement Musgrove, both a wanderer and a planter; his daughter Rosamond, both beautiful and a congenital liar; Jamie Lockhart, both bandit and bridegroom. At the beginning Clement meets Jamie at an inn and sees him as hero in an encounter with the historic Mike Fink, then begins to dream of him as a son-in-law. Jamie and Rosamond do eventually get together with a bandit kidnapping and survive the efforts of a wicked stepmother to disenchant them. They are rewarded, all three, Jamie and Rosamond with a fine mansion and a hundred slaves, Clement with the knowledge that his children have them, as he returns to the Trace on his own free will alone.

Delta Wedding (novel, 1946) is a delicate and whimsical portrait of a family: the Fairchilds, of Fairchild, Mississippi, a fictional town on the Yazoo River near Delta City. The story, or rather the situation, since there is no cohesive plot, is seen chiefly through the eyes of a little girl, Laura McRaven, who comes to Fairchild for the marriage of her cousin Dabney Fairchild with the "low-born" northern Mississippian Troy Flavin, who works as overseer on the Fairchild fields. The Fairchilds are a closely-knit clan who quarrel with each other but present an impenetrable wall to outsiders;

those who marry into the family must either accept its ways and lose their identity in it or be cast out. Their huge old house, full of sisters, aunts, cousins, and innumerable Negroes, is the center of a life of fascinatingly disorganized eccentricity; its fixtures include a demented but harmless aunt, an idiot child, a somewhat confused Negro witch-woman, and a number of precocious children. The chief events of the novel are the quarrel between an uncle, George Fairchild, and his wife Robbie, which begins when George ignores her safety to risk his life rescuing the feeble-minded Maureen, his niece, from a train (an act symbolic of the inward loyalty of the Fairchild clan); and the gradual acceptance of Troy by the clan, which admits him into its circle only on the assumption that Dabney will go on living in the family as before. None of this is related explicitly; it is conveyed chiefly through dialogue of a particularly colorful and whimsical irony, and the story is revealed only gradually and obliquely. As the novel ends Troy and Dabney move into Shellmound, a spare Fairchild mansion which has remained vacant for years, and Robbie and George agree to occupy The Grove, another family house, so that their lives will remain within the Fairchild circle.

Other characters are Battle, brother of George and head of the family; his Virginia-born wife Ellen, still an outsider after spending a generation in the family; the elder daughter Shelley; and Ellen's nine-year-old daughter India, a precocious child who is free from the smugness of most literary children of her type. A high moment in the novel is the account of the birth of Shelley, in which the bumbling Dr. Murdock anesthetizes himself with his gas machine and leaves Ellen to deliver her baby alone. This scene well illustrates Miss Welty's skill in relating broadly farcical material in a subdued and faintly ironic style. As Mr. Bryant says in his pamphlet on Eudora Welty, "In the end what makes this family a living, continuing thing is the capacity of a sufficient number of the people in it to participate with compassion, selflessness, and intensity in the daily lives of all the others, whether linked by blood or by simple affection."

The Golden Apples (connected stories, 1949) can be read either as a novel or as separate but connected stories. It has as much unity of impact as Joyce's *Dubliners* or Sherwood Anderson's *Winesburg,*

Ohio; but the threads of unity are even more subtle and more numerous. The central setting is the fictional Mississippi town of Morgana, although Morgana characters may range as far away as San Francisco in "Music from Spain." The theme of this complex and encompassing work is found in the Yeats poem about the Wandering Aengus, from which Miss Welty takes her title; the last stanza reads:

> Though I am old with wandering
> Through hollow lands and hilly lands,
> I will find out where she has gone,
> And kiss her lips and take her hands;
> And walk among long dappled grass,
> And pluck till time and times are done
> The silver apples of the moon,
> The golden apples of the sun.

The setting is authentic and contemporary, like that of *Delta Wedding*; but the fabulous enters the narrative, as it does in *The Robber Bridegroom*. Greek myth enters with the greatest of ease; the golden apples of the Hesperides, the shower of gold of the Danaë story, and the Zeus-like character himself, King MacLain, a tea and spice salesman who spends much of his time away, wandering. King fathers Castor and Pollux twins in Morgana, to be named Lucius Randall ("Ran") and Eugene. Miss Katie Rainey of Morgana tells the first story about them. Then her daughter, Virgie Rainey, who develops as a main character and at the end takes over the kingship of wanderers or seekers from King MacLain himself, enters in "June Recital" to muse and meditate with her piano teacher, old Miss Eckhart, on a picture of Perseus with the head of the Medusa. Perseus turns out to be Loch Morrison, a boy who grows up in Morgana. He too is a potential wanderer, and he watches through his father's telescope as Miss Eckhart tries to set on fire the house where Virgie and a sailor friend are making love and as King MacLain, temporarily in town, helps put out the fire. The two main wanderers, Virgie and King pass by each other here and almost meet; that meeting is reserved for the funeral of Virgie's mother in the last story. Virgie in the cemetery, with earned understanding, watches "the rain of fall, maybe on the whole South, for all she knew on the everywhere." It is a moment close to that of Gabriel at the end of Joyce's *The Dead,* watching the snowfall; but Virgie senses her participation in the perennial vibrations of earthly life rather than Gabriel's emptiness.

The Ponder Heart (novella, 1953) is presented in the form of a long monologue spoken by Edna Earle Ponder, one of the central characters, to a "captive audience," a young girl staying at the Beulah Hotel in Clay, Mississippi because her car has broken down. The listener tries to read in vain, as Edna Earle's voice dominates the long Mississippi summer "evening," or as we say up north, afternoon, telling the story of her uncle and the generosity of his give-away heart. Uncle Daniel Ponder is an old gentleman so eccentric that on one occasion he is locked up in a mental institution in Jackson for a brief period by his own father; his apparent feeble-mindedness, however, is due mainly to his benevolent impulsiveness (the Ponder heart) and to the fact that he lives in a private world of his own particular logic. The story relates chiefly his marital adventures: how in his forties he was married off by Grandpa Ponder to a local widow named Miss Teacake Magee and escaped after only a brief ordeal of matrimony when she divorced him, and how he is later tricked into marriage with the cheap, self-centered, "poor white" Bonnie Dee Peacock of Polk, who worked at the jewelry counter in Clay's ten-cent store. Subsequently Bonnie Dee dies during a thunderstorm under ambiguous circumstances (the truth seems to be that Uncle Daniel playfully tickled her to death, playing "creep-mousie") and the Peacock clan, bent on revenge, has him charged with murder. The trial is the climax of the narrative; it is an extended and skillfully related farce in which the vulgar Peacocks are contrasted with the tradition-proud and essentially upright Ponders. Uncle Daniel is acquitted, mainly because he gains the crowd's favor by passing out his entire fortune, inherited from his father, to them in greenbacks while the court is in session. This, of course, alienates most of the citizens of Clay who take the money but in the embarrassment of their spiritual poverty can't bring themselves to return it. The best of this short novel lies in the portraits of Daniel himself, of Bonnie Dee, and of Edna Earle, who is neatly characterized as the one sensible member of the family through her own rambling style of telling the story, arriving at her own gesture of generosity toward Uncle Daniel at the end as she invites him downstairs to greet the visitor.

Losing Battles (novel, 1970) takes place in what Miss Welty calls "the poorest place and the poorest time in the state of Mississippi" to reduce things to essentials, that is, on a farm and in the nearby community of Banner in the northeast hill country corner of the state during a summer of the 1930's depression. The narrative action covers one August Sunday from dawn through the next morning—just a few more hours than Joyce's *Ulysses*, but the characters remember (not interior monologue—they *tell*, impulsively, compulsively, what they remember) and there are so many of them and they all talk, at least all the women and most of the men, reaching into the past and into their neighbors' lives as well as most importantly the life of the family. Kith and kin are all here for Granny Vaughn's 90th birthday: six of her grandchildren, all Beechams, Nathan, Curtis, Dolphus, Percy, Noah, and Beulah Beecham Renfro; Mr. Renfro and the Renfro children, Jack, Ella Fay, Etoyle, Elvie, Vaughn, Jack's wife, Gloria, and her daughter, the youngest great-great grandchild living at home, Lady May Renfro at the age of one, plus assorted descendants and cousins and married kin of the Beechams and relatives of Mr. Ralph Renfro, and dogs—dogs and children. There are even unexpected guests like Judge and Mrs. Moody of Ludlow. What a reunion! Just like a painting by Breughel, only not Flemish but American. Uncle Noah Webster Beecham says to Jack's wife: "Gloria, this has been a story on us all that will never be allowed to be forgotten. . . . Long after you're an old lady without much further stretch to go, sitting back in the same rocking chair Granny's got her little self in now, you'll be hearing it told to Lady May and all her hovering brood. How we brought Jack Renfro back safe from the pen! How you contrived to send a court judge up to Banner Top and caused him to sit at our table and pass a night with the family, wife along with him. The story of Jack making it home through thick and thin and into Granny's arms for her biggest and last celebration—for so I have a notion it is—I call this a reunion to remember, all!" And it is. But that's not the whole story.

Instead of a single "character" narrator like the woman who went to live at the P. O. or Edna Earle Ponder, most of the people in this novel are narrators and they're almost all "characters" with particularities if not peculiarities. Often they want to talk at the same time; they shriek, squeal, squeak, cry, whoop, and often just ask or answer. But the crowd, the family as chorus, is center-stage all the time. Even the hero, after the build-up for his entrance, his return from two years at the penitentiary at Parchman for what the family rightly considers heroic action rather than crime, is shunted to one side because the novel is social rather than psychological. Jack is a real hero, handsome, brave, nineteen; but he's human rather than mythical, not a robber bridegroom nor a King MacLain. He seems to be competent, the real hope of his family, but his world is always going to pieces, crops, truck, or fights. He is one of those who lose battles and represents others. The biggest loser besides Jack is a character who never appears but whose presence persists; she died on the morning of Granny's birthday reunion, the schoolteacher for many years at Banner school, Miss Julia Mortimer. She had taught all the Beechams and Renfros and most of the community and even tutored Judge Moody in Ludlow. All that teaching meant losing many battles, as Miss Julia has told the Judge in her last letter which he reads aloud at the reunion in spite of protests; and, the letter continues, "the reason I never could win for good is that both sides were using the same tactics. . . . A teacher teaches and a pupil learns or fights against learning with the same force behind him. It's the survival instinct. . . . But the side that gets licked gets to the truth first." She has commanded all her former pupils to her funeral, but school is not to be dismissed, neither for hell nor high water, hurricane nor tornado. Miss Julia had held school in Banner through a cyclone and a flood herself. She had had designs on everybody, to make doctors and lawyers; she'd say "A state calling for improvement as loudly as ours? Mississippi standing at the bottom of the ladder gives me that much more to work for."

So Miss Julia fights against the impoverished but lively if unwilling-to-learn Banner farmers. She and Granny represent opposed powers; Granny as the "source" of more than fifty people present is unthinking biological renewal, while the teacher as an old maid has only a different kind of torch to pass on, a vision of learning and knowledge. Gloria Renfro is caught in the middle. Intended to carry on the teacher's work as her protegée, she had devoted herself instead to one student in Banner school, Jack Renfro, and married him. She resists both the pull of his family ("I *won't* be a Beecham!") and the pull of Miss Julia's austere idealism. But of course everybody loses in the end, and it is unlikely that Gloria can hold out much longer. Gloria wants Jack to herself, but Jack wants family. "Don't pity anybody you could love," he says and adds, "Don't give anybody up. . . . There's room for everything and time for everybody."

In a letter Eudora Welty says of *Losing Battles,* "What I was trying to do was simmer everything down to action and speech—to see if I could convey all that belonged in a novel of kinship and family to the showing forth of talk and acts, without having to explain or enlarge things by going into their minds in words." It works phenomenally well. The only mind we crawl into is that of the usually silent Vaughn, Jack's younger brother toward the end of the novel and that very briefly. The sound of the night surrounds him. "As he plodded through the racket, it rang behind him and was ahead of him too. It was all-present enough to spill over into voices, as everything, he was ready to believe now, threatened to do, the closer he might come to where something might happen. The night might turn into more and more voices, all telling it—bragging, lying, singing, pretending, protesting, swearing everything away—but telling it. . . . the world around him was still one huge, soul-defying reunion." This emphasizes the success of the huge dialogue in chorus; the words are the words of many. The author continues, "I also wanted to strip down all the worldly things, possessions, props, to the very least and to the things they made, to clear the stage for their performance. . . . I wanted to start from scratch and make up their lives as *they* made them, to show what *they* made and how and why. I really loved the people in it, which is what made all the doing matter to me."

Losing Battles is far from allegorical, but the novel suggests enlargement. If Joyce's *Ulysses* is a naturalistic novel become epic in the city of Dublin, this is a realistic novel become epic in poor old Boone County, Mississippi. Both are comic, but the country characters seem to get intoxicated on lemonade and watermelon juice and the sound of their own voices. As Howard Moss said in his *New Yorker* review, the dawn we witness at the beginning of *Losing Battles* "seems more like the first morning of the world" and the story that of the human race. In August 1970 Miss Welty was awarded the Edward MacDowell Medal in New Hampshire (previous winners include Thornton Wilder, Aaron Copland, and Robert Frost); the President of the Colony said, "Eudora Welty, who is a force of life, brings all of these qualities to the magic of her prose as one of the most remarkable novelists of our time," in making the presentation. Newspaper accounts mentioned specifically *Losing Battles.*

The Optimist's Daughter (novel, 1972) is as succinct and astringent as *Losing Battles* is expansive and mythic. In four tight little narrative sections with laconic but revealing talk we are given the conflict between Laurel McKelva Hand, the optimist's daughter and protagonist, and her surprisingly tough opponent, Fay McKelva, the optimist's second wife who is a few years younger than her step-daughter. Upon questioning Laurel admits she had been named for her dead mother's state flower (Becky had belonged to the West Virginia mountains) which brings a sneer from Fay. Both are strong women in their forties. The optimist and romantic, Judge McKelva, dies in Part One, following an eye operation in New Orleans during Carnival time. The widowed daughter, too realistic to be an optimist, squares off against Fay who apparently thoughtlessly and selfishly hastens her husband's death. Part Two presents us with the funeral in Mount Salus, Mississippi, one of the most grotesquely comic funerals in all literature but still realistic (as Finnegan's Wake is not). Fay's Snopes-like family comes in from Texas (she had denied their existence) and confronts the aristocratic and Presbyterian old Mount Salus residents and friends of Laurel (her particular friends are still referred to as the bridesmaids although the wedding must have been a good twenty years ago). The house now belongs to Fay, who accompanies her family back to Texas for a brief visit, and in Part Three Laurel has a chance to make her peace with moving out as she prepares to fly back to Chicago and her designing business. The last confrontation between Fay and Laurel takes place in Part Four with the dramatic threat of an uplifted breadboard which had been made for Becky by Philip Hand and recently desecrated by Fay's cracking walnuts. The parting of the two is final but restrained. However, we get to know and understand Laurel very deeply as she gets to know and understand herself and those around her. This novel won the 1973 Pulitzer fiction award.

Ernest Gaines (born 1933)

Ernie Gaines, one of our youngest writers, is for many readers the most promising and exciting new talent in American fiction to appear in the nineteen-sixties. With three novels and some half-dozen stories, short and novella length, he has emerged as a creative writer of serious and impressive proportions. So far he has appeared primarily as a regionalist and a naturalist, but mainly interested in individual human beings and their interrelationships, doing for the Louisiana bayou plantation country west along the Mississippi river something of what Faulkner and Eudora Welty had been doing farther north for the Mississippi east of the river. Gaines' country is an area up and down river from Baton Rouge, which enters his fiction under its own name. The smaller town, Bayonne, is fictional and may incorporate some features of Oscar, Louisiana, near which the author was born, or other nearby communities. Individual, original, and very much his own man, he nevertheless chose early in his own avid reading certain models for guides to his craft: Turgenev (then Tolstoy and Chekhov), Hemingway for paragraphs, Faulkner, Joyce, Welty, and Greek tragedy. A writer with real talent, and Gaines has it, who works with one eye on such models for style and construction, is going to have something to say which commands attention.

Not primarily a militant black writer, Ernie Gaines is a writer first, then a black and a proud one, and probably a militant in third place (whether willingly or reluctantly one can't be sure). But one must not misunderstand. Gaines is not soft, nor is he likely to refuse support to any demands for black rights. *Bloodline* is a strong and militant novella and an effective story about Christian ("Copper") Laurent, who appears as the most militant and uncompromising leader or "General" of the new forces. But it is first and above all a novella, carefully constructed, beautifully written, balanced and controlled. Its content is enclosed in a form, and they are welded by a conscious artist. In avoiding being politically didactic, although not politically unaware, Ernie Gaines believes that "literature expresses man's feelings and relationships much better than politics ever can." "Besides the conflict between the white and the black, we also carry on a full life: we love, women have children, men gamble, shoot at people, have fights, everything." And it is primarily that life that he writes about.

Gaines has a fine ear for the speech of his characters. It is clearly and realistically of the region of which he writes. The French influence is evident in the Cajuns and the Creole language which filtered into the dialect of his people. One example of his care is the occasional use of the word "Mon" for mother, not Ma, nor Mum, nor Maw, nor any other variant; but his children call for their Mon (or Gran'mon in *A Long Day in November*) almost as often, it seems, as for Mama. You can hear it, probably derived through a couple of hundred years give or take fifty from the French "Maman," abbreviated to the nasal second syllable and handed down from one generation to another. And there's the little girl, Tite, the daughter of Louise and Bonbon in *Of Love and Dust*, short for Petite. The French flavor of the dialogue when appropriate, especially for Cajuns, is effective and particularizes the locale. The spelling of dialect words is carefully thought out to indicate pronunciation, and the author refuses to let his publishers tamper with it.

Ernest Gaines has been most often compared with James Baldwin as a writer of comparable stature. They are not much like each other, except in their apparent devotion to the craft of fiction and in the finish and polish which they bring to it. They are clearly not amateurs but professional writers who have developed their individual and authentic voices.

Life: Ernest James Gaines was born January 15, 1933 at Oscar, Louisiana, the eldest of twelve children of Manuel and Adriean Gaines. He remained on the Louisiana plantation for fifteen years, learning about life and the people around him, working in the fields from the age of eight or nine, his first job picking up Irish potatoes, and going to the one-room schoolhouse described in *A Long Day in November*. In 1948 Ernie made his way via abrupt transition to

Vallejo, California, where he went to high school and junior college and read widely in the public library (here he discovered Turgenev). In the army from 1953 to 1955 he served in Guam and traveled on leave to Tokyo. In 1957 he graduated from San Francisco State and the next year won a Wallace Stegner Creative Writing Fellowship to Stanford, the following year the Joseph Henry Jackson Literary Award.

Catherine Carmier, his first novel to be published but the fourth written, was put out by Atheneum in 1964. It is modeled to some extent on Turgenev's *Fathers and Children* (sometimes called *Fathers and Sons*) but Russian realism is brought to serve Louisiana and Ernie Gaines. He had earlier published a short story, his first publication on a national basis in *Negro Digest,* "The Sky Is Gray," which took its point of departure and some of its inspiration from Eudora Welty's "A Worn Path." His second novel, *Of Love and Dust,* appeared in 1967, and a paperback edition followed two years later. Five stories collected under the title of one of them, *Bloodline,* were published similarly in 1968 and 1970. The third novel, *The Autobiography of Miss Jane Pittman,* was released in April 1971. Among his other ventures, Ernie Gaines leaves his home base in San Francisco to visit college campuses and encourage young writers. He reads well in a deeply resonant voice, and *Miss Jane Pittman* can be a spell-binder. He says his favorite activities besides writing are bowling, pool, reading, and just being lazy; but for one who averages five hours of writing every day and publishes as much quality work as he has produced in less than ten years, some doubt may be expressed at the last assertion.

Chief Novels: *Of Love and Dust* (novel, 1967) is a story that takes place in the summer of 1948. The narrator-observer is Jim Kelly, a black who has been three years on a Louisiana plantation and who is trusted by workers and their families and by the Cajun overseer Sidney Bonbon (who calls him "Geam") and owner Marshall Hebert alike. The protagonist, more folk-hero than anti-hero, is Marcus, young, handsome Negro tough from the city (Baton Rouge) who has killed a man in a knife-fight in a bar and is bonded out of jail to Marshall Hebert to work on the plantation. He hates authority, especially in his major antagonist, the Cajun overseer whom he considers white trash. Marcus works in the fields but hates it and starts looking for a woman, the most beautiful woman on the plantation is the only one for him, who happens to be Pauline, the overseer's black mistress.

Tension builds, with Jim, who had promised Miss Julie Rand, the old lady who had brought Marcus up, to take care of him, trying to keep the lid on. Marcus starts looking at Bonbon's wife, Louise, since he can't get at his mistress Pauline although he tries, and she looks back. Louise, blond, twenty-five, small, cream color of face, abandoned by her husband as far as sexual attention is concerned, is more than attracted by Marcus the young stud. Tite, the Bonbon daughter, plays knowingly around the house and yard, with Aunt Margaret, the Negro house servant doing her best to keep things in order. The inevitable happens with mad passion between Marcus and Louise. They plan to run away together, up North, taking Tite with them, mother and daughter in black face. But in a final confrontation, with Marshall Hebert trying to fix things so that Bonbon would be killed by Marcus (for his own private reasons), Marcus is killed by Bonbon with a scythe-blade. Louise has to be taken to the insane asylum in Jackson. Pauline and Bonbon apparently leave for the North. Jim has to leave the plantation because he guesses the implication of Hebert, and the threat of blackmail must be avoided—which is what Hebert was attempting to avoid in the first place. In some ways Jim Kelly seems to be a neutral character, but the reader tends to identify with his compassion and tenderness for the other characters involved in the tragedy, with his love for Aunt Margaret, with his almost grudging admiration of Marcus and Louise, with his general sympathy for all men and women caught in the tangle of living.

The Autobiography of Miss Jane Pittman (novel, 1971) is fiction which gives the impression of being history. The approach of the outside narrator is soon forgotten: "I had been trying to get Miss Jane Pittman to tell me the story of her life for several years now. . . . she was over a hundred years old, she had been a slave in this country, so there had to be a story. When school closed for the summer in 1962 I went back to the plantation where she lived. . . . I would not take no for an answer. 'You won't,' she said. 'No ma'am.' 'Then I reckon I better say something,' she said."

One proof of the success of what Gaines set out to do can be seen in the report that a slick magazine in this country had accepted the manuscript for publication and later turned it down when it was discovered that it was "fiction" (the craze being for fact)—that's realism achieving success. The author says that Gertrude Stein's *The Autobiography of Alice B. Toklas* suggested the title and perhaps it suggested the challenge of writing in the style of someone almost completely "other." The tape recorder is working and Miss Jane starts talking: When she was ten or eleven years old, she was a little slave girl named Ticey, but one day during the war a Yankee corporal coming to the gate with other soldiers renamed her Jane Brown, after his daughter in Ohio. Freed about a year later she listened to the master of the Louisiana plantation where she was born read the Proclamation from the gallery: "Y'all free. Y'all can stay or y'all can go. Y'all can work on shares, because I ain't got nothing myself since them Yankees went by here last time." The house Negroes stand behind him weeping.

Miss Jane decides to leave, to go to Ohio to find the Yankee corporal who had given her her name and an invitation to look him up. She takes off with a group of freed slaves, but they are set upon by a gang of Klansmen and rebel troops; many are killed including Big Laura who leaves her son Ned in Jane's care. Miss Jane is persistent in her quest although she never gets out of Louisiana: "Where North at?" she asks after trudging and hiding in swamps, "Where Ohio at?" This is exciting narrative and involves definitions of North and Freedom. Finally Jane and Ned wander South again with a straggling group of slaves and find work on a plantation. Later she meets Joe Pittman, a strong, sensitive cowboy and breaker of horses for a Louisiana-Texas border trader; they marry by agreeing to live together, and she becomes Miss Jane Pittman. Joe dies after being thrown, but she keeps her new name. Ned grows up to be a freedom fighter, founds a school, and is assassinated by a hired killer. Time passes and makes Miss Jane an ardent believer in Huey Long, a Dodger fan (through admiration for Jackie Robinson), and, very old now, a follower of Martin Luther King, Jr. Miss Jane joined the church after Ned's death and leaned on a God who supported her; whether He was dead or had never existed did not trouble her nor interfere with her spiritual experience or physical endurance. As one reviewer put it, though meant as a novel, this "magnificent portrait of a Southern black woman and of the vicissitudes through which she passed" emerges as history in the hands of Ernie Gaines; and it is clearly a large slice of internal American history.

Stories: *Bloodline* (1968) contains two novellas and three short stories. *A Long Day in November* is a novella told convincingly from the point of view of a five-year old boy. It is the story of the break-up and restoration of a marriage seen through the sensitive eyes of the son whose understandings have to be limited. Gaines has said that both Joyce and Faulkner helped him to achieve his purpose. In the first part of *The Sound and the Fury* Benjy uses the simplest terms to express feelings: "the gate is cold," "the fire is good," "I stamped my shoes on." Reading Joyce's *Ulysses* at the same time he got the "day" idea, added Faulkner's rhythms and his own school house experiences, and came up with *A Long Day in November,* which ends with the little boy's reactions to his parents' reconciliation: "I go to sleep little bit, but I wake up. I go to sleep some more. I hear the spring on Mama and Daddy's bed. I hear it plenty now. It's some dark under here. It's warm. I feel good way under here."

"The Sky Is Gray," a much shorter story, is told from the point of view of an eight year old boy with a toothache. The major character is his mother, a woman with a wonderful strength coming from the earth, comparable both to Faulkner's Dilsey and Eudora Welty's Old Phoenix, but with a more independent, prouder spirit, rearing her son in the same way. There is a bus trip to the dentist in Bayonne; it is cold, with no place for them to eat down town, no place to get warm. "White" and "Colored" are separated, and the inhumanity of segregation in this story is felt rather than stated.

"Just Like a Tree" is a beautiful short story utilizing a multiple point of view approach in the manner of Faulkner's *As I Lay Dying.* The assortment of characters, young and old, boy Chuckkie, parents Emile and Leola, friends and relatives gather to say goodbye to Aunt Fe, the old woman whom relatives are moving out of the house where she has lived most of her life—or think they are. But the song says, "Just like a tree that's planted 'side the water./

Oh, I shall not be moved." Aunt Lou, the last observer, realizes that Aunt Fe prefers and prepares to die rather than move. " 'Sleep on, Fe,' I tell her. 'When you get up there, tell 'em all I ain't far behind.' "

7. Realists and Naturalists: The New Generation

In the period after the Second World War there emerged an important new group of young American writers, a school basically in the realistic-naturalistic tradition of the Twenties and stemming essentially from Hemingway, Dos Passos, Faulkner, Wolfe, and Anderson. John O'Hara, the oldest of this group, was born in 1905 and began publishing well before the war; among the youngest, Norman Mailer was born in 1923 and published his first book in 1948 and Truman Capote, born in 1924, published precociously *Other Voices, Other Rooms* also in 1948. In spite of this considerable spread in time, these writers are conveniently grouped together because they represent the second generation of twentieth-century realists, a group of authors who read the naturalists of the Twenties when they were young men and started in where Hemingway and his generation left off.

CHARACTERISTICS: (1) These younger writers resemble the earlier American naturalists first of all in attitude: they are skeptical, ironic, anti-puritanical, hard-minded, and bascially materialistic, although they are not without traces of idealism. Four of the seven authors treated here wrote war novels, and with one exception they are novels in the tradition of *All Quiet on the Western Front* and Dos Passos' *Three Soldiers*: cynical, anti-heroic, antagonistic toward the professional officer class and the military mind, basically pacifistic. On the whole no American or British novel of World War II has achieved the originality and value of such World War I novels as Cummings' *The Enormous Room*, Hemingway's *A Farewell to Arms*, or Ford Madox Ford's *Parade's End*. Some view Wouk's *The Caine Mutiny* as the exception, and its special qualities will be explained under the proper heading. When these writers treat domestic scenes they tend to do so in the manner of Sinclair Lewis and Scott Fitzgerald, satirizing the banality of middle-class life and antagonistic toward the hypocrisy that stems from American puritanism. Here again Wouk is the exception.

(2) In style the group writes in the idiom which is thought of as characteristically "American" in the twentieth century, and which derives from the naturalists of the Twenties: terse, vernacular, understated, and often hard-boiled. The tendency is toward pure narrative (especially dialogue) rather than discursive exposition; the authors are concerned to make us see "how it was" at first hand instead of telling us about the action in retrospect. The outstanding impression one receives from the post-1945 war novels is the studied detachment of the author, the utter absence of emotional comment or sentimentalizing. Here the line of development of the American war novel, from Crane through Hemingway to Jones, Mailer, and Shaw, is obvious. Stylistically Salinger and Capote (*not* war novelists) are somewhat different from the others, being essentially more poetic and leaning at times toward the expressionistic (particularly in Capote's *Other Voices, Other Rooms*). *In Cold Blood,* however, as a non-fiction novel must represent a new kind of realism.

(3) In construction the group owes something to war novels like *A Farewell to Arms* and to the Jazz Age novel of manners (e.g., Scott Fitzgerald) but more to Joyce, Faulkner, and Dos Passos; the typical construction of the post-1945 naturalistic novel is complex and ingenious, with flashbacks, shifting point-of-view devices, and experiments in chronological order. Perhaps the most influential single work in this respect is Dos Passos' *U.S.A.*, which was frankly imitated by Mailer in parts of *The Naked and the Dead* and which has also obviously left its mark on Shaw's *The Young Lions.* This kind of "pattern novel" technique, with its continual switching to different characters and its flashbacks into their past, is ideally suited to a war novel which presents a number of men of diverse backgrounds and then analyzes their contrasting reactions to the experience of war.

Of the seven writers considered here, three (O'Hara, Shaw, and Salinger) are also consummate masters of the short story. In their story style the influence of their market—the commercial American magazine—is apparent. Salinger and Shaw wrote much of their short fiction for *The New Yorker,* and the well-known characteristics of this weekly (its brittle and sophisticated style, its fondness for stories of diffuse plot—or perhaps for the Chekhov-Mansfield type of realism, the slice of life where little happens, that stops rather than ends) became a part of their technique. O'Hara's magazine experience is more diversified; his stories rely more on plot and are more conventional in characterization. This peculiarly American genre, the magazine story, has reached a high stage of perfection in these three writers, as well as in others (Katherine Anne Porter, Eudora Welty) not considered in this group.

John O'Hara (1905–1970)

The relation of O'Hara to his environment is analogous to that of Thomas Wolfe. Born in a small Pennsylvania town, he moved on to a big-city culture and became a professional newspaperman and writer; yet as an author he remained fascinated with the places and the people of his boyhood, and he returns to this material consistently in his most important work. In a sense he is a kind of regionalist; his region is the south-central portion of Pennsylvania centering around Harrisburg and O'Hara's own home town of Pottsville (which he converts into the fictional town of Gibbsville). The population of this region is varied: Pennsylvania Dutch farmers, Polish coal miners, Italian shopkeepers and small tradesmen, Irish artisans, upper-middle-class townspeople mainly of Anglo-Saxon extraction, and a sprinkling of professionals (doctors, teachers) from out of the state. It is the last two groups with which O'Hara is chiefly concerned; that is to say he invariably writes from their point of view even though people from the first four groups appear as minor characters. O'Hara himself belonged to the last group; his father was a doctor who attended both the illiterate miners of the "patches" or small mining villages and the wealthy town gentry. In *The Doctor's Son* O'Hara portrays his own experience as a boy accompanying his father on his professional rounds, thus gaining invaluable knowledge of the people he was later to portray in his fiction.

O'Hara's Pennsylvania writing includes *The Doctor's Son,* the novels *Appointment in Samarra, A Rage to Live, The Farmer's*

Hotel, and *Ten North Frederick*, and various stories published in other collections. With the exception of *The Farmer's Hotel*, a minor work, all the novels in this list have the same structure: they are fictional biographies of upper-middle-class Pennsylvanians involving a more or less complete social analysis of a small Pennsylvania city. O'Hara is never content to show us an individual; he must also show us the society which produced the individual. His novels contain much detailed data on the economy and industry of the region, and the changing social conditions which are causing some families to rise and others to decline. This sort of sociological documentation, however, serves only as background: his main interest remains centered on character. His typical hero (Julian English, Joseph B. Chapin) is a man born into a superior family in a small Pennsylvania town, educated at an Ivy League college, who returns to his home town and lives a "respectable" life as a leading citizen, concealing from the public the rottenness and unhappiness of his private life. In *A Rage to Live* the protagonist is a woman, but the pattern remains the same.

As an author who "takes the wraps off the social customs, the politics, the morals of a small American city," O'Hara at first sight resembles Sinclair Lewis. But there is an essential difference: Lewis is basically a satirist, and O'Hara, although not devoid of irony, approaches his subject much more seriously. Even though he attacks the hypocrisy and banality of middle-class life, it is obvious that he is impressed himself with the distinction of families like the Chapins with their Cadillacs, their Ivy-League educations, their social position, and the general aura of importance which surrounds them. Here O'Hara resembles Scott Fitzgerald more than he does Lewis. He is consciously a portrayer of "superior" people, even when he is attacking their standards. In spite of his political and social liberalism he can never view the miners, the immigrant shopkeepers, and the Negro servants of his region as anything but supernumeraries, background figures for his central drama; the bootlegger Al Grecco in *Appointment in Samarra* is one of his few convincing *déclassé* characters, and even he seems thin and stereotyped compared with similar characters in Hemingway or Dos Passos.

As a stylist O'Hara is facile but not highly precise. His writing is all first-draft; according to his own statement in an interview with

Robert Van Gelder it goes to the printer just as it comes from his typewriter. Under these conditions its obvious finish is a tribute to his ear for dialogue and to his long experience as a newspaperman. Because of this technique, however, his construction is often awkward, his conversations, particularly intimate ones between husband and wife, gauche and unconvincing. He is not original in construction; *Butterfield 8,* the only one of his novels that shows any ingenuity in this respect, borrows its pattern from Dos Passos and Joyce. O'Hara's importance lies chiefly in his thorough knowledge of a certain region and a certain people, and his skill in recreating this private world in fictional form for the general reader.

Life: John O'Hara was born in Pottsville, Pennsylvania in 1905; his father was a physician, and O'Hara was one of seven children. Of Irish extraction, he was raised as a Catholic and educated at various schools including the Fordham Preparatory School and Niagara Preparatory School in Niagara, New York, from which he graduated in 1924. He had intended to go on to Yale, but the death of his father made further education impossible. Instead he went to work and held a number of odd jobs which provided him with valuable material for his later writing, ranging from guard in an amusement park to secretary to Heywood Broun. He gradually moved into newspaper work, serving as reporter on two Pennsylvania papers and gong on to the *New York Mirror,* the *Morning Telegraph,* and the *Herald Tribune.* At one time he was also football editor of *Time.* In 1934 he turned to screen-writing and worked in succession for four different motion-picture companies. He was married in 1931 to Helen Ritchie Petit, and again, after a divorce, to Belle Mulford Wylie in 1937. His first novel, *Appointment in Samarra,* appeared in 1934. Meanwhile he was turning out short stories at a prolific rate; a collection, *The Doctor's Son and Other Stories,* appeared in 1935. His *Pal Joey* stories, which appeared originally in *The New Yorker* as a set of sketches about New York night life, were dramatized in 1941, winning success on Broadway as a musical comedy, and were later made into a motion picture. In 1955, after the death of his second wife, he was married to Katharine Barnes Bryan. A long-time New York resident, O'Hara has lived more recently in Princeton, New Jersey.

Having published some thirty-six books, the prolific John O'Hara died in his sleep of a heart attack at his home in Princeton in April 1970. Another completed novel, *The Ewings,* was scheduled for publication in 1971, and he was working on a sequel at the time of his death.

Chief Works: *Appointment in Samarra* (novel, 1934) describes three climactic days in the life of Julian English, an automobile dealer in Gibbsville, Pennsylvania. Julian, son of the Dr. Billy English who appears frequently in O'Hara's fiction, is bitter and dissatisfied with his life and tired of the monotony of his relations with his wife Caroline; basically an individualist, he is at the point of attempting to break out of the pattern of conventional behavior that holds him fast in the respectable society of the small town. As the novel opens he does commit an act of rebellion, but it is a stupid and destructive one: at a country-club party he throws a drink into the face of Harry Reilly, who is not only his friend but also an influential member of the community who has invested money in Julian's business. Julian's collapse and destruction begin with this act. He begins drinking heavily, he insults the servants and antagonizes his wife, he flirts dangerously with the girl-friend of a local racketeer, and he gets into a low argument in his club which ends in a general brawl. At one point he considers simply driving out of Gibbsville and starting life anew somewhere else, but he lacks the character to do this. Returning to his home and finding it empty, he has a short drinking party in company with a young woman from a newspaper who has come to interview his wife; when he makes overtures to her he is repulsed. This final failure disgusts him with his life and with himself, and he commits suicide in his garage using the exhaust of his automobile to asphyxiate himself.

Other important characters in his novel include Julian's wife Caroline, oversexed and frustrated by Julian's indifference; Lute Fliegler, a contented automobile salesman who works for Julian; and Al Grecco, a cynical but competent bootlegger whose life becomes involved with Julian's at several points. There are also numerous passages filling in the economic and social background of Gibbsville. This short novel may be considered a kind of exercise for the more important treatment of similar themes in *A Rage to Live* and *Ten North Frederick*.

A Rage to Live (novel, 1949) is the fictional biography of Grace Tate, née Caldwell, daughter of the leading family in Fort Penn, Pennsylvania, an invented city roughly drawn after the capital town of Harrisburg. Grace's family is an old and proud one, and her parents raise her consciously in the tradition of aristocracy. To their surprise, however, she marries an "outsider," the New Yorker Sidney Tate, who is nevertheless considered acceptable because of his Yale background and his family's wealth. Grace and Sidney are at first happy living on a farm outside of Fort Penn, raising three children, and gradually assuming position as the most prominent family in the community. But Grace, first and foremost a Caldwell, continues to think of her husband as an outsider, and more and more her interests turn back to her own clan. In addition her character is dominated by a fierce "rage to live," a vitality so boundless that she cannot remain faithful to Sidney even though she loves him; she has a tempestuous affair with a local contractor, Roger Bannon, which soon becomes a matter for public gossip. Meanwhile the First World War comes; Sidney applies for a naval commission but is turned down for a physical defect. Shortly afterward he is stricken with infantile paralysis and dies, and a few days later Grace's small son Billy is carried off by the same disease. Struggling to reorganize her life, Grace rejects a chance to resume her affair with Bannon, but in spite of her inward struggles against her emotions she falls in love with Jack Hollister, a Fort Penn newspaperman. Although Hollister and Grace are innocent, Hollister's wife Amy senses their feelings toward each other, comes to an outdoor party where they are together, and fires several wild pistol shots at them without hitting anyone. This incident persuades Grace that her time of passions must come to an end, and that she must now resign herself to a graceful middle age. An epilogue describes her life a number of years later, in 1947; she has grown into a gracious if inwardly unhappy grandmother, living in New York and sustained by the obvious respect the young members of the Caldwell family show her. Another important character in *A Rage to Live* is Grace's brother Brock Caldwell, in his youth a playboy and a snob, who acquires character through gradual maturity and through marriage with a sophisticated Frenchwoman.

Ten North Frederick (novel, 1955) is O'Hara's most ambitious and most important work. Broader in scope than any of his previous novels, it includes a complete history of its locale and characters from Civil War times to the present. The central character is Joseph B. Chapin, the leading citizen of Gibbsville, a man whose life is dominated by a secret ambition to be President of the United States. The novel begins with Chapin's funeral and then goes back to recount the history of his life in a single long flashback. Born into the leading family in the town, Chapin never doubts his own superiority, just as he never doubts the superiority of Gibbsville and its society to all other places on earth, not excluding New York City. As a Yale student he has relations with Marie Harrison, sister of a friend; when she later dies from an abortion he feels a temporary remorse, but soon recovers from it. He marries Edith Stokes, who comes from a good Gibbsville family and is the proper and approved bride for him, and goes into a law partnership with Arthur McHenry, a boyhood friend who has also gone to Yale for his education. Chapin's law career is a success, and gradually political ambitions grow in him. In his forties he enters into negotiations with Mike Slattery, the local Republican boss, for the nomination for Lieutenant Governor. When Mike suggests that he make a large political contribution, "with no strings to it," he does so. But the Party leaders decide against his candidacy; they view him (perhaps rightly) as a snob with no appeal for the common voter. Chapin has thrown away a hundred thousand dollars on an ephemeral dream. But except for McHenry and perhaps Slattery, no one knows of his blasted ambition to be President; the world is unaware that his life has been a failure. Toward the end of his career he has a brief affair with Kate Drummond, his daughter's roommate; then he dies of a liver ailment aggravated by overdrinking.

Other important characters in *Ten North Frederick* are Chapin's wife Edith, who sees through him and is dissatisfied with her marriage but permits herself only one brief extramarital affair and then lives out her life maintaining her standards to the end; his daughter Ann, who falls in love with a musician named Charley Bongiorno and whose life is ruined when the family breaks up the affair; a son

Joby (Joseph Jr.), whose character is broken by his strong-willed father and who ends up cynical and alcoholic; and Slattery, the politician, who views Chapin's stiff family pride somewhat ironically but nevertheless admires him and sympathizes with him as a man. As in *A Rage to Live,* there is much social documentation, including a complete analysis of the economic and commercial interrelationships of the town. The core of the novel, however, is the character of Chapin and his relations with his wife, his children, and Slattery.

O'Hara's remaining novels are less important. *Butterfield 8* (1935) is laid in uptown New York City and demonstrates the intricate pattern of relationships of the people who live within the telephone exchange indicated by the title. The central figure, Gloria Wandrous, is a fast girl of the flapper age who becomes involved in a descending circle of vice and is finally killed when she falls overboard from a steamer. *Hope of Heaven* (1938), set in Hollywood, describes the unhappy love affair of a scenario writer and a girl who works in a bookstore. *The Farmer's Hotel* (1951) is a short novel in which guests in a snowbound hotel become involved in a complicated intrigue of passion and tragedy.

Stories: O'Hara's short stories are collected in *The Doctor's Son* (1935), *Files on Parade* (1939), *Pipe Night* (1945), *Hellbox* (1947), and other volumes down to *Assembly* (1961), *The Hat on the Bed* (1963), and *And Other Stories* (1968). He was beginning to seem inexhaustible. The best known of his stories are contained in the first volume. Of these, "The Doctor's Son," the title story, is a long tale based on O'Hara's boyhood experiences following his father on his medical rounds. During a flu epidemic the narrator, James Malloy, visits the coal-mining "patch" of Collieryville with "Doctor" Myers, a young medical student, and falls in love with Edith Evans, daughter of a mine superintendent. But Edith's father dies in the epidemic, and James, who has seen Myers making love to Mrs. Evans, comes out of the experience matured and disillusioned; he never sees Edith again.

The best-known stories in *Files on Parade* are the "Pal Joey" letters, written by a semi-literate but expressive night-club entertainer on the road to a friend in New York City. The dialogue style is reminiscent of Damon Runyon. These stories and others about the same characters, most of them originally published in *The New Yorker,* were collected as *Pal Joey* in 1940 and converted by O'Hara and others into a musical comedy the same year. Stories from *The Doctor's Son* and *Files on Parade* are also contained in a collection, *The Great Short Stories of John O'Hara* (1956).

Irwin Shaw (born 1913)

In spite of his occasional excursions into the drama and the novel, Irwin Shaw is first and foremost a short-story writer. Early in his career he mastered the art of a certain type of American magazine story: the mature, urban, and slightly ironic story constructed mainly out of conversations among witty and sophisticated city dwellers. Many of these stories were written for *The New Yorker,* and they show the style of brittle urbanity which that magazine has made famous. Thus his experience has made Shaw an expert stylist. His situations are often highly sentimental, but they are saved from mawkishness by the ironic objectivity of his treatment; emotion is always understated, and often the deep emotional reactions of the characters to their situations are conveyed only through implication.

Irwin Shaw's world is essentially a tragic one, even though Shaw himself is not a pessimist. He might perhaps best be termed a stoic; he is convinced of the basic hostility of the universe toward man, and he sees man himself as a selfish and egocentric creature essentially callous toward the sufferings of his fellows. Only occasionally is this grim picture relieved by some act of idealism, some unexpected attitude of unselfishness or tenderness. These isolated acts of decency illustrate Shaw's ethic: that even in a hostile universe, even in a callous and selfish society, the individual person occasionally shows impulses toward good. In *The Young Lions* the urban and detached playwright Michael Whitacre and the bitter young Jew Noah Ackerman, who have little in common on the social or intellectual plane, eventually find a basis for friendship in their common humanity, the core of decency and brotherhood they share beneath their complicated social exteriors. Shaw's attitude toward his own Jewish background is connected to this ethic of individualism. He obviously feels a certain emotional loyalty toward his race and its traditions (see the story "God on Friday Night") but nevertheless he refuses to consider himself primarily a Jew who stands in social opposition to a gentile majority. This attitude is magnificently illustrated in "Act of Faith," in which the Jewish soldier Seeger, at first troubled by a letter from his neurotically fearful Jewish father, eventually decides to sell his most precious possession to share the money on a Paris leave with his gentile friends.

Shaw is the type of author who is highly preoccupied with problems of literary technique, especially construction, and he often builds elaborate—if inconspicuous—symmetry and parallelism into his work. This tendency is most apparent in *The Young Lions,* where some critics have attacked his rather obvious ingenuity. It is not this rather pretentious complexity of construction, however, that marks Shaw as an important author; it is rather his unerring skill in dialogue and his mature urbanity in characterization, qualities which make him simultaneously one of the most cosmopolitan and the most American of modern writers.

Life: Irwin Shaw was born in 1913 in New York City and was educated in the Brooklyn public schools, later going on to Brooklyn College. As a college student he played football, wrote for the student newspaper, and wrote several plays produced by a local dramatic society. He was at one time expelled from the college for academic deficiencies (he failed calculus) but returned, after an interlude of odd jobs, to graduate in 1934. After his graduation he worked as a radio writer, producing serial scripts in a mass-production technique the demoralizing effects of which on a writer he has described in a story titled "Main Currents of American Thought." In 1936 he wrote his first work of literary importance, the play *Bury the Dead,* which was produced first by the experimental New Theatre League but soon attracted enough attention to be moved to a Broadway theatre for a successful run. On the strength of this success Shaw then went to Hollywood and wrote a number of screen plays, to which he attaches no importance whatsoever. In 1939 another play, *The Gentle People,* enjoyed a modest success and ran for four months on Broadway. Drafted in 1942 (he had requested 1-A classification although he could have been deferred), he served for the rest of the war in Africa, England, France, and Germany. Meanwhile he had achieved success as a short-story writer; his fiction was included in the O. Henry and O'Brien collections for the first time in 1940 and won numerous awards thereafter. One of his first war stories, "Walking Wounded," won the O. Henry Memorial Prize for 1944. After the war he turned again to playwriting, produced two failures, and then turned his hand to his first novel, *The Young Lions,* which appeared in 1948. It was generally considered a success, although some critics felt it did not fulfill the promise of his stories. *The Troubled Air,* another novel, appeared in 1951 and *Lucy Crown,* a third, in 1956. Shaw, whose most recent address is in London, England, has more recently published *Voices of a Summer Day* (1965) and *Rich Man, Poor Man* (1970).

Chief Works: *Bury the Dead* (drama, 1936) was written for the experimental New Theatre League, later ran successfully on Broadway, and has since been frequently produced by amateur and little theatre groups. Stylistically and structurally it resembles the drama of the German Expressionists, especially Toller and Wedekind; it is in the tradition of continental experimentalism also in its set, which is highly stylized, almost rudimentary. In dialogue, however, it is totally American, patterned after the World War literature of the type of *Three Soldiers* and *What Price Glory?* The plot is built around a sergeant and three soldiers who are detailed to bury six men killed somewhere in France in the First World War. The six dead men, however, refuse to be buried; they stand in their graves and demand an explanation of why they were "sold for twenty-five yards of bloody mud" while others live and make a profit from the war. A doctor is called to certify that they are actually dead, and a priest, a captain, and a trio of generals all try to persuade them to be buried. Finally the war department brings to France the women of the dead soldiers to persuade them to listen to reason. But one wife, the bitter and poverty-crushed Martha Webster, cries, "Tell 'em all to stand up!" As the play ends the corpses, walking over the inert form of a general, leave the stage like "men who have leisurely business that must be attended to in the not too pressing future"—i.e., to take their revenge on those who have instigated the war for their own profit. This drama is typical of the pacifism of the disillusioned Thirties, and its theme stands in sharp contrast to the attitude toward the Second World War which Shaw was later to express in *The Young Lions.*

Stories: The best of Shaw's stories are collected in *Sailor Off the Bremen* (1939), *Welcome to the City* (1942), and *Act of Faith and Other Stories* (1946); *Mixed Company* (1950) includes selected stories from all three earlier volumes. A few of the best known of these stories should be briefly described. "The Girls in their Summer Dresses" (from *Sailor Off the Bremen*) is typical of Shaw's light and urban *New Yorker* style. Michael, the hero, is happily married to Frances, whom he loves, but on the Sunday afternoon in which the story takes place a quarrel develops. It is spring, and Michael, a lover of beauty, cannot help admiring the splendid girls who pass on Fifth Avenue; but Frances, possessive and jealous, makes a scene about this, and at the end of the story it is obvious that the two are basically incompatible. "The Eighty-Yard Run" is the story of a football hero, Christian Darling, who makes a spectacular run one day in practice and then finds the rest of his life is an anticlimax. His wife Louise, who married him because he was a football hero, gradually surpasses him and becomes a magazine editor, while he is reduced to selling suits for a third-rate clothing manufacturer. Thus the story demonstrates the artificiality of "college hero" success and the way this kind of success destroys the character of a young man too immature to see it in perspective. "Act of Faith," from the volume of the same name, is a study of three soldiers in a camp in France, shortly after the end of the war, waiting to be transferred back to America. Norman Seeger, a Jew, receives a depressing letter from his father and learns that his brother Jacob has gone virtually insane through fear of anti-Semitic persecution. Meanwhile he is called upon to make a difficult decision. He and his two gentile friends Olson and Welch have a chance to go to Paris on leave, but have no money; the two ask Seeger to sell a German pistol which is his most prized possession, since he had to kill an SS major to get it (a symbol to Seeger of the Jew's triumph over Nazism). He also has a vague irrational feeling that he had better keep the pistol to defend himself against anti-Semites in America. But Seeger remembers that Olson and Welch have both risked their lives for him; when he asked them about their attitude toward the Jews he finds that they do not think of him as a Jew at all, but as a friend. Knowing now that he will be able to rely on Olson and Welch—and many others like them—when he returns to civilian life, he agrees to sell his pistol, remarking, "What could I use it for in America?" "God on Friday Night" (1939), originally published in *Story* magazine and frequently anthologized, is a portrait of a Jewish night-club entertainer, married to a blonde gentile girl, who comes home to his mother to ask her to pray for the son his wife is about to bear. The mother, who gave up her religion the day she married Sol's socialist father, nevertheless agrees to say the prayers. When the baby is born Sol and Violet, his wife, bring it to the mother, who lights candles for thanksgiving; and when her skeptical younger son Lawrence sneers sarcastically at this, she tells him, "Shut up, City College philosopher."

Novel: *The Young Lions* (1948), Shaw's most important full-length work, is a war novel following the fortunes of three soldiers, two Americans and one German, through the Second World War. Numerous other characters, all of them connected to these three, are also described in some detail. Michael Whitacre, a New York playwright, intellectual, a self-styled liberal, is rescued by the advent of the war from the vacuity and meaninglessness of his life and from an unhappy marriage. Although he could easily get a commission through influence, he joins the army as an enlisted man, serves for a time in a Civil Affairs unit, then requests combat duty and fights in the European campaign. Noah Ackerman, an unhappy young Jew, marries Hope Plowman, daughter of a rugged New Englander, and manages to overcome the old man's instinctive anti-Semitism. In the army, however, he does not have it so easy; he is constantly persecuted by ignorant and brutal draftees, and finally is forced to fight the ten biggest men in the company one by one. Emerging broken in body but not in spirit from this ordeal, he goes into combat in France and proves himself a capable and courageous soldier. Christian Diestl, the third main character, is a German soldier who enters Paris as a member of the victorious Nazi blitzkrieg, fights in North Africa under the hard and methodical Lieutenant Hardenburg, is wounded and returns to Europe, and finally retreats with the German army before the Allied invasion forces in 1944. The three meet in a symbolic and rather contrived climax in a Bavarian concentration camp just before the end of the war; Diestl kills Ackerman from ambush and is then stalked and killed by Michael, who by this time has developed from a vague and detached liberalism to a hard and angry resentment toward Nazism and everything it stands for.

This basic plot is reinforced with a complicated set of parallels and allegorical incidents. The novel opens with three chapters showing the activities of the three main characters on the same day: December 31, 1937. Diestl and Whitacre are often treated as "opposite numbers"—e.g., they are both refused commissions because of pre-war Communist associations, and they both have affairs with the same girl, Margaret Freemantle. In Chapter 4 Diestl is slightly wounded in the face in the capture of Paris, and on the same day, in Chapter 5, Whitacre is cut in the face when his neurotic wife throws a badminton racket at him. (For a more complete list of such parallels, see Aldridge, *After the Lost Generation*, pp. 151ff.) This novel has been acclaimed by some critics as the best work of fiction to be written about the Second World War; it is certainly one of the most ingenious and highly finished. Its detractors object to its "air of prefabrication and contrivance," its excessive ingenuity in construction, and the stereotyped quality of its characterizations: the ruthless Nazi, the muddled liberal, and the heroic and persecuted young Jew.

Herman Wouk (born 1915)

In the company of the other war novelists of World War II Wouk is an anomaly. He is conservative in temperament, religious in tendency, and has a great respect for stability, tradition, and established order. His most important work, *The Caine Mutiny*, avoids the clichés that have filled every war novel since *All Quiet on the Western Front*—the arrogant stupidity of officers, the superiority of the civilian soldier over the Prussianized professional, the monotonous obscenity. In fact *The Caine Mutiny* includes a specific satire on such novels in the description of *Multitudes, Multitudes*, the war novel which the pretentious and effete naval officer

Tom Keefer is writing—a novel which is not without resemblance to *From Here to Eternity* and *The Naked and the Dead.* Wouk does not admire war, but he admits its necessity under special circumstances, such as the threat of fascism, and he accepts the fact that war involves a certain amount of stupidity, incompetence, and unfairness to individuals. But he is not anti-militaristic *per se;* he realizes that a military establishment, with its professional militarists, is necessary even in a democracy if democratic ideals are going to be maintained and made secure. He goes further: he believes that the military tradition, taken in itself, is a good and fine thing, and that a man cannot rise in a military organization unless he is a man of character. These "conservative" ideas are radical in the era of Dos Passos, Jones, Mailer, and Irwin Shaw.

In literary style too Wouk is a conservative. His approach to the novel is old-fashioned; he has scarcely been touched by the literary revolution led by Joyce, Faulkner, Dos Passos, and other twentieth-century experimentalists. The most remarkable quality of the style of *The Caine Mutiny* is its decorum. It is entirely devoid of the obscene language that fills most war novels (Wouk believes that "you don't use dirty language in somebody else's home," even when you enter the home as a writer of a novel) and it contains little shocking or violent incident. Only one man is killed aboard the *Caine* during its whole war service. Yet Wouk's novel loses none of its masculine hardness in observing this decorum; it is a thoroughly male book, devoid of prissiness or sentimentalizing.

Wouk's remaining work, although less important, follows this same pattern. He stands for all the domestic and traditional virtues: he believes in the American middle class, in the family, in the integrity of marriage, in patriotism, and in traditional religious values. None of this would be remarkable if Wouk were an ordinary American citizen; but as a writer, standing in the company of Sinclair Lewis, John Dos Passos, Ernest Hemingway, and his own post-1945 contemporaries, Wouk the conservative and traditionalist is virtually unique.

Life: Herman Wouk was born in 1915 in the Bronx and except for his naval service has lived most of his life in the New York area. His parents were Russian Jewish immigrants who came to America in 1905; his father at first supported the family by washing clothes and rose to become the president of a large and modern commercial laundry firm. His mother was the daughter of a rabbi, and the family was always Orthodox. According to Wouk, the two great influences on his ideas have been those of Rabbi Mendel Leib Levine, his grandfather, and the Columbia University philosopher Irwin Edman.

As a student at Columbia Wouk edited *The Columbia Jester,* a humor magazine, and wrote two varsity shows; he graduated with honors in 1934 with a major in comparative literature. After graduation he worked six years as a radio writer, at one time serving as script writer for the Fred Allen show. In June 1941 he left this position to work for the government as a dollar-a-year man writing and producing radio shows to popularize war bonds. When America entered the war he joined the Navy as a line officer, and served four years in the Pacific. His first ship, the U.S.S. *Zane,* a DMS (destroyer-minesweeper), won a unit commendation in the Solomons campaign. Wouk served in various positions including communications officer on this ship, and was then transferred to another DMS, the *Southard.* He rose to second in command (executive officer) of the *Southard* before it was finally wrecked in the Okinawa typhoon of October, 1945. All of this experience, as can be seen, found its way into *The Caine Mutiny.*

Meanwhile Wouk had begun writing fiction. His first novel, *Aurora Dawn,* was begun while he was still in the Navy and published in 1947; it was a Book-of-the-Month-Club selection and was favorably reviewed, and Wouk was launched as an author. *The Caine Mutiny,* in 1951, was his third novel. Its success was phenomenal. It sold over three million copies in various editions and was then dramatized, by Wouk and others, to become a Broadway hit; it was subsequently made into a motion picture which won an Academy Award. The book itself won a Pulitzer Prize and was selected by each of the four largest book clubs.

Wouk was married in 1945 to Betty Brown, a Phi Beta Kappa from U.S.C. whom he met while still in the service. His religious development is important in relation to his work. Converted to a "modern" skepticism at Columbia, he later returned to the traditional values of his Jewish heritage, and in the postwar period was active in a number of Jewish organizations. His gentile wife is a

Jewish convert, and Wouk himself has taught literature at Yeshiva University in New York. *Marjorie Morningstar* appeared in 1955 to generally favorable reviews. *Youngblood Hawke* in 1962 did his reputation little good; in fact it turned off many admirers for what seemed to be a gratuitous attack on Thomas Wolfe's character. *Don't Stop the Carnival* (1965) was described as "a book that will kill time. Dead."

Chief Works: *The Caine Mutiny* (novel, 1951) is a war novel told chiefly from the point of view of the young naval officer Willie Keith, "because the event turned on his personality as the massive door of a vault turns on a small jewel bearing." A Princeton graduate and son of a wealthy doctor, Keith is uncertain what to do with his life; as the novel opens he is making his living as a night-club entertainer. He falls in love with a pretty young singer, May Wynn; but meanwhile the war breaks out, and Keith enters midshipman school at Columbia. When he gets his commission he is assigned to a decrepit converted destroyer, the U.S.S. *Caine*. Shortly after he joins the ship its captain, De Vriess, is detached and Commander Philip Queeg takes his place. Other important officers of the ship's company are Tom Keefer, a sophisticated intellectual who plans to write a novel about the war, and Steve Maryk, a San Francisco fisherman with a thorough knowledge of seamanship. It soon becomes apparent to officers and crew that Queeg is not only an unbearable martinet but apparently mentally unbalanced, especially under conditions of strain. He is over-meticulous about petty details and addicted to minor compulsions like the two ball bearings he continually plays with in his hand; he is afflicted with a mild paranoid tendency which convinces him that the ship has united in a conspiracy against him, and he tends to freeze up completely in moments of crisis to the point where he is incapable of giving orders or listening to reason. Keefer, who is well read in modern psychology, believes he is insane, and convinces Maryk of this; he tells him of Article 184 of Naval Regulations, which permits a junior officer to relieve his captain of command under "unusual and extraordinary circumstances" such as insanity. Maryk conscientiously begins to compile a notebook of Queeg's eccentricities in case such a crisis should ever arise. Meanwhile the *Caine* carries out its function as an escort ship and general errand-boy in the Pacific campaign. Queeg demonstrates his mental unbalance on many occasions. The most important of these is the "Yellowstain" incident during the Kwajalein invasion. Queeg, ordered to escort some landing boats into a beach under fire, instead deserts them, leaving a yellow dye-marker in the water to mark their point of departure; it is apparent that he did this either out of cowardice or out of temporary insanity.

The final crisis comes during a typhoon in the Philippine Sea in December, 1944. When the *Caine,* beaten by heavy seas, broaches to several times and almost founders, Queeg seems to lose command of himself and is unable to issue coherent orders. Maryk, by this time executive officer, countermands his confused orders and takes over the ship; the young Keith, who is officer of the deck, supports him. The ship is saved, and Queeg is transferred back to the United States for rest. But Maryk must undergo a court-martial; if he is found guilty of "conduct to the prejudice of good order or discipline," then Keith and Keefer will be faced with similar charges. Barney Greenwald, in peacetime a successful Jewish lawyer and now a Naval aviator, is assigned as defense counsel. His only chance lies in proving that Queeg was unbalanced, and his job is difficult; Queeg, now released from conditions of strain, is plausible and impressive, and three Navy psychiatrists declare him sane. But Greenwald, using every "smart lawyer" trick he knows of, succeeds in badgering Queeg until he breaks down in court and clearly demonstrates his paranoid personality; Maryk is acquitted. The *Caine* officers plan a party to congratulate Maryk and Keefer, whose war novel has been accepted by a publisher. Greenwald is invited, but comes only briefly to tell the group that they were wrong and Queeg was right. In a confused but eloquent drunken speech, he explains what the menace of fascism means to him as a Jew (his relatives have died in European concentration camps), and points out that while he and other civilians were hurriedly learning how to defend their country, it was only Queeg and those like him who were holding the line against the enemy. Militarism is therefore necessary and those who attempt to tear its ideals down (like Keefer with his antimilitaristic novel) are stupid and dangerous. He then throws a glass of (yellow) wine into Keefer's face and leaves.

Meanwhile the story of Keith's personal life has been woven into the novel. During a California leave in the middle of the war he meets May again and decides to marry her, but is later prevailed upon by his socially conscious mother that the marriage is beneath him and would interfere with his planned career as a scholar. At the end of the novel, however, he realizes that both loyalty and his continuing love call for him to marry her; he does so, even though her reputation has become somewhat tarnished by this time in the cynical world of night-club entertainment. Keith's character is shown developing throughout the novel; at the beginning he is a playboy and drifter without direction in life, and his war experience, along with his respect for his father, who dies during the novel, develops him into a strong and purposeful person of character.

Marjorie Morningstar (novel, 1955) is, like *The Caine Mutiny*, an anomaly among modern novels, in this case a tribute to female virtue and middle-class domesticity. Marjorie Morgenstern, the heroine, is a Jewish girl in a Bronx family which rises socially and finally moves to fashionable Central Park West. Romantic as a young girl, she dreams of a stage career and has already picked out a name for herself: Marjorie Morningstar. At a summer resort she meets Noel Airman, a fascinating and sophisticated stage producer who spends most of the rest of the novel trying to seduce her—finally succeeding in a New York hotel. But Marjorie is basically virtuous, and she is not sure she is satisfied with the effete but superficial Noel. She is courted by three other men: the steady and unexciting Dr. Shapiro, Noel's assistant Wally Wronken, and Mike Eden, a "brilliant, devastating heel—a West Side version of a Scott Fitzgerald hero" (*Time*) whom she meets on a trip to Europe. But in the end she rejects all four and marries Milton Schwartz, a young Jewish lawyer, first telling him all the details of her relations with Noel and others. As the novel closes she has settled down to a comfortable middle-class existence in a New York suburb, in every sense an "average young matron." The most memorable parts of this novel are the scenes of Jewish home life in the nineteen-thirties, related by Wouk nostalgically but with great objectivity.

Other Works: *Aurora Dawn* (1947), Wouk's first novel, is a sophisticated satire on the radio advertising business in New York

City. *The City Boy* (novel, 1948) is the story of eleven-year-old Herbie Bookbinder, who grows up in the Bronx and gradually comes to an acceptance of his own difference from his fellows (he is "brainy" and introspective) and an understanding of what he really is. It ends with his graduation into adolescence and his discovery of the adult world. *The Traitor* (drama, 1949) is an analysis of the problem of national security in the face of Communist conspiracy; its nationalistic and conservative attitude antagonized many liberals at the time it appeared, before the Hiss trial and other spy revelations.

Youngblood Hawke (novel, 1962) distorts and does violence to the life and career of Thomas Wolfe in pretending to present the story of the writer, successful with his first novel, Arthur Youngblood Hawke, sought after by rival publishers, film producers, actresses, agents, and manipulators. There are three women in his life: the virginal, devoted copy-editor Jeanne Green, sophisticated patroness of the arts Frieda Winter (who becomes his mistress), and Sarah Hawke of Hovey, Kentucky, his mother and, financially speaking, his alter ego. In the end he is the victim of the tax collector and the money lender. Wolfe himself gave us much better fictional portraits of his mother. Perhaps the less said about *Don't Stop the Carnival* (novel, 1965) the better; it was remarked that it gives the self-satisfied middle class exactly what it wants.

J. D. Salinger (born 1919)

Salinger made an excellent reputation for himself as a writer of polished and subtle short stories before he published his first novel in 1951. *The Catcher in the Rye* confirmed and sustained this reputation and gained him a position as one of the more important American writers of the younger generation. The novel owed part of its popular success to its alleged shocking passages and to its selection by the Book-of-the-Month Club, but it is nevertheless a first-rate novel and one of the most convincing studies of adolescence ever to be written by an American.

Salinger is widely thought of, with justice, as a keen student of children. "All of my best friends are children," he himself has said. His extraordinary achievement in this area rests on two principles:

first, he views children not from the adult point of view but from their own, from the inside, in a way few writers have succeeded in doing; and second, he concerns himself almost exclusively with extraordinary children. Many adult writers tend to make children seem younger than they actually are, to accentuate their babyish qualities, but Salinger does the opposite: he portrays children who are unusually mature for their age, who speak, or attempt to speak, like adults, and who wish to be accepted by adults on an adult basis. Models of this type are the little girl in "For Esme—With Love and Squalor" and Phoebe, the sister of the hero in *The Catcher in the Rye*. His adolescents speak in a curiously gauche dialect which belongs to their age, yet they too are seeking for acceptance in an adult world —in fact this is the whole plot of *The Catcher in the Rye*.

Stylistically Salinger is competent, painstaking, and precise, in the tradition of the *New Yorker* type of fiction which is his specialty. Like many other young American writers, he has an unerring ear for dialogue. His fiction is not strong on plot, and is sometimes virtually plotless; his stories are essentially character studies revealed through accurate, highly vernacular, and often clever dialogue. Yet for all his magazine-writer competence he is not stylized; there is a quality about his style that instantly identifies it as his own. Part of this is due to his characterizations, i.e., to the fact that he usually writes about the same kind of people who talk in the same way. In addition to this, however, his style is individual and original, bearing that unmistakable personal mark which is one of the characteristics of a quality writer.

Life: Jerome David Salinger was born in New York City on January 1, 1919, the son of a Jewish father and Irish mother; he was educated in New York schools and at the Valley Forge Military Academy in Pennsylvania, which presumably provided him with the boarding-school background for *The Catcher in the Rye*. He attended several colleges, including New York University and a writing class at Columbia, without completing a program for a degree. His first published story appeared in 1940 in *Story* magazine, "The Young Folks." Drafted into the Army in 1942, Salinger served in Tennessee, England, and the D-Day landings until 1946, leaving the service as a staff sergeant. The war experiences may well be responsible for his sometimes powerful feelings of alienation from modern existence. His short stories have appeared in an assortment of American magazines ranging from *The Saturday Evening Post* to *The New Yorker*. In 1951 his first novel, *The Catcher in the Rye,* won critical acclaim and also caused a considerable sensation, mainly because one or two rather frank four-letter words offended some readers; its acceptance by the Book-of-the-Month Club assured its commercial success.

A book of *Nine Stories* followed in 1953. In 1955 Salinger married Claire Douglas, an English girl, and settled in Cornish, New Hampshire, where in the sixties they have been living quietly with a son and a daughter. J. D.'s production has declined since 1953, with *The New Yorker* bringing out his most important stories. Two thin books have been published, containing two stories each: *Franny and Zooey* (1961) and *Raise High the Roof Beam, Carpenters*; and *Seymour: An Introduction* (1963). These stories focus on the Glass family, particularly Seymour, brother Buddy, Franny, and Zooey out of the seven children and the mother, Bessie. Taken all together, with the help of the reader, they almost make a novel. The most recent stories in *The New Yorker,* "Hapworth 16, 1924," for instance, in 1965 show what some critics believe to be deterioration, a tendency to diffuseness and repetition. However, if Holden Caulfield and Seymour Glass, with his wisdom instead of knowledge, are all we are going to have, plus a few stories, Salinger's work is likely to last longer than that of a good many writers who have been pouring it out in the fifties and sixties and can't seem to stop. Joining the parade of unforgettable characters we must add, of course, Esme, Phoebe, and Frannie; and thank God for such little girls.

Chief Works: *The Catcher in the Rye* (novel, 1951) is a sensitive psychological study of a prep-school boy, Holden Caulfield, whose parents live in New York. Holden in many ways exaggerates the normal tendencies of adolescence: he is hard-boiled and sophisticated in his own reveries but immature when confronted with a practical situation, he is basically good-hearted, even tender, but gruff and matter-of-fact on the outside, and he has a typical adolescent attitude toward sex: theoretically he is cynical and all-knowing, but in practice he is naive and chaste. His real difficulty, the reason he does not fit easily into the life of the Pennsylvania prep school, is that he is more sensitive and idealistic than the boys around him; this makes him bitter and unhappy, and to his teachers and others he seems a troublemaker and a misfit. In the eighth chapter of the novel he runs away from the school and goes to New York, with only a vague notion in mind of what he is going to do; actually he is homesick, and half-afraid to approach his parents for fear of their disapproval. Arriving in the city, he registers at a hotel and is fleeced of his money by a prostitute and a cynical bellboy, who recognize him as a runaway and know he cannot complain to the police against them. After various other unsatisfactory experiments in New York high-life, he secretly steals into his parents' apartment and visits his small sister Phoebe, for whom he feels a deep and protective affection, although he does not fully admit this to himself since it does not fit in with his outward pose of callousness. He also visits an old teacher, Mr. Antolini, the one adult in the world who understands and likes him; but the visit turns into tragedy through what is most probably a misunderstanding, and Holden flees under the impression Antolini has made homosexual advances to him. The next day he arranges to meet Phoebe at a museum, but she arrives with a suitcase, determined to run away with him because she instinctively understands he is unhappy. Touched by this, "so damn happy" and at the same time "damn near bawling," Holden decides to go home with her instead. In a brief epilogue (Chapter 26) he is in an institution recovering from an illness, probably a mental breakdown. Salinger's ending promises no happy future for Holden, and leaves him still struggling with the muddle of his adolescent temperament.

This novel, written in the first person, is a masterpiece of extended monologue; it is all related in Holden's own defiant, ungrammatical slangy, and cryptic way of talking, and yet manages to express great subtlety and insight. The relations between Holden and Phoebe are masterfully depicted; Holden never specifically analyzes his emotions toward his sister, yet the reader clearly sees his mixture of patronizing superiority and tender brotherly protectiveness. The dominant theme of *The Catcher in the Rye* is the helplessness of the adolescent—half child, half adult—in an adult society. Holden is too old for childish amusements, yet is punished cruelly when he tries to force his way into the adult world. He is punished as well for his finer qualities, his sensitivity; tenderness, fastidiousness, and insight are not virtues that are highly regarded by the normal inmates of prep-schools. The red hunting-hat which Holden wears through most of the novel is a symbol to him of defiant yet childish bravado in face of the conventions of the adult world.

Stories: A representative selection of Salinger's stories is contained in *Nine Stories by J. D. Salinger* (1953). These stories, like most of Salinger's work, may be roughly classified in two groups: stories of upper-middle-class life in the New York region, and studies of small children. Of the first type, "Uncle Wiggily in Connecticut" is typical. Mary Jane and Eloise, who were college roommates together, meet in Eloise's house in Connecticut and proceed to get drunk while reminiscing about times past. In the course of the conversation it becomes apparent to the reader that both of them have made a failure of their lives, and that they have turned into selfish, superficial, and ignorant women. In a sense the story is an analysis of war marriages; both women married service men during the war, and both marriages failed to survive the monotony and banality of peacetime life. There is also a remarkable child named Ramona, who at first appears rather obnoxious but who wins the reader's sympathy when it becomes apparent that she is lonely and ashamed of her mother.

"For Esme—With Love and Squalor" is a story built around the typical Salinger child, grave, grown-up, and whimsically wise. In this case the central character is a little English girl who meets the narrator while he is a soldier stationed in Devonshire. Behind her serene sophistication Esme demonstrates all the British virtues: she is heroically matter-of-fact about the death of her father, who was "slain" in North Africa, and she is proper enough to write a quite adult letter to the narrator after he is transferred to Germany. This story, virtually plotless, is built around the tenderness which the soldier feels for the little girl and the contrast between the juvenile immaturity of his fellow soldiers and Esme's own precocious maturity.

James Jones (born 1921)

As author of the most successful war novel of the period after 1945, Jones is *de facto* leader of what might be termed the Neo-Hemingway school of fiction among the younger generation of American writers. This is not to say that his style consistently imitates Hemingway's (although it sometimes does) or that he consciously took Hemingway as his model. He has admitted a debt to Thomas Wolfe, and actually *From Here to Eternity* outwardly resembles *Three Soldiers* and *What Price Glory* more than it does *A Farewell to Arms* or *For Whom the Bell Tolls.* Jones' novel nevertheless stands in the line of development in modern fiction that is commonly associated with Hemingway, and which owes a great deal to Hemingway as innovator and pathfinder. The qualities Jones shares with the older writer are those which the general public associates with the name of Hemingway: the understated and laconic dialogue, the violence presented without emotional comment, the stoic and hard-boiled view of character, the presentation of woman as a mere subjective object of masculine pleasure.

A comparison of *From Here to Eternity* with *A Farewell to Arms* or even *Across the River and into the Trees,* however, will demonstrate the differences between the two writers. Hemingway is concerned chiefly with personal and internal reactions; Jones, in spite of his subjectivity, views his characters mainly from the outside. Hemingway works on a small canvas; Jones attempts, at least, to be panoramic. Hemingway usually writes his entire novel from the point of view of a semi-autobiographical protagonist; Jones switches point of view frequently, so that each of his characters is seen in succession from the standpoint of the others. Finally, Hemingway generally uses coarse language and shocking incident in implied contrast to the higher human values in his story; Jones seems to show an adolescent fascination with vulgarity for its own sake. He does not even tacitly indicate disapproval of the premeditated murder which the hero of *From Here to Eternity* commits to revenge himself on a stockade guard. It is true that Prewitt himself is eventually destroyed through this act and that his victim is a brute and a sadist, yet Jones to the end apparently considers Prewitt merely an unfortunate victim of destiny who was ridden to the breaking point and who struck back in the way a man must if he is cornered.

Hemingway's ethics are consistent, if unconventional; but Jones' ethics seem confused, poorly thought out, and in the end damaging to the integrity of his own hero.

It is not the ethical content of *From Here to Eternity,* however, which is its most important quality. Jones has a precise memory, a masterful eye for detail, and an acute ear for dialogue; his narrative style creates the illusion of reality—of "being there"—as well as the style of any contemporary writer. His characters instantly come to life as soon as they begin to speak; their language, monotonously and conventionally obscene, nevertheless has the interest which always attaches to unmistakable authenticity. His slang is convincing, never artificial or contrived, never "cute" or ingenious. In short, his skill in characterization is based mainly on dialogue. His best characters are those closest to his own personality; his women, for example, are two-dimensional and unconvincing. Most of all he fails in his presentation of officers; here his literary skill is hampered by his obvious subjective antagonism, his "enlisted man's complex" that makes it impossible for him to view officers with any objectivity. Thus his scenes in the Schofield officers' club are mere caricature, sometimes amusing but never convincing. Jones, a soldier, wrote about soldiers and even in a certain sense wrote for soldiers; this is the limitation of his method. Yet within these limits he has produced an important book, one of the most important American war novels to be written by a member of the post-1945 generation.

Life: James Jones was born in Robinson, Illinois in 1921 in a family that had been settled in the region for several generations; his father was a Northwestern graduate and a dentist. Although the family was a respectable one, its domestic life was not always serene; as Jones himself explains he grew up "in an atmosphere of hot emotions and boiling recriminations covered with a thin but resilient skin of gentility." The family suffered a severe blow from the Depression, and at an early age Jones was made aware of the ephemeral nature of social standing and financial security. When he graduated from high school jobs were hard to get, and on his father's suggestion he joined the Regular Army. Stationed at Hickam Field in Hawaii shortly before the Second World War, he became interested in writing through the discovery of Thomas Wolfe, whose family background he recognized as essentially similar to his own. His first novel was submitted to Scribner's in 1945 and rejected by the late Maxwell Perkins, who had earlier edited Wolfe; Perkins suggested, however, that Jones write another novel, and offered him an advance to support him while he did so. Additional financial backing was provided by Mr. and Mrs. Harry E. Handy of Robinson, who by this time were operating a sort of fiction school in this small Illinois town in which they maintained promising young writers and at the same time held them to a rigidly disciplined writing schedule. The result was *From Here to Eternity,* published in 1951 and an immediate success; it was a Book-of-the-Month Club Selection and won its author the National Book Award for fiction in 1952. In 1953 it was made into a successful motion picture. Critical opinion of the novel was also generally favorable, although some critics objected to its awkwardness in structure and its excessive crudeness in language. His financial position assured, Jones embarked upon another novel, this time centered on the life of a small Illinois community; this was eventually published as *Some Came Running* (1957). Additional fiction has included *The Thin Red Line* (1962) and *The Ice-Cream Headache and Other Stories* (1968).

Chief Work: *From Here to Eternity* (novel, 1951) begins as Robert E. Lee ("Prew") Prewitt, a soldier in Schofield Barracks in Hawaii, is transferred from a bugle corps to an infantry line company at his own request. The time is late 1940, approximately a year before the Japanese attack on the Hawaiian Islands. Prewitt, a tough uneducated boy from the coal-mining town of Harlan, Kentucky, has the character to make a good soldier, but he soon finds himself in trouble. A skilled boxer, he has previously blinded an opponent in an Army tournament and has made up his mind never to box again. Unfortunately the outfit into which he transfers is one in which favor and promotion go only to athletes. Captain Holmes, the company commander, is brow-beaten by his athletic-minded colonel to win victory for his company in the Post athletic competition at all costs, and he determines to force Prewitt to box or break him in the attempt. For months Prewitt undergoes the "treatment"—he is given dirty and unpleasant tasks to do, mistreated by non-coms, punished for minor infractions, and ostracized by other members of the company. He stands this as long as he can, but finally he is forced into a corner: Ike Galovitch, an illiterate and incompetent drillmaster, pulls a knife on him, and Prewitt knocks the non-commissioned officer down. For this he is sent to the post stockade, a virtual concentration camp where prisoners are tortured by sadistic guards and in some cases mutilated or murdered. Prewitt resolves to have revenge on S/Sgt. Judson ("Fatso"), and after he serves his term he waylays Fatso in a Honolulu alley, challenges him to a knife duel, and kills him. Prewitt, badly cut himself, goes A.W.O.L. and takes shelter in the house of Alma Schmidt, called Lorene, a prostitute with whom he fell in love before he went to the stockade. While he is convalescing the Japanese attack of December 7, 1941 takes place, and the war is on; after several days of restless brooding Prewitt, still ill, leaves the house to try to regain his outfit and is shot by a sentry who takes him for a deserter or a spy.

Around Prewitt's story are woven the stories of several other characters: Angelo Maggio, a likable Italian-American who dislikes authority, beats up two Military Police single-handed, and is eventually killed by sadistic guards in the stockade; Sergeant Milton Warden, a hard-boiled but competent professional soldier who has a dangerous affair with Captain Holmes' wife Karen; Colonel Delbert, a bull-headed and anti-democratic personification of the military mind; Isaac Bloom, a Jewish soldier who commits suicide when his long efforts to win the esteem of his fellow soldiers come to nothing; and Jack Malloy, a tough and unbreakable prisoner Prewitt meets in the stockade, a philosopher and natural leader of men who gives Prewitt the courage he needs to stand up under the inhuman punishment.

Norman Mailer (born 1923)

Harvard-trained and well read in modern literature, Mailer is a more consciously skillful writer than James Jones, and his work is free from the naive awkwardness that occasionally mars *From Here to Eternity*. Yet in another sense his literary background is an impediment; his style occasionally seems imitative and contrived, as though he were writing with the examples of Hemingway and Dos Passos consciously in mind. His political sophistication and his familiarity with the principles—and the jargon—of modern psychology are also apparent, but add little to the effectiveness of his fiction. He is at his best when he writes from direct personal experience, of incidents or conditions that moved him profoundly and which he is able to recreate for the reader. As a newspaper reviewer remarked of *The Naked and the Dead,* "For sustained terror and accurate translation of complete physical exhaustion, this has no parallel in American literature." Since the great experience of Mailer's life was evidently his war service, *The Naked and the Dead* is his best novel. The weakest parts of it, as might be expected, are those not written directly from experience: the psychology of General Cummings, the inner reflections of Lieutenant Hearn, and the flashbacks ("The Time Machine") in which he fills in the civilian backgrounds of the thirteen men who make up his platoon, many of them with past histories markedly different from his own. Likewise, in *Barbary Shore,* the parts we may presume to be autobiographical —the young writer who rents a room in Brooklyn to write a war novel—are good, and most of the presumably imaginary incidents are unconvincing. Mailer surmounted this difficulty to a certain extent in *The Deer Park,* where the screen writer Charley Eitel and even minor characters like the marijuana addict Paco and the producer Herman Teppis come alive in a convincing manner. Yet the trouble with *The Deer Park*—a vastly superior novel to *Barbary Shore*—is again connected to the derivative quality of the material. Whatever his experience of Hollywood might have been, Mailer is too obviously writing in the genre of the satire on Hollywood or Southern California customs—Huxley's *After Many a Summer Dies the Swan,* Waugh's *The Loved One,* or Schulberg's *What Makes Sammy Run?* Mailer has the merits that go with his faults; although he is often too conscious of his literary background, he is a competent and subtle literary craftsman, and his feeling for minute and vivid detail and his skill in structure make *The Naked and the Dead* one of the best of the post-1945 war novels.

Life: Norman Mailer was born in Long Branch, New Jersey in 1923 and grew up chiefly in Brooklyn, where he finished high school in 1939. He went on to Harvard with the idea of becoming an aeronautical engineer. During his freshman year, however, he became interested in writing, and was soon turning out stories at a prolific rate. In 1941 he won the *Story* magazine college writers' contest with a story entitled "The Greatest Thing in the World." He graduated from Harvard in 1943, and during a period of eight months while he was waiting to go into the Army wrote a novel called *A Transit to Narcissus,* a "romantic, morbid, twisted" study of life in a mental hospital, which was never published. The Army, according to Mailer's own statement, was an invaluable experience in his development as a writer. He served for about two years in the Philippines and in Japan in various jobs ranging from regimental intelligence clerk and aerial photograph expert to rifleman in a reconnaissance platoon, most of which experience found its way in one way or another into *The Naked and the Dead.* In 1944, while still in the service, he published "A Calculus at Heaven," a novella about five American soldiers who are trapped by a Japanese platoon. Discharged in 1946, he immediately resolved to write a novel about the war. *The Naked and the Dead,* which further developed the idea he had expressed in embryonic form in "A Calculus at Heaven," appeared in 1948. This novel, one of the most successful books to come out of the war, was favorably greeted by critics and established Mailer as one of the leading American writers of his generation. *Barbary Shore* (1951) was less successful; an excursion into a romantic and analytical style, it disappointed readers who expected another novel like *The Naked and the Dead.* Meanwhile Mailer traveled; he studied for a winter in Paris (1947–48), made visits to England, Spain, Switzerland, and Italy, and on his return wandered around America for some time while he worked on *Barbary Shore.* His third novel, *The Deer Park,* appeared in 1955 and was more favorably reviewed than any of his books since *The Naked and the Dead.* Mailer has been married once (1944) and later divorced; his political leanings are leftist but independent, and he describes himself as an "anti-Stalinist Marxist." Recent publication has included *An American Dream* (1965), *Cannibals and Christians* (1966), *Why Are We In Vietnam?* (novel, 1967), and *The Armies of the Night* (1968). Both Jones and Mailler publish frequently in the American slick magazines, *Esquire* included; a recent satirical article on Women's Liberation has the merit of being amusing.

Chief Works: *The Naked and the Dead* (novel, 1948) is built around the structure of the typical war novel of World War I, e.g., Remarque's *All Quiet on the Western Front* or Barbusse's *Under Fire*: it follows a typical squad of men, of diverse backgrounds and character, into a combat situation and analyzes their individual reactions to the experience. Mailer's chief characters include a group he intends as a cross-section of American life: Julio Martinez, a Mexican boy from San Antonio; Sam Croft, product of an illiterate Texas cracker family who becomes a competent but callous professional soldier; Red Valsen, son of a Montana miner who "went on the bum" during the Depression and who joined the Army because "in the war you keep on moving"; Roy Gallagher, a South Boston Irish boy who had become involved in right-wing racist movements and was developing into a petty hoodlum before the war intervened to make him a soldier; Robert Hearn, a sensitive and over-mothered young lieutenant from a middle-class background, Harvard-educated, a half-hearted intellectual radical before he joined the Army to escape the boredom of his life; Woodrow Wilson, a Southern hillbilly who has passively drifted through life before the war; Edward Cummings, the division commander, West-Pointer and right-wing militarist from a conservative Midwestern family; Joey Goldstein, a Brooklyn Jew who is annoyed and tormented in petty ways by Croft and others because of his race; Willie Brown, in civilian life a salesman married to an unappetizing wife; "Polack" Czienwicz, a petty Chicago criminal; Roth, another Jew, more intelligent and analytical than most of the other enlisted men; and Steve Minetta, an Italian-American who is afraid he lacks the character to endure the discomfort and danger of combat. The action of the novel takes place on the imaginary Pacific island of Anopopei, which General Cummings' division captures from the Japanese after a long and muddled campaign. Hearn, who is Cummings' aide, rebels against the petty personal discipline which the general inflicts upon him and in punishment is put in charge of a reconnaissance platoon including most of the enlisted men among the characters listed above. This platoon is thereupon given an impossibly difficult task: to land on the far side of the island, march across the jungle, and conduct a reconnaissance of the Japanese forces to see whether an amphibious attack is feasible. Hearn takes command of the platoon but is resented by Croft, who shrewdly maneuvers the platoon into a position where Hearn is killed by the Japanese. Croft then takes over, tough and brutal, hated by the others but admired for his obvious competence as a soldier. Roth is killed in a fall from a mountain and Wilson is wounded by a sniper; four men are detailed to carry the wounded man back to the other side of the island. Two drop out, and finally Goldstein and a naive and religious Southerner named Ridges carry the backbreaking burden to the coast, following their orders out to the end even though Wilson dies on the way. When the survivors return to their base they find that their heroic struggle has been unnecessary; Japanese resistance has collapsed unexpectedly in a single day when General Cummings happened to be absent from the island, and the campaign is virtually over.

The attitudes in this novel are those implicit in most war novels by enlisted men: war is an obscene and meaningless sacrifice, most officers are incompetent and lacking in character, and the chief characteristic of combat is its senseless and ironic waste of effort. Another idea (expressed by General Cummings but perhaps shared by the author) is that a poor standard of living produces good soldiers, and vice versa. The pampered youths like Hearn fail to rise to the challenge of combat, while underprivileged boys like Croft and Martinez, the latter of whom distinguishes himself by a courageous single-handed reconnaissance behind enemy lines, find their true vocation in the army. Mailer's political radicalism is expressed through the arguments of Hearn in his conversations with Cummings; the general himself is intended as a caricature and psychological study of the military mind, with its ruthless disregard of human values and its right-wing and racist political principles.

The structure of *The Naked and the Dead* is intricate and carefully planned. Scenes involving the enlisted men in the reconnaissance platoon are alternated with conversations between Hearn and Cummings, in which the ideas latent in the situation are developed. As the novel proceeds to its climax an ironic contrast is apparent between the dogged and futile struggles of the platoon and the muddled strategy of the high command. Sprinkled throughout the narrative are two types of fictional vignettes imitated from Dos Passos' U.S.A.: "The Time Machine" presents brief flashbacks into the civilian lives of the various characters (Dos Passos' "Camera

Eye"), and "Chorus," a slightly more original device, consists of small conversational interludes in dramatic form.

Barbary Shore (novel, 1951) is markedly different in style, decadent, analytical, and overrefined. The chief character and narrator, Mikey Lovett, is a young author who rents a room in a Brooklyn boarding-house to write a novel about the war. There he encounters four people whose lives become involved with his: the landlady Guinevere, a neurotic and unhappy nymphomaniac; McLeod, a former Communist and an amateur philosopher; Hollingsworth, a mysterious young man who seldom comes out of his room; and Lannie, a moody and impulsive young girl who has evidently just been released from a mental institution. These five people, along with Guinevere's three-year-old daughter, enter into a set of intricate and somewhat perverted relationships with each other. The mystery which Lovett at first does not understand is that McLeod is secretly Guinevere's husband; a second mystery, only gradually uncovered, is that McLeod, at one time a government employee, is suspected of having stolen "a little object" from his office in the interests of the Communist Party, and that Hollingsworth is an agent assigned to stalk him and produce a confession from him. McLeod, however, is suffering from a guilty conscience at having betrayed his political ideals; he agrees at one point to return the "little object" to its proper owners, but when Hollingsworth calls upon him to deliver, he refuses and Hollingsworth kills him. Lannie, by this time insane again, is presumably arrested for the murder. This novel is intended as an allegory of the anti-Communist witch-hunt as well as a general comment on the neuroticism of post-war America. The characters, each wrapped in his private egotism and pursuing his private lusts, are destroyed in the end through their lack of purpose or ideal, and only the heroic self-sacrifice of McLeod lends a positive note to the pessimistic ending. An interesting and original experiment, this novel is nevertheless less successful than *The Naked and the Dead,* and in his third major work Mailer returned to his earlier style.

The Deer Park (novel, 1955) is set in Desert d'Or, a mythical California desert resort somewhat resembling Palm Springs and populated with a grotesque and colorful set of Hollywood characters. The chief character and narrator is Sergius O'Shaugnessy, an Air

Force veteran who has won a small fortune in a Tokyo poker game and comes to Desert d'Or to spend it. There he meets Charley Eitel, a Hollywood screen-writer who has been fired because he refused to identify former Communist associates when he was investigated by a Congressional committee. Sergius enters into an unsatisfactory romance with Lulu Meyers, an actress whose best days are over; and meanwhile Eitel, once married to Lulu, falls in love with Elena Esposito, mistress of a producer named Collie Munshin. The novel is devoted chiefly to the conversations of these people and their friends as they pursue their pleasureless and debauched amours and try to find some meaning in their cynical lives. The dialogues, vernacular, ironic, and sophisticated, are the best part of the book. Also memorable is the farcical scene (Chapter 20) in which the overbearing movie executive Herman Teppis tries to persuade Teddy Pope, a homosexual, to marry Lulu, not knowing she is already married to somebody else; the characterization of Teppis is a masterpiece of parody. As the novel ends Eitel agrees to cooperate with the Communist-hunters and regains his position in Hollywood; partly as an expiation of this he marries Elena, who has been injured in an automobile accident and is now penniless and helpless. Sergius goes off to New York to study and write, later opening a school for bull-fighters. *The Deer Park,* in spite of its cynicism and its chaotic plot, is an interesting and well-written novel; the characters of Eitel and Lulu are vivid, and the many minor characters are all well drawn. The title refers to the "Parc des Cerfs" in which Louis XV maintained a household of concubines, and a quotation from Mouffle D'Angerville implicitly identifies this depraved Deer Park, "that gorge of innocence and virtue in which were engulfed so many victims," with Hollywood, which brings even the sincere Elena and the idealistic Eitel, to depravity.

Truman Capote (born 1924)

Often considered by critics in relation to Carson McCullers and Eudora Welty, either as a Southern regionalist or a writer of the grotesque (and there are interesting individual parallels: the passages on love from *The Ballad of the Sad Café* and *The Grass Harp,* and "Why I Live at the P. O." and "My Side of the Matter"), Truman Capote is probably of slighter stature than either but not negligible, a kind of major-minor author, whose range is wider than one might have supposed in the mid-fifties. Paul Levine points out that even his supporters "have to admit that Capote's stories tiptoe the tenuous line between the precious and the serious."

His early fiction from *Other Voices, Other Rooms* (1948) through *A Tree of Night, The Grass Harp,* and the later *Breakfast at Tiffany's* concentrates on the genre of fantasy, one of the most elemental fictional forms. But these stories, long and short, are of two distinct patterns and concerns: the nightmarish "inverted nocturnal world" (of *Other Voices, Other Rooms*), grotesque and frightening and violent; and the fanciful "realistic, colloquial, often humorous day-time" world (of *The Grass Harp*), whimsical, cheerful, heartwarming. But having established himself as a writer of subjective fantastic fiction, Capote turned his descriptive talents to the most objective kind of reporting (with good effect inverting the journalist to novelist development as in Hemingway) beginning with *Local Color* (1950) and going on to *The Muses Are Heard* (1956), an account of the American *Porgy and Bess* company tour of Russia, sponsored by the State Department, and reaching its ultimate expression in what Capote has called a new form, the "non-fictional novel" represented by *In Cold Blood* (1966).

If Capote is a writer "from" the South, he is not a southern writer in the same way McCullers is. In "McCullers and Capote: Basic Patterns," Mark Schorer says, "Truman Capote's talent is more urbane, more various, and more extravagant than Carson McCullers', and his work has always seemed in danger of being overwhelmed by the stylish and the chic in a way that hers never has."

Life: Born in 1924 in New Orleans of Spanish descent, Truman Capote spent much of his childhood in Alabama but went to Greenwich High School in New York City for his secondary education. His first story, "Miriam," appeared in *Mademoiselle* in 1944, and his first novel, *Other Voices, Other Rooms,* was published in 1948. Writing serious fiction at an early age is something else he shared with Carson McCullers. *A Tree of Night,* a volume of short stories, followed in 1949, with *The Grass Harp* (later dramatized by the author) in 1951. After *Breakfast at Tiffany's,* stories published in 1958, Capote seized upon the idea for his "non-fiction" novel. An article in the *New York Times* on November 16, 1959 about "Wealthy Farmer, Three of Family Slain" in Holcomb, Kansas led him to over four years of on the spot research and interviews initially with the assistance of Harper Lee, "a lifelong friend" who had recently completed her first novel, *To Kill a Mockingbird.* The result was *In Cold Blood,* published in 1966. In 1968 a very small novel or novella by Truman Capote appeared under the title *Thanksgiving Visitor,* which represents a return to earlier fictional approaches.

Chief Works: *Other Voices, Other Rooms* (novel, 1948) is the story of a boy's search for his father (for someone to love him), the incredible misfortune of finding him, and an initiation into an adult world of evil and deformity. The education of thirteen-year old Joel Knox bearing his mother's maiden name, far from sentimental, is a nightmare. Joel, separated from the father he never knew by divorce, travels after the death of his mother from New Orleans to Noon City and Skully's Landing with a letter from his father, Edward Sansom, apparently written to an aunt with whom he had been staying. The trip is difficult, hitchhiking the last twenty miles into swamp country and the almost inaccessible Landing; and the people he meets are extra large, grotesque, and sinister. The most monstrous of all is Cousin Randolph, sexual deviate who helps "educate" Joel. There is also the cold and cruel Miss Amy, nurse-wife to Joel's paralyzed father, not the athlete of Joel's fantasies, but a bed-ridden invalid with eyes full of tears, having been shot by Cousin Randolph. Here is no model for Joel, and he loses the power to distinguish reality from unreality. The "heart of darkness" journey continues to the private dream ruins of Cloud Hotel, the characters of tomboy Idabel (who thwarts his latent masculinity) and her "good" twin Florabel, the dwarfish Miss Wisteria, Little Sunshine, the Negro servant Jesus Fever and his daughter Zoo. Treading the edge between reality and unreality, Joel emerges no longer a boy but ready, perhaps, with the insights to become an artist.

The Grass Harp (novel, 1951) is a daylight novel, altogether more cheerful than the story of Joel. Characters may be as queer, but the normal ones are sinister, not the strange ones. The "harp" of the title is a field of dry grass, with the wind speaking as it passes, "gathering, telling, a harp of voices remembering a story." The story is about five people up a tree, in a literal tree house in Alabama: the narrator Collin; Aunt Dolly, also called Dollyheart; Catherine, a Negro servant; Judge Charlie Cool, retired and practically driven from home by his daughters-in-law; and a "loner" of eighteen named Riley Henderson. The tree house is a little crowded; the first three have fled from Dolly's sister, the other aunt with whom Collin has been living, Verena, loveless, practical, hard, and terribly organized. Dolly, on the other hand, is affectionate, gentle, soft in heart and a little in the head.

She has a secret remedy for dropsy which Verena and a business associate, Morris Ritz, from the city try to get for a money-making enterprise. That's why they have moved out to the tree house by the field which is the grass harp. Conventional and indignant townsfolk, led by Verena and the sheriff, try to force the odd ones back to normalcy. But when Morris skips town with Verena's money, the war against the tree house inhabitants collapses. Verena sees the error of her ways and begs, "It's too long to be alone, a lifetime. I walk through the house, nothing is mine: your pink room, your kitchen, the house is yours, and Catherine's too, I think. Only don't leave me, let me live with you. I'm feeling old, I want my sister." They go back home; and Collin thinks, "No matter what passions compose them, all private worlds are good."

In Cold Blood (non-fiction novel, 1966) is the record of a multiple murder in the American mid-West, put together from lengthy interviews with all those connected with the crime, especially the two murderers, and not published until after their execution. The question arises, did their death change the "novel" from fact to fiction? It has been suggested that documentary material, non-fiction, must offer the possibility of verification, while fiction by its very nature is impossible to verify. In any case the novelist in dealing with his material selects, arranges, and focuses upon imagery to convey meaning above and beyond "cold facts."

The facts are relatively simple: On 15 November 1959 in Holcomb, Kansas, Richard Hickock and Perry Smith shot four members of the Clutter family with shotgun blasts in the head for no apparent motive, profit, or purpose. But Capote, following an injunction by Thoreau apparently, tries to get at the mythic significance of the facts by simply stating them, to so observe realities, that "reality is fabulous," as Thoreau put it. He felt "that journalism, reportage, could be forced to yield a serious new art form: the 'non-fiction novel'" and cited the work of Rebecca West and Lillian Ross (of *The New Yorker*) as pointing the way. The "literary photographer" must be the opposite of the subjective novelist. Hersey's *Hiroshima* is not quite what he means; the Lillian Ross *Picture* or his own *The Muses Are Heard,* with comic short novel techniques, is closer. Although he rejects the idea of the "documentary novel" (presumably that developed by a pseudo-scientific naturalism), the non-fiction novel that he is talking about seems close to the "documentary film"; and film techniques in selection, arrangement, and focus can be seen in *In Cold Blood,* which was transferred to that medium with some ease.

Capote has said that many readers see the book as a reflection on American life, a "collision between the desperate, ruthless, wandering, savage part of American life, and the other, which is insular and safe, more or less," which had a kind of inevitability. He hasn't quite recovered from the writing; it churns in his head "like the echo of E. M. Forster's Malabar Caves, the echo that's meaningless and yet it's there: one keeps hearing it all the time." It has been said that here, to paraphrase Marianne Moore, Capote has put "real toads in a real garden" in his study of "motiveless malignity."

8. Regionalism and Naturalism in the City

The city is a region too. Many modern writers find their cultural and emotional ties in a metropolis, which may be both inimical and threatening but which also provides for some whatever salvation, if any, may be found. Hawthorne is reported to have found

New England quite as large a spot of earth as his heart could hold; this is the feeling of the regionalist. James Joyce certainly felt this way about Dublin, and wherever he went Dublin went with him in his creative imagination. Other great European cities have had their artists and lovers in modern fiction. (Dickens probably got in early with London, and Gogol and Dostoevsky with St. Petersburg.) Alfred Döblin tried to do for Berlin what Joyce had done for Dublin. Of all those who have given us Paris we must remember Proust, in a sense both an urban regionalist and a rural one (with Combray for Illiers). It may be odd, but Hemingway has made Madrid "The Capital of the World" and conveyed the feeling that here is the center, the axis. Camus used Oran and Durrell used Alexandria as microcosms of the world. In America the cities which have emerged in our twentieth-century fiction as engaging a kind of regional devotion even in the midst of naturalistic reporting and critical despair are Chicago and New York. To be sure Marquand following Howells can picture Boston for us, but it seems somewhat thin and washed-out.

If regionalism is more than emotional attachment to a place and the deep understanding that comes with knowing well that place and its people, it usually means a certain kind of provincialism too; but in twentieth-century America many of our most "provincial" people live in the big cities. Some years ago one of our magazines published a New Yorker's map of the United States. The distortions were significant: Yankee Stadium was larger than West Virginia and Ebbetts Field (the Dodgers were still in Brooklyn then) larger than Ohio, in fact everything between New York and Los Angeles was compressed and distorted and misplaced. The provincialism of the city-dweller may be challenged but not very successfully.

Of those writers included in Volume III as belonging primarily to pre-1930 American literature, Theodore Dreiser should certainly be considered as an author who worked the Chicago vein, and John Dos Passos as one who presented New York City both in *Manhattan Transfer* and the *U. S. A.* trilogy. Following Dreiser, the one American novelist who is most clearly both naturalist and Chicago regionalist is James T. Farrell. When he moves from the Chicago slum area and the lower-class Catholic Irish of Studs

Lonigan and Danny O'Neill, his writing loses power (just as much as Faulkner moving away from Yoknapatawpha County). Richard Wright would have to be considered an adoptive Chicagoan, but of all the stages in his journey (Mississippi, Memphis, Chicago, New York, Paris) it is Chicago where he feels the most excitement and exultation of spirit. He gives us black Chicago in *Native Son* and *The Man Who Lived Underground.*

New York City is all things to all men. Its writers who have used, abused, and presented it to us have included natives like Malamud (born in Brooklyn) and those who have come to it from elsewhere. James Baldwin clearly is not restricted to the city for his most effective fiction, although he was born there. (*Giovanni's Room* proves that.) But *Go Tell It on the Mountain* and *Another Country* among his other work present a New York that has a telling reality. Ellison, a stranger, soaks up New York City in *Invisible Man,* and although its naturalism is shot through with surrealism, the feel of the city is there. Saul Bellow, who imported himself from Quebec via Chicago, while like Baldwin not restricted to New York for his settings, nevertheless conveys regional reality and naturalistic detail in *Seize the Day* and *Mr. Sammler's Planet.* Malamud of course is equally free to range abroad, but *The Assistant* seems tied to New York City and cuts through it in a beautifully perceptive way.

As Ihab Hassan has noted of post-war (World War II, that is) American fiction, "naturalism and symbolism, comedy and tragedy, picaresque and romance, even surrealism, crowd into the form of the recent novel," and he cites Ellison's *Invisible Man* among other works. So the "naturalism" of our sectional title is loose. It is possible, he says, to draw distinctions between the agrarian South and the dense industrial cities of the North. "The two most active centers of contemporary fiction in America are situated in the Gentile rural South of Carson McCullers, Flannery O'Connor, Truman Capote, and William Styron, and the Jewish urban North of Saul Bellow, J. D. Salinger, Bernard Malamud" and others. "It may very well be that the Southern novelist and the Jewish writer have both emerged from the tragic underground of our culture as the true spokesmen of mid-century America." It seems unfortunate and somewhat shortsighted not to have included the Negro writers from the "tragic underground of our culture" as well, but with that inclusion the statement may stand as a partial justification for the group of writers presented to you.

James T. Farrell (born 1904)

Farrell is often treated as a disciple of Dreiser, and certainly there are many parallels between the two authors in attitude and style. There is an even closer resemblance, however, to Zola. Farrell is a model naturalist in the pseudo-sociological European tradition; his writing is more ruthless and callous than that of either Dreiser or Dos Passos, and he accepts the environmental doctrines of the European naturalist school. Nevertheless, Farrell is totally American in content; he has a sure touch for the slang of the Chicago slums, and he has never lost his contact with the lower-class Catholic Irish who make up the greater part of his characters. Though his technique may have been influenced by European examples, Farrell's experience and material are totally native.

According to his own statement, Farrell's writings are intended as an integrated panorama of American life in the form of a series of novels similar to Zola's *Rougon-Macquart* series, in which the influence of environment and heredity on a lower-class city population are demonstrated in detail. In practice his plan is a good deal more modest than Zola's; he is interested primarily in the lower class, where Zola sought to depict an entire nation, and his locales have been chiefly restricted to the Irish-populated slums of Chicago. He is less objective than Zola; his major works are essentially fictionalized autobiography, whether he calls himself Studs Lonigan or Danny O'Neill. Farrell also differs from Zola and many other naturalists in that he writes of the lower class from first-hand experience. He is not obliged to do research to document his novels; he has a wide fund of personal experience, involving many different occupations and activities, to draw upon. This experience gives to his naturalism a force and authenticity lacking in more academic authors.

Farrell's lower-class origins have contributed two other qualities to his work. In the first place he has little respect for decorum or gentility; his style is blunt, even vulgar, and the incidents he relates often approach the pornographic. In addition Farrell has developed into a bitter social partisan; he is critical of capitalism, respectability, even success in its ordinary forms, and his bitterness has in some instances brought him close to communism. He is too violently individualistic in personality to align himself with a program of any specific party; he has preferred to maintain a position as a vigorous foe of the inequality he encountered in the South-Side Chicago of his youth.

In addition to Zola, Farrell has cited as his favorite authors Dostoevsky, Turgenev, Tolstoy, Gogol, Chekhov, Stendhal, Balzac, Flaubert, Proust, Joyce, and Dickens. The list is a significant one; with the possible exception of Proust all the authors are realists of one kind or another and not a single American is included. The omission of Dreiser is striking. But Farrell no doubt disliked the gauche dialogue, the emotional empathy with his characters, and the tendency toward sentimentalism which are Dreiser's weaknesses. As literary models Flaubert and Zola are more hard-minded and more objective; in addition they share the belief in environmental determinism which Farrell derived from his philosophical Marxism, and which Dreiser never grasped except in a muddled way. "If there is any hatred in my books," Farrell wrote, "it is not directed against people but against conditions which brutalize human beings and produce spiritual and material poverty." Such a credo cannot always be taken at face value; a good deal of Studs Lonigan's failure is due not to the environmental influence of the Chicago slums but to his own stupidity and innate lack of character.

In style as well Farrell shows not so much the European influence as the inspiration of European models. His style creates the illusion of a brutal and unpretentious spontaneity, although it is actually carefully worked; he is a slow writer and a careful one, and a stickler for detail. The chief defects in his work are those which come inevitably attached to his merits: his painstaking documentation often produces a tedious and repetitious prolixity, and his ruthless realism sometimes alienates more sensitive or idealistic readers. Yet *Young Lonigan,* which shocked readers in 1932, seems fairly innocuous in the age of James Jones and Norman Mailer, and a 1937 obscenity charge brought against *A World I Never*

Made was thrown out of court. Like Bernard Shaw, Farrell has lived to outgrow his own radicalism; he is today a conservative writer. Yet the Studs Lonigan books, the major work of his career, remain as an invaluable document of the world and the time they describe, as well as one of the more interesting naturalistic experiments of the Depression era.

Life: Farrell was born in 1904 in the Chicago South Side, at that time one of America's most brutal slums. As a pupil in a Catholic high school he was an enthusiastic athlete; his dominating interest was in baseball, but he also won letters in football and basketball. Because of his education in parochial schools he has always retained an interest in priests, churches, and religious experience; his personal attitude, however, has remained independent and secular. Farrell attended the University of Chicago for about three years and for a time attended night classes at De Paul University, but his education remained incomplete; his personality was too active for him to sit quietly in a classroom for long. Meanwhile he had held a variety of odd jobs which later provided him with valuable literary material: gas-station attendant, express company clerk, clerk in a cigar store in New York City, and advertising salesman. He began to write around 1929; *Young Lonigan,* his first novel, appeared in 1932. It was only moderately successful, however, and real fame came to Farrell only with the obscenity charge brought against *A World I Never Made* in 1937. The same year he won the $2500 Book-of-the-Month-Club prize for the *Studs Lonigan* trilogy. From that time his writing has generally been popular both with the public and with critics, although criticism has tended to view his later work as not up to the quality of the Lonigan books. As his writing became successful Farrell moved to New York; he is married and the father of a son. He has made outspoken, even radical statements on politics from time to time, but he has never publicly espoused the cause of any particular party or group. In *The League of Frightened Philistines* (1945) he developed a rather unorthodox set of Marxian ideas on literary criticism, and roundly condemned the manner in which literary and publishing activities are presently carried on in capitalistic countries. In the nineteen-sixties Farrell was living in New York

City, working on a new series of novels, including *The Silence of History* (1962), *What Time Collects* (1964), *When Time Was Born* (1966), *A Brand New Life* (1968). The series has the overall title, *A Universe of Time.* Unfortunately away from Chicago Farrell seems to lose some of his authenticity, without which a naturalist is lost.

Chief Novels: The central work of Farrell's career is the trilogy *Studs Lonigan,* which consists of *Young Lonigan* (1932), *The Young Manhood of Studs Lonigan* (1934), and *Judgment Day* (1935). Studs Lonigan, the protagonist of the series, is far from a conventional hero; he is ignorant, brash, pugnacious, and at times brutal. He is intended, however, to serve as Farrell's personification of the Chicago South Side, and to a certain extent the entire American city proletariat. But Lonigan is less a worker than a loafer and ne'er-do-well; in this respect he resembles the "drifter" side of Farrell's own personality minus the detachment and creativity which have made him a major novelist.

In the first novel of the trilogy Lonigan, still a boy, is healthy, intelligent, and basically decent; the trilogy records his gradual corruption by his environment. The great struggle of his life is the incompatibility between the sense of sin instilled in him by his Catholic rearing and the brutal cynicism of the South Chicago streets. There are good influences in Lonigan's life: his mother encourages him to become a priest, and a girl, Lucy Scanlon, attempts to regenerate him. But inevitably he slips into the society of pool rooms, gambling, sexual degeneracy, and alcoholism of the young ruffians he encounters in the streets. Before *Young Lonigan* is finished it is apparent that his degeneration is inevitable. *The Young Manhood of Studs Lonigan* shows the completion of his transformation into an adolescent tough. He dabbles in petty crime, turns increasingly to alcohol, and narrowly escapes prison through an orgy in which members of his gang are incriminated in a rape. In *Judgment Day* his decline is complete. Another woman, Catherine Banahan, attempts to rescue him, but the process has gone too far. Lonigan, now approaching his thirties, has become a typical and unredeemable loafer and petty criminal of the South Side. Brooding over his weak heart, partly the result of his dissipations, he ruins himself through a series of bad judgments; he loses his small savings gambling on stocks, enters into an affair with Catherine and is unable to persuade her to have an abortion when she becomes pregnant, and finally finds himself unemployed and drifting in the early years of the Depression. At the end of *Judgment Day* he dies of heart disease at the age of twenty-nine, still ignorant of the forces—within him and in his environment—which have made him into a punk and a failure and finally destroyed him when his youth was scarcely over.

The best parts of the *Studs Lonigan* trilogy are those that are closest to Farrell's own experience. The characters of Studs and his father are well drawn; the women including Studs' mother and the two girls who attempt to regenerate him, are stereotyped and less convincing. But although Studs is drawn largely from the experience of Farrell's own youth, the author and his character should not be confused; Studs is less Farrell than the sum of all the loafers, petty criminals, and ne'er-do-wells that Farrell observed in the Chicago of his youth. He has, however, put himself into the novel in another form; Danny O'Neill, the protagonist of Farrell's later novel cycle, appears in *The Young Manhood of Studs Lonigan* as a gas-station attendant and college student whose sensitive perceptions and more reasoned judgment raise him above the environment which has produced him. The main literary flaw in the trilogy is its profuse and repetitious detail, which often seems included merely to build up a feeling of authenticity; the three books might well have been compressed into a concise novel of one volume.

The second Farrell novel series centers around Danny O'Neill, a South-Side boy who succeeds in raising himself above the influence of the slums. Danny, more sensitive and thoughtful than Studs, eventually becomes a writer like Farrell himself. This series is generally considered inferior to the Lonigan material; Farrell's obvious sympathy for his character has blunted his powerful realism. The series includes *A World I Never Made* (1936), *No Star Is Lost* (1938), *Father and Son* (1940), *My Days of Anger* (1943), and *The Face of Time* (1953). These volumes are not consecutive; for example *The Face of Time* finds Danny five years old, while *A World I Never Made* shows him as an adolescent.

Mention should also be made of several other novels which do not form a part of either series. *Tommy Gallagher's Crusade* (1939) is the story of a Catholic boy who is drawn by an anti-Semitic priest into a sordid right-wing political organization and finds himself on street corners passing out racist literature; the novel is the only literary treatment of any importance of the reactionary and racist movement within the Catholic Church in the Thirties, a movement which was eventually suppressed by the Church itself. *Ellen Rogers* (1941) is another story of adolescence on the Chicago South Side, but this time the protagonist is a girl; Ellen, from a good Catholic family, is ruined by her experiments in promiscuity with the boys of the South Side and finally commits suicide.

Bernard Clare (1946) begins a new series of novels, this time about a Chicago boy who comes to New York to become a writer. In *The Road Between* (1949) the character's adventures are continued, although his name is changed to Carr; and *Yet Other Waters* (1952) completes the series.

None of these post-1939 novels is considered up to the quality of *Studs Lonigan*, although *Ellen Rogers* is perhaps the best of them. A recurring difficulty is that Farrell, at the bottom an autobiographical writer, has difficulty conveying the emotions of the opposite sex. His women are never as convincing as his men, and in *Ellen Rogers* the character of Ed Lanson, the tough South Side boy who cheats Ellen and abandons her, is more believable than the heroine herself.

Richard Wright (1908–1960)

Richard Wright is perhaps most important as a pioneer. His novel, *Native Son*, published in 1940, was an immediate success, chosen as a selection by the Book-of-the-Month Club and a best seller, adapted for the stage by Orson Welles and made into a film-script by Wright himself. This was the first major breakthrough for Negro writers, not only for this author; after this date publication of black literature becomes easier. As Robert Bone says, "He had gained a hearing, claimed a territory, challenged the conscience of a nation." His second major success, *Black Boy* (1945), was a work of autobiography that in many places reads like fiction. Only one other work can be considered of real literary significance, a novella entitled *The Man Who Lived Underground,* written and published in three versions (1942, 1944, and in the posthumous *Eight Men* of 1961), although Wright tried to find the creative impulse again after removing to Paris in the last decade of his life, publishing seven books in that time. For whatever reason the spark had gone. But his best writing seems to have prepared the way for Ralph Ellison, in the themes of isolation, of repression by white and black alike, of identity crisis, of the feeling of not even being seen, and even in the somewhat expressionistic techniques of the *Man Underground,* leading to the *Invisible Man.* Wright's best work had dealt with his own Mississippi boyhood and flight to the North; his fiction centered in Chicago, a city which captured his imagination. The tough, vital, raw metropolis impressed him by its size and the tempo of its life. His style was generally naturalistic; he had schooled himself in the fiction of Sinclair Lewis, Stephen Crane, and Theodore Dreiser.

Life: Richard Wright, born in 1908 on a cotton plantation near Natchez, Mississippi, struggled through a difficult, almost impossible, childhood. His father deserted the family when Richard was five. Some years later his mother suffered a series of paralyzing strokes. His grandmother, a stern Seventh-Day Adventist, turned him by her evangelism and excessive prayers into eventual rejection of religion. Although getting through the ninth grade at the age of sixteen, Richard missed and lacked even the formal education of high school. The next year he made his first step to escape the repressions of both white and black society in Mississippi by getting as far as Memphis, Tennessee. It was here that he devised a stratagem to get books from the public library which then barred lending to blacks. He wrote a note: "Dear Madam: Will you please let this nigger boy have some books by H. L. Mencken?"

In 1927 Wright and his remaining family "migrated" to Chicago where he stayed for ten years working when he could as porter, dishwasher, postal clerk, life-insurance salesman, at other times on relief. He joined the Communist Party in 1932 and kept his membership until he was expelled in 1944. Moving to New York in 1937 Wright never felt the same emotional involvement with this city as he had for Chicago. Having served a literary apprenticeship in work for the party, he now became seriously concerned with techniques, looking for answers in Dostoevsky, Conrad, Henry James. His concern led him to the success of his first novel in 1940, *Native Son.* After *Black Boy* in 1945 a long period of public silence followed. His review of Gertrude Stein's *Wars I Have Seen* in *PM* so pleased Miss Stein that she initiated a correspondence with him. Wright mentioned that he would like to visit France, and a formal invitation by the French government and the most famous French writers was forthcoming. In the spring of 1946 Gertrude Stein received the Wrights, introducing them to her friends. After this visit the Wrights moved to Paris permanently in 1947, living principally in an apartment near the Luxembourg Gardens, rue Monsieur le Prince. There was perhaps too much admiration and lionizing. He was probably most impressed by the existentialists, Jean-Paul Sartre and Simone de Beauvoir. After the relative failure of *The Outsider* in 1953 (note that he thought of "No Entrance" rather than "No Exit"), his following books continued the decline. In 1960 Richard Wright died of a heart attack.

Chief Works: *Native Son* (novel, 1940) is the story of a Negro boy's crimes, of what part society played in those crimes, and of how the boy, Bigger Thomas, paid the penalty. Mr. Bone calls urban nihilism its real subject: "We have spawned in the city slums a breed of men who are radically alienated from the dominant values of their culture. And this rough beast, its hour come round at last, slouches toward the ghettoes to be born." Its plot occasionally moves over thin ice: Bigger Thomas seems in a confusion that baffles even his creator (which may be the result of trying to make him a combination of the Clyde Griffiths of *An American Tragedy* and the Raskolnikov of *Crime and Punishment,* the rationalist determinism of Dreiser and the existential demonism of Dostoevsky); but these are negligible imperfections on the surface of great narrative. From the moment a giant black rat steals into the Thomas family's one-room flat at the beginning of Book I, "Fear," culminating in the "accident" murder of the white girl Mary Dalton who likes Negroes, through Book II, "Flight," in which the now "heroic" Bigger compounds horror by murdering Bessie, one of his own, and is captured, to Book III, "Fate," where

Bigger in his death cell bids his attorney Max farewell, the novel is shocking, brutal, frank, and sordid, but it moves with power. The only parts that don't work are the occasional didactic and rhetorical "agitprop" speeches in Book III. Jan Erlone the Communist and Max are the weakest of the characters. In fact the only authentic character to emerge is Bigger, but he *is* a big one. Mr. Bone sees his name as symbolic of his aspirations; this is "the first authentic portrait of the stranger in our midst."

Black Boy (1945), subtitled "A Record of Childhood and Youth," has been called autobiography. It might now be called an autobiographical "novel" or even "energized biography." It is not an "up-to-now" life story. It stops at the point where Richard Wright says "Goodbye" to the South, heading North. These early years supply vivid details, the "grim bare bones" of what it feels like to be a lower-class Negro youth growing up in the Black Belt. He does describe sordid scenes with neither delicacy nor reticence. Where melodramatic and didactic fiction sometimes crippled Wright's prose, truth in autobiography liberates his narrative.

The Man Who Lived Underground (novella, appearing in final form in *Eight Men,* 1961) is obviously modeled on Dostoevsky's *Notes from Underground.* But it was conceived in Chicago, which is its setting. The main character whose name we discover later typed by him one finger at a time on a stolen typewriter is freddaniels and whose subterranean world is a symbol of black social marginality runs from the police, dodges down a manhole, and finds himself in the municipal sewer system, a place for discarded, filthy, and rejected things. Far from being a Jean Valjean, he explores that system in a fabulous plot and surrealistic style, looking through a hole into the basement of a Negro church, breaking through at one point to rob a jewelry store, setting up "home" in a cave which becomes a mock symbol of the white world as he papers the walls with hundred-dollar bills. Fred Daniels then emerges into the upperworld, but nobody will notice him. (Wright had quoted William James on another occasion: "No more fiendish punishment could be devised . . . than that one should be turned loose in society and remain absolutely unnoticed by all the members thereof.") He is first taken for a sewer workman and ignored. Entering a Negro church, he is tossed out. Turning himself in to the police, he finds himself cleared of any crime. Finally, pretending to believe his story, they accompany him to his manhole and shoot him down. Bone calls this novella "an existentialist fable based on the absurdities of American Negro life."

James Baldwin (born 1924)

Attention has been called to James Baldwin's relationship with his "spiritual father," Richard Wright. After the death of his own father in 1943, James met Wright for the first time within a year and, as he tells us in his essays, adopted the older man as a father figure. This involved opposition as well as admiration; if Wright were committed to protest fiction, Baldwin would respond satirically with the essay, "Everybody's Protest Novel." After Wright's death in 1960, Baldwin was free of his second father.

Undoubtedly the most important Negro American writer to emerge in the Fifties, James Baldwin has worked primarily in three areas: the essay, the novel, and drama. The last area is the weakest, with only one competent apprentice play, *The Amen Corner,* produced at Howard University in 1955. The better known *Blues for Mr. Charlie* (1964) is little more than propaganda and not very good at that. But as essayist and novelist, Baldwin has achieved a brilliant reputation. Edmund Wilson, in *The Bit Between My Teeth,* speaks of him as one of three of the only younger American fiction writers he always reads. "James Baldwin I think most remarkable. He is not only one of the best Negro writers that we have ever had in this country, he is one of the best writers that we have. He has mastered a taut and incisive style—which is what Negro writers often lack—and in writing about what it means to be a Negro he is writing about what it means to be a man." That is high and justifiable praise. Concerned as much as any with the Negro problem, Baldwin transcends it by style and intellect. Wilson continues, "He concentrates on himself or his principal character an intense kind of isolating spotlight, which makes him stand out against his sordid background—or, rather, he makes this individual seem to shine and throw everything else into shadow."

Critical opinion varies widely on individual novels, of which there have now been four, but most agree that one of his very best is *Go Tell It on the Mountain* (1953) where he writes about his own experience in the Harlem ghetto and gives us a New York City which pulsates with reality and reappears in *Another Country* (1962) and *Tell Me How Long the Train's Been Gone* (1968). He is a naturalist and an urban regionalist, although certainly not always a happy one. Baldwin has become such a celebrity in his own time that it is not always easy to disengage the artist from the public figure.

Life: Baldwin's father had come to New York from New Orleans and his mother from Maryland, a part of the Great Migration, as it has come to be called. James was born in 1924 in Harlem, the first of nine children. His father, a factory worker and a lay preacher, brought up his family under the two disciplines of poverty and the store-front church. In his fourteenth year James "saw the light" and entered a ministry that was to last for three years; then the second crisis, the turn away from religion, the break with his father's values, occurred to give him subsequent material for first novel and first play. Graduated from De Witt Clinton High School in 1942, Baldwin left home shortly afterwards and tried to support himself as a writer without much initial success. He left America for Paris in 1948, intending not to return. Perhaps his greatest creative period took place now during the nine years he remained abroad. *Go Tell It on the Mountain, The Amen Corner,* a series of probing essays, and *Giovanni's Room* explore his own identity, examined from the perspective and aesthetic distance of Europe. In 1957 Baldwin returned to America. In his work since that time he seems to have assumed a more prophetic voice, a kind of apocalyptic vision, and a new stridency. Perhaps he has lost some of his aesthetic "cool" (temporarily, it is hoped), particularly when compared with the work of Ernest Gaines.

Chief Works: *Go Tell It on the Mountain* (novel, 1953), generally considered a major contribution to American fiction, cuts through the store-front church in Harlem to essential Negro experience in America. The powerful and authoritative prose is colored by the rhythms and substance of the Bible, especially when the father, Gabriel Grimes, is invoked: "So he fled from these people, and from these silent witnesses, to tarry and preach elsewhere—to do . . . in secret, his first works over, seeking again the holy fire that had so transformed him once. But he was to find, as the prophets had found, that the whole earth became a prison for him who fled before the Lord." The main event of the novel is the religious conversion of an adolescent boy, John Grimes. The action begins on the morning of his fourteenth birthday; before the night is over he is reborn in Christ. The first part, "The Seventh Day," introduces the boy and his family and the Temple of Fire Baptized in Harlem during the spring of 1935. The second, "The Prayers of the Saints," flashes back in series to the private lives and deepest thoughts of his Aunt Florence, his mother Elizabeth, and his "legal" father Gabriel. Through the histories of the adults we see the boy's conversion in new perspectives. John had been an illegitimate child, born after Elizabeth had gone to Harlem from the South, following her lover Richard, who is arrested wrongly by the police, beaten, and hysterically commits suicide. It is Gabriel, who has a long history of first wife dead, mistress and illegitimate son dead, who marries her and takes Johnny as his own son. Royal, John's half brother who followed, has turned his back on God; and Gabriel feels that he is Abraham and John as Ishmael is standing in his conversion where Isaac-Royal should be. (The guilty father and rejected son stand as symbol of American race relations, says one critic.) The third and last part, "The Threshing-Floor," completes the conversion in the present. John Grimes lies before the altar, and dream fragments and Freudian sequences pass before his vision. There is a hint of the despair that will cause the second crisis or turning away, the sound of blues in the background, the ultimate inadequacy of traditional Christianity for the Negro because its color symbolism is all wrong: black is evil, "wash me . . . whiter than snow."

Giovanni's Room (novel, 1956), about equally damned and praised and neither faintly by the critics, treats the theme of homosexual love with all white characters in the setting of Paris and the south of France. It does so artistically, not pornographically, with a technique that suggests André Gide or Marcel Proust (*The Cities of the Plain*). Perhaps what disturbs most readers most is the casting of the homosexual in a priestly role. David, an American young man in the south of France, recalls his experiences in Paris, where he had met a girl from home, Hella, and asked her to marry him. To think it over she goes to Spain, and in her absence David meets Giovanni, a proud, handsome Italian bartender in a questionable café run by Guillaume, "a disgusting old fairy." With reluctance and some fear on David's part, he and Giovanni are attracted to each other; they fall deeply in love and have a passionate affair—in Giovanni's room. Jacques, a friend, has told David, "Somebody, your father or mine, should have told us that not many people have ever died of love. But multitudes have perished, and are perishing every hour—and in the oddest places!—for the lack of it." He adds that the only "way to be really despicable is to be contemptuous of other people's pain." When Hella returns, David has to choose between his American fiancée and his male lover. He leaves Giovanni to the homosexual underworld, where after a series of humiliations, the young Italian strangles Guillaume, is tried for murder and eventually executed at the guillotine. David, in the south of France with Hella, cannot forget Giovanni and, tortured by self-doubt and guilt, tells his fiancée everything, breaking off the engagement.

This is a compact novel, focusing on the triangle Hella, David, Giovanni. Robert Bone says, "It is the purity of Giovanni's love for David—its idealized, transcendent quality—that protects him from a kind of homosexual Hell. David is the string connecting him to Heaven, and when David abandons him, he plunges into the abyss." David betrays his calling, questioning his "vocation," "but ironically he has been ruined for both the priesthood and the world." There is suggested a central distinction in all of Baldwin's work: between a relatively innocent *laity*, novices in human suffering and including Americans, whites, heterosexuals, and squares, and a fully initiated *clergy*, intimate with pain and including Europeans, Negroes, homosexuals, hipsters, and jazzmen.

Another Country (novel, 1962) continued to disturb readers but on a larger scale. The setting is New York City; Harlem and Greenwich Village bound the tale except for brief, inserted episodes in France and the South. It, too, has been called failure and success, but unusually ambitious and "rich in thematic possibilities."

Granville Hicks called the book "an act of violence" which is visited upon the reader. The story concerns a crucial year in the lives of people who struggle to avoid the quicksand of an "aimless, defeated, and defensive bohemia." They inhabit a kind of underworld of interracial, intersexual relations. Two of the most important characters are Negroes: Rufus Scott, jazz drummer, and his younger sister Ida, aspiring singer. Others are white: Vivaldo Moore, a young unpublished writer and Rufus' closest friend; Cass Silenski, a woman whose marriage is failing; Eric Jones, a homosexual actor from the South; and the pathetic white Southern woman, Leona, whose passionate affair with Rufus ends as he is driven to suicide by racist pressures, jumping from the George Washington Bridge, and she is driven to insanity by the torment. Rufus, who has been called Baldwin's most impressive character, is missing in the last half of the novel except for the long shadow of his memory in the minds of other characters. After his death his sister Ida falls in love with Vivaldo; they live together, but Ida is unfaithful, and Vivaldo, though not homosexual, spends a night with Eric. Even the virile Rufus had once had an affair with Eric, who also crosses the line for an affair with Cass.

According to Norman Podhoretz, who admires the novel, "Baldwin's intention is to deny any moral significance whatever to the categories white and Negro, heterosexual and homosexual." The mixed couplings, "none of it involving casual lust or the suggestion of neurotic perversity, and all of it accompanied by the most serious emotions and resulting in the most intense attachments," lead to this conclusion: "the only significant realities are individuals and love," and nothing should prevent their free operation. Baldwin puts the voltage back into this simple liberal proposition until it burns. Among other things, if you believe "that racial prejudice is wrong, that all men are created equal, that individuals must be judged on their own merits," then you must surrender objections against miscegenation. If love is the supreme value, it must be recognized under whatever guise it appears. Bone, who doesn't really like the novel, talks of the striking images of New York, "the moral chaos of contemporary urban life:" the Villagers with their drinks and buried despair, cash registers, neon signs. "The tense subway crowds and the ubiquitous police convey a sense of latent violence. The furtive scribblings on lavatory walls provide a chilling commentary, in their mixture of raw lust and ethnic hate, on the scope and depth of our depravity."

Tell Me How Long the Train's Been Gone (novel, 1968), which has been called a "careless" book and "beautifully formed," a "masterpiece by one of the best writers in America" and "not successful," "one dimensional," seems less powerful as fiction than the first three novels; nevertheless Harlem is again evoked "more convincingly" than in any other writer, to quote still another critic. The narrator-hero is a highly successful actor named Leo Proudhammer. Thirty-nine years old and at the height of his career as the story begins, he is stricken by a heart attack. As he lies in the hospital he recalls his childhood in Harlem, his tender mother, his fierce father, his adored brother Caleb; he recalls his struggles when young, his love affair with a white girl Barbara King, who also has had a great career in the theatre. At the end Leo leaves the hospital with his young lover and protégé, black Christopher. Traditional songs, Fats Waller, and W. H. Auden give Baldwin epigraphs for the novel and its sections.

Ralph Ellison (born 1914)

Like J. D. Salinger, Ralph Ellison rests his present reputation on a single novel, *Invisible Man* (1952), an impassioned, compelling, and original book which won on its appearance the National Book Award for fiction. Encomiums have been plentiful: "it shows an energy of *mind* comparable only to Bellow's;" "the shifting perspective in which Ellison reveals the Negro is unparalleled even by Faulkner;" "*Invisible Man* is not a great Negro novel; it is a work of art any contemporary writer could point to with pride;" "richly, wildly inventive;" "not only representative of America, white and black, but also of twentieth-century man, and, indeed, man in any time." And yet this novel and its reputation have grown steadily more impressive with the passing of time. In 1965 some two hundred writers, editors, and critics in a Book Week poll voted it the most distinguished novel of the preceding twenty years. Jack Ludwig wrote ten years after its publication "that his may turn out to be the most alive fictional talent of his generation, and perhaps, with Faulkner and Melville and Twain, of American writing of all time."

Life: Born in Oklahoma City March 1, 1914 to Lewis Alfred and Ida Millsap Ellison, Ralph Waldo lost his father, a construction worker and tradesman, who died when he was three; the mother worked as a domestic to support herself and her son. In high school he played trumpet in the band; he loved jazz and started reading Hemingway and T. S. Eliot, later Stendhal. He studied music at Tuskegee Institute in Alabama for three years beginning in 1933. In 1936 Ralph went to New York City to study sculpture, met Langston Hughes and Richard Wright; the latter led him to read Conrad, James, and Dostoevsky. During World War II Ellison served with the United States Merchant Marine; after the war a Rosenwald Fellowship permitted him to work on *Invisible Man.* The history of that publication is referred to above. He worked on a sponsored project with Karl Shapiro which came out as *The Writer's Experience* in 1964, also the year of publication of a book of essays, *Shadow and Act.* Reviewing this book in London, Philip Larkin (see Volume II) wrote, "Ellison was 'freed' not by the Negro Freedom Movement but by Marx, Freud, T. S. Eliot, Pound, Gertrude Stein, and Hemingway." A second novel, of which only a fragment has appeared as "And Hickman Arrives," is still awaited (much as Katherine Anne Porter's novel was announced and delayed); whether it appears or not is unlikely to affect Ellison's position. Since 1964 he has been a visiting professor of writing at Yale University. He and Fanny McConnell were married in 1946 and live in New York on Riverside Drive with their dog Tucka. Ralph Ellison is very warm, humane, a scholar and a gentleman, much in demand as a lecturer.

The Work: *Invisible Man* (novel, 1952) obviously owes something in the way of inspiration to Dostoevsky, to Richard Wright, to existentialists, and perhaps to others, but it presents in its own highly original way themes of marginality and alienation, creating myth rather than simply mythic parallels. Its epigraphs from Melville's *Benito Cereno* and T. S. Eliot's *Family Reunion* place it in a literate and literary tradition. The opening sentences are as memorable as Melville's "Call me Ishmael." "I am an invisible man. No, I am not a spook like those who haunted Edgar Allan Poe; nor am I one of your Hollwood-movie ectoplasms. I am a man of substance, of flesh and bone, fiber and liquids—and I might even be said to possess a mind. I am invisible, understand, simply because people refuse to see me." The Prologue continues to place the anonymous figure of the narrator in a basement coal-cellar (where better for a black to be invisible?) in Harlem. "The joke, of course, is that I don't live in Harlem but in a border area. . . . Now, aware of my invisibility, I live rent-free in a building rented strictly to whites, in a section of the basement that was shut off and forgotten during the nineteenth century, which I discovered when I was trying to escape in the night from Ras the Destroyer."

This man has descended into the pit, or womb, or subconscious, waiting to reemerge: "And remember, a bear retires to his hole for the winter and lives until spring; then he comes strolling out like the Easter chick breaking from its shell. I say all this to assure you that it is incorrect to assume that, because I'm invisible and live in a hole, I am dead. . . . Call me Jack-the-Bear, for I am in a state of hibernation." Flashbacks now take the hero through the experiences that led him here. As a boy in a Southern town he had dreamed of becoming educated and pleasing the white community, remembering the voice of his grandfather, "I want you to overcome 'em with yesses." If invisibility is inevitable in the North, agony is the necessary condition in the South. The boy, initially following his grandfather's advice, wants to make a speech on humility at a white "smoker," but first he must take part in a battle royal with his schoolmates "as part of the entertainment;" "I suspected that fighting a battle royal might detract from the dignity of my speech. In those pre-invisible days I visualized myself as a potential Booker T. Washington." The humiliations include being forced to pick coins off an electrified rug. The hero is seen at the next stage in a Southern Negro college, supported by do-gooders from the North. He tends to identify with the college president Bledsoe (long suffering, hence bled-so, says one critic), but this man is only a tempter in his path, an Uncle Tom educator. The fall from the college Eden comes when he conducts on a tour of the environs a college trustee and benefactor from the North named Norton:

this becomes a voyeur's perverse fantasy, and the boy is virtually expelled.

Bledsoe gives him letters to influential Northern whites to "help" him get a job, but they prove to be traitorous exposés of his disgrace. We now move to Harlem and the New York City area. The boy does get a job through the pity and hint of an understanding assistant (and son) to Mr. Emerson (one of the college trustees to whom he had a letter)—at Liberty Paints on Long Island: "Keep America pure with Liberty Paints." The factory is famous for its color "optic white" (symbol of the theme of sight and blindness, visibility and invisibility, white and black); the "job" is to make white paint by adding the right amount of a solution to cans of black liquid. Our hero can't make it white enough, only grey. Lucius Brockway, another Negro plant worker and now furnace man, knows the secret and has created the company slogan: "If it's optic white it's the right white" out of the folk song refrain, "If you're white you're right, but if you're black, get back, get back, get back." After altercation with Lucius and a furnace explosion, the young man finds himself in the factory hospital, with an expressionistic vision of birth, castration, and lobotomy; here begin his most serious identity problems. Upon release he's mothered by Mary Rambo, who picks him up outside the Harlem Men's House. He enters the Brotherhood, changing clothes, name, family, and makes speeches for them which appear to be "raving" if initially effective. The Brotherhood comes to regard his assertion of individuality over the unity of the organization as a crime. Tod Clifton, who had turned against the Brotherhood and now sells dancing minstrel dolls on the streets of New York, is brutally murdered; the hero wants to exploit him as a sacrificial victim, but the committee is opposed.

Toward the end of the narrative the hero falls between the opposing forces of the Brotherhood and Ras the Destroyer (sometimes called Ras the Exhorter), the Negro nationalist leader. A riot grows out of the conflict. The hero runs through the streets, trying to get back to Mary, his glasses broken, still carrying his briefcase which contains a broken bank, a grinning comic Negro image. He escapes running from Ras and his men only when he falls into the coal cellar where he can remain invisible, bringing us full circle to the Epilogue. Here as he prepares himself to return aboveground, the invisible man confesses, "I *have* to love. I sell you no phony forgiveness, I'm a desperate man—but too much of your life will be lost, its meaning lost, unless you approach it as much through love as through hate." And so he becomes representative of America, white and black, of twentieth-century man, asking at the end, "Who knows but that, on the lower frequencies, I speak for you?"

Saul Bellow (born 1915)

Of a large number of American Jewish writers who have emerged with best-seller success since World War II, the best according to many perceptive critics seem to be Saul Bellow and Bernard Malamud. One Jewish professor has explained the phenomenal success of the group as the money-purchase of conscience-ridden and guilt-stricken masses of people who are aware of the Nazi Jewish genocide, the concentration camps and the gas chambers, and who feel lost innocence simply because they are still alive. These writers cultivate their Jewishness (often excessively) and speak as representatives of a minority; but as Ralph Ellison has observed, in a sense all American writers belong to one minority group or another. There are ways in which Bellow and Malamud lift themselves above exploitation of a phase of success, by searching for and reaching a kind of myth for modern man irrespective of race or creed, by underplaying without ignoring cultural differences, by facing the universal human problems as they reveal themselves now.

As Keith Opdahl has said in his book on Saul Bellow, influenced by the proletarian novel, he "assumes a direct connection between art and society. He examines the injustice of religious prejudice and the effect of war on the middle class. He explores the place of the individual in a capitalistic society and the meaning of a vast population to the private life." Bellow, in the tradition of Dreiser and Farrell, is, as Maxwell Geismar pointed out, "one of these few surviving figures of the 1930's who have not repudiated their heritage and their link with a central literary tradition of the past." But besides sociology, he is interested in psychology as well; he moves from the public to the private and passes to a metaphysical view. Earl Rovit calls him "probably the most significant American novelist to come to maturity since World War II."

Life: Born in 1915 of Russian-Jewish immigrants in Lachine, Quebec, the youngest of four children, raised in one of the poorer ghetto sections of Montreal until he was nine, Saul Bellow and his family moved to Chicago in 1924; and Saul attended public schools and came of age during the depression. He went to the University of Chicago and took a degree from Northwestern in anthropology and sociology in 1937. Close to his family and having received an orthodox religious education, the young man nevertheless experienced a relaxation of traditional ties, as they "dissolved in the secularism" of his surroundings. Rovit has noticed that family and religion play "ambiguous roles" in his novels: they are an additional burden for his protagonists to carry, as they seek to "evade attachment" while holding on to a kind of nostalgic possession.

Bellow's earliest writing achieved publication with *Dangling Man* in 1944 and *The Victim* in 1947; but he arrived at maturity in the fifties with *The Adventures of Augie March* in 1953, *Seize the Day* (1956), and *Henderson the Rain King* (1959). The sixties have produced two more significant novels, *Herzog* (1964) and *Mr. Sammler's Planet* (1969), also a play, *The Last Analysis* (1965) and a number of pieces of short prose fiction and non-fiction. Saul Bellow has also taught at New York University, Princeton, and the University of Minnesota. During the Arab-Israeli conflict of 1967 he was a special correspondent for *Newsday*. He has received several book awards for his fiction.

Chief Works: *The Adventures of Augie March* (novel, 1953), Bellow's first major success, is a kind of first-person *Bildungsroman*, written "catch as catch can," in which the narrator (already a semi-anti-hero) thinks back on the picaresque adventures of his youth when as an ostensible protagonist he was "an uncommitted wanderer upon the face of the earth." He seems to have gone through everything but undergone nothing, and emerges a neutral and indifferent man. This is a pattern characteristic of a number of Bellow's novels, even when the narrative pattern is more complex chronologically as in *Herzog*. Augie March grew up in Chicago, with an older brother Simon, a younger idiot brother Georgie, his mother abandoned by the father, and a number of Machiavellian characters whose influence Augie in the end rejects, the first being his grandmother, a fascinating character ruling the home with guile and malice but happy and carefree, Grandma Lausch. Augie soon becomes more of a traveling victim than rogue (or picaro). It is Grandma who gets Georgie into a state home, and Simon and Augie drift off to the Chicago streets to avoid the "dinkier, darker, smaller" house. As Augie goes to work for William Einhorn, crippled, courageous, brilliant, ambitious, and petty, he soon finds another Machiavellian on his back. When he loses his job in the depression, he goes to work for a third dominant figure, a Mrs. Renling whose husband owns a sporting goods store in Evanston. Pushed to the wall, Augie leaves, wanders to Buffalo, upper New York, a jail in Detroit, and back to Chicago. Simon, his brother, becomes the fourth Machiavellian when, having married money, he tries to persuade Augie to work for him and eventually do the same. Augie escapes by going to Mexico with Thea Fenchel, after having tried his luck as a labor organizer in Chicago. They try to find love, but she is something of a grotesque and possessive. Augie turns toward another woman, Stella; the break-up is completed; Augie and the novel "go limp." As the war comes he undergoes a hernia operation so that he can join the merchant marines, marries Stella although she tries to warn him not to, is wrecked at sea, and after the war makes money in the European black market while he learns of Stella's unfaithfulness. Augie is a good man, but his goodness is biological; he gains understanding, but he is passive.

Seize the Day (novella, 1956) has been called "the painfully exact American tragedy of our affluent day." Many critics consider this Bellow's best work; it is tight and the symbols like the Gloriana Hotel, the elevator, the movie house with its marquee, the tide of Broadway traffic, New York City itself, function both with economy and a raying-out of meaning. The main character, Tommy Wilhelm, who has changed his name and is still "Wilkie" Adler to his old eighty-year old father, the severely independent retired doctor, is a salesman in a period of bad luck (worse off than Willy Loman), out of a job, separated from wife and children still demanding support, from his Catholic mistress who can't marry him, but still dreaming of financial success in a big way and being taken in by a mysterious and phony psychologist, Dr. Tamkin, losing what little money he has left in the commodities market. He is a drowning man, being submerged in failure. His father tells him (but offers no money), "You make too much of your problems. They ought not to be turned into a career. Concentrate on real troubles—fatal sickness, accidents." Dr. Adler is clinically right but morally wrong, except perhaps for himself. Tommy is concerned with the debilitating quality of daily life between the accident of birth and the fatal sickness of death.

"Oh, God," Wilhelm prayed, "let me out of my trouble. Let me out of my thoughts, and let me do something better with myself. For all the time I have wasted I am very sorry. Let me out of this clutch and into a different life. For I am all balled up. Have mercy." There is no mercy from father or wife or Dr. Tamkin. Wilhelm, who has been looking for Tamkin, stumbles into a funeral home, dark, cool, with organ music. Forgetting himself and Tamkin, he looks at the dead man, a stranger in the coffin, and begins to weep, sobbing. People wonder who he is, could it be the cousin from New Orleans? Nobody else is crying. The music pours into him "where he had hidden himself in the center of a crowd by the great and happy oblivion of tears. He heard it and sank deeper than sorrow, through torn sobs and cries toward the consummation of his heart's ultimate need." This is an ambiguous drowning, perhaps like the end of Eliot's Prufrock, "human voices wake us and we drown."

Mr. Sammler's Planet (novel, 1969) has been viewed by critics variously as "not as accomplished" as earlier books or as Bellow's masterpiece. It is timely. The action takes place on a day, a night, and the next day in April of 1969 in New York City, just before the first Apollo lunar landings when everybody was talking about life on some other planet. The main character, Mr. Artur Sammler, a Polish-Jewish displaced person in his seventies, born in Cracow, blind in one eye having survived being buried alive in Poland during the war, educated at Oxford and having known H. G. Wells in Bloomsbury days, is living in New York on the hospitality of a niece Margotte and the liberality of a nephew Dr. Elya Gruner. But the earth is his planet all the same, and he defends it along with human discipline and decency, although it isn't easy in this place at this time. He *has* endured, with some impairment of physical but not mental powers. He is a displaced person, but perhaps we all are (all of Bellow's protagonists seem to be).

Mr. Sammler, threatened and fascinated by the latent violence, the harsh pursuit of happiness in sex and protest, of New York City, gets up in the morning; makes a fiasco as a guest lecturer at Columbia (talking about George Orwell at the invitation of a graduate student, Lionel Feffer); is on his return dogged and threatened by a sinister and allegorical Negro pickpocket he has observed; finds in his room an unpublished manuscript on "The Future of the Moon" by Dr. Govinda Lal, Hindu scientist working with NASA, which had been "stolen" by his daughter Shula who tries to get her father to use it for research on a Memoir of H. G. Wells; and leaves to visit the hospital to see his nephew, Dr. Gruner, near death with an aneurism. He talks with Dr. Gruner's spoiled ungrateful children, Angela in her thirties and libertine in her sexual life and Wallace, a friend of Feffer's but given to hair-brained schemes and accident prone. After the visit (Elya is a man of kindness and principle), Mr. Sammler discovers the manuscript missing from his room, police bulletins looking for Shula, and decides to look for his daughter in the Westchester home of Dr. Gruner. She is slatternly, collects things, and is divorced from a half-mad Israeli, Eisen; but she is his daughter. He finds her but she had hidden the manuscript in a Grand Central locker. Margotte and Dr. Lal appear; with explanations they have supper and an oration on the moon. Mr. Sammler (he and Lal find each other sympathetic) begins a defensc of the human condition on this planet:

"It has only been in the last two centuries that the majority of people in civilized countries have claimed the privilege of being individuals. Formerly they were slave, peasant, laborer, even artisan, but not person. It is clear that this revolution . . . has also introduced new kinds of grief and misery. . . . We have fallen into much ugliness. It is bewildering to see how much these new individuals suffer with their new leisure and liberty. . . . The idea of the uniqueness of the soul. An excellent idea. A true idea. But in these forms? . . . Dear God! With hair, with clothes, with drugs and cosmetics, with genitalia, with round trips through evil, monstrosity, and orgy, with even God approached through obscenities?" Time will help, but we have to learn.

Mr. Sammler is not just a commentator but "a judge and a priest" to his family, to advise, mediate, guide, impart and uphold ethical standards, to meet with rejection and scorn. His second visit to the hospital is delayed by a street fight between Feffer and the pickpocket and Eisen almost kills the Negro; at the hospital he stops to lecture Angela on promiscuity with no success. Elya has been dead for two hours, but Mr. Sammler speaks his words of eulogy over the body of a man who was kind and met his contract. One could wish that some of the language of the book were not as offensive as it is, particularly Angela's, but that is part of the ugliness that Mr. Sammler stands out against. He is a good man who sees things clearly, perhaps a great man.

Bernard Malamud (born 1914)

The only other American Jewish novelist in a position to challenge seriously Saul Bellow's eminence is Bernard Malamud. The others seem to be drowning in the Jewish mother-chicken soup tradition of humor or wallowing in sex sensationalism and the new freedoms. Malamud like Bellow writes about the American Jew as a symbol of man's struggle in the modern world; he is closer to Kafka in the exploration of the theme of alienation than might be initially supposed. But Malamud is a quieter writer than Bellow; he is even more mythic and insinuates his ideas often less obtrusively into the fabric of his books. He seems to deal with the core of the good and moral life, refusing to differentiate Jewish ethics from Christian or humanistic ethics.

Life: Bernard Malamud was born in 1914 in Brooklyn, New York, the son of Bertha and Max Malamud. After the usual public school education he went on to receive degrees from the City College of New York and Columbia University. By 1940 he was working as a clerk in the Census Bureau in Washington and subsequently taught evening classes at Erasmus Hall High School where he had himself studied and started writing short stories. In 1945 he married Ann de Chiara. From 1949 to 1961 he was a member of the faculty of Oregon State College in Corvallis, Oregon. After the magazine publication of various short stories his first novel, *The Natural,* a brilliant and mythic baseball fantasy, appeared in 1952. It was followed in 1957 by what has been called his "most intense novel," the problematic, sombre and bittersweet *The Assistant. A New Life* (1961) turns toward the comic, the story of Seymour Levin's progress as an instructor in an Agricultural College from weakness to strength, from fear to courage; but it is less successful artistically than the novel it followed. At this point in his career Malamud joined the faculty at Bennington College in Vermont. During these years he occasionally traveled in Europe, England, and the Soviet Union. His next major novel, historical in focus this time, was *The Fixer* (1966), based on the trial of a Jew, Mendel Beiliss, for the alleged ritual murder of a Christian child in Kiev half a century ago. In 1969 he published *Pictures of Fidelman; an Exhibition,* which has been called his finest comic work, a proper rival to *The Assistant.*

Chief Works: *The Assistant* (novel, 1957) is the story of a conversion; the Italian Frank Alpine, brought up in a Roman Catholic orphanage on the west coast comes to New York and an initial life of crime, climbs out of evil into good, and becomes a Jew, complete with circumcision in the last paragraph. There are two major literary works in the background: Joyce's *Ulysses* with Stephen Dedalus, another lost Catholic in search of an unacknowledged Jewish father, and Dostoevsky's *Crime and Punishment,* which Frankie reads and gets the point of. There is also his affectionate attachment to stories of Saint Francis which prepares him in many ways for his conversion.

The novel opens and closes within the tomb-like confines of a run-down little grocery story in New York City (proprietor Morris Bober, aging and ailing but the ethical center of the novel) with a rather miserable five-room apartment above it. Morris lives there with his wife Ida, a nagging woman with weak legs, and his daughter Helen, twenty-three, working for Levenspiel's Louisville Panties and Bras but dreaming of escape. At the end of an initial chapter describing a typical day, two accomplices in crime, Frankie Alpine and Ward Minoque, enter the store for robbery. Ward strikes the old man with the butt of his pistol, and he falls. Frankie is at once caught up by his conscience and begins the long struggle, not easy and not rapid, from evil toward good. Ward says to Frankie, "You stinking kike."

However, to expiate his crime Frankie returns to the store, unmasked this time, and begs for a job as an assistant. The confining atmosphere of the store with its shelves of canned goods holds in the characters with only occasional and fitful release for two years while frustrations mount. Frankie learns much from Morris; they both like the store in spite of themselves. Frankie and Helen have a tentative affair which grows into love. Even Ida, a nay-sayer, comes to appreciate Frankie eventually. In the two years Frank Alpine goes through a pattern that parallels the history of the Jews: the Prophets' way of gentleness, the sins of the people, punishment, exile, and return. In the Dostoevsky parallel Ward Minoque is the Svidrigailov to Frank's Raskolnikov and Helen is a much modified Sonia. But ambiguities prevail. The store, threatened with ruin by new competition; Morris, after a narrow brush with accidental death, taken to the hospital with pneumonia by Frank—only Frank remains to work furiously in the store and to no avail. On the death of Morris, Frank falls into the grave on the top of the coffin, which may be the symbol (as in *Moby Dick*) for his taking over as grocer and ultimate conversion. But the novel does not end with unambiguous affirmation. Frankie makes efforts to send Helen to college and perhaps out of his life. The inconclusive final stages of his "career" are convincing; to "live happily ever after" is simply not possible in our world.

Pictures of Fidelman; an Exhibition (six discrete stories which make a novel, 1969) suggests Pictures at an Exhibition (Fidelman is a would-be painter and artist) and exhibitionism as a mild sexual deviation. Robert Scholes calls it the "Portrait of the Artist as an Escape Goat" (which brings to mind other variations of the Joyce novel: Dylan Thomas "as a Young Dog," Michel Butor "as a Young Monkey"); and he also calls it "an allegory of the artistic and moral life" which follows the protagonist's Hogarthian progress from "down and out to salvation." Arthur Fidelman is caught in six stories or pictures frozen in crucial postures on the way to an esthetic Calvary, six comic stations of the cross. This could suggest blasphemy, but that is not the impression Malamud intends or produces for most people. (It is similar to his use of Saint Francis material in *The Assistant.*) Fidelman plays the roles of both Jesus and Judas, betrayed and betrayer, until the ultimate betrayal which is salvation. Many critics consider "Still Life" the best individual story of the six; but the last story, "The Glass-Blower of Venice," is climactically important for in it Fidelman, sometime critic, imposter, forger, pimp, and Judas, is "saved" by giving love rather than taking it, and by letting go the pretenses of art for the honesty of craftsmanship. There is the suggestion of outrage, salvation through sodomy (Beppo), but Malamud wants to shock us only enough to wake us up; he is writing about love, a love which is never a "normal" or automatic thing like heterosexuality. Translated he seeks craft rather than Art and the love of men and women rather than Love.

Fidelman, as Scholes has said, gives us as universal a rendition of the artist's progress as the Catholic Stephen Dedalus or the Protestant Gulley Jimson (*The Horse's Mouth*). Malamud (like Saul Bellow) is a traditional novelist of social and psychological behavior, forthrightly and gratefully a Jewish novelist.

9. The Reaction to Realism: Psychological, Ideological, and Romantic Fiction

One of the outstanding characteristics of the twentieth century is its cultural heterodoxy: it is an era in which a confusion of contradictory systems, attitudes, and philosophies exist side by side. It is difficult to form a neat judgment of a century which produced both Adolf Hitler and Albert Schweitzer, or to summarize the philosophy of an age in which John Dewey, Jean-Paul Sartre, and Jacques Maritain were all considered leading philosophers. This heterogeneous quality is found as well in twentieth-century literature. The dominant movement of the century is unmistakably realism, including its sub-movements of naturalism and regionalism.

A small but important minority of writers, however, rejected this basic tendency and experimented instead with various forms of analytical, romantic, psychological, or ideological literature. Such writers tend to be highly individualistic and therefore difficult to classify under the traditional headings of literary history. In general, however, they may be said to fall into three groups:

Psychological Literature: The term "psychological literature" is used in many different senses. In the France of the seventeenth century it referred to the analysis of moral sentiments and the conflict of ideas of right and wrong in the minds of tragic heroes, i.e., the kind of literature represented by Racine's *Phèdre* or Corneille's *Le Cid.* In the nineteenth century the term "psychological novel" was applied to novels of the type of Stendhal's, in which the hero's inner conflicts were analysed minutely for the reader. Later in the century the works of Poe, Baudelaire, and Dostoevsky were termed "psychological" because they were preoccupied with unusual or abnormal states of mind. All these tendencies are revived in the psychological literature of the twentieth century. Writers like Thornton Wilder treat moral problems from the psychological point of view; Wilder and Katherine Anne Porter concern themselves with internal analysis of the motivations of their characters, and others including Carson McCullers and William Styron give attention to the sexual or neurotic problems popularized by the Freudian and other schools of psychoanalysis. These authors differ widely in content and technique, but they are essentially alike in their purpose: to present human motivations from the inside, from the point of view of the mind concerned, rather than from the point of view of an external observer in the realistic tradition.

It is immediately apparent that many other writers, including some commonly considered realists or naturalists, come partly under this heading: the names of Henry James, Edith Wharton, William Faulkner, Eudora Welty, and J. D. Salinger come immediately to mind. There are indeed elements of psychological analysis in the work of all these writers, and in the end the question is only one of degree.

Neo-Romanticism: The history of twentieth-century European literature is marked by a curious revival of romanticism, which stands in direct opposition to the mainstream of realism in the period. The authors who participated in this romantic revival shared an interest in the exotic or unusual as opposed to the prosaic or ordinary, a certain flamboyance or preciosity of language, a liking for fantastic, heroic, or superhuman characters, and an inclination toward fantastic plot material. The movement included a number of European authors of first-rate importance: Maeterlinck, Cocteau, Saint-Exupéry, Rostand, Christopher Fry, Stefan George. In American literature the movement is not as important, although a number of authors already treated (Elliot Paul, Thomas Wolfe, Willa Cather) demonstrate certain romantic qualities which serve to modify their basically realistic approach to literature. Thornton Wilder has many romantic characteristics. But the romantic interest in the fantastic has reemerged in American fiction primarily in a preoccupation with the grotesque, the Gothic School, best represented here by Flannery O'Connor, Carson McCullers, and Nathanael West (although the latter is not *Southern* Gothic), but also seen in Edgar Allan Poe, Erskine Caldwell, Faulkner, Tennessee Williams, and Truman Capote. John Hawkes (born 1925), whose fiction shows clear affinities with both writers, has coupled West and O'Connor: "But if Nathanael West wrote less effectively whenever he attempted to take into account the presence or absence of God, while Flannery O'Connor would not write at all without what she calls the 'attraction for the Holy,' . . . the 'pitch' of their comic fictions is very nearly the same. Both writers are demolishing 'man's image of himself as a rational creature'. . . . Both writers are reversing their artistic sympathies, West committing himself to the creative pleasures of a destructive sexuality, Flannery O'Connor committing herself creatively to the antics of soulless characters who leer, or bicker, or stare at obscenities on walls, or maim each other on a brilliant but barren earth." This in a sense places West and O'Connor in all three of our categories: psychological, romantic grotesque, and religious ideological.

Ideological Literature: As part of a general reaction against the aims, narrowly viewed, of realism and naturalism which almost accompanied these movements, there occurred a small but important revival of religious idealism and fervor in literature. A general disillusionment with science and democracy added to this movement, as did a reaction against the late nineteenth-century fads of evolution, agnosticism, and socialism. After 1914 Europe and Britain produced what is known as the Catholic Revival movement: Mauriac and Claudel in France; Chesterton, Waugh, Graham Greene, and Muriel Spark in England. America's belated contribution to this fervor can best be seen in Flannery O'Connor. But not all the writers who have devoted themselves to religious renewal have been Roman Catholic. T. S. Eliot among poets and dramatists advocated traditional, conservative Anglicanism. The American William Styron seems to be more like the British William Golding in revitalizing a Protestant rather than a Roman ethic. That both Styron and Flannery O'Connor are viewed in this context of religious writers is witnessed by pamphlets on both included in the series, *Contemporary Writers in Christian Perspective.* For the picture of religious-ideological writers to be complete one should certainly reconsider Bernard Malamud in this context for his renewed Judaism and perhaps even the Zen Buddhism of some of the novelists of the Beat Generation.

In addition to the religious and generally conservative authors referred to above there are a number, somewhat more secular and iconoclastic, who are devoted to humanitarian and liberal ideas which inform their writing. Thornton Wilder might well be considered one of these, and Steinbeck, Maxwell Anderson, Robert Sherwood, Arthur Miller, and E. E. Cummings could be included with a host of others. Ideas may be compelling motives for literary composition. The fact that individual writers may be placed in more than one category should disturb no one by this time.

Thornton Wilder (born 1897)

Wilder stands in marked contrast to his American contemporaries, especially the Hemingway-Dos Passos school of naturalism. He is consistently romantic (*The Cabala, The Bridge of San Luis Rey*) or fantastic (*Our Town, The Skin of Our Teeth*) in subject matter, and restrained, subtle, and highly polished in style; perhaps the best term to apply to his prose is classic. He is a highly intellectual writer in an age of proletarian or pseudo-proletarian naturalists, and an educated man in a time when even those American writers who have a liberal education strive assiduously to conceal the fact from their reading public. In fact, aside from his occasional use of American settings, there is little to mark Wilder as an American writer at all; in his literary and philosophical attitudes he is more properly a representative of the wider European tradition of letters. Here he resembles Henry James, his literary godfather and a writer he imitated in one of his most important novels, *The Cabala.*

Wilder has a warm regard for American life and expresses it in *Our Town* and *The Skin of Our Teeth,* but this does not lead him into chauvinism or naive provincialism. His real subject is humanity, and the long cultural tradition which has led it from the cave to the Europe and America of today. He is not interested in setting down a chronicle of his time; to him all times and places are equally important. He has therefore been attacked by left-wing critics who believe that modern literature must be a document, that it must engage the pressing social problems of the day. Wilder believes that literature must press beyond these immediate exigencies to attain the essential and the universal. This attitude has caused him to be viewed in some quarters as an escapist and a sentimental romantic. The accusation, fair in the case of Cabell (see Volume III), is unfair when applied to Wilder.

Wilder's philosophy is a sort of broad and tolerant Christian humanism. He is little concerned with theology; he stands like Tolstoy for the brotherhood of man and for the spirit of tolerance and understanding. Christianity itself does not play a major part in his work, although it is commended by implication and contrast in *The Woman of Andros* and hovers like a shadow over *The Skin of Our Teeth.* In a 1928 preface Wilder declared his desire to present the highest and most basic religious principles of humanity without falling into "a repellent didacticism."

In actual practice his works are not primarily concerned with ideas. His characters are real flesh-and-blood creatures, and their main problems are moral and psychological ones; Wilder is interested chiefly in the internal life of his subjects. There is little documentation, even in his historical *Bridge of San Luis Rey* and *The Ides of March.* The latter work is precise as to historical fact, but nevertheless literary rather than scholarly; the documents involved are secondhand research materials, the very sort of data the Zola school sought to avoid.

Wilder differs from many of his American contemporaries as well in his careful attention to style. His models are Anatole France, James, Proust, Gide, and Mme. de Sévigné, each an acknowledged master of prose technique. He is a conscientious craftsman; he writes slowly and turns out a relatively small volume of work, but what he does produce is carefully polished. In fact some of his novels appear even too carefully wrought; in any case he does not err on the side of clumsiness. His strongest qualities are irony and subtlety. The first is seen at its best in the gravely satirical exposition of *The Cabala* and the adroit farce of *Heaven's My Destination,* and the second in the intricate emotional relationships of *The Bridge of San Luis Rey* and in the nuances of attitude and psychological reaction in *The Ides of March.* Finally, he is highly educated, especially in Western European history and literature, and he has no compunctions about incorporating his cultural background into his work. The nuances of social convention, of ecclesiastical procedure, and of aristocratic genealogy in *The Cabala* are worthy of Proust, and *The Skin of Our Teeth* is virtually an allegorical Survey Course in European civilization. Of course he had also read James Joyce and uses an excerpt from the *Portrait* in *Our Town* and the basic idea of the whole of *Finnegans Wake* in *The Skin of Our Teeth.* In the case of the latter, Wilder was even rather stupidly accused of plagiarism; he acknowledged his indebtedness to Joyce but turned the Irish stew into palatable American fare, making available to a large public in the theatre in good American English what only a few will be able to find in the multilingual *Wake.* When Wilder's background and attitude are considered, the popular success of his work, especially *The Bridge of San Luis Rey* and *Our Town,* is even more remarkable than it seems at first sight.

Life: Thornton Wilder was born in Madison, Wisconsin in 1897. His father, a newspaper editor, was later appointed Consul-General in Hongkong and took the nine-year-old boy with him to China. Wilder was educated in China, at the University of California, at

Oberlin, at Yale, at the American Academy in Rome, and finally at Princeton, where he took an M.A. in 1926. From 1921 to 1928 he worked as a teacher in the private Lawrenceville School near Princeton, but from that year on he was able to live on the income from his writing. His first novel, *The Cabala,* appeared in 1925, but he won wide recognition only with *The Bridge of San Luis Rey* in 1927. This novel won him a Pulitzer Prize, became a best-seller, and was made into a successful motion picture. He was awarded another Pulitzer Prize for *Our Town* (1938), a popular success which has reappeared in the theatre with some frequency and repeated its success in the late sixties; this drama, along with *The Skin of Our Teeth* (1942) won him recognition as a leading American dramatist as well as an important novelist. A more recent novel, *The Ides of March* (1948), was received with less enthusiasm by the general public but won critical praise.

An interesting example of revised opinion can be seen in the play originally produced as *The Merchant of Yonkers* in 1938. It failed as theatre in the same year that *Our Town* went to town. Only slightly modified it reappeared as *The Matchmaker* in 1954, which was a hit at the Edinburgh Festival and the following year in both London and New York. In 1964, with music, it became *Hello, Dolly!* and outlasted a string of Dollies beginning with Carol Channing. In 1967 Wilder published his first novel since *The Ides of March.* It was called *The Eighth Day* and was received with less enthusiasm by some of the critics than by the public. Thornton Wilder, who has never married, has made his home in recent years in New Haven, Connecticut. His sister, Isabel Wilder, sometimes acts as his secretary, takes care of his affairs, and protects his writing time. She writes gracious letters of regret to the universities that try to get her brother to come to their campuses.

Chief Works: *The Cabala* (novel, 1926) is an intricate and subtle novel which may be read on at least three levels: as a Jamesian intrigue of social relationships in a European setting, as an analysis of decadent nobility in the manner of Proust, and as an allegory of Christianity, paganism, and modern civilization. The action takes place in Rome and is seen through the eyes of a young American student known only as "Samuele." Accompanied by his friend James Blair, a scholar and writer, he comes to visit the Italian capital and is soon introduced into the circle of "the Cabala," a mysterious social group which is said to wield wide power. The Cabala's members include Miss Grier, its ostensible organizer and leader; the Princess d'Espoli, a Frenchwoman whose obsession is the restoration of the Bourbon throne to France; Mlle. de Morfontaine, another French royalist whose dream is that France should again become a Catholic country; the Cardinal Vaina, a retired missionary to China and a universally respected churchman and scholar; and the Duchessa D'Aquilanera, member of the proud Colonna family and a "malignantly resourceful woman" famous for her sarcasms. Samuele agrees to try to rescue the Duchessa's son Marcantonio from the dissipations into which he has fallen; but the young American's puritanical indignation at Marcantonio's vices deranges the Italian boy, and he commits suicide. Samuele's other adventures with the Cabala are hardly more satisfactory. The Princess d'Espoli falls in love with Blair, who flees from her in chaste horror; meanwhile Samuele himself has secretly fallen in love with her. The Cardinal, a truly devout person but somewhat unconventional in doctrine, upsets the conventionally pious Mlle. de Morfontaine so greatly that she hysterically fires a pistol at him; he flees from Italy to return to China and dies aboard ship en route. At the end of the novel Samuele visits Miss Grier to demand an explanation from her of the curious mystery behind the Cabala, and she answers in a parable, refusing to say whether it is literally true or not: that the gods of ancient Greece did not die with the coming of Christianity, but still wander the earth, carefully concealing their identity from outsiders and consoling themselves with their own company. Thus the two parallel themes of the novel are: (1) the decadence or obsolescence of the anachronistic feudal nobility, with its ideals of Universal Catholicism and the divine right of kings, in the twentieth century; and (2) the "ghosts" of the past—including even the demons of paganism—which linger over the European soil. At the end the poet Virgil, appearing to Samuele in an apparition, tells him to "seek some city that is young"—i.e., to look to the future in some new and uncorrupted nation like America.

The Bridge of San Luis Rey (novel, 1927) is a pattern novel in which the lives of the various characters are linked together by a single catastrophic incident. The central theme is that of love; several types are portrayed and analysed. On a certain day of July, 1714 a precarious bridge across a gorge in Peru breaks, killing five persons who happen to be on it. These are the Marquesa de Montemayor; Pepita, her maid; Esteban, an Indian; Uncle Pio, coachman of a popular actress; and Jaimé, son of the actress La Périchole. Each of these persons loves another human being intensely and hopelessly; the types of love range from that of the Marquesa (drawn from the historical figure of Mme. de Sévigné) for her selfish daughter Clara to that of the primitive Esteban for his brother Manuel. The falling of the bridge occurs at the climax of each of these lives; it is, in fact, the only answer to the predicaments of the characters. The inhabitants of San Luis Rey attach no particular significance to the accident, but a scholarly monk, Brother Juniper, becomes interested in the incident and makes it his business to investigate the lives of the victims. His researches at last lead him to a profound respect for the omniscience and benevolence of the Providence which arranged so ingenious a solution to human problems.

This novel, which brought first fame to Wilder when it was published, is still his best-known work. Its chief literary affinities are with James and Proust, although the latter author probably had little direct influence on Wilder. The style of Mme. de Sévigné's letters is also frequently cited as an influence on the style of the novel.

The Woman of Andros (novel, 1930) is an idyll of classic Greece based partly on Terence's *Andria*. The scene is laid shortly before the birth of Christ on the Aegean island of Byrnos. A woman from the island of Andros, Chrysis, a hetaira or courtesan, has come to the island and totally bewitched all the young men, who banquet at her house and enjoy intellectual conversations in the Socratic manner. Pamphilus, son of Simos, is one of the youths attending these symposia. His father wishes to marry him to Philumena, a local maiden. Her father, Chremes, objects to young Pamphilus' relations with Chrysis and demands that he break them off. Pamphilus, however, refuses to give up his attachment to the fascinating woman, and it soon becomes evident that Chrysis herself is in love with him.

The knot is drawn tighter when Pamphilus discovers that Chrysis has a younger sister, the virtuous Glycerium; he transfers his love to her and soon gets her with child. Chrysis, ill, is shaken by the news and soon dies; her household is sold, and Glycerium narrowly escapes being bound into slavery. Simos, pitying her, buys her from the slave-dealer, but she dies in childbirth. Pagan love and stoic virtue are mingled with pagan cruelty in this novel; the final lines tell how "the stars shone tranquilly down upon the land that was soon to be called Holy and that even then was preparing its precious burden." The nebulous reference to the advent of Christianity seems to condemn the decadent Greek culture by implied contrast.

Heaven's My Destination (novel, 1935) is an adroit and subtle satire on two facets of American life: the "mythology of salesmanship" (as in Miller's *Death of a Salesman*) and the tradition of fundamentalist evangelism (as in Lewis' *Elmer Gantry*). The hero, George Brush, is a devoted, idealistic, but priggish young man who makes his living as a textbook salesman but considers his work as an amateur evangelist more important. Essentially George's difficulty is that he is completely logical by nature and that he literally believes the Christianity of the Bible; he thus tries doggedly to live in the twentieth century according to the spirit of the Gospels, which involves him in a series of farcical mishaps. Typical of these is the story of his relations with Roberta Weyerhauser, a farmer's daughter who seduces him in a hayloft and whom he therefore conscientiously regards as his wife. He pursues her to Kansas City and insists on marrying her, even though he does not love her and she candidly hates him; when the marriage turns out to be a failure George is sincerely surprised and disillusioned. George also has a genius for getting locked up in small-town jails, usually because of his philosophy of non-violence (which he borrows from Gandhi) or because the local rustics misinterpret one of his frequent twenty-four-hour vows of silence and consider him either mad or criminal.

Wilder's attitude toward his hero has caused much controversy. The novel is obviously a satire, even a farcical one in spite of its restrained and mock-solemn style. Yet Wilder evidently sympathizes with George, who at worst is only a monomaniac and who may from another point of view be considered a sincere idealist who takes seriously the religion his fellow-men mouth hypocritically but lack the character to practice. George is in the end likeable, as maddening as his priggish earnestness may be to the other characters of the novel as well as the reader.

Our Town (drama, 1938) is a tribute to American life, a microcosm of life and death, love and marriage in a typical American village. The play is based structurally on the device of breaking down the "theatrical illusion" and letting the audience into the production of the play, which is also used in Pirandello's *Six Characters in Search of an Author* and in much of Brecht. There is a Stage Manager, an effective character with authentic New England diction and rhythm in his speech, who serves as a sort of narrator or chorus; he introduces the story's characters and comments on the action which takes place in Grover's Corners, New Hampshire, from 1901 to 1913. The plot, a cliché situation made fresh by its treatment, centers about two neighboring families, those of Editor Webb and Dr. Gibbs. In the first act Dr. Gibbs comes in from a maternity case (the theme of birth), the Webbs cook breakfast and the children go off to school. The young George Gibbs and Emily Webb play at puppy-love. In the second act, three years later, the couple are about to be married; their courtship and wedding are described (the cycle of life at its center). In the third act, nine years later, Emily has died in childbirth; the cycle has completed itself. Emily's ghost appears; she abandons the living and joins the group of the dead in the cemetery (a simple row of folding chairs on the bare stage), who advise her to forget her past existence and prepare for the future.

This play attempts to demonstrate that even the humblest lives partake of the divine cycle of birth, love, and death. But that isn't all. In emphasizing the wonders of ordinary daily living, it does not rest in a sentimental position; there is a snake in the garden. Most of the characters are essentially good and love Grover's Corners, but there is Simon Stimson, a man with an artistic temperament, driven to drink and suicide by our town. The town does have a jail. And the newsboy, young and promising, will be killed in World War I. The Stage Manager, as Minister, expresses his doubts about marriage. But the end result is affirmation, not absurdity; it's just that the simple life is not treated simplistically.

The Skin of Our Teeth (drama, 1942) is a fantastic *tour de force* resembling nothing else in Wilder's work but foreshadowed by the Joyce *Wake.* The hero is all humanity, personified in the figure of George Antrobus. He is Adam, Noah, in fact every great hero of humanity; he invents the wheel and the alphabet, lives through the Fall, the Flood, various wars, the Ice Age, and countless other catastrophes, and yet his life somehow struggles on. His wife Eva or Maggie bears him two boys and a girl, but Henry, or Cain, the elder, murders his brother. A maid, Lily Sabina, serves as a sort of Lilith or personification of female sensuality. The first act takes place simultaneously in the Ice Age and following the American depression of the thirties, when the family is living in comfortable circumstances in Excelsior, New Jersey, with pet dinosaur and mammoth. It is so cold they are burning pianos in Hartford; gradually the wall of ice creeps southward. Refugees crowd into the home, including Homer, Moses, and the Muses. The second act takes place immediately before the Deluge. The scene is Atlantic City; the convention of the Ancient and Honorable Order of Mammals, Subdivision Humans, is taking place, and George is to address the gathering. His theme is "Enjoy Yourselves." The Flood begins as the act closes; the family scrambles into a boat.

The third act returns to the suburban home. A war has just ended; Henry or Cain (the personification of brute force) was the enemy. Sabina, of course, was a camp-follower. The father, George, is now the tired but still creative and inventive spirit in humanity, and continues with trying to build a new life after the calamity and almost complete destruction of the war as long as he has his books left. And we hear the words of Spinoza and Plato and the Bible as the play comes to an end, which repeats circle-fashion the beginning, "This is where you came in. We have to go on for ages and ages yet. You go home." The style of *The Skin of Our Teeth* is light and fast moving, and the theme—which is nothing less than the survival of the human race by the skin of its teeth—is less heavy and more exhilarating than one might think. The walls of the setting tilt, almost fall, correct themselves, or fly up into the air; an actress complains of her lines to the audience; the audience is asked to participate in the action by passing up chairs for burning. Wilder always sees the stage as stage; theatre is not so much a slice of life as life is like the theatre.

The Ides of March (novel, 1948) concerns the events leading up to the assassination of Julius Caesar. The story is told entirely through documents, proclamations, and letters of the participants. The material is divided into four books as follows:

Book I mainly concerns Clodia Pulcher, patrician daughter of a respected Roman family. Her mind has been disturbed by a variety of experiences; she is violated by an uncle, and her beliefs are upset by Caesar's skepticism. She is loved by the poet Catullus, but despises him.

Book II depicts the arrival of Cleopatra in Rome and her relations with Caesar; it describes her rôles both as a woman and as a queen. Clodia discovers a plot whereby Marc Antony is to be discovered embracing Cleopatra. Caesar happens along too soon, however, and the plan is thwarted.

In Book III is related an incident which historically happened some time before; Wilder concentrates the chronology for dramatic effect. Clodia arranges for her wild young brother, Clodius, to be spirited into the highly secret women's ritual of the Bona Dea. In the ensuing scandal Pompeia, Caesar's wife, is accused of connivance, or even of adultery with Clodius, and Caesar divorces her.

Book IV deals with the conspiracy to assassinate Caesar. Catullus writes broadsides attacking him, and Brutus and Cassius plan the actual murder. The novel closes with a description of the historical assassination borrowed from Suetonius.

The Matchmaker (comedy, 1938, 1954, 1964 as *Hello, Dolly!*), which is more slapstick farce than anything else, centers around the game played by Dolly Levi, a matchmaker. She leads the merchant of Yonkers, Horace Vandergelder, to believe she's arranging a marriage for him to a beautiful and rich young orphan (made up in her own mind) while manipulating things so that she can marry him herself. The farce rushes through the early 1880's with trapdoors, asides, hiding under tables and in cupboards, hats left behind, overhearing behind screens, men disguised in women's clothes to escape detection, and with highly amusing lines. Dolly teaches Vandergelder that he's wrong to live only for the accumulation of money. Money should circulate like water rather than lie idle or frozen. He has long felt that the world is made up of fools who can be used to pile up wealth. She counters that the best way to keep us fools out of harm's way is to allow us a few human pleasures, which takes money but not too much of it. The difference, she says, between poverty and a little money is great "and can shatter the world." The difference between a little money and a whole lot of money "is very slight—and that also, can shatter the world." Money, like manure, is useless unless spread out to encourage young things to grow. Dolly tries to spread it. She attempts to alter life a little here and there like an artist. When she has finished, everyone feels better, and Dolly has achieved her mission.

The Eighth Day (novel, 1967) although somewhat diffuse, labyrinthine, and a mystery story, begins explicitly enough: "In the early summer of 1902 John Barrington Ashley of Coaltown, a small mining center in southern Illinois, was tried for the murder of Breckenridge Lansing, also of Coaltown. He was found guilty and sentenced to death. Five days later . . . he escaped from his guards on the train that was carrying him to his execution." With somewhat allegorical overtones this work echoes most of the themes of his earlier novels and plays, chiefly the human capacity to survive disaster, to get on improvisationally if necessary, with the daily business of living. Abstract matters are always tied to a specific, concrete, detailed story. The Ashley family (he represents the "good" man) and the Lansing family (he was generally "evil," although he concealed it well) are followed into genealogies, ancestors and descendants; geography and geologic history are explored. Coaltown, U.S.A. becomes Everytown, Universe. The children of John and Breck are seen in their careers. And all the while there are three unanswered questions: What happened on the Sunday afternoon when Breck Lansing was shot in the head during rifle practice by his best friend? Who were the six men, blacked up and disguised as Pullman porters who effected Ashley's escape from the train taking him to Joliet? What happens in the subsequent life of Ashley to permit pattern and meaning to emerge? The answers to the first two questions at the end of the novel are not completely satisfying to the mystery story reader. But Wilder's humanistic affirmation persists in the unwinding of the third.

Dr. Gillies, resident philosopher of Coaltown, explains that each of the seven days of God's creation stands for millions of years and that the present age represents only the beginning of the second week: "We are children of the eighth day." History may be seen as a tapestry, reminding one of Maugham and a figure used by Cronshaw in *Of Human Bondage*; some people see a design or a pattern in it and are strengthened; "some find strength in the conviction that there is nothing to see. Some." The dying fall of the last isolated word leaves no doubt where Wilder stands. There are absurdists, completely negative, in modern literature; but he is not one of them.

Nathanael West (1903–1940)

Relatively little known during his lifetime except to a small group of critics, friends, and important writers like Quentin Reynolds, S. J. Perelman (who married his sister Laura in 1929), William Carlos Williams, Erskine Caldwell, Dorothy Parker, James Thurber, and Edmund Wilson, Nathanael West achieved a mushrooming reputation after his accidental death in 1940. He wrote four novels, the first and third not very good, showing little more than scatalogical and sexual obsession (of a kind of *Naked Lunch, Candy* variety), which very soon becomes boring. But the second novel, *Miss Lonelyhearts* (1932), has come to be recognized as a great novel, translated into French in 1946 as *Mademoiselle Coeur-Brisé* and visibly influential on subsequent French fiction. The last novel, *The Day of the Locust* (1939), is spotty and probably fails in a final analysis, but it contains good things and is a brilliant satire on the Hollywood scene of the Thirties. West is viewed in some circles as one of the most important American novelists of this period.

Stanley E. Hyman writes of him: "The world West shows us is for the most part repulsive and terrifying. It is his genius to have found objective correlatives for our sickness and fears: our maimed and ambivalent sexuality, our terror of the idiot mass, our helpless empathy with suffering, our love perverted into sadism and masochism." As suggested earlier John Hawkes has an equally high opinion of West's work.

Life: Nathanael West, born Nathan Weinstein in New York City in 1903 of German-Russian-Jewish immigrants, evolved his pen name from an intermediate Nathaniel von Wallenstein Weinstein, uniting his mother's family name with his father's and, perhaps because of Schiller's heroic play, tacking on the extra "von." He had two younger sisters, Hinda and Laura. In public school in Manhattan and in DeWitt Clinton High School, Nathan showed no talent, leaving the latter in 1920 without graduating. Apparently on a forged transcript he entered Tufts and later as a transfer Brown University, where he did graduate. He received but little education in the Jewish religion and subsequently threw off what Jewishness he could. Perelman, a college friend, remembers him as the first man on campus to read *Jurgen* by James Branch Cabell (see Volume III). From 1924 to 1926 West spent two happy years in Paris and returned to take up hotel management. At the Sutton in 1928 he put up at special rates such guests as Erskine Caldwell and James T. Farrell. His first novel, *The Dream Life of Balso Snell,* was privately printed in 1931, the first work to appear under the name Nathanael West. He told William Carlos Williams he got the name from Horace Greeley's injunction, "Go West, young man." "So I did." His own anti-Semitism was considerable at this point.

Miss Lonelyhearts, on which he had worked for some time, was published in 1933 to enthusiastic reviews, but the publisher declared bankruptcy shortly thereafter and the books were not available for sale when they would have sold. West wrote *A Cool Million* (1934) in a hurry, hoping to make money, but it was unfavorably reviewed and sold poorly. Having been in Hollywood briefly in 1933, West now returned there to work as a script writer. The most he got out of that was the experience and material for *The Day of the Locust* (1939). Bennett Cerf told him the reason this novel didn't sell (fewer than 1500 copies) was because women didn't like it. In April of 1940 West surprised everyone who knew him by marrying Eileen McKenney, the protagonist of *My Sister Eileen* by Ruth McKenney. They were apparently very happy. Returning from a hunting trip in Mexico on December 22 of the same year, West driving and as usual poorly, they went through a stop sign near El Centro, California. There was a collision. Eileen died instantly; her husband an hour later.

Chief Novels: *Miss Lonelyhearts* (1933) is a short novel which begins: "The Miss Lonelyhearts of the New York *Post-Dispatch* (Are-you-in-trouble?—Do-you-need-advice?—Write-to-Miss-Lonelyhearts-and-she-will-help-you) sat at his desk and stared at a piece of white cardboard. On it a prayer had been printed by Shrike, the feature editor.

"Soul of Miss L, glorify me.
Body of Miss L, nourish me.
Blood of Miss L, intoxicate me.
Tears of Miss L, wash me. . . .
Help me, Miss L, help me, help me.
In saecula saeculorum, Amen."

Immediately one sees the basic grotesque irony that holds the book together. The real work of Christ, of deeply felt religious impulse, must be done or perhaps may best be done in our modern American world by an Advice to the Lovelorn columnist. The anonymous journalist who takes on the job casually finds himself facing the needs he had tried to avoid or ignore. He becomes a tormented, reluctant priest in effect. He attempts to explain to his fiancée Betty: "A man is hired to give advice to the readers of a newspaper. The job is a circulation stunt and the whole staff considers it a joke . . . , but after several months the joke begins to escape him. He sees that the majority of the letters are profoundly humble pleas for moral and spiritual advice, that they are inarticulate expressions of genuine suffering. He also discovers that his correspondents take him seriously. For the first time in his life, he is forced to examine the values by which he lives. The examination shows him that he is the victim of the joke and not its perpetrator."

Betty is "an innocent Eve" unable to save Miss Lonelyhearts as the "fallen Adam." Most of the other characters are caricatured. Shrike, the columnist's boss, is the isolated "cynical intelligence" of Miss Lonelyhearts himself, "master comedian and ironist," brilliantly witty in his monologues, improvisations, and games. He has been called the Buck Mulligan to the Stephen Dedalus-Miss Lonelyhearts, the spirit that denies. The correspondents, some of whom sign themselves Desperate, Sick-of-it-all, Harold S., Broad Shoulders, asking for guidance really want gospels. "Why is there evil in the world?" "What are the principles of religion?" asks the Roman Catholic wife with seven children and pregnant again, who is quite literally "Sick-of-it-all." "What good is love?" Miss Lonelyhearts stops reading. "Christ was the answer, but, if he did not want to get sick, he had to stay away from the Christ business. Besides, Christ was Shrike's particular joke." With two correspondents the columnist becomes particularly and climactically involved, Fay Doyle whose letter of sexual invitation he responds to, and her husband Peter Doyle the cripple who at the end of the novel shoots Miss Lonelyhearts in an embrace that was intended to produce a miraculous cure, the "Christ business," as they roll down the stairs toward Betty.

Many allusions to the Bible and to modern literature have been pointed out; they do give a double and effective frame of reference. The letters cry "Help! Help!" and Shrike answers "Jug! Jug!"—having read Eliot. West referred to *Miss Lonelyhearts* as a "novel in the form of a comic strip." But the pain and suffering of the book comes to its sharp point in the Christ complex. The pace is frantic, the imagery grotesque. The letters from readers are "stamped from the dough of suffering with a heart-shaped cookie knife," and the sky has a look "as if it had been rubbed with a soiled eraser." Some of the many puns are so extreme that they seem to violate sensibility, as when Shrike comments on a letter from an old woman who sells pencils in order to live, "She has rheum in her eyes. Have you room in your heart for her?" There seems to be no book like this one in American literature before its time, but it seems to influence many that come after: Carson McCullers to some extent, Flannery O'Connor even more. Hyman thinks it ranks with *The Great Gatsby* of Fitzgerald and *The Sun Also Rises* of Hemingway as "one of the three finest American novels of our century." It is perhaps a mistake to try to choose three instead of a dozen. Not everyone would agree with this selection, but it is not an absurd one.

The Day of the Locust (novel, 1939), a flawed work but West's second best, is most effective as a satire on the Hollywood scene and by extension on twentieth-century American life and manners. Some of its most outrageous scenes, incidents, descriptions, we are assured by some critics, are almost literal transcriptions of what was there, in the "Caliphonia" of the Thirties—which seems to connect this novel with Evelyn Waugh's later *The Loved One* (see Volume II). Tod Hackett, a young painter, is ostensibly the main character; he works as a set and costume designer for a Hollywood movie studio but dreams of painting a picture, "The Burning of Los Angeles." Tod fades before other characters at times: Faye Greener (whom he loves) and her father Harry (an old vaudeville comic), cowboy Earle Shoop and his Mexican friend Miguel (who works with fighting cocks), the dwarf racetrack tout Abe Kusich, and Homer Simpson from the Midwest to whose rented house in Irish peasant style and the party thrown there the action shifts until murder and riot erupt and end the novel with a vision associated with the Burning of Los Angeles. The title refers to the plague of locusts in Egypt in the Biblical account of the exodus. But unity is lacking and unlike *Miss Lonelyhearts* this novel has no moral core or singleness of image. Any surrounding frame of reference is broken, even splintered. Second thoughts might see in these novels by Nathanael West the kind of Black Humor that we were looking forward to in the Introduction. In that case a backward glance can be useful. Alan Ross wrote in *Horizon,* "Perhaps the savagery of West's portrait, his making of the whole political and economic racket so undisguisedly repulsive and meaningless, was too near the bone for an American audience with a mass neurosis, and a guilty conscience." *The Day of the Locust* was originally called in a first draft *The Cheated* (the common middle-class people who have come to California mostly from the mid-west to die—even the California sun is a joke—"They have slaved and saved for nothing.")—in which case the Hollywood figures connected with the movie industry are the cheaters. Their comic and pathetic plight is indicated by the spurious houses they live in, "Mexican ranch houses, Samoan huts, Mediterranean villas, Egyptian and Japanese temples, Swiss chalets, Tudor cottages."

Carson McCullers (1917–1967)

The fiction of Carson McCullers, which has been the subject of considerable critical controversy, seems likely to hold a firm if small place in the American renaissance of southern writers. Comparisons, which may be unfortunate, are almost inevitable with Faulkner, Truman Capote, Eudora Welty, Flannery O'Connor, Erskine Caldwell, and others. The range of her fictional themes is narrower than in Faulkner or Welty: consistently she writes about the center of loneliness in people in a world where other people are as lonely as themselves. Love is never equal and reciprocal, and the imagination creates its own chamber of horrors, where a physical defect or an emotional perversity is blown up into a freak show. If the lack of communication between one human being and another creates the overriding anxiety of our time, then Carson McCullers rides that wave; no better symbol and no more representative character than the deaf-mute Singer of *The Heart Is a Lonely Hunter* has been achieved. The filmed version with Alan Arkin in this role in 1968 makes this crystal clear. Flannery O'Connor and Truman Capote work variations on much the same theme; but Miss O'Connor, like Graham Greene, has a Roman Catholic perspective which, if it doesn't attenuate the loneliness, at least provides an ultimate out.

One kind of character Carson McCullers has created superbly well, the adolescent girl more than half-tomboy who experiences deep joy and frustration in the impossible business of growing up; Mick Kelly of *The Heart Is a Lonely Hunter* and Frankie (F. Jasmine Addams) of *The Member of the Wedding* may in some sense be autobiographical characters but they are fully realized and living. One must quickly add the character of Berenice, the Negro servant who represents the voice of experience in Frankie's hesitant search for maturity. Having published the novel, *The Member of the Wedding,* in 1946 and encouraged by Tennessee Williams in the effort, Mrs. McCullers transformed the whole thing, with hints from *Glass Menagerie,* into a "mood" play which opened on Broadway in 1950 with Julie Harris as Frankie and Ethel Waters as Berenice, a tremendous success. It received the Donaldson Award and the prize of the Drama Critics Circle the following year, ran for more than five hundred performances, and was filmed by Stanley Kramer.

The best of Carson McCullers' other work is her second novel, *Reflections in a Golden Eye,* which appeared in 1941, the year after *The Heart Is a Lonely Hunter* (and which, in spite of a poor reception by critics at the time, was filmed by John Huston in 1967 with Marlon Brando and Elizabeth Taylor) and the strange, rather Gothic, but powerful novella, *The Ballad of the Sad Café* (1943), which Edward Albee subsequently dramatized in 1963. All her best work has the local flavor of the south Georgia region. Critics continue to pull and tug at Mrs. McCullers' literary reputation. She is either at the bottom of the list or, as V. S. Pritchett and Gore Vidal have thought, at the top. Perhaps she will take her place somewhere between the two.

Life: The life of Carson McCullers, although her young years were outwardly uneventful, reads almost like her fiction and seems even more improbable. Born Lula Carson Smith in Columbus, Georgia in 1917, she gave up the "Lula" when she learned to dislike it, a process which didn't take long. Her father of French Huguenot ancestry, Lamar Smith, was a watchmaker and jeweler who had come from Alabama (three watchmakers appear in her fiction); her mother, of Irish descent, had been born in Dublin, Georgia. An odd, lonely, obviously talented girl, she developed a passion for music (at five she was given a piano for lessons) and fantasy and writing (at fifteen her father brought her home a typewriter). While still small she suffered an attack of rheumatic fever, misdiagnosed by the family doctor as growing pains. Taller than other girls her age and a tomboy at heart, like Mick and Frankie, she muddled into adolescence. At twelve, having outgrown the talents of her piano teacher, she found a more advanced teacher in the wife of a Colonel Albert Tucker who lived on the post of nearby Fort Benning, where she was taken for more lessons. What she observed until she was seventeen entered into the garrison background of *Reflections in a Golden Eye*.

She made her way to New York City at eighteen; a roommate from her home town lost all her tuition money for the Julliard School of Music in a subway. Carson had to work at odd jobs, study creative writing at Columbia and N.Y.U., and write furiously; her writing, especially after her initial success, the publication of "Wunderkind" in *Story* magazine in December 1936, the story of a prodigy by a prodigy, became her lifetime dedication. The following year, after a trip back home, she married a young Georgia soldier from Ft. Benning, Reeves McCullers, and found a pen name more satisfying than Smith. Living happily in Charlotte, North Carolina, where Reeves worked as a credit manager, Carson worked on her first novel, originally called "The Mute"; her publishers changed the title (probably for the better) and *The Heart Is a Lonely Hunter* came out in 1940. Reviews were generally enthusiastic, but critics couldn't believe that a twenty-two year old girl could probe that deeply. Having moved to Fayetteville, Reeves picked up the story of a Peeping Tom at Fort Bragg which he related to Carson and which became the inciting incident for the second novel. But by this time the marriage was in trouble, and Carson was planning an eventual divorce. In late 1940 she left the New York apartment where they were then living and took up residence in an old brownstone house in Brooklyn Heights, which came to be known as February House, with an odd but fascinating and coming-and-going group of friends, a kind of cooperative "Brook Farm" experiment. For the most of five years she lived here with George Davis, editor of *Mademoiselle,* W. H. Auden, Louis MacNeice, Paul and Jane Bowles, Christopher Isherwood, Richard Wright, Benjamin Britten, Golo Mann (Thomas Mann's second oldest son), Gypsy Rose Lee, and others at various times, including such guests as Salvador Dali and Aaron Copeland. Domestic details were usually managed by Mrs. McCullers, Auden, or Gypsy Rose Lee. The house, No. 7, Middagh Street, surely became one of the most interesting bohemian cénacles this side of 27 rue de Fleurus. For the Georgia girl this was spirited if somewhat fatiguing company and fine material for stories. In a bar near the Brooklyn Navy Yard Carson met a little hunchback who strutted in every evening, was petted, given free drinks, and was a favorite of an imposing old prostitute named Submarine Mary. She put him into *The Ballad of the Sad Café* as Cousin Lymon.

In the winter of 1940–41 back in Columbus, Georgia for a rest, Carson suffered the first of three strokes that combined to cripple her. Corresponding with the divorced Reeves who was wounded fighting in Europe, she married him a second time when he came back to the States. They were together in Paris in 1947, and she experienced another stroke which impaired the vision of the right eye and later partly paralyzed one side of her body. The success of *Member of the Wedding* as a play cheered her up. She and Reeves bought a house at Bachvillers near Paris, but much of the next two years was a nightmare. Reeves, a heavy drinker, took drugs, became wildly abusive; Carson returned alone to a house in Nyack to live with her widowed mother and learned that Reeves had committed suicide in a Paris hotel in December, 1953. Her mother died two years later of a bleeding ulcer. Considering the stresses, the play and the novel published in 1958, *The Square Root of Wonderful* and *Clock Without Hands,* were stoic triumphs but artistic failures or relatively so. With gallantry and spirit Carson McCullers in the sixties underwent a heart attack, breast cancer, paralysis, pneumonia, and a bone-crushing fall, shattering her left hip. Yet she traveled, received guests, worked fitfully at manuscripts. In August of 1967 another stroke put her into a coma and she died in September.

Chief Works: *The Heart Is a Lonely Hunter* (novel, 1940) is set in the deep South with estranged and disadvantaged characters; its theme is loneliness and the inevitable frustrations of love. John Singer, the central character is a deaf-mute, active, neat, and quick-witted, who has been joined for ten years in a close but strange friendship with another deaf-mute, Spiros Antonapoulos, impassive, sloppy, fat, and feeble-minded. Singer works as a silver-engraver, Antonapoulos in a fruit store; they play chess, go to the library, to the movies, happy with each other in this depressed factory town. But Spiros suddenly becomes a menace to society, stealing, jostling strangers, urinating in public; he is sent to an asylum two hundred miles away. Singer, with love, follows him to the distant city, renting a room with a family named Kelly, taking his meals at a nearby café. Four people focus in on Singer, trying to complete their own fragmentary and obsessive dreams: Mick Kelly, a twelve-year old tomboy with a love of good music, especially Mozart; a Negro doctor, Benedict Copeland, surprised by this rare instance of white compassion; Jake Blount, a radical agitator who seeks refuge in alcohol; and Biff Brannon, the café owner with a half-ironic, half-compassionate interest in people. The deaf-mute who can read lips makes an ideal listener; although he seems bewildered by their interest in him, he offers his left-over love freely. When Antonapoulos dies, Singer commits suicide, and his four disciples are left to grieve and wonder. Although religious symbolism has been read into the novel, it is not vital to it. It has been suggested that Singer owes something to Dostoevsky's Prince Myshkin in *The Idiot.* The honest sentiments of the story can come perilously close to sentimentality.

Reflections in a Golden Eye (novel, 1941), a whipping post for critics, takes place at an army camp, still deep South, in the late 1930's with its characters listed as "two officers, a soldier, two women, a Filipino, and a horse." Captain Penderton, a repressed, latent, up-tight homosexual, infatuated by his wife's lovers, and Major Langdon, a charmboy who beds Leonora Penderton within hours after their first meeting, are the officers. The soldier, Private Williams, not too bright but attractive as a D. H. Lawrence primitive, is the Peeping Tom who is fascinated by the nude body of Leonora; actually he is at his best with the horse, Firebird. The Major's wife, Alison, having cut off her nipples with garden shears, finds solace with the Filipino houseboy, Anacleto. The horse, tended by Williams, adored by its owner, Leonora, and despised by her husband who can only with difficulty hide his love for Williams, is finally ridden by the Captain and throws him with a sickening humiliation, in view of the soldier-groom. Driven by love and hate toward the silent Williams, he discovers that the private has affections only for Leonora and murders him. Sensational and shocking in outline, somewhat in the manner of Faulkner's *Sanctuary,* the novel has been severely criticized because the characters do not relate and react with each other—which may, of course, be the theme, that they cannot do so. As one critic said, "Not even the horse is normal."

The Ballad of the Sad Café (novella, 1943), which divides honors with *The Member of the Wedding* as Mrs. McCuller's best work, restricts itself to three main characters, Miss Amelia Evans, a large, rough, masculine woman; Cousin Lymon, a hunchbacked dwarf; and Marvin Macy, a handsome, vicious criminal, who had been married for ten stormy days to Miss Amelia some years before the appearance of Cousin Lymon. It also focuses in on a restricted, alien, legendary ballad world which happens to be at the same time a dingy southern town, realistically presented as cut off from society by the boundaries of swamp, black pine-woods and general inaccessibility. There is absolutely nothing to do. You might just as well "go down to the Forks Falls Road and listen to the chain gang." The hunchback arrives from nowhere, claims to be a cousin of Miss Amelia, and disappears into the house. Local people think he has been murdered, but they discover that Miss Amelia has taken him in, fallen in love with him, and showers him with favors. Changes occur; as a lover Miss Amelia becomes softened, communicative, and decides to start a café on the premises to amuse Cousin Lymon; as the beloved, the dwarf becomes proud, demanding, difficult. After six years Marvin Macy, who had been deeply in love with Amelia, rudely repulsed by her, and sworn revenge, returns to town from prison. Cousin Lymon falls in love with Marvin, who will have nothing to do with him although he is willing to use him in accomplishing his revenge. The triangle of love relationships, not one of them reciprocated, builds tensions. Amelia is forced by Lymon to let Marvin move in with them; "once you have lived with another . . . it is better to take in your mortal enemy than face the terror of living alone." Amelia and Macy prepare for hand-to-hand combat; the townspeople gather; at seven o'clock they begin to fight. After boxing and wrestling, Miss Amelia is about to crown her victory by choking her opponent, when Cousin Lymon flies at her back and pulls her off. The two men smash up the property and take off, even leave poisoned food for her. For three years she waits for the hunchback to return, then has a carpenter board up the house which is falling into decay and becomes a recluse. The town returns to desolation, the road is empty; "the soul rots with boredom. You might as well go and listen to the chain gang." The text seems to be that the lover and the beloved come from different countries. Anybody can be a lover, and the most outlandish people can be the stimulus for love. The beloved, however, fears and hates the lover. But love does not have to be reciprocal to benefit and change the one who loves, even if the change is subject to time.

The Member of the Wedding (novel, 1946; play, 1950) is about a twelve-year old girl (much like Mick Kelly but the center of the story this time), Frankie the tomboy who daydreams of herself as F. Jasmine Addams. When her brother Jarvis comes home as an army corporal to marry his girl friend Janice, Frankie falls "in love with her brother and his bride and wants to become a member of the wedding." This was what Carson McCullers is reported to have shouted at Gypsy Rose Lee one Thanksgiving when the idea for the novel coalesced. At the end of the first part of the novel (or play) which takes place mostly in the kitchen of her widowed father's house in a Georgia town much like Columbus, the tomboy has pestered the cook, four-times married and very black Berenice, whose wisdom tells Frankie, "I believe the sun has fried your brains," and the fantast decides to take over. Part two is the day before the wedding, and F. Jasmine puts on a pink dress instead of blue-jeans, lipstick and perfume, and wanders about town with tales of the wedding. Wanting to be somebody new and romantic, she rejects Berenice's theory that we're caught, "I born Berenice. You born Frankie. . . . Me is me and you is you." In part three, disappointed because she could not go with the bride and groom on the honeymoon, Frankie does show signs of growing up into Frances and chooses a girl friend, Mary Littlejohn. Frances is more reasonable than, but not really as attractive as, Frankie or Jasmine; but that's the way growing up is.

Flannery O'Connor (1925–1964)

There is some sharpness in the disparity of critical opinion on Flannery O'Connor's work. For instance, when Stanley Hyman undertakes evaluation he states: "Two points must be made immediately. The first is that despite the prevailing opinion, she was primarily a novelist, not a short story writer, and consequently her novels are better and more important than even the best of her stories." This is pompous and flies in the face of some very sensitive judges among "the prevailing opinion." The kind of thing Miss O'Connor does is not only easier to take in small doses; it works best in the shorter forms. This is no disgrace. Katherine Anne Porter has survived very well with it, among others. Robert Drake, whose critical pamphlet on Flannery O'Connor appeared in the same year as Mr. Hyman's (1966), more judiciously states, "her real *forte* is the short story—and for reasons which are perhaps not difficult to ascertain. The violent but fiercely controlled intensity with which she wrote is extremely difficult to sustain for the length of a novel, and the ironic reversals on which so many of her plots turn seem to demand the shorter fictional form. Her prose style itself is . . . perfectly adapted to her highly compressed story form . . . ; in her novels . . . too much of the canvas remains empty after the bold outline has been violently brushed on." Stated most simply, Hyman is wrong and precisely the opposite is true. This kind of red flag to the bull reaction is something Miss O'Connor does to people (and *that* perhaps is good), probably because she writes about religion and religious beliefs almost exclusively—which touches most concerned persons on sensitive areas, where they live. Perhaps Mr. Hyman who refers to Flannery O'Connor's being an outsider as a Roman Catholic in the South as a parallel to Nathanael West's alienation as a Jew alienated from other Jews, is leaning over backward to do justice to her alien religious views. Reading her fiction is somewhat like a contest between fascinated curiosity and repulsion; in most cases curiosity can win out for up to forty pages. Getting back to his *second* point, "that any discussion of her theology can only be preliminary to, not a substitute for, aesthetic analysis and evaluation," the only response is "of course"—if you can get that far.

In Flannery O'Connor the Hound of Heaven (a perfectly legitimate and effective image in the poem by Francis Thompson) seems sometimes more like a monstrous wolf with blood-dripping fangs. Christ the Tiger is somehow a cleaner, swifter destroyer than the "bleeding stinking mad" Jesus of the O'Connor fiction. The particular combination of her Catholicism and the closely observed Southern Bible-belt Protestantism has been partly responsible for her particular and peculiar grotesque. Even if she takes "a grim ironic pleasure in siding *with* the Southern fundamentalists" and their eccentricities against the modern indifferent intellectuals of the North and elsewhere, as Robert Drake seems to believe, there still seem to be barbs for non-Catholic blindness, for the Baptists and Methodists particularly, rather than simply "condescension" in her fiction. The London *Times* early identified Flannery O'Connor as a "theological" writer, which evidently pleased her. It is not always easy to tell whether she is using theology for fictional purposes or fiction for theological purposes, but perhaps it doesn't matter. She has been called the most radical Christian dualist since Dostoevsky; her subject seems to be Vocation, "that the way to sanctity is through the greatest sinfulness." As long as one wins through, this is all right; but in most of her fiction the outcome of the struggle remains highly doubtful. Far too often the double question must be asked of a particular character or a particular symbol (like the Dragon in the epigraph to *A Good Man Is Hard to Find*): "Is it the Devil who has many protean forms . . . ? Or is it perhaps even Christ the tiger . . . ?" One may admire ambiguity, even seven types thereof, but in a writer to whom the Christian questions and answers have the only validity one might expect greater clarity on such an issue. Is Hazel Motes anti-Christ or Christ, or one becoming the other? Some readers might be damned in trying to figure it out.

John Hawkes, speaking in tribute to Flannery O'Connor and again coupling her name with that of Nathanael West whose work she so much admired and whose "cartoon" effects she copied, calls attention to a certain Satanism: "I would propose that Nathanael West and Flannery O'Connor are very nearly alone today in their pure creation of 'aesthetic authority,' and would also propose, of course, that they are very nearly alone in their employment of the devil's voice as vehicle for their satire or for what we may call their true (or accurate) vision of our godless actuality." She has tried to justify the violence and grotesquerie of her writing in this symposium statement:

> The novelist with Christian concerns will find in modern life distortions which are repugnant to him, and his problem will be to make these appear as distortions to an audience which is used to seeing them as natural; and he may well be forced to take over more violent means to get his vision across to this hostile audience. When you can assume that your audience holds the same beliefs as you do, you can relax a little and use more normal ways of talking to it; when you have to assume that it does not, then you have to make your vision apparent by shock—to the hard of hearing you shout, and for the almost blind you draw large and startling figures.

Louise Gossett in her book on *Violence in Recent Southern Fiction* (1965) says of this, "Implicit in this method of enlargement is the danger of creating caricatures who evoke no response from the reader instead of characters who provoke pity and compassion or even disgust." When lusts and afflictions are exaggerated, people may be dehumanized. To those who say that Miss O'Connor's use of sexuality (in some of its more violent and repulsive manifestations) is a surrogate for religious experience one need only point out that Hosea did it much more effectively, and so did the church commentators on *The Song of Songs.* Haze Motes in the arms of his whore and the sodomitic rape of the young Marion Tarwater do nothing at all for most readers to suggest the experience of the holy spirit. The Cult of the Gratuitous Grotesque is a phrase that often serves, particularly in the novels, to explain an excessive violence of conception.

The initial impact of Flannery O'Connor may be greater than her staying power. Almost any reader does "a double take" upon first reading a story by her (it refuses to be ignored). But there is a very real danger in overplay or overkill or overwrite—second readings do not lead to the third, except perhaps for the very devoted. Perhaps Miss O'Connor misjudged her fellow men, her audience, after all; certainly she did not judge them kindly. It is almost silly to speak of her characters; they are almost all caricatures. Perhaps the clue to her is a Swiftian misanthropy. Interestingly enough she regarded herself, after the religious position has been understood, as a regionalist. Of New York cosmopolites she is reported to have said, "You know what's the matter with all that kind of folks? They ain't frum anywhere!" And she claimed interest in the Old Adam (sin, it is supposed), "He just talks Southern because I do." She has been called a "Roman Catholic Erskine Caldwell," which isn't bad from many points of view: Georgia-centered stance, grotesque technique, poor-white characters (although Flannery has a larger collection of types, a more crowded canvas), largely rural settings (again Miss O'Connor can add the city), relative evaluations, and both essentially short story writers—even when episodes are strung together for novel length. The third Georgia writer in the trio is, of course, Carson McCullers, with the larger dimensions of Flannery O'Connor and not limited by the restrictive subject matter of religious perspective.

Mr. Hyman says that Protestant Fundamentalism is "Miss O'Connor's metaphor, in literary terms, for Roman Catholic truth (in theological terms, this reflects ecumenicism)." To deny the malice in Miss O'Connor's picture of the Protestant South is to ignore the overall tone of her work and, indeed, the strength of her gift for caricature and cartoon. (Have you ever known a spiritual political cartoonist?) To say that she is ecumenical in her views is equally strange. She is about as ecumenical as the masses of Dublin Catholics who have resisted strongly the efforts of Pope John and Pope Paul in this direction. To add that this author abhors sentimentality (a good modern characteristic) and thus is objective in her portraits is not to excuse her for the absence of some honest sentiment and human feeling. Her generation gap between parents and children is brutal, and in most cases you can't even regard the children as innocent. It is possible that she is a Black Humorist like Nathanael West before the term became current.

One of Mr. Hyman's best observations is that "If the male characters are all God-intoxicated, the female characters in Flannery O'Connor's fiction are mainly self-intoxicated. Smugness and self-satisfaction, often represented by women, is another important theme." She gives the impression at times of having become a character in her own fiction, one of these women. Certainly her work most closely resembles that of Nathanael West, but there is a major difference. One might say that even with his caricatures, there is much kindness in the Jew, but not in the ungentle Gentile. Her chief flaw may well lie in an apparent lack of compassion ("the only way to be really despicable is to be contemptuous of other people's pain," said one of Baldwin's characters)—this has been called her "objectivity" and "aesthetic distance," God forbid. (And Faustus said, "God forbade it indeed; but Faustus hath done it . . ."—there is here a kind of pact with Satan.) To say this is not to be anti-Catholic, although it might seem so; for full measure of compassion (and objectivity) one need only look at James Joyce and Mary Lavin (see Volume II). In certain ways Flannery changed her name quite deliberately from Joy to Hulga; Mary should have been a harder name to give up than it was. Which came first, the life or the fiction, would be difficult to determine. Perhaps, to paraphrase the old injunction, Be careful what you pray for—you might get it, one should be careful what kind of fiction one writes—it may become the habit of the soul. R. I. P. Which came first, the chicken or the egg? It is hard to forget the exhibitionism of that chicken that walked backward, and its possible effects on a five-year old child. To hazard a guess, Miss O'Connor's place in American fiction is likely to be seen one day as that of a major-minor writer with a handful of short stories that, despite some flaws, will be regarded as classics in the form, and distinctly her own.

Life: Mary Flannery O'Connor (who dropped the "Mary" be-before entering the University of Iowa in 1945) was born the only child of Edward Francis and Regina Cline O'Connor on March 25, 1925 in Savannah, Georgia. Both families were Roman Catholic, and their daughter attended parochial schools. An aunt once gave her a bantam chicken that walked backward. As Flannery later wrote, "When I was five, I had an experience that marked me for life. Pathé News sent a photographer from New York to Savannah to take a picture of a chicken of mine." It was a kind of Ripley "Believe It or Not" sequence. She started collecting fowl, feeling a special affinity for them, moving from chickens eventually to peacocks and peahens. The peacock is "The King of the Birds," which charming essay appeared in *Holiday,* September 1961, as "Living with a Peacock." In 1938 it was discovered that Edward O'Connor had an incurable disease, disseminated lupus, and the family moved to his wife's home, the Cline house in Milledgeville, Georgia. The father died in 1941. The daughter graduated from Peabody High School in her new home town and there attended Georgia State College for Women, receiving her degree in 1945.

On the basis of some writing she had done, she was awarded a Rinehart Fellowship at the Writers' Workshop of the University of Iowa where she spent two years, publishing her first story, "The Geranium," in *Accent* in the summer of 1946. Other publication followed pretty regularly, with Flannery O'Connor working at Yaddo and in New York and with her Roman Catholic friends, the Fitzgeralds, in Connecticut until her first serious sickness, diagnosed in Atlanta in 1950 as disseminated lupus. Blood transfusions and a method of treatment that made her a cripple saved her life. Flannery and her mother moved to Mrs. O'Connor's country place four miles north of Milledgeville, Andalusia, a dairy farm where she was able to resume writing. *Wise Blood,* her first novel, was published in 1952; *A Good Man Is Hard to Find,* a collection of ten short stories, in 1955; and the second novel, *The Violent Bear It Away,* in 1960. Early in 1964 Flannery O'Connor had to have an abdominal operation. Although the tumor was benign, the lupus returned, and she died at the age of thirty-nine in Milledgeville on August 3, 1964. A fourth volume, the nine stories collected under the title *Everything That Rises Must Converge,* was published posthumously in 1965. Her tragic early death, like that of Nathanael West, probably stimulated increased public interest in her work.

The Works: *Wise Blood* (novel, 1952) is Flannery O'Connor's first venture into the form; it is too full of incidents that refuse to hang together. Her first novel is perhaps the least successful of her more ambitious works. The "hero" or at least the "agonist" is Hazel (Haze) Motes—the name grotesque and allegorical is easy to interpret, the mote in the eye makes things hazy—who loses his fundamentalist faith in the army, goes from his native east Tennessee to Taulkinham (obviously Atlanta) and with an inverted Calvinistic conscience preaches the Church Without Christ, "the church peaceful and satisfied!" This sequence makes an effective satiric thrust at today's smug and secular church (although possibly more telling in the Fifties than in the Seventies). As Haze says, "the blind don't see and the lame don't walk and what's dead stays that way." Then he passes from the rejection of his childhood faith through a series of violent events and self-inflicted mutilations toward a final peace, through blasphemy, seduction, and murder pursuing the truth. He blinds himself and faces God in the darkness because a rival "evangelist," Asa Hawks, has falsely claimed to have done the same thing and failed in his trust. When Haze goes on to put rocks and broken glass in his shoes and wears barbed wire around his chest (like a good Catholic medieval flagellant?), his landlady notes, "You must believe in Jesus or you wouldn't do these foolish things."

The novel is loose in structure; there are too many gratuitous and unrelated incidents of outrage; the language is often garish and distracting. But there are at least two good sequences which might have been extracted to make excellent short stories: Enoch Emery, a boy who works as a city park guard and has his own religious mysticism (a sect unto himself), dresses up as a gorilla and parades in front of a movie house; the second is the relationship between Haze and his automobile (the author has a "thing" for automobiles), an old rat-colored Essex that becomes his religious mystery—almost a fantastic parody of Dante's looking on the church as chariot. Part of Flannery's explanation of what *Wise Blood* was meant to be (prefixed to a second edition in 1962) is worth looking at: "The book was written with zest and, if possible, should be read that way. It is a comic novel about a Christian *malgré lui,* and as such, very serious, for all comic novels that are any good must be about matters of life and death." Perhaps. But whether the *malgré lui* (in spite of himself) turns out to be *manqué* (lacking or wanting) is another matter. Mr. Hyman points out that *Wise Blood* is in many ways deliberately modeled on West's *Miss Lonelyhearts,* "with many specific reminiscences of it." But it doesn't work as well, possibly because it lacks the universal modern metaphor of the West novel.

The Violent Bear It Away (novel, 1960) is better unified than *Wise Blood,* since everything centers on Francis Marion Tarwater, the boy who is a reluctant prophet (Moses' and Jonah's reluctance form background reference) and who would be the central character if he were not so caricatured and two-dimensional. The theme at least is clearer, but the vocation does not seem significantly sacred, or for that matter even human or humane. Hyman establishes the meaning of the title and its context with ease: "the violent are enemies of the kingdom, capturing it from the righteous, as a sign of the imminent coming of the Messiah." But when young Tarwater is left at the end "entirely violent and mad," it is difficult to see him as a true prophet, certainly not in the tradition. There are fewer "characters" in this novel and we are in rural Georgia, only heading toward the city at the end. Young Tarwater has as much of a split personality as his predecessor, Haze Motes, half godly, half satanic, although it is not always easy for the reader to tell which is which. The great-uncle, Mason Tarwater, a mad prophet who made bootleg whiskey, brings up the boy to the vocation of prophecy, the boy alternately resisting and submitting in stages marked by violence. There is another uncle, George Rayber, plain nephew to Mason, who is the "secular antagonist," the rationalist (called Satanic, but aren't they all?), and his idiot son named Bishop whose baptism Marion has been ordered to carry out.

Young Tarwater first rebels against vocation by getting drunk and burning the house down instead of decently burying his great-uncle who has died at table before the first sentence: "Francis Marion Tarwater's uncle had been dead for only half a day when the boy got too drunk to finish digging his grave and a Negro named Buford Munson, who had come to get a jug filled, had to finish it and drag the body from the breakfast table where it was still sitting and bury it in a decent and Christian way, with the sign of its Saviour at the head of the grave and enough dirt on top to keep the dogs from digging it up." The baptism of Bishop turns out to be a drowning as well. Hunger and thirst torment young Tarwater as he walks back to his home clearing. He is picked up by a young man in a lavender shirt (either the devil or an angel of God, take your pick), is drugged and sodomitically raped. At this point it would be interesting to compare O'Connor's Tarwater with Malamud's Fidelman in a similar situation—to the advantage probably of Fidelman (and Malamud) who learns something from the experience. Finally Tarwater sees a burning tree flaring up out of the forest fire he has set; this is the burning bush of Moses and he moves off toward the city to prophesy.

Mr. Hyman thinks this novel Miss O'Connor's masterpiece, but this will not be an acceptable judgment for many people. To view arson, murder, and sodomy as preparation for the prophetic profession seems a little much. Granted that sinners make good preachers. Saint Augustine and John Donne prove that wasted youth may be no waste at all and that a knowledge of the world, the flesh, and the devil may be a basis for desire of the other world. But we see neither works nor faith acceptable in the sight of the Lord in any of the Tarwaters, nor any deepening of insight either. It is true that both fire and water, universal symbols of a double baptism, are used in original ways to represent both destruction and salvation, but they seem here a travesty of Dante's vision and even of Eliot's more modern use in *The Wasteland.* This novel is short as novels go (the language is under better control and the situation tighter than in the first one), but it seems curiously long. Could anyone desire to meet any character in either novel under any circumstances? It is hard to imagine. But this demurrer does not necessarily hold for the short stories.

Short Stories: Considerable difference of opinion as to the best of Miss O'Connor's shorter fiction is probably to be expected. Mr. Hyman's preferences are sound ones. The most often anthologized, the title story "A Good Man Is Hard to Find," is less impressive than many of the others: a "melodrama about a family casually wiped out by an escaped criminal called the Misfit, and in spots it is cruelly funny." The talkative grandmother and the criminal have the most interesting exchange of conversation for the author's purpose. " 'If you would pray,' the old lady said, 'Jesus would help you.' . . . 'I don't want no hep,' he said. 'I'm doing all right by myself.' " When her son Bailey Boy is shot, she "carries on." The Misfit tells her, "Jesus was the only One that ever raised the dead, . . . and He shouldn't have done it. He throws everything off balance." The story is a little off balance too.

"The Artificial Nigger" from the same volume is one of her best stories and is reported to have been Miss O'Connor's own favorite. Here we have exceptionally two characters who come alive as persons, two country people, Old Mr. Head and his grandson Nelson who take a trip to Atlanta by train and return that night. The two live alone and have only each other, Mr. Head's wife and only daughter, after giving birth to Nelson, having died. For the old man at sixty it is his third trip to the city. Nelson at ten insists it is his "second" trip since he has been told that he was born there. They have a good relationship, although Nelson shows some impudence. The grandfather wants him "to see everything there is to see in a city so that he would be content to stay at home for the rest of his life." One of the most terrifying aspects of the city is the sewer system; to offset the boy's pride in having been born in the city, his grandfather has him stick his head into a sewer entrance and explains how it is full of rats and undermines everything. Nelson has never seen a Negro before, and he has several encounters with them during the day, half repelled but inexplicably attracted to a large Negro woman he wants to hold him. The most important part of the story is the estrangement and reconciliation of grandfather and grandson. Nelson accuses the old man of losing their lunch and their way as they walk. When, running, he knocks down an old white woman and her groceries on the street, she yelling for a policeman, Mr. Head panics and reenacts the denial of Christ by Peter: " 'This is not my boy,' he said. 'I never seen him before.' " After the separation—at least twenty paces—of Nelson's contempt and his grandfather's guilt and shame and the coming on of dark, Mr. Head cries to a fat man approaching, "I'm lost and can't find my way and me and this boy have got to catch this train and I can't find the station. Oh Gawd I'm lost!" Finally the reconciliation of the pair occurs when they see on a lawn the shabby plaster figure of a Negro about the size of Nelson eating watermelon; both exclaim "An artificial nigger!" And they could feel a new communion, "dissolving their differences like an action of mercy." There is a bit of theological explication at the end, but it doesn't interfere with the story, which is quiet and believable and feelingly presents the only two characters in O'Connor fiction to find anything like peace this side of the grave.

"Good Country People" is one of the more grotesque stories; Hyman calls it "the author's cruelest self-caricature." There is hostility between a mother Mrs. Hopewell and her daughter Joy, a large blonde thirty-two with an artificial leg and glasses, thoroughly unpleasant, unattractive, and well educated (with a Ph.D.), who had changed her name legally at twenty-one from Joy to Hulga, having thought long to find "the ugliest name in any language." Hulga wears a yellow sweat shirt with a cowboy's picture on it and is a confirmed atheist who vaunts her views whenever possible. When a Bible salesman appears on their farm ("I'm a country boy") Hulga sets out cynically to seduce him, but it works in reverse. When they climb to the loft of a barn, the boy with the Bibles with much persuasion gets her to remove her artificial leg. His hollow Bible contains a flask of whiskey, pornographic playing cards, and a package of condoms. As he leaves Joy-Hulga taking her leg as a souvenir (he once got a glass eye that way), he tells the professed intellectual atheist, "you ain't so smart. I been believing in nothing ever since I was born!" The story ends precisely where it should with a picture frame return to Mrs. Hopewell talking with Mrs. Freeman, as they watch the young man in the bright blue suit moving toward the highway.

"The Displaced Person," the longest, most ambitious story in the volume *A Good Man Is Hard to Find,* is a candidate for best story provided one doesn't push too hard the religious interpretation; it's there but should rest easy. Mrs. McIntyre, three times married (once widowed, twice divorced) runs a dairy farm, has problems with her help and personal problems. Her chief confidante is the wife of the hired man, Mr. Shortley; as a matter of fact the first third of the story seems to be seen through Mrs. Shortley's eyes with their narrow fundamentalist Protestant squint. A priest, Father Flynn (it's good to see one among the other caricatures), has persuaded Mrs. McIntyre to take on a Polish refugee family, the Guizacs, apparently in the post-World War II period. Mr. Guizac, the displaced person, is of course Roman Catholic, and the priest uses his visits to Mrs. McIntyre to offer instruction in attempting to convert her. Mrs. Shortley offers a classic definition of Displaced Persons (rather like Frost's definitions of "home" in "The Hired Man") to the old Negro Astor, "It means they ain't where they were born at and there's nowhere for them to go—like if you was run out of here and wouldn't nobody have you." When she overhears Mrs. McIntyre threaten to give Mr. Shortley his month's notice (Mr. Guizac has been such a good worker that he has shown up the others), she packs up her family and in the car when they drive away has a stroke and dies and becomes a displaced person; her dead eyes "seemed to contemplate for the first time the tremendous frontiers of her true country."

Mrs. McIntyre becomes most disturbed when she learns that Mr. Guizac is trying to arrange a marriage between the Negro Sulk and his sixteen-year-old blonde cousin who is still in a displaced persons camp in Europe and will do anything to get to America. Trying to express her displeasure and uneasiness to Father Flynn, she says of Guizac, "He didn't have to come in the first place." The priest who has been talking of Christ answers, "He came to redeem us." They usually talk past each other. " 'As far as I'm concerned,' she said and glared at him fiercely, 'Christ was just another D.P.' " And in

His human nature he was; but in His divine nature the priest sees him in the peacock who wanders through most of the story and spreads his tail in glory—"Christ will come like that!" But Christ in the conversation embarrasses Mrs. McIntyre "the way sex had her mother." Mr. Guizac becomes further displaced when rehired Mr. Shortley with the connivance of others allows a tractor to run over and kill him. Finally Mrs. McIntyre, collapsed, bedridden, and alone, becomes a displaced person at the end of the story. She had said earlier of Mr. Guizac as a good and efficient worker, "that man is my salvation." Of course he might have been; but it seems going too far to see his death for which she shares the guilt as "redemptive for her insofar as it abases her pride and prepares her to accept the burden of the world's misery." It is exactly this that she never does accept.

"Parker's Back" from the volume *Everything That Rises Must Converge* is certainly one of the best stories in Miss O'Connor's fiction and an unusual one by any standards. It is reminiscent of Kafka's "In the Penal Colony" without any suggestion of influence. A young man, O. E. Parker has had himself tattooed just about everywhere except for his back from the age of fifteen through five years in the navy, adding to his collection of pictures indiscriminately. He marries a woman Sarah Ruth, a plain, even ugly woman, because she wouldn't let him have her any other way. She marries him possibly because in her piety she meant to save him (her father was a Straight Gospel preacher), possibly because she discovers that his initials stand for Obadiah Elihue. She does *not* like his tattoos, in contrast to the other women he has known. After increasing tensions—she is pregnant; he has work problems—in a flash of inspiration Parker runs off to the city to the tattoo artist to have a Byzantine mosaic Christ reproduced on his back—literally becoming *christophoros* or Christ-bearing, "witnessing for Jesus," although he denies this, apparently only wanting to please his wife. However, Parker's life *is* changed; he resumes the name of Obadiah which he had hidden. He passively allows his wife to beat him for "idolatry" until large welts had formed on the face of the tattooed Christ. Obadiah Elihue is last seen in the yard leaning against the tree, crying like a baby. Notice that "against the tree" is not underlined. Hyman calls this metaphor of tattooing for the Christ-marked man, ludicrous though it is, a truly metaphysical conceit. This is a weird story, if you will, but effective.

William Styron (born 1925)

Although William Styron has already been placed in divergent categories, notably the group of southern novelists who in the tradition of regionalists and rural naturalists write of violence (Caldwell, Faulkner, Robert Penn Warren, Flannery O'Connor, Truman Capote, Carson McCullers among others as discussed by Louise Gossett in *Violence in Recent Southern Fiction*) and the existentialists, as in Robert Gorham Davis' essay "The American Individualist Tradition: Bellow and Styron," it is perhaps too early to feel secure about any classification. The close of his first novel, *Lie Down in Darkness,* incorporates the interior monologue of Peyton Loftis which has been admired as an extreme form of stream of consciousness technique.

Perhaps one of the most interesting suggested frames of reference is that of the critical essay by Robert H. Fossum in *Contemporary Writers in Christian Perspective*: one of the novelists " 'more vitally and directly concerned with religion in fiction than any preceding age.' " He couples his name with that of Flannery O'Connor, who certainly represents an American Southern Catholic extension of the return to tradition and faith of Mauriac, Waugh, Claudel, and Graham Greene. (Bernard Malamud might well represent an American Jewish "return to the faith.") The Protestants are not as well represented, perhaps because their form of belief and more diffuse rituals do not lend themselves as effectively to fictional needs, symbols, pegs to hang a story on, as Catholicism and Hebraism. Styron, however, might be considered a representative of Protestant concern. Although suspicious of "systematic theology and institutionalized faith," he reveals in his first four novels the feeling "that America is suffering from a disease of the spirit which 'cries out for a religious interpretation, an interpretation in terms of finitude, anxiety, sin, guilt, despair, grace, repentance, faith, regeneration, and eschatological interpretation.' "

As a Southern writer Styron is not rural; he is middle-class, urban, and contemporary—which means post World War II. As an existentialist he is clearly of the religious rather than atheistic tradition. One other thing is clear: since the publication of *The Confessions of Nat Turner* in 1967 Styron is in the vortex of a controversy which shows few signs of diminishing. This novel has been highly praised and as deeply damned, the split generally between interpretations of the white and black communities. In it Styron turns to the materials of an "historical novel," with perhaps some additional attempts to make it "documentary" in the manner of Capote's *In Cold Blood*. Its "most daring and brilliant feature . . . : the first-person point of view from which we see the novel's focal center—the mind of Nat Turner himself" is also the center of attack by black critics for its inauthenticity, whether deliberate or inadvertent. The subject, the Turner-led Negro insurrection in Tidewater Virginia in 1831, has, as everyone recognizes, relevance to "more recent, more massive Negro rebellion." Fossum puts the author's intentions this way: "Determined to confront directly the racial specter of his Southern heritage, Styron felt that for a man of his generation a third-person account would be both morally and artistically evasive. He had to understand the psychology of the black slave; he had to abandon the objective stance . . . assumed by Faulkner, his literary master, in depicting Negroes; in short, he had to see and feel what Turner saw and felt."

In *William Styron's Nat Turner: Ten Black Writers Respond*, edited by John Henrik Clarke in 1968, the opposition has stated its case most succinctly: the Nat Turner created by Styron "has little resemblance to the Virginia slave insurrectionist who is a hero to his people." The claim is that historical facts are ignored. "Is there a difference between William Styron's stereotyped portrayal of Nat Turner and the current racial bigots' opinion of civil rights leaders?" H. Rap Brown and Stokely Carmichael, for instance. One of the greatest points of sensitivity seems to be sexual—"to degrade and emasculate the character of Nat Turner," denying him a father and a black wife. There are frequent references to "The Confessions of Willie Styron." "Nat Turner still awaits a literary interpreter worthy of his sacrifice."

Without wishing to take sides in racial controversy, it can be said that Styron has spent much time and energy in recent years appearing in panel discussions around the country, followed by a "black tornado" released from the Ajax bottle of Nat Turner. It is to be hoped that he can someday return to the writing of fiction.

Life: Born in 1925 in Newport (or Newport News), Virginia, William Styron comes from the Ellen Glasgow part of the South. Educated at Davidson College and Duke University (where he received a degree in 1947), he interrupted his education to serve in the Marine Corps. His first novel, started at Duke, *Lie Down in Darkness,* was published in 1951 and received immediate critical attention. There were still visible influences of Faulkner and Fitzgerald (an interesting combination) and perhaps Thomas Wolfe. The second novel, *The Long March,* much shorter as a novel and directed against war as well as against stupidity in the marines, appeared in 1955; the third, *Set This House on Fire,* in 1960. Having married Rose Burgunder in 1953, Styron lived for some time abroad, including Italy, then moved with his family to Roxbury, Connecticut. The publication of *The Confessions of Nat Turner* in 1967 brought him the Pulitzer Prize in 1968.

Chief Novels: *Lie Down in Darkness* (novel, 1951) has a title from Sir Thomas Browne's *Urn Burial* and an epigraph from *Finnegans Wake*: "Carry me along, taddy, like you done through the toy fair." It begins "Riding down to Port Warwick from Richmond" in Virginia Tidewater country on the funeral day of Peyton Loftis, being brought "home" from her suicide in New York City; time present is the journey from the railroad station to the cemetery, but through the memories of unhappy people in the interrupted funeral procession, even at the end Peyton's recreated consciousness, we traverse the sad and tangled lives of the Loftis family and a few associates: Milton Loftis, Peyton's sometime lawyer father who loved her too well, even incestuously when drunk—which was most of the time; Helen Loftis, the mother who has the money but also a father-fixation problem—the daughter tells her "The terrible thing is that you hate yourself so much that . . . you hate everything;" Dolly Bonner, Milton's mistress and a childish woman who keeps him thinking himself young (he's rather like Tommy Wilhelm in Bellow's *Seize the Day*); and the Reverend Carey Carr, representing the church and trying to reconcile the secular and the sanctified with "good taste."

As Peyton grew up her mother was more concerned about her sister Maudie, physically and mentally defective. At Maudie's death Milton had gotten drunk and attended a homecoming with Peyton at the University of Virginia. Perhaps it's for this desertion that the jealous Helen refuses so long to attend Peyton's funeral. Peyton, having discovered her father's infidelity with Dolly, marries in some haste without love, and takes another step toward suicide. Both Milton and Helen tend to confuse God with their own fathers. They are aware that in the country-club living of the between-wars period, many of the values of the older generation in Tidewater Virginia have been lost, but they are too much the victims of confusion and apathy to find them again. Although the moments before the suicide of Peyton, also confused, apathetic, and lost, are the climax of the novel before the end of the funeral, there is a kind of appendage in the picture of the Dilsey-like Ella Swann, the maid in the Loftis household, engaged in a revivalist (Daddy Faith) affirmation as a kind of answer to the negative conclusions of Helen and Milton. Their last cries had been "Nothing! Die, damn you, die! . . . Nothing! Nothing!" Ella can say, "Yes Jesus! Yeah! Yeah!" From the bottom there is no place to go but up.

The Confessions of Nat Turner (novel, 1967) is a *tour de force* not only as an imaginative reconstruction of historical events in the insurrection of Nat Turner in 1831 in Tidewater Virginia in which blacks killed fifty-five whites in two days before suppression but as the reconstructed thoughts and motivations of Nat Turner himself, the "black John Brown," as Edmund Wilson called him. The structure of the book is somewhat similar to the time scheme of *Lie Down in Darkness.* It begins with "Judgment Day" when Nat Turner, having been captured in a cave in the Dismal Swamp, is given his death-sentence. The next section, "Visions, Dreams, Recollections," leads back to the childhood and growing up of Nat Turner in "Old Times Past." Then comes the story of the massacre in "Study War," ending with "It Is Done . . ." as the execution is carried out. Nat Turner sees himself both as Christ and as an Old Testament prophet, leading the Negro slaves like the ancient Jews out of an Egyptian bondage.

As he remembers his past, and many of his thoughts are sexual as well as religious, he talks about his first Master Samuel Turner who helped him learn to read, about the book taken from the library, Bunyan's *Life and Death of Mr. Badman* rather than its companion volume, *Grace Abounding*. Other characters are numerous: Willis, another slave for whom Nat feels real affection; the evil Reverend Mr. Eppes; a new master, Joseph Travis; Richard Whitehead and his sister Margaret, who becomes the subject of a sexual and obsessive fantasy; and Will, who becomes a kind of second-in-command of the rebellion, hating and terrible in his anger. After his capture Nat Turner dictates his "confessions" to a lawyer, Thomas Gray, at best a devil's advocate, at worst an anti-Christ or false prophet. Styron's purpose seems to have been a "kind of religious allegory" in which slaves "exercise their powers of moral and spiritual choice by destroying their owners" with a warning, "that those who are heedless of the lessons of history are doomed to repeat its mistakes." His purpose, perhaps, has not been achieved; but there should be room for many different fictional portrayals of historical figures. Styron seems honestly disturbed by the uproar he has caused.

AMERICAN DRAMA: MID-CENTURY

III

10. Modes and New European Influences

American drama had come of age by 1930. With the award of the Nobel Prize to Eugene O'Neill in 1936, everybody knew it. For an account of the coming of age of American drama you are referred to Volume III. The dominant modes had been established in realism and naturalism, and experiments in anti-realism and expressionism (both the Strindberg and Kaiser-Toller varieties) had been initiated with some success. But in the period after 1930 two new European influences gave the American theatre new directions and new techniques: the theatre of Bertolt Brecht and later the Theatre of the Absurd (for a fuller discussion of these see Volume I). Of course by this time influences were moving in both directions across the Atlantic, and plays like *Death of a Salesman* (1949) created in Europe almost the kind of sensation that German expressionist dramas created in America in the Twenties.

Bertolt Brecht (1898–1956), the German left-wing dramatist whose earliest plays (1918–1927) grew out of the school of expressionism, particularly influenced by Wedekind, Toller, and Kaiser, soon evolved his own style and techniques which he talked about as Epic Theatre and Alienation-effects (*Verfremdungseffekt*). These were to create a "non-Aristotelian" theatre, without cathartic emotions for the audience but rather "preachment, protest, and persuasion." He intended to be seriously didactic. Epic Theatre, or "non-dramatic drama," was really rather episodic and directed at a thinking audience who should never be allowed to forget that they were in a theatre. Alienation-effects, the use of narrators, placards, non-realistic sets (or none at all), acting that breaks up empathy (with direct address to the audience and comments on the action), were to be used for distancing, for shattering the illusionism and emotionalism of realistic, naturalistic, or romantic drama. In his best plays, *The Threepenny Opera* (1928), *Mother Courage and Her Children* (1939), *Galileo* (1938–39), *The Good Woman of Setzuan* (1940), and *The Caucasian Chalk Circle* (1945), his theories did not always work according to plan. The plays are more dramatically effective, even with emotional involvement, than he proposed; the new techniques created a fresh approach to the stage, and Brecht came to have his primary appeal to the intellectuals rather than instructing and influencing the masses in accordance with his announced aim.

In 1941 Brecht escaped the Nazi arms that were reaching out for him in Denmark, Sweden, and Finland, by coming to the United States where he remained until summoned in 1947 before the Committee on Un-American Activities. With his airline reservation in his pocket he lied to the Committee, received their thanks, went to New York, and left for Europe. While living on the edge of Hollywood he had worked with Charles Laughton on a version of *Galileo* in English which opened in New York in December of 1947. Whether Thornton Wilder knew Brecht's work or whether he developed quite independently the techniques of *Our Town* (1938) and *The Skin of Our Teeth* (1942), there is clearly a similarity of dramatic approach in both writers (Wilder has been highly inventive, but he has also read widely and quickly the best modern literature which he has not hesitated to adapt—*Finnegans Wake* (1939) into *The Skin of Our Teeth*, for instance). Brechtian influence continues to affect the staging of such plays and the writing of "protest" drama in the Sixties like Kenneth H. Brown's *The Brig* (1963), Van Itallie's *America Hurrah* (1966), and Megan Terry's *Viet Rock* (1966).

The Theatre of the Absurd developed in Paris in the Fifties and Sixties and very soon reached into England and America. The adaptation of Kafka's *The Trial* for the stage by André Gide and Jean-Louis Barrault in 1947 may have been an inciting cause, but Eugène Ionesco with *The Bald Soprano* (*La Cantatrice Chauve*), billed as an "anti-play" in 1950, followed by *The Chairs* (1951), *The Killer, Rhinoceros,* and *Exit the King* (1963) and Samuel Beckett with *Waiting for Godot* (1952–53), *Endgame* (1957), and *Krapp's Last Tape* (1959) established Theatre of the Absurd as something very serious indeed. This has been reaffirmed by the awarding of the Nobel Prize to Beckett in 1969. Absurdist drama reflects the philosophical despair of much of existentialism, but its theatrical principles are primarily reductive (not only anti-Aristotelian like Brecht but anti-play): characters are reduced almost to non-entities (in fact there is almost always an "identity" crisis), plot is minimal if there is any, place and time are often reduced to any place and any time, language or dialogue is minimized, made absurd, close to being eliminated (actually eliminated in Beckett's *Act Without Words*—which shortens a play considerably). The English modify absurd theatre by making it English (giving it a setting in England with recognizably British dialogue, however minimal) as in Harold Pinter and David Storey (see Volume II). In America our chief dramatist to be influenced by Theatre of the Absurd is Edward Albee. His first play, *The Zoo Story,* was presented as one half of a double bill with Beckett's *Krapp's Last Tape* quite appropriately.

Albee, however, also modifies absurdist drama by making it American. *The Zoo Story* is set in Central Park in New York City and belongs there. The characters, more fully developed than most in this kind of play, express a kind of minimal or potential optimism which breaks through the levels of despair. Albee is pretty clearly the most significant new American dramatist of the Sixties and takes his place easily with Tennessee Williams and Arthur Miller. Other young talent in the American theatre, like Sam Shepard, are apparently taking off from Brechtian and Absurdist bases to move (who knows where for sure?) at least in the direction of satire and social comment.

11. The American Theatre after 1930

The period of American drama which began around 1930 and continued through the Forties and Fifties, was an era of assimilation and refinement, a period in which the radical new techniques of the Twenties were popularized and perfected by a new generation of dramatists. There is scarcely anything new in the drama of this period which cannot be traced to the Twenties; yet some of the post-1945 dramas of Arthur Miller (*Death of a Salesman*) and *Tennessee Williams* (*The Glass Menagerie* and *A Streetcar Named Desire*) far surpass the more awkward experiments of the earlier era in their subtlety and maturity. These plays especially represent an essentially new combination of realism-naturalism and expressionism in which the elements of both are so welded together as to be inseparable. One of the innovations of Tennessee Williams, the presentation of a "Memory" play, although it has roots in dream play technique, combines the easy fade, "dissolve," flashback approach of the films (which began with such devices as slipping back through the pages of a calendar) with devices of screen, music, and lighting to make *The Glass Menagerie* (1944–45) what has come to be seen as a pioneer effort. The Memory plays that follow, *Death of a Salesman,* Hugh Leonard's *Stephen D.* (1962), and Brian Friel's *Philadelphia, Here I Come* (1965), make this clear in retrospect.

Naturally many of the old generation of the Twenties continued to produce plays. Eugene O'Neill, the old master-dramatist, had a new creative period—almost an independent career in the Forties and Fifties and posthumously: *The Iceman Cometh* (1946), *A Moon for the Misbegotten* (1953), *Long Day's Journey into Night* (1955), *A Touch of the Poet* (1957), *More Stately Mansions* (1962). In the period from 1930 to 1960 certain highly competent, major American dramatists established themselves as dominating the field, just below but often touching O'Neill himself: Maxwell Anderson, Lillian Hellman, Arthur Miller, Tennessee Williams, Thornton Wilder (who must not be forgotten although included elsewhere), and T. S. Eliot (with the same parenthesis). To get the full spectrum of American drama in this period one must add

William Saroyan as well, and such other novelists and poet-dramatists who may have written only one or two plays, William Carlos Williams, E. E. Cummings, Archibald MacLeish, for instance. This was a rich era of American drama.

In the Sixties Williams and Miller have continued to write drama. The big new star is Edward Albee, but there are other important new dramatists too. Lorraine Hansberry with *A Raisin in the Sun* (1959) and *The Sign in Sidney Brustein's Window* (1964) gave every indication of being a major talent. Her promise was cut off by death at the age of thirty-four in 1965. In many ways her newly oriented problem plays suggest the quality of Lillian Hellman. At the end of the Sixties signs of promise have been seen in Jean-Claude Van Itallie for *America Hurrah* (1966) and in Sam Shepard (born 1943—his one-act plays like *Chicago, Red Cross, Icarus's Mother* seem more exciting than his longer *La Turista* and *Operation Sidewinder*); but their talent has yet to crystallize. Very frequently these days a first play will stir up real excitement—*The Basic Training of Pavlo Hummel* (1971) by David Rabe, or *Museeka* (1968—"full of Brechtian tricks") and the second play, *The House of Blue Leaves* by John Guare (1971), for instance. The problems of Broadway production in the last thirty years have contributed first to Off-Broadway and then to Off-Off-Broadway theatre. In these equivalents of left-bank experimental drama are probably the future directions of the American stage.

Sidney Kingsley (born 1906)

Kingsley is a deliberate and conscientious craftsman who works slowly, produces a relatively small quantity of work, and polishes each play to perfection before he is done with it. His creative method is essentially that of the European naturalists, as much as he sometimes differs from them in content. He bases his writing on painstaking research; he customarily spends from two to five years gathering material before he writes a play. In preparing for the writing of *Men In White* he spent many months in New York hospitals, sometimes actually attending surgical operations disguised as an intern in order to obtain authentic basic data for his play. Likewise, before he wrote *Detective Story* (1949) he spent two years visiting police stations and detective squad rooms in New York City. In these plays and others like them his research method resembles that of a sociologist; the plays are virtually documentaries, based on first-hand data and organized into artistic form. In *The Patriots* (1942), on the other hand, his research method is that of the historian, based chiefly on books and documents. In either case he invariably accumulates a copious mass of data before he begins the actual writing of a play.

Although plays like *Dead End* and *Ten Million Ghosts* are in a sense exposés of modern "capitalistic corruption" and other evils of civilization, Kingsley is not exactly a political radical. He is, in fact, virtually without politics when compared with dramatists like Odets, Anderson, and Rice; his work shows a general humanitarian tendency and he shares with the Marxists the theory of environmental determinism, but he is reluctant to offer a neat solution for society's ills in the form of any political program or philosophy. He is not a polemicist; he is first of all a professional playwright, concerned primarily with questions of dramaturgy and stagecraft. He operates on the principle that dramatic effectiveness can be obtained only through authenticity, and that authenticity is achieved through painstaking research. This formula has won him a position as one of America's leading dramatists of the post-1918 generation, and in addition has brought him financial success achieved by few other legitimate dramatists of the era.

Life: Sidney Kingsley (pseud. of Sidney Kieschner) was born in New York in 1906 and educated in New York City schools. While still a student at Townsend Hall, a secondary school, he began writing one-act plays; upon graduation he won a scholarship to Cornell, where he continued with his playwriting and gained valuable experience acting in student productions. In 1928 his *Wonder-Dark Epilogue* won a prize as the best one-act play of the year by an undergraduate writer. After college he worked briefly as an actor in a New York theatrical troupe, then spent several years as a scenario writer for Columbia Pictures. In 1933 the Group Theatre produced his *Men In White* (originally titled *Crisis*), and overnight Kingsley had won a reputation as a significant playwright. The play won a Pulitzer Prize in 1934 and was produced in London the same year; it was subsequently staged in many other European capitals, and was frequently revived in later years by small theatre groups. Sold to Metro-Goldwyn-Mayer, it was made into a successful motion picture. *Dead End* (1935) was an even greater critical and financial success; the New York stage production was acclaimed a sensation (partly due to its *succès de scandale*) and the expression "Dead End Kids" became a part of American slang. The script was again sold to Hollywood, and again a successful motion picture resulted. Nothing in Kingsley's later work matched the success of these two plays. *Ten Million Ghosts,* a pacifist drama in a semi-expressionistic technique, closed after eleven performances in 1936, and subsequent plays barely managed to break even. The play Kingsley intended as his third major work was *The Patriots,* a complicated historical drama based on the life of Thomas Jefferson which finally appeared in 1943. The play was acclaimed by reviewers and won the New York Drama Critics Circle Award for 1943, but lacked the dramatic interest to win box-office success; it was essentially a historical pageant rather than a conventional drama of conflict. Meanwhile Kingsley was serving in the army; after his discharge he wrote motion picture scenarios for a few years while gathering material for another play. This was *Detective Story,* which appeared in 1949 and was again successful both as a stage play and a motion picture. In 1951 Kingsley completed *Darkness at Noon,* an adaptation based on the Arthur Koestler novel; the play won another Critics Circle Award and was generally favorably reviewed. In 1954 appeared *Lunatics and Lovers,* a farcical comedy which demonstrated Kingsley's supple versatility as a stylist. Kingsley and his wife, the actress Madge Evans, have lived in recent years on a New Jersey farm.

Chief Works: *Men In White* (drama, 1933) presents a detailed picture of the daily routine of a modern hospital as well as a study of ethical conflict in the mind of a young doctor. George Ferguson, a young intern training in surgery under the noted specialist Hochberg in a New York hospital, is in love with the wealthy Laura Hudson and hopes to marry her soon and take her with him to Vienna, where he plans to continue his studies. At present, however, he has little time for her because of the demands of his hospital position.

Laura, jealous and annoyed, quarrels with him, and George has a brief affair with Barbara Dennin, a nurse. Laura and George soon make up their differences, but meanwhile Barbara finds she is pregnant. She seeks escape from her situation through an abortion, which results in a dangerous infection. When she is brought by coincidence to George's hospital for treatment the young doctor is faced with a moral dilemma: should he stand by Barbara and admit his guilt for her condition, or should he sacrifice Barbara to his future with Laura? But the matter is decided for him: Laura, learning of the affair, breaks off the engagement. He resolves to marry Barbara, even though he does not love her. But Barbara's illness is fatal, and George now believes his passing folly has lost him both women. Then, however, the wise surgeon Hochberg talks to Laura and convinces her that George's affair with Barbara was only an ephemeral passion; he explains also that George's devotion to his work, the original cause of the misunderstanding between the two young people, is a splendid and admirable thing and in no way incompatible with his love for her. The young couple are reconciled; George, now wiser and more steadfast in his ideals, goes off alone to Vienna, promising to marry Laura on his return.

Dead End (drama, 1935) is a bitter Depression play somewhat resembling Elmer Rice's *Street Scene* (1929) but more convincingly authentic in its use of slang and big-city local color. The setting symbolically contrasts the elegant apartments of the New York wealthy with the slum tenements in the dead-end streets behind them; the street in front of the apartment houses is temporarily closed for paving, and thus its tenants are forced to come and go via the rear entrance, the unsavory Dead End. The central character is Gimpty, a young cripple who grew up in the slums and struggled to win an education as an architect but is at present unemployed. He is in love with Kay, a prostitute who is the mistress of Jack Hilton, a wealthy tenant of the apartment. Other important characters are the "Dead End kids"—five young slum hoodlums named Tommy, Dippy, T.B., Angel, and Spit, all of them incurably warped by their environment. The climactic event of the drama is the visit to the street of Baby-Face Martin, a gangster who grew up in the neighborhood. After an inner moral conflict Gimpty decides to betray Martin to the police for the reward in order to be able to marry Kay and save her from her sordid life; when he does so, however, she convinces him that "This isn't the miracle we were looking for"—that the money would last them only a year or so, and then they would be at the mercy of the slums again. Kay goes off with Hilton, who has promised to marry her, on a yachting trip. Meanwhile a secondary plot has followed the fortunes of the Dead End kid Tommy and his sister Drina, who is in love with Gimpty. When Tommy, in a brawl, slightly wounds Mr. Griswald, a pompous tenant of the apartment building, Griswald threatens to prosecute and have him sent to a reform school. Drina unsuccessfully tries to convince Griswald that the reform school is only a school for crime, but he is adamant. Finally she appeals to Gimpty, and he agrees to use his reward money to hire a lawyer to defend Tommy. The play ends as Gimpty and Drina go off arm in arm, leaving the street to the obscene and raucous horseplay of the Dead End kids.

The chief importance of *Dead End* lies in its daringly frank picture of slum conditions and in the coarse and slangy dialogue of the Dead End kids themselves. The Gimpty-Kay story is somewhat melodramatic, and Gimpty himself is less believable than the more typical slum inhabitants. The symbolic contrast between slum and expensive apartment is ingenious, extending not only to the set and characters but into the plot itself; the apartment tenants, especially Mr. Griswald and his son Philip, attempt to ignore the corruption under their feet but are finally dragged down and soiled by it in spite of their hypocritical fastidiousness. The theme of environmental determinism is free from any political or partisan message; Kingsley offers no solution to the "problem of juvenile delinquency" other than the abolition of slums and the awakening of human tolerance in "respectable" people like Mr. Griswald.

Maxwell Anderson (1888–1959)

At first glance Maxwell Anderson is an anomaly in twentieth-century literature: a romanticist whose chief contribution to the theatre has been in the virtually obsolete form of the verse drama. There is, however, a thoroughly modern quality to Anderson's work, even when he is treating Elizabethan subjects in an archaic dramatic form; he invariably converts his characters into modern personalities with modern psychologies, and his political liberalism and cutting irony mark him as a typical American writer of his generation. Like Faulkner, Jeffers, and O'Neill, he was dissatisfied with the limited possibilities of prose realism, and he sought to break away from realistic conventions through some more subtle literary form. Instinctively romantic in temperament, he turned naturally to the lyrical verse drama which had grown steadily out of favor since the seventeenth century.

In practice Anderson's plays fall into three distinct groups. The first, the realistic prose dramas, begin with *What Price Glory* in 1924 and continue through *Truckline Café* in 1945 and his dramatization of William March's *The Bad Seed* in 1954. The second group, the historical dramas in verse form, includes *Elizabeth the Queen, Mary of Scotland, Joan of Lorraine,* and *Anne of the Thousand Days.* The best-known of these plays are concerned with the English sixteenth century, especially the reigns of Henry VIII and Elizabeth, and their style is a combination of the modern and the Shakespearian; even their form and structure follow the pattern of the Elizabethan drama. The third group comprises plays with a modern setting but in verse form, and includes *Winterset,* perhaps his most important play, and a number of minor dramas such as *High Tor* and the war play *Eve of St. Mark.* The plays of the first group are written in the style of modern naturalism, with realistic dialogue often spiced with slang and contemporary allusions. The second and third groups are more similar than might be expected; Anderson makes a deliberate effort to modernize his historical characters, and conversely he imparts a "classic" quality to the speech of the characters in his modern verse dramas. Like the Elizabethan dramatists, he often writes the speeches of his heroes and the more exalted portions of his action in a kind of blank or free verse, and the comic, satirical, or vulgar portions of his play in prose. The technique is seen at its most typical in *High Tor* and *Knickerbocker Holiday.* Other plays like *Winterset,* which has no comic relief and which substitutes a bitter irony for satire, are written almost entirely in verse. His realism (and Anderson is in one sense a realist) lies almost entirely in the area of content and attitude. He is not the kind of romanticist represented by Robinson Jeffers, living in isolation in a remote part of the world and detached as much as possible from contemporary events; he is in intimate contact with current events and his interests are deeply involved in contemporary life. Two of his plays (*Gods of the Lightning* and *Winterset*) are concerned with that great *cause célèbre* of his generation, the Sacco-Vanzetti case, and even so fantastic a comedy as *Knickerbocker Holiday* was intended as a satire on the New Deal. For Anderson verse is a living form which may, and ought to, be used for subjects of pressing interest for a modern audience. The success of *Winterset* showed that his judgment was not entirely wrong.

Life: Maxwell Anderson was born in Atlantic, Pennsylvania in 1888, the son of a Baptist minister. Educated in various parts of the middle west as his father was transferred from one church to another, he received his B.A. from the University of North Dakota in 1911. He went on to take a Master's degree at Stanford (1914) and to work at a variety of teaching and newspaper jobs. During the First World War he maintained a rigidly pacifistic stand, which got him into considerable difficulty before the war was over; he was dismissed from a teaching position at Whittier College and fired from an editorial job on the *San Francisco Bulletin*, but refused to compromise his ideals even in the face of hostile public opinion. This attitude, undoubtedly connected to his Christian background, is part of a wider religious enthusiasm which Anderson has maintained throughout his career in spite of his political liberalism (although the two are not necessarily incompatible); he once referred to the theatre as "a religious institution devoted entirely to the exaltation of the spirit of man."

In 1918 Anderson went east to New York, where he worked intermittently for various publications including the *Evening Globe* and the *New Republic* until 1928. Meanwhile he had begun writing dramas; his first play, a verse drama in a contemporary setting entitled *White Desert*, appeared in 1923. His first success came with *What Price Glory?*, which he wrote in collaboration with Laurence Stallings in 1924. The play, which starred William Boyd and Louis Wolheim in rôles which became permanently associated with their names, was an instant success; the characters of Sergeant Quirt and Captain Flagg became a part of American folklore, and the story was later made into a successful motion picture. In 1930 appeared *Elizabeth the Queen,* the first of his verse dramas to achieve box-office success; he followed it with *Mary of Scotland* (1933) and *Winterset* (1935), which won him acclaim as a leading American playwright. During the Thirties he joined with Elmer Rice, Robert Sherwood, and others to organize the Playwrights' Group, a co-operative venture formed to produce plays written by its members. Anderson has won numerous awards and prizes during his career, including a Pulitzer Prize (1933) and two Drama Critics' Awards (1936 and 1937). He has been married twice, the second time (1933) to Gertrude Maynard. For many years a New York City resident, Anderson lived subsequently on a farm in Rockland County, N.Y. He died in Stamford, Connecticut of a stroke on February 28, 1959 at the age of seventy. At the time of the stroke he was engaged in arranging for the production of his thirty-third play, *Madonna and Child.*

Chief Works: *What Price Glory?* (drama, with Laurence Stallings, 1924) is the first American drama in the new realistic school of war literature represented by such novels as *All Quiet on the Western Front* and Dos Passos' *Three Soldiers.* The action is built around a long-standing feud between Sergeant Quirt and Captain Flagg, hard-bitten members of a U.S. Marine company in France during the First World War. When Flagg goes off to Paris for a week he leaves the company in charge of Quirt, who seizes the opportunity to appropriate Flagg's French girl Charmaine to himself. When Flagg returns he finds that Charmaine's father Cognac Pete has brought charges of seduction against Quirt and demands five hundred francs compensation plus marriage of his daughter to the sergeant. Flagg threatens to force Quirt into the marriage, but the war intervenes; the company is suddenly sent into action. Combat-weary, they are promised a month's leave if they can capture a German officer needed for intelligence purposes. Before they do, however, Quirt is wounded and sent back to the rear, where he escapes from a hospital and happily begins consorting with Charmaine again. When the German prisoner is captured Flagg returns to the rear area with the rest of the company and discovers Quirt's trick. They quarrel, then decide to gamble for the girl. Flagg wins, but at that moment new orders arrive sending the company back to the front in spite of the promised leave. Flagg, cursing, cedes Charmaine to the still invalided Quirt. But as the play ends Quirt, whose final loyalty is to the Corps and who is determined not to be outdone by Flagg, abandons the girl to follow his outfit back into the fighting.

In spite of its ostensible realism *What Price Glory?* is in many respects a romantic play. Its interest centers around the colorful characters of Flagg and Quirt and their perpetual friendly enmity; the constant quarreling between the two cannot disguise the fact that they respect each other and are really—perhaps unconsciously—close friends. The play differs from pacifistic war novels such as *All Quiet on the Western Front* in that it does not show war as totally brutal and meaningless, and indeed imbues it with a certain romantic aura of adventure. As Gassner remarks, "It is, indeed, far from certain that the authors were not themselves captivated by what they set out to deprecate." Most of the war color in the play was provided by Stallings, who served as a captain in the Marines during the war and lost a leg in combat at Château-Thierry; Anderson's contribution was mainly in dialogue and dramatic structure. It was the salty, realistic, and unerringly accurate dialogue which chiefly accounted for the stage success of this play.

Saturday's Children (drama, 1927) is typical of Anderson's prose comedies of manners. The theme is marriage, or rather the ironic contrast between the ecstasy of young love and the banality of the marriage which is its inevitable result. Florrie and Willie Sands, a young married couple, enjoy a typical American marital bliss of the lower-middle-class variety, that is to say they are constantly plagued by bills and quarrel petulantly in the intervals of their love-making. They accept their lot and make the best of it, however, and Florrie even undertakes to help trap a husband for her younger sister Bobby. Through Florrie's adroit strategy Bobby manages to trick Rims O'Neil, a likable but rather confused young man, into proposing to her. They marry, and immediately find themselves in the thick of the problems which have previously harassed Florrie and Willie: bills, dirty dishes, in-laws, petty deceits, quarrels, and banality. "What we wanted was a love affair," Bobby complains, "and what we got was a house and bills and general hell." Refusing to accept this, she leaves Rims, moves into a boarding house, and gets her old job back. When Rims comes to the boarding house to implore her to return, she refuses. Later that night, however, after the landlady has banished visitors from the house, Rims climbs stealthily in through the window, and she accepts him—as a lover and not as a husband. This wry but amusing study of middle-class marriage succeeds chiefly through its dialogue, which is cleverly and accurately vernacular.

Elizabeth the Queen (verse drama, 1930) is the best known of Anderson's historical dramas. The action is laid in the latter years of Elizabeth's reign (1599–1601) and the plot concerns the rebellion led by the Earl of Essex. The aging queen, suppressing her natural affection for Essex, tricks him into dissolving his army and then imprisons him in the Tower. She offers him pardon in return for renunciation of his ambitions, but he refuses, unwilling to be content with second place in the kingdom and preferring death to ignominy. This play, written in traditional English blank verse, represents an attempt to achieve a stylistic compromise: Anderson sought to revive the splendor and high poetry of the Elizabethan drama and at the same time remain natural and idiomatic enough to be acceptable by modern audiences. *Mary of Scotland* (1933) and *The Masque of Kings* (1937) are similar in style and treatment.

Both Your Houses (drama, 1933) is a satirical attack on political chicanery, one of the first serious criticisms of corruption in the Federal government in American literature. Alan McClean, an idealistic young congressman, is appointed to an Appropriations Committee because other members consider him too naive and inexperienced to cause any trouble. But McClean soon discovers that almost all the members of the Committee represent corrupt vested interests, and that an appropriations bill originally intended for a Nevada dam has actually been laden with graft through the old tradition of log-rolling. When he tries to expose the corruption he finds that the evidence will prove damaging to Simeon Gray, another congressman whose daughter Marjorie is Alan's sweetheart. He persists in his efforts, however, and opposes the bill to the end even though the others succeed in getting it passed. As the play ends he resolves to begin a vigorous personal campaign to expose the log-rolling and corruption which are the traditional means of getting legislation passed in the Congress.

Winterset (verse drama, 1935) is usually considered Anderson's most important play. Set in a New York tenement district near the river, it deals with people and places much like those in Rice's *Street Scene* or Kingsley's *Dead End,* but does so with an entirely different technique; its mood, tragic and highly poetic, is the antithesis of naturalism. Thirteen years before the action begins an Italian workman and anarchist named Romagna has been unjustly executed for a murder committed during an attempted payroll robbery. The murder was actually committed by Trock Estrella, who has just been released from prison as the play opens. Garth, a young musician and son of the Jewish scholar Esdras, was a witness to the crime; and the killer Trock, who is ill and has only six months to live, suspects him of wanting to give evidence to the police. He threatens Garth, who protests that he has no intention of talking and that his interests are the same as Trock's, since he is technically guilty of murder too. Then Mio, the young son of the executed Romagna, arrives on the scene, wandering about the world seeking evidence which will cleanse the name of his innocent father. He falls in love with Miriamne, Garth's sister, before he realizes her relation to his natural enemy Garth, and is then faced with a cruel moral dilemma: to restore his father's reputation he must destroy the brother of the girl he loves. Meanwhile, through a coincidence, Judge Gaunt, who had sent Romagna to the electric chair, appears, distraught and half insane with remorse and obsessed with the idea of justifying himself before the world; Esdras temporarily takes him into his home to protect him. The crisis of the play occurs when Trock has Shadow, an obnoxious gunman, shot and thrown into the river; Shadow, not yet dead, appears wounded and bent on revenge in the Esdras tenement, and Trock is forced to kill him again for good, this time in the presence of Esdras, Garth, Mio, and Miriamne. When the police arrive Mio, knowing Trock as the criminal who should have died instead of his father, denounces him for the murder of Shadow. But Garth and the others, fearing Trock's vengeance, fail to back Mio up, and the police depart with the demented Judge Gaunt, leaving Trock untouched. Mio, now knowing he faces certain death at the hands of

Trock, goes off to meet his fate; when he is killed Miriamne also exposes herself to fire and is struck down by a bullet from the gangsters' machine gun. As the play ends Esdras tells the dead Mio that the glory of man is "not to cringe, never to yield, but standing, take defeat implacable and defiant." The implied reproach to the sensitive but cowardly musician Garth is obvious. *Winterset*, in structure a tragedy in the Elizabethan manner, is highly refined and artificial in style, rich in metaphor and in the ironic turns of language which Elizabethans called "conceits." Its diction is archaic and imaginative, making little attempt to imitate the modern vernacular.

High Tor (verse drama, 1936) is a fantasy or allegory contrasting traditional American individualism and self-reliance with the aggressive business-philosophy of the twentieth century. Van Dorn, a fiercely independent young man who lives alone on High Tor, a peak overlooking the Hudson River in upstate New York, quarrels with his fiancée Judith, who wants to live a normal domestic life and tries to persuade him to sell his mountain to entrepreneurs who wish to mine its valuable trap-rock. Two pompous business-men, Biggs and Skimmerhorn, arrive on the mountain to deal with him, hoping to trick or coerce him into surrendering the valuable rights, but become involved in a farcical imbroglio involving a set of Dutch ghosts left over from a seventeenth-century ship and a gang of incompetent bank-robbers, Dope, Elkus, and Buddy. A satchel full of money stolen by the bank-robbers comes eventually into the hands of Biggs and Skimmerhorn, who are then trapped in the scoop of a steamshovel and arrested by the police for the crime. Meanwhile Van has romanced with the attractive Lise, one of the phantoms from the Dutch ship, who serves as a symbol of his desire for a pure love uncontaminated by banality and materialism. After the two unscrupulous business-men are arrested, however, Lise goes off in her ship leaving Van to Judith, who now repents of her mean decision and agrees to accept Van on his own terms. Van finally agrees to sell the mountain for a large sum to Skimmerhorn's father, a business-man of a blunter and more honest sort, and go west with Judith to seek an unspoiled new region where he can retain his individualism. John, an Indian who is about to die and who makes Van promise to bury him on the mountain, provides philosophical comments through the play, concluding at the end, "Nothing is made by men but makes, in the end, good ruins." Thus modern American "progress" and materialistic aggressiveness are repudiated completely. Unlike *Winterset, High Tor* is not written completely in verse; comic scenes and speeches of characters like Biggs and Skimmerhorn are in vernacular prose similar to that of Anderson's realistic dramas.

Robert Sherwood (1896–1955)

Sherwood is an acknowledged master of the technique of high comedy, but he writes high comedy of a very special kind, resembling the philosophical comedy of Bernard Shaw more than the Noel Coward "comedy of manners." His *Road to Rome,* in fact, is essentially the same kind of play as Shaw's *Caesar and Cleopatra,* a comedy of ideas in which historical figures are converted into modern characters with modern psychologies. Although Sherwood is by no means as partisan and dogmatic a thinker as Shaw, there is a consistent thread of idea running through his work: he is a pacifist and humanitarian (although his pacifism at one period turned into militant anti-fascism) and he is an advocate of natural human behavior as opposed to social convention. These two concepts are epitomized in *Idiot's Delight*; the polyglot Europeans and Americans who meet in the remote Italian hotel are friendly and tolerant as long as they follow their natural instincts, but when they are infected with the mass hysteria of nationalism they turn into stereotypes of war-mongering patriots. In *The Petrified Forest* and *Reunion in Vienna* natural action is contrasted with artificial (social or conventional) action; Sherwood believes that a genuine individual impulse which comes from within, even if it is what society condemns as immoral, is wiser than conduct determined solely by external morals, laws, or conventions. Amytis in *The Road to Rome* is the model Sherwood heroine in this respect: she is unmoved by the hysteria of Roman chauvinism which infects her husband Fabius, she gives herself to Hannibal when it seems natural and proper for her to do so, yet in the end she violates the stereotyped conventions of romanticism by going back to her husband rather than becoming Hannibal's concubine.

When the play is over it is apparent that she has acted rightly in each case, and that Rome, her husband's career, and her own destiny have been served by her feminine intuition.

Sherwood spent a number of years of his life in Europe, and he always retained an admiration for European civilization and a respect for the European cultural tradition. Almost half his plays are either laid in a European setting or based on European characters; in his best-known American play, *The Petrified Forest,* the heroine is half French and the chief male character a former American expatriate who constantly contrasts European and American culture to the detriment of the latter. Yet this apparent rejection of "the American way of life" is merely the normal iconoclasm of a writer who grew to maturity during the Twenties. Sherwood's later work—especially his *Abe Lincoln in Illinois* and *Roosevelt and Hopkins*—shows him to be a writer who is deeply concerned with American problems and conscious of his American heritage, which he views from the standpoint of a sincere humanitarian and liberal.

Life: Robert Emmet Sherwood was born in New Rochelle, New York in 1896. He evidently inherited his artistic inclinations from his parents; his father was an investment broker with an enthusiastic interest in the theatre and his mother a talented painter and illustrator. The family was well-to-do, and Sherwood had an excellent education, first at Milton Academy and then at Harvard. In 1917, however, he left college in his junior year to enlist in the Canadian Black Guards; he saw the worst of the combat on the Western Front, was wounded at Amiens, and spent many months in hospitals. From this experience came his lifetime detestation of war, which found its way in one way or another into most of his plays.

Sherwood had begun writing plays while still an undergraduate at Harvard, and had also wirtten for student publications including *Lampoon,* for which he wrote a particularly ingenious parody of *Vanity Fair.* When he was mustered out of the service in 1919 he was invited to join the *Vanity Fair* staff, and served on the magazine as dramatic critic until the next year, when he resigned in protest against the firing of Dorothy Parker, whose criticisms were considered too caustic by the publishers. During the following years he wrote for a number of periodicals including the old *Life* and *Scrib-*

ner's. Meanwhile, he had retained his interest in playwriting, and 1927 saw the production of his first play, *The Road to Rome.* The production was a success, and thenceforth he was able to make his living as a playwright, achieving both critical and popular success; he received three Pulitzer Prizes between 1936 and 1941, and served from 1937 to 1941 as president of the Dramatists' Guild.

A lifetime liberal, Sherwood took an active part in politics under the New Deal administration of Franklin Roosevelt, especially after 1940; during the war he served as chief of the overseas branch of the Office of War Information, and is credited with writing many of Roosevelt's best speeches. A close friend of Harry Hopkins, he inherited his voluminous papers after his death; out of this mass of material he compiled an important historical study of the New Deal, *Roosevelt and Hopkins: An Intimate History* (1948). This work, over a thousand pages long, not only became a best-seller but won Sherwood a reputation as a first-rate researcher and historian.

Sherwood was married twice, to Mary Brandon in 1922 and to Mrs. Madeline Connelly, former wife of the author Marc Connelly, in 1934. Toward the end of his career he wrote extensively for television and motion pictures; one of his movie scenarios, *The Best Years of Our Lives,* won an Academy Award. He died of a heart attack in New York in November, 1955. "In the American theatre," wrote Maxwell Anderson in a funeral sermon prepared for reading by the actor Alfred Lunt, "the death of Sherwood has an effect comparable to the removal of a major planet from the solar system."

Chief Works: *The Road to Rome* (drama, 1927) is a philosophical comedy laid in Rome in the period of the Second Punic War (*ca.* 216 B.C.). Fabius, newly elected Dictator of Rome, is a typical political windbag and chauvinist who boasts emptily of the victory the Romans will win over the invading Carthaginian forces led by Hannibal. His half-Greek wife Amytis, however, has no interest whatsoever in politics and can see little sense in a useless war which will kill thousands of men and bring no gain to either side. She is intrigued, however, by descriptions of the ruthless Hannibal, who sounds to her much more attractive than her prosaic husband. When news comes that the Roman legions have been defeated in the disastrous battle of Cannae and that Hannibal's forces will shortly sack Rome, she flees, ostensibly to go to take shelter with her mother on the seacoast. Actually, however, she steals secretly with two trusted slaves into the camp of Hannibal, curious to see what he is like and perhaps hoping for an escape from her humdrum and conventional existence. Hannibal at first orders her put to death, then is intrigued by her beauty and obvious intelligence; she willingly surrenders herself to him. The next day Fabius, with his chief general Scipio, comes to the Carthaginian camp to treat for terms. But Hannibal has already been convinced by Amytis of the senselessness of destroying the city and slaughtering all its inhabitants; his unthinking soldier's nationalism has been shattered completely by her woman's common sense. He withdraws his army from the city and goes instead to raise the siege of Capua, inviting Amytis to come with him and share his life. But she refuses, telling him that he must not spare Rome to win her but because "every sacrifice made in the name of war is wasted." She goes back to rejoin her husband Fabius, who announces bombastically that the Carthaginians have retreated because "Hannibal, with all his elephants all his men, could not subdue the high moral purpose of Rome."

In spite of its setting *The Road to Rome* is no historical drama. It makes no attempt to achieve an authentic Roman atmosphere, and uses the historical background only as a convenient frame for a philosophical comedy. Much of the Roman setting, in fact, is actually a satire on the modern American state (e.g., the clichés repeated by Fabius, a parody of the speech of a modern politician), and the Greek attitude which Amytis upholds bears a certain analogy to modern European culture, especially the French. The psychology of the chief characters is thoroughly twentieth-century, and even minor characters like the Carthaginian soldiers are treated as satires on their modern equivalents.

Reunion in Vienna (drama, 1931) is a study of social transition, the passing of the old Hapsburg order in Austria and the coming of a new and modern generation to replace it. The story is laid in Vienna in 1930 on the hundredth anniversary of the birth of the late Emperor Franz Joseph I. The handful of aristocrats left in Vienna plan a party for the occasion at a fashionable hotel, and invite Frau Elena Krug, famous before the war as mistress of the Crown Prince Rudolf Maximillian and now wife of the eminent psychiatrist Anton

Krug. Elena at first refuses, but when she learns that her old lover Rudolf, exiled for years, is actually going to enter Austria illegally to attend the dinner, she comes to the hotel. Rudolf proposes a renewal of their love, but she refuses, telling him that an era has passed and that now she is another woman, the wife of Dr. Krug. Rudolf is unable to understand her attitude; he pursues her to her home, where he meets Anton and cynically reveals his desire to him. Anton leaves the matter up to Elena; meanwhile he leaves the couple alone in the house while he goes off to consult with the political authorities about plans for the safe re-exiling of Rudolf, who will probably be shot if he is captured by the police. Rudolf is so impressed with his courtesy, and with the implied trust Anton has shown in Elena, that he willingly agrees to leave the country and renounce his rights over his old mistress. He has comprehended what his fanatic followers and hangers-on have not: that the day of the Hapsburgs is gone and can never come back, and that the future belongs to Dr. Krug and his kind. Sherwood wrote this realistic "romantic comedy" especially for Alfred Lunt and Lynn Fontanne, who played Rudolf and Elena respectively in the original production.

The Petrified Forest (drama, 1934) is a study of decadent Western civilization, a culture in which the intellectuals who have been dominant for so long are finally at the point of extermination through self-induced sterility. The play is evidently influenced by Eliot's poem *The Waste Land,* which is referred to twice in the course of the action. The setting is the interior of a gas station and lunch stand on the Arizona desert. The proprietor, Jason Maple, is a pompous self-appointed patriot who conceals his lack of character under an American Legion uniform. The remaining important characters are his daughter Gabrielle (Gabby), whose French mother has despaired of life on the bleak desert and gone back to Europe; his father Gramp, an old pioneer who is disgusted with twentieth-century culture; Boze Hertzlinger, a former star athlete and now employee of the café; Alan Squier, a "lost generation" American expatriate who has lived for several years on the French Riviera, married to a wealthy woman, but who has now come back to hitchhike his way through America in search of some meaning in life; and Mr. and Mrs. Chisholm, a pair of middle-class travelers from Ohio. The plot centers around the capture of the café by Duke

Mantee, a killer and fugitive from the law, and his gang; this crisis brings out the latent qualities of each of the characters and brings their lives to the climactic point. Alan, who has fallen in love with Gabby, willingly allows himself to be shot by Mantee in order that the young girl may use his insurance money to escape from her dull life and go to France to study art. Mrs. Chisholm who is also bored with her life, offers to "crawl into the hay" with Mantee, but a gun battle intervenes to prevent this; meanwhile, however, she has seen through her husband's insipid conventionality. Jason is unmasked as an incompetent coward, and Duke Mantee, the anti-social criminal, is typified by Alan before he dies as "the last great apostle of rugged individualism" in the Petrified Forest of outmoded ideas. The final message of the play is a plea for a life of wider experience than the usual existence dominated by convention and banality; even Duke seems more admirable than the blustering "patriot" Jason, who does only what society expects of him and parrots second-hand ideas in place of a philosophy. It should be noted that Alan is not the "hero" of the play in the ordinary sense; he is intended as a personification of the decadent generation of the Twenties, which can only talk instead of act and which confines its intellectual leadership to presiding over the degeneration of culture.

Idiot's Delight (drama, 1936) is set in a remote Italian hotel on the Austrian border on the eve of a hypothetical war. In this microcosm are assembled a set of symbolically contrasting characters: Dr. Waldensee, a German scientist consecrated to the study of the cause of cancer; Quillery, a French socialist and pacifist; Mr. and Mrs. Cherry, English newlyweds preoccupied with their own personal happiness; Harry Van, an American nightclub entertainer, with his troupe of six showgirls; Achille Weber, a French munitions manufacturer; and Weber's mistress Irene, a self-styled White Russian refugee. Other characters important in the plot are Pittaluga, the proprietor of the hotel; the Austrian waiter Dumptsy; and Captain Locicero, an Italian officer in command of the nearby airfield. In the first act the characters are friendly and tolerant toward each other and indifferent to the clouds of a major European war which are gathering on the horizon; Quillery is a professional pacifist, Dr. Waldensee holds science and humanity above his loyalty to Germany, and the others are mainly concerned with their individual search for happiness. Then war breaks out suddenly and news comes that Italian planes from the airfield have bombed Paris; immediately all the main characters are caught up in the hatreds of the war. Quillery speaks out violently against the bombing of Paris and is shot by the Italians; Dr. Waldensee decides to go back to Germany to contribute his knowledge to germ warfare, and the others plan to return home to join their respective armies. It is not Weber, the "warmonger" and target of Quillery's pacifistic diatribes, who is responsible for the war but humanity itself, normally peaceable but irrational and fanatic as soon as the war fever is whipped up. As the play ends Irene denounces Weber and he abandons her; she joins forces with Harry, who recognizes her as a girl he met long ago in Omaha, and they begin "Onward Christian Soldiers" as the first French bombs crash down on the hotel. This play, written in 1936, is a remarkably accurate prediction of the outbreak of the Second World War. It is also interesting that Sherwood was able to predict the change of heart of many liberals who turned from pacifism to militant anti-fascism between 1932 and 1939, and ironic that he himself was to undergo this same change of opinion; by 1940 he was an impassioned anti-Nazi and anti-communist who attacked the Russian invasion of Finland in *There Shall Be No Night* and supervised anti-fascist propaganda as a high official of the O.W.I.

Abe Lincoln in Illinois (drama, 1938) is a historical play in twelve scenes following the career of Lincoln from his period as a New Salem storekeeper to the time of his departure for Washington as President-Elect. Sherwood treats Lincoln as a personification of the American ideal of humanitarianism plus personal ambition and self-realization, and attempts in the play to show the development of the idea in Lincoln himself. The play was awarded a Pulitzer Prize in 1939.

Clifford Odets (1906–1963)

The talent of Clifford Odets burst dramatically onto the American theatrical scene in the middle of the Depression era. In a single year, 1935, he wrote four plays and won a reputation as the outstanding member of the new left-wing school of young American dramatists. Odets today is still remembered chiefly for these 1935 plays, especially *Waiting for Lefty* and *Awake and Sing.* His subsequent work, while less important in the development of American drama, has nevertheless shown him as a playwright with a great deal of versatility. *Paradise Lost* (1935) and *Rocket to the Moon* (1938), along with *Night Music* (1940), are satires of middle-class American domesticity, usually involving a love plot but virtually devoid of political comment; *Golden Boy* (1937) is a penetrating study of the American cult of success, symbolized through the figure of an Italian boy who cannot decide whether he wants to be a prizefighting champion or a violinist. The most important of Odets' post-1945 plays is *Country Girl* (1950), in which the central conflict is again personal and domestic rather than social. Taken as a whole, Odets' work reveals him as a dramatist whose talent lies mainly in the portrayal of the inner conflicts and struggles of the big-city American middle class—a class which in the Thirties shaded off imperceptibly into the tenement proletariat of the Bronx.

Odets was a professional actor for several years before he wrote his first play, and he has an intimate technical knowledge of the theatre. With the possible exception of *Waiting for Lefty,* which borrows some of the technical innovations of European expressionism, his plays are not experimental or radical in technique; they are sound and competent in construction and written always with an eye to the practical limitations of dramatic production. As is often the case with dramatists with an extensive theatrical background, Odets' plays do not read as well as they play; they sometimes seem gauche or oversimplified in book form and come to life only when put upon the living stage. This is particularly true of *Waiting for Lefty,* which is a sort of visual pageant rather than a purely "verbal" drama and must be seen in production to be properly appreciated.

Odets' most striking talent, however, and the quality which chiefly accounted for the success of his early plays, is his skill in dialogue. He has an unerring ear for the speech of the big-city masses—brash, colorful, cynical, enriched by the influences of a half-dozen immigrant languages and seasoned with a poetic bitterness born from the poverty and hopelessness of life in the metropolitan tenements. His command of this idiom, the language of his own people, makes the parallel efforts of Kingsley (*Dead End*) and Rice (*Street Scene*) seem amateurish by contrast. He is naturally at his best in the Jewish dialect—*Golden Boy* with its Italian hero is less successful in dialogue than *Awake and Sing*. This idiom is strongly influenced by the underlying Yiddish substratum of its speakers, even using Yiddish syntax ("Please, I'm making a story? I fell in the chair like dead."). In Odets' drama the dialect seems colorfully foreign and at the same time deeply and characteristically American; above all it has the unmistakable ring of authenticity. The same criticism may be made of his characterizations—they are best when they are closest to his own background, and weakest in characters (like the doctors in Episode V of *Waiting for Lefty*) who are farther from his own experience. Likewise *The Country Girl* is the best of his later plays because he is writing about what he knows—the backstage lives of actors in the big-city theatre. Odets' permanent place in the American theatre is assured, not by his efforts at left-wing propaganda, but by his skill in dramatic composition and his mastery of the idiom of an important segment of American culture.

Life: Clifford Odets was born in Philadelphia in 1906; both his parents were Jewish Lithuanian immigrants. He was raised in New York and Philadelphia and attended schools in both cities. At fifteen, however, he left high school to work as a radio writer and announcer; at nineteen he was earning a living by reading dramatic poems over the radio. By 1928 he had established his career as an actor, working in stock companies and obtaining an occasional minor part in Theatre Guild productions. In 1930, along with Harold Clurman and Herbert Biberman, he helped to organize the Group Theatre, which was conceived as a sort of junior Theatre Guild to produce plays by younger dramatists and which began under the protection of the older organization. At this time Odets' ambitions were still confused; he dreamed vaguely of becoming a concert pianist and also experimented tentatively with writing novels. He worked as an actor in Group Theatre productions for three years before he wrote his first play. This was *Awake and Sing*, which he wrote to express the "strangulations of family life" as he had known them in his own youth. The Group rehearsed the second act of the play but decided not to produce it; meanwhile they went on to stage Kingsley's *Men In White*. The following year (1934) Odets wrote *Waiting for Lefty* in three days for a one-act play contest sponsored by the New Theatre League. Staged by the League, the short play created an enormous sensation and made Odets a celebrity overnight. The Group Theatre now reconsidered his work; it produced *Waiting for Lefty* on Broadway in early 1935 and commissioned another short play, *Till the Day I Die,* to complete the bill. In February the Group also produced *Awake and Sing,* which achieved a considerable box-office success. Odets, his reputation made, went to Hollywood, where he stayed for three years, contributing to the scripts for such important films as *The General Died at Dawn.* In 1937 he was married to the motion-picture actress Luise Rainer; the union was a stormy one, and the two were divorced in 1940. Odets subsequently spent several periods in Hollywood, where he worked both as screenwriter and as director. Meanwhile his political attitudes had changed with the changing atmosphere of the times. His early plays adhered closely to the Communist Party line; *Waiting for Lefty* is probably one of the most violently partisan proletarian dramas ever to be produced on the Broadway stage. Even as late as 1939, writing a preface to his first six plays, he remarked, "We are living in a time when new art works should shoot bullets." But by 1942 he was content to describe himself as "some kind of a socialist" and had disavowed formal Party connections. In 1952, at the height of the Congressional anti-Red "purges," he testified before the House Committee on Un-American Activities that he had been a Party member briefly in 1934 but had resigned when pressure was put upon him to write party-line propaganda. Odets was married for the second time in 1943 to the actress Bette Grayson; she died in 1954. After the war he divided his residence between New York and California. He died August 15, 1963 in Los Angeles. Obituaries suggested that his failure to outgrow the adjective "promising" was partly because he had "sold his soul" to Hollywood like his character in *The Big Knife* (1949), played by John Garfield.

Chief Works: *Waiting for Lefty* (one-act drama, 1934) consists of six "Episodes" plus a number of incidental scenes, all played on a bare stage without benefit of scenery. The sequence of action is outwardly disconnected and the general mood is fantastic, suggesting the Continental expressionistic drama of Kaiser and Wedekind and the similar American experiments of O'Neill and Rice. The action is concerned with a strike of New York taxicab drivers during the Depression, and approximately half the scenes take place in a drivers' meeting in which the theatre audience is addressed over the footlights as though it were the membership of the meeting. Retorts, heckling, and comments are frequently heard from this audience, thus effectively breaking down the conventional barrier between stage and theatregoer. The play opens as Harry Fatt, a corrupt union leader who actually serves the capitalistic bosses, tries to persuade the drivers not to go out on strike. Flashback scenes then show typical incidents in the lives of the strikers. The driver Joe is exhorted by his wife Edna to strike to provide food for his starving children, and the young Sid tells his fiancée Florence he cannot marry her until the drivers' wages are increased. Meanwhile the drivers await the arrival of Lefty Costello (symbol of aid from the international workers' movement), the one leader they trust and respect. When news comes that Lefty has been found dead, murdered by the bosses' police, the workers turn into a howling mob which chants, "Strike, strike, strike!" as the curtain comes down. In addition to its interest as an extreme example of proletarian drama, *Waiting for Lefty* is important as one of the first American plays to utilize the bare-stage technique and the breaking down of the audience barrier which were later used in such important dramas as Thornton Wilder's *Our Town* (1938).

Awake and Sing! (drama, 1935) was written before *Waiting for Lefty* but produced slightly later. All the action takes place in the Bronx tenement flat of the Bergers, an impoverished Jewish family including three generations. Jacob, the grandfather, is a philosophical and studious old Jew who has been unable all his life to convert his idealism into action. Bessie, his daughter and the real head of the family, is aggressive and hard-working but unhappy, obsessed with a desire for bourgeois prosperity and respectability; her husband Myron is a "born follower" who lacks the character to seize what he wants out of life. Their son Ralph, an impractical thinker and dreamer, resembles his grandfather in character. Their daughter Hennie, a stenographer, is an individualist who "travels alone" and feels loyalty to no one, even to her own family; she is made for love and motherhood, but so far has been unable to find a husband. Also frequently present in the flat are Uncle Morty, a self-made man and successful clothing merchant who patronizes the Bergers but does little to aid them, and Moe Axelrod, a bitter and cynical sensualist who lost a leg in the war and is now out only for himself; he loves Hennie, but she despises him. The crisis of the action arises when Hennie announces she is pregnant by an unknown lover. The hard Bessie, taking the situation in hand, forces her into a marriage with Sam Feinschreiber, a recently arrived immigrant whom Hennie does not love. Meanwhile Bessie works to break up Ralph's romance with his fiancée Blanche, whom she dislikes because she is a moneyless orphan. The two idealists in the household, Ralph and the old Jacob, seem helpless before the cynical ruthlessness of the others. Then Jacob, who owns a three-thousand-dollar life insurance policy made out to Ralph, takes the dog up on the roof for an airing and leaps to his death, presumably in order to give Ralph a new start in life. The family immediately begins squabbling over the money, but Ralph, disgusted, willingly hands it over to Bessie. By this time Blanche has abandoned him; he resolves to go out into the world alone and struggle for his living, exulting in the new strength that his freedom has given him. Hennie, bored by her monotonous life with Sam, elopes with Moe to go on "a big boat headed south," and the dissolution of the family is complete. The title of this drama comes from an Old Testament passage quoted by Jacob before he dies: "Awake and sing, ye that dwell in the dust, and the earth shall cast out the dead." Thus the play demonstrates the viciousness of a certain kind of family, which sacrifices everything, even happiness, to material success and ruthlessly suppresses the individual needs and longings of children. The wise grandfather Jacob, with his combination of Old-Testament humanitarianism and Marxist criticism of bourgeois capitalism, serves as a spokesman for the ideas Odets himself held during the period.

S. N. Behrman (born 1893) Since the success of *No Time for Comedy* in 1939 and the relative decline of Philip Barry (see Volume III), Behrman has assumed a position as the leading American writer of high comedy. The difference between high comedy and comedy of manners is a subtle one, but it may be perceived by comparing *End of*

Summer or *No Time for Comedy* with Noel Coward's *Private Lives,* or any of the more sophisticated comedies of Kaufman and Hart. Both types achieve their humor through character contrast and verbal wit, but Behrman's comedy is based in the end on significant social, moral, or personal problems, problems which might equally well serve as subjects for tragedy or serious melodrama. Behrman is not a "social dramatist," nor is he a profound philosopher; but the superficial and attractive surface of his comedy invariably conceals a serious comment on life which is the more effective for being presented in witty and engaging form. A typical example is *No Time for Comedy,* which at first glance appears to be a mere "triangle story" about a man who cannot decide which of two women he loves. Underneath, however, are fundamental problems: the duty of an artist to strive for the amelioration of his society versus his duty to his own artistic principles, the rôle of feminine inspiration in the life of an artist, and—most basic of all—the attitude of an individual toward corrupt social forces over which he has no control.

It is often remarked that Behrman sprang almost full-blown into maturity as an artist; he had no discernible formative period, and *The Second Man,* his first major drama, is as mature in idea and technique as his most recent work. Although his work is generally consistent both in attitude and in style, he does show a considerable versatility. In addition to his own comedies he has adapted three European dramas for the American stage, the most important of which is Werfel's *Jacobowsky and the Colonel* (1944), a play which Behrman might well have written himself. In 1954 he adapted Marcel Pagnol's trilogy *Fanny* as a Broadway musical, and he has also published two major non-fiction works: a biography of the New York art dealer Joseph Duveen, and a set of autobiographical reminiscences about his early family life in Worcester, Massachusetts. Both originally written for *The New Yorker,* they were later published in book form as *Duveen* and *The Worcester Account* respectively.

Behrman is neither a political polemicist nor a dramatist of idea, yet there is a consistent thread of attitude running through his work. Like most important American writers of his generation, he is a liberal and humanitarian and thus an anti-fascist; he deals frequently in his drama with the radical movement of the Depression era (e.g., in *End of Summer*), but he treats it with great objectivity. His obvious sympathy for the cause of the masses never leads him into the partisan radicalism of Odets or Maxwell Anderson. Moreover, he differs from these two playwrights and their kind in his suspicion of conventional heroism; the iconoclasts, the rebels, and the prophets in his dramas are often revealed at the end as hopelessly incompetent. When the young lover Austin, in *The Second Man,* attempts in a high moral passion to shoot Storey, who he believes has seduced his fiancée, he only makes a fool of himself, for two reasons: he is a poor pistol shot, and he is wrong about the seduction. In the end it is the sophisticated, blasé, and compromising Storey who is right. Likewise in *No Time for Comedy* the dramatic romanticism of Amanda is contrasted with the level-headed realism of Linda, who realizes that, heroic gestures aside, it is more important to know how to live than to know how to die. In Behrman's view heroism and high comedy are mutually incompatible; as soon as the merciless light of satire is turned onto heroism it is exposed as nothing but dangerous and irrational bluster.

Life: Samuel Nathaniel Behrman was born in Worcester, Massachusetts in 1893 in a simple middle-class Jewish family he has skillfully described in *The Worcester Account.* An avid reader in his youth, he began to write at an early age; he wrote a one-act play while still in high school, sold it to a vaudeville circuit, and then got a job acting in it himself. After attending Clark College in Worcester he went on to Harvard, where he studied playwriting alongside Sidney Howard in Baker's "47 Workshop" (1916). Unable to find a job after he left Harvard, he took an M.A. at Columbia, studying under Brander Mathews and John Erskine. Meanwhile he had written his first important play, *The Second Man.* It was basically ahead of its time, and the theatre was in a period of doldrums; Behrman worked for eleven years before he succeeded in getting it produced. During these intervening years he worked on two dramatic collaborations, with J. Kenyon Nicholson and Owen Davis, and served intermittently as a book reviewer and theatrical press-agent. *The Second Man* was finally produced by the Theatre Guild in 1927. The production was a success, and Behrman was established as a Broadway playwright. He continued to turn out approximately one comedy every two years until the period of the Second World War. He also visited Hollywood several times to work on screen plays (*Queen Christina, A Tale of Two Cities*) and adapted a number of foreign works for the American theatre including Somerset Maugham's story *Jane,* Giraudoux's drama *Amphitryon 38,* and Werfel's *Jackobowsky and the Colonel.* Most of these works, along with his own plays, were box-office hits as well as critical successes. Married in 1936 to Elza Heifetz, sister of the violinist Jascha Heifetz, Behrman has lived a quiet and retired life in comparison with most other New York dramatists; he has frequently contributed short stories and articles to popular magazines and has revealed a secret ambition to write a novel. In 1954 his adaptation of Marcel Pagnol's *Fanny* was the hit of the Broadway season. In 1959 he published a play, *The Cold Wind and the Warm,* and he has continued to be productive in the Sixties: *Portrait of Max* (a biography of Beerbohm); *Lord Pengo* (1963), a comedy based loosely on his studies of Duveen; *But for Whom Charlie* (1964); *The Suspended Drawing Room* (1965), a collection of essays and pieces done for *The New Yorker*; and that novel, *The Burning Glass* (1968). No grass grows under Mr. Berhman's feet.

Chief Works: *The Second Man* (drama, produced 1927) is built around a romantic intrigue involving two couples who shift relationships in the manner of Noel Coward's *Quadrille.* The chief characters are Clark Storey, a writer of slick commercial magazine stories; Monica Grey, a vivacious young girl of twenty; Austin Lowe, a dedicated young scientific researcher; and Mrs. Kendall Frame, a wealthy dilettante. The plot depends on the fact that Kendall and Austin have money, while Storey and Monica do not, and that Kendall and Storey are practical while Monica and Austin are romantic. As the play opens both Kendall and Monica are in love with Storey, although Kendall is annoyed at him because of his careless and independent ways and because she believes he is interested in her only for her money. The latter charge is true: Storey, who is normally sexed but incapable of love, knows through his common sense that he and the wealthy Kendall would be happy together but that a marriage with Monica would be stifled by poverty. Austin, fumbling and incompetent in personal life, is unable to win Monica; and she, meanwhile, is open and shameless in confessing her love for Storey. Storey tries to throw the young pair together by leaving them alone in his apartment and ordering a dinner for them, but they quarrel, and for a time Austin develops an interest in Kendall. Monica makes overtures to Storey but is rejected; in a last desperate effort she accuses him, in the presence of the other two, of being "the father of her unborn child." Storey, defeated, agrees to marry her, and the angry Kendall plans to leave for Europe for an indefinite stay. But the next morning Austin appears in the apartment, distraught, and tries to kill Storey with a pistol. Missing, he is overcome with humiliation and despair, and goes to another room to sleep off his fatigue. When Monica arrives at the apartment and learns of Austin's rash and "heroic" act she believes in his love for the first time, and falls in love with the new man he has become. The lovers depart, and the cynical and sophisticated Storey appears to be beaten at last. But he quickly calls up Kendall on the phone and comes to an understanding with her; worldly and free from sentimentalism, the two realize that they can best find happiness with each other. The dramatic interest in *The Second Man* lies in the contrast between the attitudes of the two pairs of lovers: Storey and Kendall, wiser than the younger couple, realize that money is as important as love in making marriage succeed. The title refers to a remark Storey makes about himself, explaining why he is incapable of sentiment or sincerity: "There's someone else inside me—a second man—a cynical, odious person, who keeps watching me, who keeps listening to what I say, grinning and sophisticated, horrid . . ." Yet it is this "second man" who is the wiser of the two parts of Storey's personality, sensing that a romantic marriage with Monica would be doomed to disillusionment and failure.

End of Summer (drama, 1936) is a somewhat more serious play than *The Second Man*, involving a contrast in social classes in addition to its theme of personal conflict. Paula Frothingham, a wealthy young heiress, is in love with Will Dexter, a college student of radical tendencies who plans on editing a left-wing magazine after he graduates. He quickly makes friends with Mrs. Wyler, Paula's grandmother and a member of the vigorous Victorian generation which rose from poverty to make the millions on which the Frothingham family now lives in luxury. Mrs. Wyler dies during the time covered by the play, leaving her money to Paula, and the young couple plan to use the inheritance to found Will's magazine. Leonie, Paula's mother, represents the middle generation, lacking Mrs. Wyler's vigor but also lacking the idealism and social consciousness which mark Paula and her contemporaries. Frivolous and impractical, Leonie is nevertheless a charming representative of the late Victorian millionaire class, which achieved an unmatched elegance and sophistication in its time but is already being destroyed by social change. Leonie, a natural flirt, has an extremely complicated romantic life; still married to Paula's father Sam Frothingham, she plans an affair with the Russian refugee Count Mirsky and then falls in love with Dr. Kenneth Rice, a psychiatrist whom she engages to treat Count Mirsky's neurosis. Meanwhile the younger generation is struggling against the older; Will's college chum Dennis McCarthy, a brash and sarcastic young intellectual, taunts Kenneth about his alleged medical omniscience, and Will finds Paula's father inalterably opposed to her marriage with a "radical." The drama begins to resolve itself when it becomes apparent that Kenneth, the suave opportunist of psychiatry, is cynically plotting to win Leonie for her money. When Paula discovers that Kenneth is actually attracted to her instead of her mother, she tricks him into confessing his "love" in front of Leonie, and thus succeeds in having him banished from the house. Will and Paula, denied Mrs. Wyler's money by Sam, who is the executor of her estate, nevertheless (presumably) marry and strike out to make a living through their own efforts; and Leonie, in a final romantic gesture, promises to back Dennis in publishing the radical magazine. Thus the "end of summer" has seen the complete collapse of the Frothingham clan and their way of life: Mrs. Wyler is dead, Paula has willingly descended into the working class with Will, and even Leonie has joined forces with the proletariat by supporting Dennis, who jokingly tells her, "Come the revolution—you'll have a friend in high places." *End of Summer* is thus an allegorical study of the shifting American social classes in the period from the nineteenth century through the Depression era.

No Time for Comedy (drama, 1939) is usually considered Behrman's most important work. Built basically around the conventional love-intrique which also forms the plot of *The Second Man,* it is in another sense an extremely personal and subjective work in which Behrman attempts to work out his own attitude toward the violent political events of the late Thirties. The central figure, Gaylord ("Gay") Esterbrook, is a successful writer of comedies much like those of Behrman's early work; he is married to Linda Esterbrook, an actress who has played in most of his dramas, skeptical by temperament and ironic in her attitude toward her husband's talent. Gay, fallen into a creative impasse, imagines he has found new stimulation in Amanda Smith, a wealthy society woman who seeks to "develop his latent powers" and inspire him to greater and more profound works. Linda, who discovers this platonic but dangerous relationship through Philo Smith, Amanda's husband, resolves to fight for Gay, and thus the basic conflict of the drama is established. Amanda represents the positive inspiration which a woman can provide for a creative artist, seeking always to encourage him to greater and more significant work; with her assistance Gay plans a pretentious and falsely profound drama entitled *Dilemma* which is to explore the mysteries of immortality. Linda, who actually loves Gay more than Amanda does, nevertheless realizes his limitations and tries to prevent him from "living beyond his intellectual means"; she knows he is an excellent writer of entertaining comedy, but fears he would produce only pompous claptrap if he tried to be profound. Thus she is a "negative" influence on his talent, but a healthy one, an influence which will encourage his true talents and save him from his own weaknesses. A social issue is also involved: under Amanda's influence Gay convinces himself that the grim political events of the time (fascism, the war in China, the Spanish Civil War) demand a more serious attitude toward art, in short that the Thirties are "no time for comedy." The conflict is debated by Gay and Linda in a long dialogue in Act III; Gay is undecided whether to go off with Amanda to fight in the Spanish War or stay with Linda to write more comedies to make the time seem a little less gloomy. As the curtain falls he is on the telephone, still agonizingly undecided; but the presumption is that he will stay with Linda. If he does he will write a play called *No Time for Comedy,* that is, precisely the play in which he is now acting. The attitude of Linda—and of Behrman—toward the question of evils like fascism is expressed in a speech in Act I: "I gather the besieged Spaniards love the American films . . . Why grudge them a little fun in their last moments? . . . We can only laugh at our plight. That's what distinguishes us from the animals . . ."

Lillian Hellman (born 1905)

If Lillian Hellman had written only *The Little Foxes* and *Another Part of the Forest,* she might well be classified as a regionalist; she was born in New Orleans and has a genuine insight into Southern manners and culture, and these two plays treat social movements and processes discussed by other Southern writers from Ellen Glasgow to William Faulkner. She is also, however, the author of *The Children's Hour,* a drama built on abnormal psychology and set in an Eastern girls' school; *Days to Come,* a play involving American labor-management conflicts; *The Watch on the Rhine,* one of the best anti-Nazi plays of the war period; and *The Searching Wind,* laid partly in a European setting and concerned with diplomacy and international intrigue. Here conventional classification breaks down. Miss Hellman is sometimes treated as a "social dramatist," and there is some justification for this label too; almost every one of her plays makes apparent the social attitudes, tendencies, and processes which lie behind personal destinies. At the same time her plays are not "sociological" dramas in any sense; her characters are genuine individuals, not social symbols, and her interest remains centered on the individual conflict of personality which arises out of the contrasting natures of her characters. Thus in *Watch on the Rhine* Teck and Kurt come into conflict not so much because one is a Nazi sympathizer and the other an anti-fascist as because one is depraved and unscrupulous and the other a man of character. The central interest is always on persons rather than on social ideas. If it can be said that in a sense all modern realistic drama derives from Ibsen, Miss Hellman follows in the tradition of *Hedda Gabler* rather than *A Doll's House* or *An Enemy of the People.*

In spite of her sex Miss Hellman is anything but a feminist; in fact it would be difficult, through mere reading of her plays, to identify the author as a woman. Here she differs from Ellen Glasgow, or from female playwrights like Clare Booth (who incidentally resembles Miss Hellman in both subject matter and political attitude). Not only is her interest equally distributed between male and female characters, but she often shows a remarkable knowledge of the male side of life and insight into the masculine mentality. With the possible exception of Tennessee Williams, few male dramatists of her generation have demonstrated such a convincing understanding of the psychology of the opposite sex. This is perhaps best demonstrated in *Watch on the Rhine,* which is almost wholly a masculine story in which the female characters play only peripheral parts.

Politically Miss Hellman is a liberal, an anti-Nazi and antifascist who "believes more in the rights of the working man than in any other rights" and who has undergone Congressional scrutiny for her alleged left-wing associations. In spite of this bias her plays are never didactic. Even *The Searching Wind,* her most sweeping indictment of fascism and appeasement, is tolerant and objective; the diplomat Alexander Hazen, who argues for appeasement, is more misguided than sinister and is at the bottom motivated by humanitarian principles.

Stylistically Miss Hellman's drama is noteworthy for its sophistication and polish, for its adroitly vernacular dialogue, for its unerring accuracy in transcribing the manners of diverse cultures from the small Southern town to the diplomatic circles of pre-war Rome. In spite of its obvious intelligence her drama is invariably facile and easily comprehensible to the ordinary audience, a quality which has enabled her to achieve an impressive box-office success with at least three plays and at the same time to win the praise of serious dramatic critics.

Life: Lillian Hellman was born in New Orleans in 1905; her family background was Jewish. The family moved to New York when Miss Hellman was five, but returned to New Orleans intermittently; she attended schools in both cities. She studied at New York University for three years but left without a degree; she later studied for a semester at Columbia. After leaving N.Y.U. she went to work in the publishing business and simultaneously began writing short stories, only a few of which were published. She first became interested in playwriting through a job as a reader for a dramatic publisher. Her first play, *Dear Queen,* written in collaboration with Louis Kronenberger in 1931, was unproduced. In 1934, however, she wrote *The Children's Hour,* which created an enormous sensation in its Broadway production; it ran for 691 performances—virtually a record for a "problem play"—and was widely thought to have missed winning a Pulitzer Prize only because of its alleged indecency. After her next play, *Days to Come* (1936), a strike story typical of the Depression era, she visited the Soviet Union (1936–37) and spent some time in Hollywood as a screenwriter; she subsequently returned to Hollywood frequently on writing assignments and collaborated on motion-picture versions of *The Children's Hour* and *Watch on the Rhine.* This latter play, which appeared on Broadway in 1941, won her the annual Critics' Circle Award and also achieved a considerable box-office success. In 1945 she visited the Soviet Union for the second time. In the following years she was active in several organizations described as "left-wing," and in 1952 she was called to testify before the House Committee on Un-American Activities. She denied she was a Communist at the time, but refused to discuss her previous political experience. In a subsequent letter to the Committee she stated that for ethical reasons she was obliged to refuse to testify about the political activities of her friends and associates or persons she had known in the various organizations to which she had belonged; the Committee did not pursue the matter. Miss Hellman has been married once, to Arthur Kober, and was divorced in 1932. During recent years she has lived on a farm near New York. Another play, *Toys in the Attic,* was published in 1960; and in 1969 Miss Hellman put out *An Unfinished Woman: A Memoir.*

Chief Works: *The Children's Hour* (drama, 1934) is set in a girls' boarding school operated by two young unmarried women,

Karen Wright and Martha Dobie, who first met in college and who have labored and saved for several years to get the school on its feet. Also teaching in the school is Mrs. Lily Mortar, Martha's aunt, a former actress and a woman of somewhat dramatic temperament. A problem arises when a pupil, Mary Tilford, who has always been somewhat unstable, develops a fit of hysteria when punished for a minor offense. The young Doctor Joseph Cardin, Karen's fiancé, examines Mary and announces that her supposed "heart attack" is only shamming. That night Mary escapes from the school and goes home to her grandmother, Mrs. Amelia Tilford, and for revenge reveals to her an involved web of gossip, partly taken from remarks made by Mrs. Mortar and partly pure fabrication, suggesting that Karen and Martha have been sexually intimate. Mrs. Tilford believes the story, since she imagines Mary to be an innocent child who could only be telling the truth; actually Mary has heard hints of female homosexuality from several other sources, including an illicit reading of Gautier's novel *Mademoiselle de Maupin.* Shocked, Mrs. Tilford spreads the news, and the school is ruined. When another pupil, Rosalie Wells, comes temporarily to stay in the Tilford home, Mary, through knowledge of a minor theft Rosalie has committed, blackmails her to back up her story. Thus complete disaster falls on Karen and Martha; their libel suit against Mrs. Tilford loses in court, and Karen's fiancé Cardin, confused and now half-suspecting the rumors are true, abandons her. Then Martha confesses to Karen her secret guilt: that she actually had felt an unnatural affection for her, although the impulse has never taken an overt form. Rejected by the shocked Karen, Martha commits suicide. Shortly afterward Mrs. Tilford arrives to beg forgiveness of the pair; she has discovered Mary's duplicity and now knows they were innocent. Karen, her life ruined, agrees to accept Mrs. Tilford's sincere contrition and her financial aid in starting over again in a new life.

As a psychological portrait of an abnormal child *The Children's Hour* bears comparison with Henry James' "The Turn of the Screw" and with the less important *The Bad Seed* by William March, later dramatized by Maxwell Anderson. Miss Hellman borrowed the idea for *The Children's Hour* from the Scottish crime writer William Roughead's book *Bad Companions* (1930), which contained a chapter entitled "Closed Doors, or The Great Drumsheugh Case" relating an 1809 Edinburgh scandal caused by a child who claimed two head-mistresses at her school had "an inordinate affection" for each other.

The Little Foxes (drama, 1939) portrays the decline of the Southern aristocracy and the rise of an aggresive new social class in a small Alabama town. The central characters are the Hubbard family—the hard, cynical, avaricious Ben; his weak-willed brother Oscar, and his ambitious sister Regina. Oscar is married to the former Birdie Bagtry, daughter of the genuine ante-bellum aristocratic family of the town; Regina's husband is Horace Giddens, an honest and philosophically inclined banker who as the play opens is away in Baltimore under treatment for a heart ailment. Ben, the natural leader of the family, has found a scheme to make them all rich, involving a partnership with the Chicago financier William Marshall in a plan to build a cotton mill in the town. Ben and Oscar each put up $75,000 and demand an equal contribution from Regina; she cynically tricks her ailing husband Horace to come home in order to get the money out of him. When Horace refuses, Ben encourages Oscar's weak-willed son Leo, who works in Horace's bank, to steal $88,000 worth of bonds from Horace's safe-deposit box. In return for this favor Regina is to marry her daughter Alexandra to the dissolute young Leo. Horace, however, sees through this plot and detects the theft. The bitterness of this family quarrel is too much for his heart, however, and he dies, as Regina, calmly looking on, refuses to bring him the medicine he needs. This is a scene of the greatest cruelty, but circumstances permit Alexandra to guess what has happened. Through Regina's knowledge of the theft she forces Ben and Oscar to give her the dominant share of the partnership; then she turns to her daughter Alexandra who understands her full wickedness for the first time and decides to leave these little foxes "that spoil the vines." Alexandra's rebellion closes the play. Tallulah Bankhead created the role of Regina in the Broadway production, and Bette Davis played the part in a memorable film.

The chief character contrast in this play is that between the Hubbards and Birdie, who represents the true Southern aristocratic tradition which has gone into decline since the disaster of the Civil

War. Horace, along with the faithful Negroes Addie and Cal, is on Birdie's side, deploring the selfish and pushing ambition of Ben and Oscar, believing, as Addie says, that "There are people who eat the earth and eat all the people on it," and that it is not even right for others to "stand and watch them do it."

Watch on the Rhine (drama, 1941) is set in an average American middle-class home, that of the widowed Fanny Farrelly, who has living with her a son, David, and a pair of house guests, the Roumanian refugee Count Teck de Brancovis and his American-born wife Marthe. As the play opens Fanny welcomes to the house her daughter Sara, who is returning to America after a long residence abroad with her husband Kurt Müller, a clandestine German fighter against Nazism, and her children Joshua, Bodo, and Babette. Although Fanny and David cannot understand the fanatic political consecration of Kurt, which has caused much physical suffering and hardship to himself and his family, they greet him warmly and attempt to make him and his family feel at home. The conflict, however, is provided by Teck. A weak character and a failure in his own career, he is jealous of Kurt and also sees in him a chance to make a small fortune. He pilfers Kurt's luggage for evidence which he takes to the German Embassy, and as a result several of Kurt's companions are arrested in Europe. Soon Kurt finds himself at the complete mercy of Teck, who demands a ten-thousand-dollar bribe before he will keep quiet in order that Kurt may return secretly to Germany to aid his imprisoned friends. Kurt at first promises to comply, but he knows that cooperation with the unprincipled Teck is useless. Only violence can resolve the situation; he strikes Teck down and drags him offstage to murder him. The Farrellys, who are of course indignant at Teck's perfidy, are nevertheless shocked at first by this act, but finally realize that evil based on violence (e.g., Nazism) can be fought only on its own terms. They assist Kurt to escape in Fanny's car, although they realize that the eventual revelation of the murder will cause trouble for them with the police. A sub-plot is concerned with the personal relations of Teck and Marthe, who married him because she was dazzled by his title but was soon disillusioned. She turns instead to David, who has previously flirted superficially with her but now accepts her sincerely in a gesture symbolic of his new-born sympathy for the liberal struggle against fascism in Europe.

The Searching Wind (drama, 1944) is a structurally intricate play exploring the reasons for the democratic appeasement of fascism in the Thirties and the human factors which went to make up this social attitude. The plot utilizes the flashback technique; the first and last scenes take place in Washington in 1944 and the intervening scenes fill in the lives of the characters from 1922 to 1938. The chief characters are Alexander Hazen, an American diplomat; the talented Catherine (Cassie) Bowman, his fiancée in 1922; her best friend Emily Taney, whom he eventually marries; and Sam, the son of Alex and Emily, a soldier during the Second World War. As the action proceeds it becomes apparent that Alex's life is one of compromise and rationalizing, in spite of his basic good nature and idealism; the pattern extends from his betrayal of Cassie and marrying of Emily to his career as a diplomat, in which he contributes importantly to the American policy of appeasement which reached its climax at the time of the Munich Conference in 1938. In the last scene Sam reveals that his leg, which has been damaged by a war wound, will have to be amputated; the family realize that Alex's political attitudes of years before have finally caused this tragedy in their own circle. As the play ends Cassie remarks, "I don't want to see another generation of people like us who didn't know what they were doing or why they did it . . . We were frivolous people." Moses Taney, Emily's father, also provides philosophical comment on the action. This play, written at the height of the Second World War, is remarkable for its objectivity and detachment toward the political issues involved; Alex is portrayed as a sincere idealist who is far from a villain, merely, as Cassie remarks, a man who "didn't know what he was doing."

Another Part of the Forest (drama, 1946) is a "sequel in reverse" to *The Little Foxes*; it portrays the earlier history of the Hubbard family in the period around 1880. At this time the family is headed by the hard and ambitious Marcus Hubbard, who made a fortune through illegal commerce during the Civil War and is now replacing the aristocratic Bagtry clan as the chief force in the region. His family, however, provides little assistance to his ambitions; his wife

Lavinia is weak-minded and preoccupied with religion, his son Oscar is a half-witted roué, and his elder son and heir Benjamin is a rebellious and ambitious enemy who opposes him at every turn. His daughter Regina is conducting a secret affair with John Bagtry, scion of the aristocratic family, and Oscar has fallen into a vulgar concubinage with a prostitute named Laurette Sincee. Meanwhile Marcus, encouraged by Ben, plans to gain control of the Bagtry plantation through secretly lending money to the daughter of the family, the childish and light-headed Birdie Bagtry. He leaves the affair in the hands of Ben, who tries to trick him by pretending that the loan is for ten thousand dollars but keeping five thousand for himself. When Marcus discovers the deception a fierce struggle breaks out between father and son. Then Ben discovers, through the maundering of his mentally incompetent mother, the secret disgrace of his father's life: that he had not only operated as a smuggler during the War but that he had once led Union troops through a swamp to slaughter twenty-seven Confederate boys in a hidden training camp. Armed with this knowledge, Ben forces his father to sign over to him all his wealth and surrender control of the family; in his ambition and ruthlessness he has proved himself Marcus' equal. Ruling his family with an iron hand, he marries Regina to Horace Giddens, a young clerk who lives in Mobile and is thus far away enough not to have heard the scandal of her affair with John. He also (as we learn in *The Little Foxes*) forces Oscar to marry Birdie in order to get control of the Bagtry wealth. Miss Hellman evidently considered *The Little Foxes* and *Another Part of the Forest* as part of a trilogy; in a 1952 interview she announced she was contemplating a third play to complete the series.

Arthur Miller (born 1915) Along with Eugene O'Neill, Tennessee Williams, Thornton Wilder, and Lillian Hellman, Arthur Miller represents the best of the American theatre which had evolved and matured in the remarkably short period from 1920 to the mid-fifties. Although as a playwright he is not simply realistic or naturalistic (indeed his best and most theatrical devices seem to be borrowed from expressionism), he nevertheless is closer to Ibsen in ideals, approaches and effects than to any other dramatist. He even adapted Ibsen's *An Enemy of the People* for presentation in 1950 at the center of his own creative work. He is at least as much of a naturalist with his interest in society and social problems as Ibsen himself. Miller's work is not highly original in technique; it represents an organic synthesis, an end product in which the diverse elements are not always apparent on the surface. Basically a realist-naturalist, he concerns himself (unlike Tennessee Williams) with the typical and outwardly normal in American life, and his style is straightforward and vernacular. He deliberately creates characters who are ordinary instead of extraordinary. Miller's typical heroes, Joe Keller of *All My Sons* and Willy Loman of *Death of a Salesman,* are normal American businessmen and husbands; their tragedy provokes sympathy precisely because it is the tragedy of average American life.

Yet Miller's realism is not simple. It is a complex form of art, a technique that uses in one form or another most of the devices developed by the experimentalists of the Twenties: the free verse of Maxwell Anderson, the fluidity in space and time of the Expressionists, the breaking down of the audience barrier of Brecht, Wilder, and others, and the inner psychological analysis of O'Neill's *Strange Interlude. A View from the Bridge* well demonstrates this heterogeneous quality of Miller's work. But since Miller's "experimental" devices are ones which have been stylized and perfected by a generation of use in the theatre, they are conventional enough to be easily grasped by the average audience; Miller in no sense appeals primarily to an avant-garde public. Thus his drama demonstrates the process of filtering-down through which the radical experiments of avant-garde literature eventually reach and influence popular art.

Miller's favorite material, and the setting for the majority of his important plays, is the American middle-class family. *All My Sons* and *Death of a Salesman* are built chiefly around father-son relationships, and *A View from the Bridge* around the tension between a father and step daughter. Although it cannot be said that any of these families are strictly speaking "normal" ones, they are at least "typical"; any playwright is usually obliged to exaggerate the normal for dramatic conflict. Willy Loman is not an "average" American salesman; he is the symbolic archetype of the American salesman, just as Gregor Samsa of Kafka's *Metamorphosis* is the symbol and type of his European counterpart, the commercial traveler. Another theme found almost invariably in Miller's work, connected to his interest in the family, is the American Dream of material success—the cult of the dollar. It is this neurotic avarice, this frenzied effort to provide for the family and rise in the world, which helps destroy both Joe Keller and Willy Loman in spite of their basic decency. And intermingled with these two themes is often found a third: the warped and distorted passions which result from the suppression of the sex drive in puritanical society. This last element is seen most obviously in *A View from the Bridge*, Miller's least realistic play. In spite of his apparent simplicity Miller is a complex artist, one who has carefully integrated his experimental techniques into a personal and original form of realism.

Life: Arthur Miller was born in New York in 1915; his father, an Austrian immigrant, was a well-to-do manufacturer by the time the son was born, although he later lost his money in the crash of 1929. A poor student, more interested in football than algebra, Arthur graduated from high school in 1932, worked in an automobile parts warehouse for fifteen dollars a week, and saved up enough money to attend the University of Michigan where he began writing plays and twice won the Avery Hopwood award for them. After graduation in 1938 he returned to New York, joined the Federal Theatre Project in its last months, and turned to radio writing for a living. His second Broadway play, *All My Sons*, in 1947 brought him acclaim from critics and a certain amount of success with the public. Two years later Miller came into his own with *Death of a Salesman*, thought by some critics to be one of the most significant of modern tragedies; the drama won a Pulitzer Prize and a Critics' Circle Award, enjoyed a phenomenal run on Broadway, later toured the country with considerable success, and eventually, with Mildred Dunnock and Lee J. Cobb of the original cast, was given a classic television production. In 1953 appeared the timely and controversial play, *The Crucible*, a somewhat allegorical and historical drama built around the Salem witch trials of the seventeenth century (which had been dramatized in a forgotten play by Longfellow, *Giles Corey of the Salem Farms*), drawing an ironic parallel to the anti-Red "witch hunts" and McCarthyism of the Fifties. Although important beyond the immediate political situation, *The Crucible* was relevant, and life imitated art when Miller was brought before the congressional un-American investigating committee in 1956 for his liberal political views. He was convicted the following year in a Federal court on contempt charges arising out of his refusal, like his character, John Proctor, to reveal the names of associates in alleged left-wing activities of earlier years. During these stormy political years Miller's first marriage to Mary Slattery, whom he had met in college and by whom he had two children, ran into difficulty and ended in divorce.

His second marriage, to the film actress Marilyn Monroe, in 1956, was certainly more newsworthy (one remark was that it seemed as if Albert Einstein had married Gypsy Rose Lee); after working together on a film for Miss Monroe, *The Misfits,* they found life together impossible and divorced in 1960. Two years later Miller married his third wife, Ingeborg Morath, a photographer for Reuters, and completed his new play, *After the Fall,* as the initial presentation of the Lincoln Center Repertory Theatre. This play, semi-autobiographical, reflecting both personal and political aspects of the dramatist's life, appeared in 1964, with the memory of Marilyn Monroe's suicide two years earlier very much in the public mind. There was certainly more searching for the personal and the shocking in the text of the play than could be legitimately found. In 1967 Miller published a volume of short stories under the title *I Don't Need You Any More.* One of his most recent plays, *The Price* (1968), is much better than the reception it had in the theatre.

Chief Works: *All My Sons* (drama, 1947) is a study of the effect of the Second World War in a typical American family. Joe Keller, the central character, is a sixty-year-old manufacturer and small businessman; his son Larry, a flyer, was reported missing during the war, and Joe's wife Kate has ever since nourished an obsessive and neurotic belief that her son will some day be found alive. Another son, Chris, brooding and idealistic, fought in the war in the infantry and now works in his father's plant. As the play opens Ann Deever, formerly Larry's fiancée, comes to visit the

Kellers, and the secret shame of the family is revealed: during the war Joe had been in partnership with Ann's father in a concern which had shipped defective cylinder heads to the Army Air Corps, causing the deaths of several young men; both had been arrested, but Joe had been exonerated while Deever was sent to prison for a long term. Now Chris, who has long loved Ann, plans to marry her, but his mother is opposed; clinging to her belief that Larry is still alive, she tells Chris that marrying Ann would be an act of betrayal to his brother. Then George Deever, Ann's brother, arrives; he has just visited his father in prison and has become convinced that Joe is also guilty of the crime. He angrily accuses Joe and attempts to take Ann away with him. But the mother Kate, his old friend, succeeds in placating him. As the action proceeds, however, a doubt begins to grow in the mind of the idealistic Chris about his father's innocence. By persistent questioning he finally elicits the truth: that Joe had known about the defective parts and had approved their shipment, later denying his part in the fraud when he was accused. Joe tries to defend his action by arguing that many others did the same thing during the war, that in fact all war procurement was based on the profit system and was basically selfish, and that he committed the fraud solely to win financial security for his family and his sons. Yet it was Joe who symbolically killed his own son Larry; Ann produces a letter to prove that Larry, in disgust over news of his father's fraud, virtually committed suicide in his own plane. Joe finally realizes that the American boys who fought in the war were "all his sons," and that he was as responsible to them as to his own family; he now knows himself to be a murderer. Tormented with guilt, he commits suicide; the mother, before neurotic but now the strongest member of the family, tells Chris, "Don't take it on yourself. Forget now. Live." Thus *All My Sons* demonstrates the basic ethical weakness of the American busines morality, which justifies all through success and often ignores human values; Joe, setting out to succeed in the typical American way, has murdered his own son and brought destruction on himself and his family.

Death of a Salesman (tragedy, 1949) treats a similar theme more expressionistically: the conflict between business ethics and the emotional relationships of a family. The action takes place in Willy Loman's house and yard and various places he visits in New York and Boston, moving with the greatest of ease through an unfixed and scaffolded setting whose spatial reality is in flux. We move back and forth freely in time in Willy's mind which toward the end of his life is subject more than ever to instability. Uncle Ben is hallucinatory and an effective symbol for part of Willy's American dream—the rags-to-riches, get-rich-quick scheme; he is a completely expressionistic character and, with music, objectifies the interior state of Willy's mind. Loman, the traveling salesman with a home in Brooklyn, covers a New England territory by automobile; the action covers the last two days of his life, but events many years back are filled in through flashbacks. An apparently successful salesman in his youth, Willy has gradually become tired and ineffectual; in spite of the encouragement of his wife Linda, he knows his life has been a failure. His two sons, Biff and Happy, are a disappointment; Happy is bogged down for life in a dull and monotonous job, and Biff has turned into a drifter and petty criminal. As the flashbacks are presented they gradually reveal the root of this tragedy: Willy's dogged faith in the magic of salesmanship, his conviction that personality, a glad hand, "contacts," a quick smile, and good clothes will bring you everything you want in life. Biff, a champion athlete in high school, was his favorite of the two boys, and he had ruined his character by pumping him full of this philosophy. "I never got anywhere," says Biff, "because you blew me so full of hot air I could never stand taking orders from anybody!" The climax of the action is a flashback scene in a Boston hotel room, where Biff surprises his father in a clandestine meeting with another woman. Shaken and disillusioned, he drifts gradually into the life of a loafer.

Willy's American dream is more complicated than the simple idea of getting rich some day. It centers most significantly on his sons and his hopes for them. They weren't much as students and their morality is weak, too. When they were young, Willy alternated between excessive pride and a deep worry. Now in their thirties they have not realized the potential Willy thought they had. He blames them and himself alternately, finally driven brutally by Biff to realize his own failure and responsibility for it. As he is fired by the company for which he had worked for thirty-six years, and in the period of grace on his life insurance policy, Willy understands that he is worth more dead than alive. He commits suicide for the twenty-thousand dollar insurance money. Miller said of him, "He gave his life, or sold it, in order to justify the waste of it." There seems little point in arguing whether the play is a tragedy or not. Willy Loman (low-man on the totem pole) is no prince, except perhaps in the American slang use of the word; he is undistinguished, common, often vulgar. But attention must be paid, as Linda says. He does bring upon himself a catastrophe that appears out of proportion to his flaws of character and errors of judgment. He represents *us,* definitely American, twentieth-century man. In business today anybody who doesn't try to succeed is aberrant—Mr. Business-Man, as the song says. But the universality of the play forces us to participate whether we're in business or not. This is our life. You build a house in the country and what happens? It becomes suburbia and then city and then slum. We all have to buy refrigerators, whether we're salesmen or teachers or lawyers or anything. And cars. And they break down before the last time payment. There are lots of contradictions in Willy's life, and ours: pride in the automobile and cursing the machine when it needs repairs—"that goddam car." There is Willy's need to praise himself, and underneath it his feeling of inferiority. Many Americans exhibit bluster over emptiness. Catharsis in experiencing this play is easy.

The Crucible (tragedy, 1953) is about a man's good name and public responsibility during the Salem witchcraft trials of 1692. Mass hysteria places John Proctor, the hero in a dilemma, but he is responsible for his own fall. His past folly, which he has been trying to live down but not with notable success in the eyes of his wife Elizabeth, is his seduction of Abigail Williams, serving-girl in his household, and this fault destroys him when Abigail turns and accuses him of witchcraft. The play's center, however, is his dilemma about commitment. In the beginning John Proctor refuses to have anything to do with the town's problem, to become involved in the absurd charges of witchcraft being made by a group of hysterical, frightened girls. In the second act when Abigail denounces his wife, Elizabeth, as a witch with the help of Mary Warren who introduces a poppet, a doll stuck through with a needle, into the Proctor home, John is pushed into involvement. In the next act John tries to set the court straight by getting Mary Warren to confess the plot of the girls, to prove the whole witchcraft accusation a hoax, to win Elizabeth's freedom without involving himself. But Abigail is too crafty and it doesn't work. Finally he reveals his adultery with Abigail, and that Elizabeth dismissed her from their service when she found out about it. Elizabeth, however, brought in from prison, lies this one time to save her husband's good name; and he himself becomes one of the accused. After suffering for some months in prison, Proctor makes a confession of witchcraft shortly before his scheduled execution, claiming, "I cannot mount the gibbet like a saint. It is a fraud. I am not that man. My honesty is broke, Elizabeth; I am no good man. Nothing's spoiled by giving them this lie that were not rotten long before." But at the last moment he refuses to let the lie stand, tears up the confession, and goes to his death with his good name intact. The victory is not an easy one, but it is a victory.

A View from the Bridge (tragedy, 1955) is actually a short full-length play in structure. Its hero, Eddie Carbone, a longshoreman of Italian descent working on the New York docks, and his wife Beatrice have brought up a niece, Catherine, now seventeen, as their own daughter. Still loyal to relatives in Italy, Eddie and Beatrice agree to take into their flat a pair of illegal Italian immigrants, Marco and Rodolpho, who plan to work on the docks. Marco, the elder, is married and has a tubercular wife, but his younger brother, Rodolpho, blond and handsome, is unmarried. Catherine and Rodolpho fall in love, but Eddie angrily opposes the match. The real reason, however, is that Eddie is himself secretly in love with his niece, and cannot bear to think of letting her go. He first realizes this latent feeling one day when he comes home drunk and finds Rodolpho and Catherine making love; in an angry scene he seizes and kisses her, then fights inconclusively with Rodolpho. Half-crazed with his mixed emotions and ready to do anything to prevent the marriage, he violates the code of his people by betraying Marco and Rodolpho to the Immigration authorities. The two are arrested, but Marco suspects Eddie of the betrayal. When the two are released on bail they come to get

Catherine to take her to be married; a fight breaks out and Eddie is killed by a blow from Marco. He is destroyed by the ignorance of his own passion and by his sin of betrayal.

After the Fall (drama, 1964), which has been called Miller's most intellectually probing play, is gradually emerging from the autobiographical elements which colored its original reception, with Barbara Loden playing the role approximating the character of Marilyn Monroe and Jason Robards, Jr. playing Quentin, the stand-in for the author. Quentin as the central character is complex and the play takes place inside his mind, telling what happens to a man after the loss of intellectual innocence, after the Fall. Quentin has lost his innocence as an individual, with the wreckage of two marriages; as a member of the family where he has seen the failure of love, his mother betraying his bankrupt father whom he himself had deserted; and as a member of society as well, his friend Mickey betraying friends to the House investigating committee and the ultimate betrayals of the Nazi concentration camp for which Quentin feels guilt. As a matter of fact, he is completely guilt-ridden, "I loved them all, all! And gave them willingly to failure and to death that I might live, as they gave me and gave each other, with a word, a look, a truth, a lie—and all in love!" Told by Quentin to an invisible narrator, who might be Quentin's analyst or God or Quentin himself, this is an excoriating examination of conscience in confession. Holga, who may become Quentin's third wife and the most hopeful character in the play, says of the concentration camp, "no one they didn't kill can be innocent again"; but in describing a recurrent dream of an idiot child with a broken face, her own life, that she had to kiss, she adds, "But it somehow has the virtue now . . . of being mine. I think one must finally take one's life in one's arms, Quentin." The note of affirmation is bleak and weak, but it is there. As Quentin screams to Maggie, the second wife, "see your own hatred, and live!" The damned and blasted and fallen man does not live "in some garden of wax fruit and painted trees, that lie of Eden, but after. . . . And the wish to kill is never killed, but with some gift of courage one may look into its face when it appears, and with a stroke of love—as to an idiot in the house—forgive it; again and again." It has been suggested that this may be a kind of conclusion like Faulkner's "They will endure."

The Price (drama, 1968), which opened at the Morosco Theatre in New York City, received indifferent reviews at best and closed relatively soon. It is not a negligible play, however. The story is about two brothers, one Victor Franz, an ordinary policeman who has had an uphill struggle for existence, his wife Esther, and the other Walter Franz, a successful surgeon. They have been separated for several years with apparent hard feelings since Victor had helped Walter finish medical school, dropping out of college himself and joining the police force during the Depression to support their father after financial reverses. Victor, now in the shadow of fifty, finds it too late to start a new career. The father died sixteen years ago, but now it becomes necessary for the brothers to meet to dispose of the property, ten rooms of family furniture crowded into an attic room of a Manhattan brownstone soon to be torn down. This setting is as cluttered as in some of the absurdist dramas of Ionesco (*The Chairs*) or Pinter (*The Caretaker*) but is effectively symbolic of the clutter of American things accumulated by a family over the years. Gregory Solomon, a man nearly ninety, with a Russian-Yiddish accent, comes to assess and possibly buy the furniture. He completes the cast of characters and dispenses wisdom. Victor's resentment comes out, "Like my brother; years ago I was living up here with the old man, and he used to contribute five dollars a month. A *month!* And a successful surgeon." But everytime that Walter came around, not often, the old man showed him respect! The price for the furniture is fixed at eleven hundred dollars; and Walter, who had not responded to Victor's telephone calls, suddenly walks in.

The second act continues with no break in the action (but in the theatre an intermission)—Walter is releasing Solomon's hand which he started to shake at first act curtain. All has not gone well with Walter and his family, disappointments in the children, divorce from his wife. They go back to the price. Walter has an idea how they can get more—it involves cheating on his income tax with an official estimate, a charitable contribution to the Salvation Army, a fee for appraisal to old Solomon, all perfectly "legal." And Victor would get at least six thousand as his share. "How would I list it on *my* income tax?" asks Victor. Walter tells him easily, "Call it a gift. Not that it is, but you could list it as such. It's allowed." Walter thinks Victor made the choice of a real life, without the rat race for money. He tells Victor that their father exploited him, because he had four thousand dollars on the side that Victor didn't know about when he approached his medical brother for a loan to finish school. Walter had finally phoned agreeing to the loan; the father took the message and never delivered it. We all make our choices, some for self-sacrifice, some for success—and pay the price. The antagonisms and selfishness of the brothers and the father are not oversimplified nor minimized (a triangulation frequent in Miller); there are no villains; the confrontation is heated and prolonged, but there are no resolutions, only greater knowledge and a feeling of exhaustion. And as Solomon says, "Good luck you can never know till the last minute, my boy." This may be a great play.

Tennessee Williams (born 1911)

Considered from the standpoints of both critical and popular success, Williams is undoubtedly the most important new dramatist to emerge onto the American theatrical scene in the period after the Second World War. A highly original playwright who has a knack for creating vivid and striking characters, he is not easy to classify by conventional literary standards. He is a regionalist whose interest in the South is incidental to his central concern: human character, personal emotions, the crisis of personality. He is a naturalist who has created some of the most sordid settings and the most debased characters in the modern drama, yet he has a fairy-tale touch that imparts an air of fantasy to his most realistic plays. "Everyone should know nowadays the unimportance of the photographic in art," he wrote in the preface to *The Glass Menagerie:* "that truth, life, or reality is an organic thing which the poetic imagination can represent or suggest, in essence, only through transformation, through changing into other forms than those which were merely present in appearance." This is a clear-cut rejection of traditional realism in the theatre. On the other hand, while his interest in exotic settings and strange and perverted personalities might be considered romantic qualities, his objectivity, his total detachment from his characters and their struggles, sets him apart from romantic dramatists like William Saroyan or Maxwell Anderson. Like Arthur Miller, he utilizes many of the experimental devices of the expressionists and other avant-garde dramatists of the Twenties, but he integrates them into a style which is wholly personal and individual. Like most first-rate authors, Williams belongs to no clear-cut school.

The dominant theme of Williams' work is one which constantly recurs in twentieth-century literature: rejection of the American middle-class Protestant culture and its standards, especially its puritanism and its hypocritical standards of respectability. Like Saroyan and Steinbeck, Williams turns for dramatic material to the exotic and foreign elements in the American population: the Italians and Creole whites of Louisiana, and the decayed aristocrats of a declining Southern culture. Behind the action of most of his plays a social process can be seen in operation: the southern plantation class, vigorous and highly cultivated in the ante-bellum period, declines with the economic decline of the South, becomes corrupt and characterless, and is finally absorbed into the energetic commercial class (often of foreign extraction) which is gradually assuming control of the economy. In *The Glass Menagerie* the dominant class is still the aristocracy, decadent as it is; a mother, lost in escapist reveries of her aristocratic youth, perverts and destroys the happiness of her middle-class children. In *Twenty-Seven Wagons Full of Cotton* a virile Sicilian cotton gin operator symbolically defeats a characterless plantation-owner and seduces his childish and mentally incompetent bride; in *A Streetcar Named Desire* and *Cat on a Hot Tin Roof* members of the former landowning class are seen in various stages of decline. *The Rose Tattoo,* with its virile, hot-blooded, and hedonistic Sicilians, frankly champions physical love in its most violent and unsophisticated form; the two middle-class housewives who appear briefly in the play provide an ironic contrast between Latin vigor and prurient middle-class puritanism.

But mere social change by itself is unrewarding as a source of dramatic conflict. For his immediate plot material Williams makes use of a subject of more immediate interest: the sexual passions, especially in their exaggerated or frustrated form. Sexual maladjustment plays a part in almost all of his major dramas, and the most important of the plays (*A Streetcar Named Desire, The Rose Tattoo*) implicitly contrast uninhibited sexual behavior, which Williams admires, with the perversions, neuroses, and hysteria which arise from frustration of this basic human need. This is not to say that Williams is a "psychological dramatist"; his work is free from the vocabulary and dogma of modern psychiatry, and he owes almost nothing to Freudianism and its related schools of psychopathology. In this respect he resembles D. H. Lawrence more than he does Robinson Jeffers or Eugene O'Neill; it is when his characters follow their "blood instinct" (e.g., the Stanley and Stella of *A Streetcar Named Desire*) that they are happy and satisfied, whatever their social position, and it is when this instinct is denied or misdirected (as in the Blanche of the same play) that neurosis and unhappiness result. And, like Lawrence, Williams has no interest in the sensational aspects of sex, no desire to shock merely for the sake of shocking, or in order to attract attention. He is so supicious of this kind of sensationalism, in fact, that he deliberately cut a number of profane speeches out of *Cat on a Hot Tin Roof* when he heard that rumors were spreading in the theatrical world that he had written a shocking play. Here he stands in sharp contrast to such writers as Henry Miller, who, whatever his basic intent, seems to take an impish pleasure in shocking the complacent and conventional through words banned in polite usage. Williams chooses his language, as he does his material and his characters, because it seems fitted to the poetic concept he has of the play.

Life: Tennessee Williams was born Thomas Lanier Williams in the town of Columbus, Mississippi in 1911. Later at the University of Iowa he changed his name for a number of reasons, according to his mother; his friends there knew he was from the South, couldn't remember Mississippi, and called him Tennessee; he thought Thomas Lanier Williams sounded too much like William Lyon Phelps; and Tom was just too common. In 1918 his father, Cornelius Coffin Williams, traveling salesman who did a lot of traveling, and his mother, Edwina Dakin, daughter of an Episcopal rector, who had been living with her parents accompanied by her two children, Rose and Tom, moved the family to St. Louis. The deplacement was especially difficult for Rose, two years older than her brother, and Tom. They had a southern accent, and neither was robust, Tom limping from recent diphtheria. The boy felt lonely and unwanted in the stodgily respectable middle-western city, and the experience undoubtedly contributed to the aversion toward lower-middle-class respectability which is apparent throughout his work. He began to write at an early age, publishing some poetry under his real name when he was still in his boyhood. Meanwhile he completed his schooling in St. Louis and went on to college in the middle of the Depression; unable to continue because of the financial situation of the family, he dropped out after two years. There followed a long period of monotonous work as clerk in a shoe factory, while he continued with his writing in his free time. Under the combined strain of job and writing his health failed, and he went to live with his grandparents in Memphis. Gradually his writing, mostly stories at this time, began to sell, and he became self-sufficient enough to reenter college. He graduated from the University of Iowa in 1938, went on with his writing, and worked at a succession of odd jobs. In 1940 he was granted a Rockefeller Fellowship which enabled him to write *Battle of Angels,* his first mature play; staged by the Theatre Guild, the play was opened for trial in Boston, but was abandoned during the trial run. Classified 4-F by the draft, Williams went back to his writing and his odd jobs. Then a Hollywood screenwriting contract provided him with enough money to write *The Glass Menagerie*; it was produced on Broadway in 1945, achieved a box-office success, and won the Critics' Circle Award for that season. In 1947 *A Streetcar Named Desire* brought him even greater success, and his reputation as a leading playwright was established. Between 1945 and 1955 he won two Critics' Circle Awards and two Pulitzer Prizes, the latter for *A Streetcar Named Desire* and *Cat on a Hot Tin Roof.* Several of his plays during the period were made into successful motion pictures. In spite of his frequent residence in New York and California, Williams prefers to live in New Orleans, in the Creole quarter he used as the setting for *A Streetcar Named Desire.* Politically independent, he claims to be merely a "Humanitarian."

Among a large number of other plays written during the Fifties and Sixties the most interesting have been *Camino Real* (1953), *Orpheus Descending* (1957), *Suddenly Last Summer* (1957), *Sweet Bird of Youth* (1959), and *The Night of the Iguana* (1962). None has been as successful in the theatre as *Menagerie, Streetcar,* or *Cat,* but *Night of the Iguana* did win another Critics' Circle Award. Effective and off-beat productions have been made of *Camino Real,* which is a different kind of play for Williams (more clearly fantasy) and makes good reading as well as good viewing. *Summer and Smoke* (1948) has been made into an opera with music by composer Lee Holby with premier production scheduled for summer 1971 at St. Paul, Minn. The 1972 Williams play, *Small Craft Warnings,* received some rather hostile reviews (it has become fashionable in the Seventies to attack Williams and Arthur Miller, often in backhand fashion for not being absurdist), but its publication has brought a somewhat more thoughtful reaction. A Tennessee Williams play for two characters, *Out Cry,* was scheduled for spring production in New York in 1973.

Chief Works: *The Glass Menagerie* (drama, 1945) is a "memory play" involving the technique of broken chronology in which the recollections of a narrator present on the stage introduce and comment upon incidents taken from his earlier life. This narrator is Tom Wingfield, a somewhat bitter young man who spent years working in a St. Louis warehouse before he finally became a merchant marine sailor. The other important characters in the seven scenes are his mother Amanda Wingfield, an impoverished widow who nostalgically recalls the youth in which she was a vivacious southern belle with many suitors, and a daughter Laura, crippled, moody, and unattractive to men. Like her mother, Laura lives in a world of illusion; she finds her escape in the "menagerie" of glass animals which she cherishes in the sordid St. Louis flat. Each of Laura's pitiful attempts to face reality has come to nothing; her mother has sent her to business college, but the atmosphere of the school made her physically ill, and Amanda discovers that she has not been attending her classes for several weeks. Tom, who is an avid reader and dreams of becoming a poet, is forced to work at a monotonous job in a shoe warehouse to support the family; he grows rebellious when he sees no way out of the impasse and turns to petty dissipation. A constant bicker goes on between him and Amanda over his way of life. Finally Amanda persuades him to invite one of his fellow-employees from the warehouse to dinner; when Amanda learns that Laura is to have a "suitor" she is filled with a nervous elation, and makes a pitiful attempt to tidy up the flat. Jim O'Connor, the guest, is "a nice, ordinary young man" who gets along well with Laura; by coincidence it happens that he is a secret beau for whom Laura had a clandestine admiration in high school. As her desperate need for a lover becomes apparent, however, Jim grows apprehensive; finally he confesses to her that he is engaged to another girl and will soon be married. After Jim leaves, Amanda bitterly upbraids Tom for bringing an engaged man as a suitor for Laura. Tom, his disgust at the sordid family situation rising to the point of rebellion, storms out of the flat—ostensibly to go to the movies, but actually to go off to sea. As the play ends Tom, now a detached narrator of his own life drama, confesses to the audience the feeling of remorse toward his sister which has pursued him ever since he abandoned her to her lonely spinsterhood.

In addition to the unrealistic device of the actor-narrator, *The Glass Menagerie* utilizes another surrealistic or expressionistic trick: a screen on which are projected magic-lantern slides bearing images or titles which comment ironically on the action. This device, intended to "give accent to certain values in each scene," was omitted in the Broadway production.

A Streetcar Named Desire (drama, 1947) is set in the Creole quarter of New Orleans "on a street which is named Elysian Fields" and which is reached by taking a streetcar named Desire and transferring to one named Cemeteries—i.e., an analogue of life itself. Stela DuBois, daughter of an old but now impoverished southern family, has come to New Orleans and married Stanley Kowalski, an artisan of Polish extraction, strong, virile, a heavy drinker and a great poker player. As the play opens Stella's sister Blanche, who has remained home in the family mansion in Laurel, Mississippi, comes to "visit"—actually she is coming to live with them, since everyone else in the family has died and Blanche, through incompetence and debauchery, has lost the family mansion to creditors. Although Blanche has pretensions to elegance and pretends to feel a fastidious repugnance for the surroundings in which Stella and Stan live, it soon becomes apparent that she is not only a neurotic but an alcoholic and a shameless nymphomaniac. She at first attempts to vamp Stan, but he, content with his satisfying relations with Stella, ignores her. Then she takes up with Harold Mitchell ("Mitch"), an unmarried friend of Stan, somewhat younger than she (Blanche is apparently in her late thirties and anxious over the approach of middle age). At first this affair goes well, and Mitch's interest in Blanche seems to be based on genuine love. Once when they are alone Blanche confesses to Mitch the secret tragedy of her life, which has left her guilt-ridden and lonely ever since: married at sixteen, she accidentally discovered that her young husband was a homosexual, and drove him to suicide through her recriminations. Mitch accepts her in spite of this, and a marriage, the solution to Blanche's problems, seems in the offing. But meanwhile she has made an enemy of Stan through her haughty air of superiority, her hypocritically fastidious ways, and her secret drinking. When Stan learns the truth about her past—that she was virtually banished from Laurel after she had taken up a life of debauchery—he tells the full story to Mitch, who breaks off relations with her. To complete his revenge Stan roughly attacks her one night when Stella has gone to the hospital to have a baby. Her "fiancé" gone and her pose of superiority toward Stan shattered, Blanche relapses into a psychotic world of self-delusion, consoling herself with an imaginary friend, the wealthy Shep Huntleigh, who is shortly to invite her on a yachting cruise of the Caribbean. Stella has no choice but to send her to a mental hospital; a doctor and a matron call for her, she struggles frantically against the female matron, but is led away quietly by the male doctor.

Two themes are interwoven in *A Streetcar Named Desire:* (1) the decline of the landowning southern aristocracy, symbolized by Blanche and Stella, and its defeat at the hands of the modern commercial-industrial class, personified in Stan; and (2) the contrast between hysterical female sex-frustration (Blanche) and normal and healthy physical relations (Stella and Stan). As a human being Blanche is pitiable, especially when we understand the past history which has made her what she is; but as a visitor in the house of Stan and Stella she stands for evil, and she brings evil to everyone she touches. Particularly obnoxious is her ingrown and perverted delicacy, which contrasts strongly with Stan's hard-drinking, profane, vulgar, but basically healthy attitude toward life.

The Rose Tattoo (drama, 1950) centers around the character of Serafina delle Rose, a Sicilian dressmaker who lives with her daughter Rosa in a small Gulf Coast village. Happily married to Rosario, a virile Italian truck driver who has a rose (evidently a symbol of physical love throughout the play) tattooed on his chest, she is expecting another child as the play opens. When she is visited by Estelle Hohengarten, a harlot, she agrees to make a rose-colored shirt for Estelle's sweetheart without realizing that Estelle is actually intimate with her Rosario. Then news comes that Rosario, smuggling narcotics in his truck under a load of bananas, has been killed in a fight with the police. Serafina, morbidly brooding on her grief, locks herself in her house and for months refuses to dress or to attend to her business. Cherishing her dead husband's ashes in an urn, she regresses constantly farther into her melancholia. When Flora and Bessie, two priggish middle-class ladies, call for a blouse they have ordered, Serafina is rude to them, and for revenge Flora repeats to her the common gossip about the unfaithfulness of her husband; Serafina, stunned, becomes even more sullen and brooding. Her daughter Rosa, seventeen and just graduated from high school, picks this moment to introduce to her mother her boyfriend, a sailor named Jack Hunter. Serafina, skeptical over the faith of men, forces Jack to swear before an image of the Virgin that he will "respect the innocence of the daughter, Rosa, of Rosario delle Rose."

In Act II a complication is introduced: by accident a young truck driver, Alvaro Mangiacavallo, calls at the house, and Serafina in spite of herself is struck with his resemblance to her dead husband. When Alvaro clumsily makes advances to her she rejects him, then gives him permission to return that night. Act III begins with a farcical courting scene in which Alvaro, hot-blooded but inept, is constantly repulsed by the inwardly confused Serafina. When Alvaro learns that her resistance is caused by loyalty to her dead husband, he proves through a telephone call that Rosario had actually been unfaithful to her; in a torment which fast becomes a passion, Serafina then gives her love to him. The next morning Alvaro arises stupefied with a terrible hangover and confusedly makes advances to the sleeping Rosa, who has meanwhile returned from a date. A terrible three-cornered argument results; but in the end Serafina blesses Rosa's marriage with Jack and forgives the clumsy Alvaro for his mistake. Life has triumphed over the cult of death in the Delle Rose household: Serafina's long dead love has been reborn in the person of the handsome young Alvaro. The success of *The Rose Tattoo* is the triumph of the characterization of its heroine. Alternating between an animal-like brooding and a fiery and hot-blooded passion, Serafina is simultaneously a vividly original human being and a symbol of healthy and unashamed womanhood, uninhibited by Anglo-Saxon puritanism and the middle-class bugbear of respectability.

Cat on a Hot Tin Roof (drama, 1955) is set on a Mississippi plantation owned by "Big Daddy" Pollitt, an energetic planter who rose from a "red-neck" overseer to become a multimillionaire. As the play opens Big Daddy is dying of cancer, a fact known to everyone in his family but his wife Big Mama. His children, who have gone to college and become "respectable" and successful, now gather around to fight over the spoils. An elder son Gooper and his wife Mae have brought their five children to the plantation to win Big Daddy's sympathy, but the howling and ill-mannered brats only set his nerves on edge. His younger son Brick, an alcoholic, takes little part in the controversy; but Brick's wife Margaret, the "cat on a hot tin roof," nervous and sexually frustrated, determines to fight vigorously for her husband's rights. The climactic scene occurs when Big Daddy, who has been assured that his illness is curable and that he will soon be well, has a conversation with Brick in which he begins to probe into his son's reasons for drinking. This reason Brick has scarcely admitted even to himself: it is a secret fear that his affection for a college friend, Skipper, was an unnatural one. Margaret, angry over Brick's failure to make love to her, has accused him of this, and now under his father's grilling he realizes it is true. In his desperate effort to get back at Big Daddy he tells him the truth that he is incurably ill of cancer. In a mixture of despair and hot-tempered anger at the lies that have been told him, Big Daddy shuts himself up in his room. Then, in a family conference, the truth about Big Daddy is told to Big Mama, and Gooper attempts to wheedle her into giving him control of the property. Margaret, seeing her cause failing, tries to rally Brick to help her, but he is apathetic. Finally, in a last desperate effort to win Big Daddy's sympathy, she sends word to him that she is going to bear Brick's baby. As the play ends she has determined to make this lie a reality, and in her dogged strength of character she finds the means to force Brick into serving as the father for her child. The ending is inconclusive, but the implication is that the flighty but courageous Margaret has won her battle against the hostility of her relatives and the apathy of her husband.

For the Broadway production of *Cat on a Hot Tin Roof* (1955) Williams was induced to write a new third act which differed considerably from the original printed version, chiefly as the result of suggestions from the director Elia Kazan. The chief difference between the two versions is that the Broadway ending is more specific and leaves less to be conjectured, also that a definite change is shown in the character and attitude of Brick. Some ambiguity was also felt about the characterization of the heroine in the original version. As Williams later wrote, Kazan "felt that the character of Margaret, while he understood that I sympathized with her and liked her myself, should be, if possible, more clearly sympathetic to the audience." This sentence is an important clue to the character of Margaret; she is by no means a dangerously hysterical neurotic like the Blanche of *A Streetcar Named Desire,* merely a healthy and normally sexed young woman who has been turned into a "cat on a hot tin roof" by her husband's inattention. In the Broadway version of the play this point is made clear by Big Daddy's acceptance of Margaret in the final scene.

Williams' plays have received interesting and imaginative productions abroad as well as in the United States. A Dublin experimental theatre production of *The Rose Tattoo* brought riots and a closing of the theatre, which almost always means good drama in Dublin.

Edward Albee (born 1928)

Edward Albee whose first play, *The Zoo Story,* was not produced in America until 1960 has in the space of some ten years written ten plays, collaborated on another, adapted Carson McCullers' *The Ballad of the Sad Café* and other novelistic works for the stage, and become a celebrity. His plays are attacked and praised with almost equal vigor. But he is America's chief writer within the general framework of Theatre of the Absurd, which he has modified in American ways even as Pinter made it English.

Probably Albee's greatest commercial success came with *Who's Afraid of Virginia Woolf?* in 1962, the long run on Broadway followed by the Richard Burton–Elizabeth Tayor film which was appropriately bitchy, debauched, and profound simultaneously. But there are other plays by Albee that repay close reading and careful viewing: *The Death of Bessie Smith* and *The Sandbox* (1959), *The American Dream* (1960), *Tiny Alice* (1965) and *A Delicate Balance* (1966) in particular. They show many specific influences from Beckett and Ionesco, but add up to a distinctly American criticism of American absurdities.

Life: Abandoned shortly after his birth on 12 March 1928, Edward Albee was adopted by foster parents when he was two weeks old and brought up in the lap of luxury (not an unmixed blessing) by Reed and Frances Albee, the former the millionaire heir to the Keith-Albee chain of movie theatres. Frances, a former model, was twenty-three years younger than her husband. Spoiled but given little parental understanding, Edward was sent to various expensive boarding schools, somewhat like Salinger's Holden Caulfield, it has been suggested. At Choate he began to write poetry and fiction.

At twenty he left home, breaking with the parents and an atmosphere of discord as well as the money, and spent the next several years hand-to-mouth mostly in Greenwich Village. He says it was Thornton Wilder, met in 1953, who suggested he write plays, but he did not do so until almost five years later. Then for his thirtieth birthday, as a present to himself, he wrote *The Zoo Story*. Refused in New York, it was sent abroad to friends and made its way to a first performance in German in West Berlin. In January of 1960 it was produced as half of a double bill off-Broadway with Samuel Beckett's *Krapp's Last Tape,* a highly successful combination. His productivity seems not to have exhausted his invention. Apparently Pinter and Albee have not reached the point of no return of a Beckett or an Ionesco.

Professional theatre people, by which is meant actors, directors, designers, not the critics, have always regarded Albee's work as eminently theatrical. Uta Hagen chose to play the role of Martha in *Who's Afraid of Virginia Woolf?* Sir John Gielgud, John Heffernan, and Irene Worth played *Tiny Alice* in 1964–65. *A Delicate Balance* (1966), dedicated to John Steinbeck, had the services of Jessica Tandy and Hume Cronyn; *Everything in the Garden* (1967), of Barbara Bel Geddes and Beatrice Straight. Even the 1971 production of Albee's *All Over,* directed by Sir John Gielgud with set by Rouben Ter-Arutunian, starred Jessica Tandy, Neil Fitzgerald, and Betty Field among others. Between the last two plays mentioned came the rather experimental two interrelated plays, *The Box* and *Quotations from Chairman Mao Tse-tung,* first performed by the Studio Arena Theatre in Buffalo, N.Y. in 1968. Even the critics usually concede that "Albee is our best playwright" at the present time. "*Who's Afraid of Virginia Woolf?* was about the emptiness that surrounds and threatens to swallow our relationships; *Tiny Alice* was about the void lurking behind our deepest beliefs; now, *A Delicate Balance* is about the nothingness of it all—it is a play about nothing." "*Everything in the Garden* is both extraordinarily flawed and extraordinarily engrossing." "At the heart of the play [*All Over*], Mr. Albee has sedulously carved a huge hollow, and he has then seen to it that the hollow does not reverberate." Yet the same critics will applaud Beckett and Pinter for similar qualities. Perhaps it is the American frame of reference for the Theatre of the Absurd that disturbs them; it shouldn't happen to us. The hollowness of American types, from the Mommy and Daddy of *The Sandbox* and *The American Dream* on down (with only the dying grandmother having any vitality), is an important message, and Albee tells us it is meant as "an examination of the American Scene, an attack on the substitution of artificial for real values in our society, a condemnation of complacency, cruelty, emasculation and vacuity; it is a stand against the fiction that everything in this slipping land of ours is peachy-keen." Even *King Lear,* according to Jan Kott, is a play about the absurdity of our existence, about nothingness, and might have been renamed *Endgame* (Beckett).

Representative Plays: *The Zoo Story* (one-act play, 1959) is a play in one scene, a bench in Central Park, Manhattan. It has only two yin and yang characters, Jerry the outcast, sensitive, somewhat feminine, eager to establish genuine contact with someone, anyone, and Peter the conformist bourgeois, respectable but square, defensively masculine, lonely without knowing it. Peter has a book; Jerry has a knife. This is a zoo story in more ways than one: Jerry has just come from the zoo ("I took the subway down to the Village so I could walk all the way up Fifth Avenue to the zoo. It's one of those things a person has to do; sometimes a person has to go a very long distance out of his way to come back a short distance correctly."); they both live with animals, Jerry in a house with a vicious dog, and Peter with two parakeets, two cats, two daughters, two TV's and a conventional wife; man is animal with animalistic violence just beneath the skin surfacing at the end of the play; and the zoo symbolizes "the caged isolation of modern man."

The dialogue of the two men in their fortuitous meeting in the park reaches a climax with Jerry's compulsive telling of the story of Jerry and the Dog; how he tried to make friends with it and, not overcoming its antipathy, how he tried to kill it, equally unsuccessful in his offers of love or hate. To be human you have to make contact with somebody, with some animal, with something. Peter is wary. Jerry pushes him into anger, into violence. He draws his knife, and Peter is afraid, "You're stark raving mad! You're going to kill me!" Jerry throws the knife at his feet and taunts him into picking it up, then runs to impale himself on the knife that Peter is holding defensively. In death, a suicide-murder, he makes contact with another human being on an animal level.

There are all sorts of lightly placed Biblical allusions: Peter's name, Jerry's "So be it" and "It came to pass," the exclamations "For God's sake" and "Oh my God," and the ubiquitous Dog anagram for God that has appeared so often since Joyce's use of it in *Ulysses*. Jerry has staged his own death, but Peter may have learned something from it—his illusions have been penetrated and he may carry the message, the zoo story of man's caged animality.

Who's Afraid of Virginia Woolf? (play, 1962) is a play where murderous dialogue leads to murder, if only of a fictive son. The setting is a college campus in New Carthage, Anywhere in America. "Fun and games" concentrate on verbal fencing. There are four characters, the two most important the married couple George and

Martha, whose hatred and love for each other are intense and inextricably mixed. Honey and Nick, a much younger faculty couple, serve only to listen, to stimulate sexual desires and jealousies, and to make up a foursome. George and Martha at the peak of their sado-masochistic marriage battle it out. Martha begins by taunting George with his failures, professional and sexual; George tries to drown her out singing, "Who's Afraid of Virginia Woolf?" In a gin, brandy, and bourbon soaked evening with "musical beds" as the faculty sport, we find that George and Martha have cemented their sterile marriage with the fiction of a child. In an upsurge of hatred they declare total war, both hitting below the belt, George striking back at Martha's age, drinking, and promiscuity.

As they reveal the truth about their imaginary child to Honey and Nick, it is obvious that the child must die, illusions must be destroyed. After the "Walpurgisnacht" of the second act and "The Exorcism" of the third, George and Martha reach a kind of tentative "hint of communion." In spite of their malice they need each other, a need that might be called love in the absence of anything else. Honey and Nick may be saved by what they have seen. George and Martha may be too old and boxed-in to change very much. But like the novel George doesn't dare publish while he teaches, Albee's play may be "an allegory, really—probably." It is exhausting, and passion is spent even if there is no concurrent calm of mind.

Tiny Alice (fantasy play, 1964) is Edward Albee's attempt to present a sensitive modern American's religious experience to its ultimate conclusion. If it seems sometimes thin, often confused, racked with doubts, and mixed up with literature, sex, and psychiatry, that's the way it is. His protagonist is Julian, a lay brother (aren't we all?), who is marked out and pursued to a martyrdom in death as relentlessly as any character in Flannery O'Connor; but there is compassion and pity for Julian—almost too much at the end where it takes him too long to die. The death itself has suggestions of Ionesco's *Exit the King* (see Volume I), the departure of everybody else, the covering of the furniture, leaving Julian quite alone in a man's ultimate confrontation with nothingness. "To be left alone—suddenly!" Julian has always wanted to serve and has sometimes dreamed of martyrdom, like Eliot's Thomas of Canterbury. Only one part of his life is blank in his dossier, when he spent six years in a mental home because he had lost his faith. He was placed, on voluntary commitment, in a section of the asylum for the "mildly troubled," which he found ironic, not considering the loss of faith a mild matter. But his concept of God is very personal, not Man's, not the church's. "I could not reconcile myself to the chasm between the nature of God and the uses to which men put . . . God." At the sanitarium Julian remembers having hallucinated—which may be what happens again when he goes to meet Miss Alice. The Catholic church is rather bitterly satirized (but by extension the Protestants and Jews as well) in the opening scene with the accommodations it makes in its greed for money.

The major setting, except for the Cardinal's garden, is the mansion of Tiny Alice, a castle brought to America from England stone by stone but including as its central feature a complete, huge model of itself on display in the reception hall. Looking into the reception hall of the model, one sees another model (a series of Chinese boxes). The castle thus becomes a symbol of the cosmos, the wonders of the world. Miss Alice, who first poses as a deaf old woman with two canes but proves to be relatively young and sexual, the Lawyer, and the Butler, named Butler, play games (cruel games and ultimately deadly serious—as in Dürrenmatt?) with Julian who is being sacrified in marriage to Miss Alice as a surrogate for Alice who is either a destructive god (*dio boia* in *Ulysses*) or nothing at all, sold in effect by the Cardinal whose secretary he had been for two billion dollars. This is the entire "establishment," a suggestive phrase in contemporary literature, but still Alice is awesome and not entirely without pity. The play as printed is too long (it was cut for production, especially at the end), but the role of Julian was sufficiently intriguing to attract Sir John Gielgud. The combination of almost "open-air" menace (as opposed to Pinter's closed room kind of thing) and exaltation with sudden shifts from malevolence to benevolence and return, dropping down shafts to nothingness, is particularly and characteristically Albee; it may be a prolonged adolescent syndrome, a mild schizophrenia, but is theatrically effective in any case.

All Over (play, 1971) may have multiple meanings in its title. The play is about a gathering of people all devoted to "grisly self-revelation" who are waiting for the slow death of a pretty important man, The Wife, The Mistress, The Best Friend, his cowed and unloving children, and of course reporters, ubiquitous carrion-seekers. The doctor in attendance finally announces the event. Ironically the interrelationships of the relatives and friends, exacerbated by their being together in the death-watch, are far from "all over." But the Pirandello-like use of the words at the end of the play refers doubly within and without to the life of the man and the evening in the theatre. It has been suggested that Albee may also have been deliberately handing the critics who have not always been kind to him a handle for discussing his career, a wry pleasantry that is more likely to backfire than not. The play, carefully plotted and written, uses language suggestive of Henry James and Ivy Compton-Burnett, perhaps in the acerbity of conversational exchange. The absurd emptiness, epitomized in the apparent hollowness of the dying man's international reputation—one never knows why he is famous, is here a more public emptiness than in the earlier plays of private experience.

Lorraine Hansberry (1930–1965)

Lorraine Hansberry achieved sudden, almost instant, recognition with her first play, *A Raisin in the Sun,* in 1959. It won the New York Drama Critics' Circle Award as best play for the 1958–59 season, the first time a play by a Negro playwright had been so honored. Her second play, *The Sign in Sidney Brustein's Window* (1964), opened to mixed critical reviews; but critics notwithstanding, it is a better play, even a great play.

As in the case of Edward Albee, professional theatre people were more aware of its greatness than reviewers. In "The 101 'Final' Performances of *Sidney Brustein*" Robert Nemiroff gives credit to the professional people who with contributions and appeals kept the play running at the Longacre Theatre in New York including members of the cast, Alice Ghostley in particular offering her savings, Sidney Kingsley, Shelley Winters, Viveca Lindfors, James Baldwin, Paddy Chayevsky, Julie Harris, Lillian Hellman and many others. John Braine, the English novelist among the Angry Young

Men who wrote *Room at the Top,* saw the play partly by accident, "it was the only new Broadway play I could easily obtain a ticket for" and wrote a foreword for the published play in which he insists it is "a great play" because "It is drama of such clarity that one may return to it again and again . . . each time more illumined." The characters are "larger than expectation," all real, "diverse, illuminatingly contradictory, heart-breakingly alive."

Miss Hansberry, like Carson McCullers and Flannery O'Connor, had her career cut short after a valiant fight against disease, only she was younger than either of them at thirty-four when she died. Her idea for a third play, partly written, *Les Blancs* was brilliant (to show the conflicting reactions of Negroes and whites living in an African land emerging from colonialism), but the finished product executed by others in 1970 did not succeed. Her reputation must depend on two plays, one good and the other great. (*To Be Young, Gifted and Black,* 1969, is an attempt to put together a "biographical play," using for its most effective scenes excerpts from *Raisin* and *Sidney Brustein.*)

Life: Born in Chicago on May 19, 1930, Lorraine Vivian Hansberry grew up there. Her father, Carl A. Hansberry, in real estate and banking, bought a house in a white neighborhood when she was eight. She became interested in the theatre while still in high school but decided to study art instead, first at the Chicago Art Institute, then at the University of Wisconsin and, finally, in Guadalajara, Mexico. In 1950 Lorraine moved to New York City, married Robert Nemiroff, a music publisher, in 1953, and living in Greenwich Village began to write *A Raisin in the Sun* after reacting with distaste to a whole body of material about Negroes—cardboard characters, cute dialect, or big-swinging musicals. *Raisin,* a phenomenal success in 1959, has been called not a Negro play but a play about people who happen to be Negroes. For two years before her death from cancer, Lorraine Hansberry had been in and out of the hospital. *The Sign in Sidney Brustein's Window* was in production and opened on Thursday, October 15, 1964. Reviews were disappointing. Two days later Lorraine was back in the hospital and on the 20th she lost her sight, then went into convulsions. Her husband read to her a letter from a stranger, "You have written a beautiful—a painfully beautiful work of art. Please, if *Sidney* fails, please keep writing . . . I don't know why or how it missed being received as one of the modern theatre's greatest achievements. . . . For my own part, let me tell you that I felt everything that was happening on stage yesterday . . . I believed in everyone, and I hurt—and I saw the beauty in each. Thank you!" Contrary to medical predictions Lorraine pulled out of her near collapse, recovering sight, partial movement, comprehension and speech, even being able to sit in a chair. But the end came on January 12, 1965. She has been described as a "slim, cheery, talkative young woman with a gay, flashing smile"; she sided, like Sidney Brustein, unequivocally with involvement.

The Plays: *A Raisin in the Sun* (drama, 1959) takes its title from a poem by Langston Hughes, "What happens to a dream deferred?/ Does it dry up/ Like a raisin in the sun?" The role of Walter Lee Younger was created by Sidney Poitier who later transferred it to the film which won an award at the Cannes Festival. Ruby Dee, Diana Sands, Claudia McNeil, and Ivan Dixon (of the TV Hogan's Heroes sequence) also had major roles. The setting is Chicago's Southside sometime after World War II. Tensions erupt in the middle class Negro Younger family when Mama (Lena Younger) comes into possession of the insurance money from her husband's death, ten thousand dollars. Almost everybody in the family has a dream, involving Mama's money—Walter Lee wants to invest in a liquor store business; his sister Beneatha wants to go to med school to become a doctor; Mama and her daughter-in-law Ruth, pregnant again, dream of buying a house with some land for a garden to get out of their rent-eating, cockroach infested, apartment, a place where the grandson Travis can grow up with fresh air and sunshine. But even ten thousand dollars won't do everything. Beneatha has a college boy friend from Nigeria whose name is Asagai; they seem very much in love and committed to issues of racial pride and civil rights. One of the best scenes in this otherwise realistic play is a semi-expressionistic one at the beginning of Act II. Beneatha comes out dressed in the Nigerian costume Asagai has brought her, dances to Nigerian folk music on the phonograph, and Walter, drunk, comes in to join in a war dance. Ruth comments,

"Africa sure is claiming her own tonight." Mama is the strongest character in the play, but that doesn't mean the others are weak. She makes a down payment on a house (in a white neighborhood in Clybourne Park) but, seeing Walter's discouragement gives him the rest of the money, three thousand for Beneatha's education, three thousand five hundred for him to bank in his own name to restore a male pride. When Mr. Lindner of the Clybourne Park Improvement Association comes to "buy them out" at a profit, they reject him with dignity. But Walter loses the whole sixty-five hundred in a "business deal" when he trusts one of his own bar buddies. Asagai asks Beneatha to marry him and go to Africa—an unresolved offer. Mr. Lindner may be a way out for Walter, but he finally stands firm and becomes a man in the eyes of his wife Ruth, his son Travis, and his mother. As the family moves out of the apartment at final curtain Lena carries her favorite potted plant.

Raisin is almost a realistic problem play in the Ibsen tradition, but the problem is modern, American, and racial, open housing, with an emphasis on the worth of individual human beings. Mr. Lindner is the only caricature. Mama in her wisdom leans a little toward the sentimental in the total portrait. But the play is a good play with authentic dialogue and fully realized characters in Walter, Ruth, and Beneatha.

The Sign in Sidney Brustein's Window (drama, 1964) proves that like Baldwin Miss Hansberry is enough of a master artist that she doesn't have to restrict herself to writing about Negro life and problems. In that sense *Giovanni's Room* and *Sidney Brustein* are not so much *tours de force* as pioneering work by black artists. They have overcome. Sidney Brustein is the protagonist and if not heroic in the old sense he is not an anti-hero either; in the end he seems a believable and affirmative hero for an American of the mid-twentieth century. He is, of course, a minority figure too, a Greenwich Village intellectual Jew who, with his friends, supports a reform candidate in a local election, after which, miraculously won, the candidate Wally O'Hara proves to be not purely altruistic, has in fact sold out. The main characters, Sidney Brustein, his wife Iris, her sisters, Mavis Bryson and Gloria Parodus (the unmarried one), the Negro friend Alton Scales, the homosexual playwright David Ragin living in an upstairs apartment, and Max who helps with Sidney's newspaper, are all strictly and individually real, not just sounding boards for Sidney. As John Braine wrote, "the play becomes Sidney Brustein's personal odyssey of discovery, a confrontation with others in the process of which he discovers himself." The scene is a basement apartment in the Village and the life there is very bohemian and casual and authentic. Alton because of his color has always lived a victim in a world of injustice. But although he has asked Gloria to marry him, when he discovers the truth that she has been a call girl as well as a model, he is just as prejudiced and as cruel as the world which has persecuted him. Intelligent, warm, sensitive, he still abandons Gloria, behaving as badly as a white man might in the same circumstances. The playwright does not make him a hero because he is black. Mavis is another brilliant characterization; by natural instinct a segregationist and anti-Semite she is nevertheless generous, brave, intelligent, and gentle, and grows in stature in a highly effective scene with Sidney. David gives the playwright an opportunity to talk about writing plays. Sidney says, "David is engaged in the supreme effort of trying to wrest the theatre from the stranglehold of Ibsenesque naturalism." Sidney shouts at Iris, "Is that all you can ever say? Who cares, who cares? Let the damn bomb fall, if somebody wants to drop it. . . . Well, I admit it: I *care!* I care about it all. It takes too much energy *not* to care. . . . And you, David, you have now written fourteen plays about not caring, about the isolation of the soul of man, the alienation of the human spirit, the desolation of all love, all possible communication." This is an answer to Theatre of the Absurd, and a pretty good one.

Scene One of Act II is a beautifully non-realistic dream sequence with Sidney as dreamer. But the play's tensions mount as good drama demands: Iris leaves Sidney to do crass TV commercials; Gloria appears and, struck by Alton's desertion and the despair of her situation, commits suicide; Wally shows his true dark colors. Sidney out of desperation decides to fight. If you don't like the world, you can change it. When he lifts his glass of water and takes his ulcer medicine he gives the toast L'chaim! (To life!) And we all get the lift of a little affirmation. Later at the very end of the play when called a fool by Wally, Sidney answers: "Always have been. A fool who believes that death is waste and love is sweet and that the earth turns and men change every day and that rivers run and that people wanna be better than they are and that flowers smell good and that I hurt terribly today, and that hurt is desperation and desperation is—energy and energy can *move* things . . ." If this is a problem play, the problem is commitment, and Lorraine Hansberry says Yes for all of us.

AMERICAN POETRY: MID-CENTURY

IV

12. New Directions and Traditional Values

The directions of twentieth century American poetry had been pretty well established by 1930. The verse naturalism of Robinson, Sandburg, and Frost with its tendencies to avoid artificiality and achieve a natural vernacular idiom continued to be written without exciting new developments until it moved into the area of protest poetry where a Langston Hughes could use it to hammer at racial injustice. In the Sixties extensive areas of protest produced song lyrics by a number of people but not a single outstanding poet; he may be around the corner. The technical experimentation, symbolism, reconstruction of language, new forms of prosody, associated with Pound, T. S. Eliot, William Carlos Williams, E. E. Cummings, and others, seemed to gain the upper hand (that's why these poets appear here rather than in Volume III); MacLeish, Wallace Stevens, Marianne Moore, and Theodore Roethke, even Robert Lowell seem to be closer to this tradition and are certainly major American poets. Sometimes, of course, the two modes are combined, even in Eliot. *The Wasteland*, one of our more difficult poems, contains passages of almost transcribed vernacular: "He's been in the army four years, he wants a good time,/ And if you don't give it him, there's others will, I said . . ."

But Eliot felt that modern poetry had to be difficult in order to express its age: "Our civilization comprehends great variety and complexity, and this variety and complexity, playing upon a refined sensibility, must produce various and complex results. The poet must become more and more comprehensive, more allusive, more indirect, in order to force, to dislocate if necessary, language into his meaning." Two critical phrases evolved by Eliot have already passed over into our critical language often without reference to Eliot himself: 1) the objective correlative, which means finding the precise sensuous object or image or metaphor to stand for and in place of a bare idea; 2) the shock of heightened awareness, which is the proper effect of a successful work of art. To be sure, the average citizen after a single glance at the obscurity of Pound's *Cantos* or Eliot's *Four Quartets* turns back to his newspaper, but the average citizen doesn't read much poetry anyway. Like modern music and modern painting, modern poetry demands a higher effort from any reader who wishes to appreciate fully its more complex modes of expression.

It is interesting that Ezra Pound, who was so influential on the Imagist poets of the 1914–24 period (see Volume III), on Eliot, Yeats, and a host of poets through the time leading to World War II, seems to be, with William Carlos Williams and E. E. Cummings, the major influence on the new American poets of the Sixties, particularly those associated with the "Projectivist" movement. They like to talk about Pound's *periplum* (leaving aside the Eliot objective correlative), or "image of successive discoveries breaking upon the consciousness of the voyager." Much post World War II poetry is seen as "confessional," a kind of neo-romanticism. The fragmentation of the long poem may be an aspect of alienation, and the development of the *sequence*, "that single real contribution to the art of the longer poem by the modern age," may be the attempt of recent poets to find a substitute for what they can no longer accomplish or find viable. There is also talk of "minimal" poetry, but in an earlier time we would have called this understatement and traditionally figurative. Terms change but one impulse slides into another. Influences from abroad are not as easy to pinpoint as they were; most may be going the other way. British poets spend much time in the United States, often on university campuses, and leave themselves open to Americanization. Yevtushenko (born

1933) and George Seferis (born 1900, Nobel Prize 1963) are probably the most vital of living European poets with admirers but no discernible disciples in America.

13. American Poets After 1930

One of the first things we must acknowledge is the artificiality of the 1930 dividing date, particularly for American poets. Of those included in the preceding volume, principally Frost, Sandburg, Aikin, Jeffers, and Ransom, many made significant new contributions to our poetry after that date. It seems almost wrong to separate Ransom and Robert Penn Warren, who must certainly be reconsidered in this section for a major contribution to American poetry. As mentioned earlier Pound, Eliot, Williams, Cummings, even Wallace Stevens wrote important poems before 1930. But overlapping is inevitable. Of this group it is probably now safe to place Eliot and Stevens as the two top-flight American poets of the twentieth century who must be considered in the field of world literature with Yeats, Rilke, and Valéry as co-equals. But there is still a lot of jockeying for position to be done. It also seems to represent a consensus of critical opinion to speak of Robert Lowell as the most important living American poet with productive years still ahead. Certainly as the poets' poet who has had the greatest historical and technical influence in the century Pound would have to be given place; and there are individual preferences that each must uphold for himself.

Richard Kostelanetz has written recently: "There are probably more publishing poets, by sheer numbers, in America today than in both any previous time of our history and any culture of the world." Not maiden-aunt versifiers of the Longfellow tradition, they stem rather from Whitman and Poe through Robinson Jeffers and T. S. Eliot to Robert Lowell. "Most of these poets earn their livelihood at American universities, either as permanent staff members usually teaching courses in creative writing or as peripatetic professors and lecturers; and most would consider themselves at odds with 'the establishment,' whatever that may be in this pluralistic culture." A large number merit critical interest and acclaim, but one must choose representatives for discussion or be inundated. One of the most hopeful signs for the future of poetry is the enthusiasm of the young.

Ezra Pound (1885–1972) Except for the notoriety of his 1946 indictment for treason and the public debate over the Bollingen Prize affair, Pound has remained throughout his career virtually unknown to the general public. Yet he has exerted a tremendous influence on the whole movement of modernist verse; Eliot has referred to him as "the most important living poet of the English language." Pound invented the term Imagism and founded the school that bore the name; he played a large part in forming the styles of Eliot, Hart Crane, MacLeish, and the generation that followed them, and he vigorously championed the work of Eliot, Joyce, Tagore, and other writers when they were relatively unknown. His own poetry is a subject of great controversy; Allen Tate called the *Cantos* "one of the three great works of poetry of our time," but Edward Fitzgerald along with many others found Pound's work hung about with "a dismal mist of unresolved confusion." Of three qualities of his poetry, however, there can be no controversy; its tremendous erudition, its striking originality, and its technical and intellectual brilliance.

It is Pound's erudition that most discourages the average reader who first approaches his poetry. He is, among his other accomplishments, a competent comparative literature scholar familiar with literary history from its earliest beginnings to the present time, conversant with the prosody of Anglo-Saxon, Provençal, medieval Italian, and Chinese poetry, and adept at most of the ordinary modern languages. Moreover he has no desire to hide these accomplishments; in fact he wears them like so many badges. The *Cantos* are an intricate network of allusions to, and quotations from, hundreds of obscure and esoteric literary works ranging from Latin poetry to the *Analects* of Confucius. "Thus it is clear," comments a critic, "that we cannot *know* everything about *The Cantos* until we have read not only everything Pound has written, but everything he has read as well." Not many readers are willing to subject themselves to such a discipline.

Among the many literary and philosophical influences which found their way into Pound's work may be cited a few of primary importance: 1) Homer, whose epics Pound knew intimately in the original language, and whose *Odyssey* provides one of the main thematic threads for the *Cantos*; 2) the medieval Italian poets, especially Dante, whose *Divine Comedy* also influenced the structure of the *Cantos,* and Cavalcanti, whose sonnets and ballades Pound translated in 1912; 3) classic Chinese poetry, a volume of which Pound edited and translated under the title *Cathay* in 1915; 4) Browning, who suggested to him the basic form for his *Personae,* and whose hero Sordello reappears frequently in Pound's work; 5) the American Orientalist Ernest Fenollosa (1853–1908), whose essay *The Chinese Written Character as a Medium for Poetry,* edited by Pound in 1936 but read by him much earlier, provided him with basic aesthetic concepts which he incorporated into his poetry; 6) the German anthropologist Leo Frobenius (died 1938), who furnished Sir James Fraser with much of the anthropological data for *The Golden Bough* and whose theory of mythology Pound used in his own work; and 7) Thomas Jefferson, whose economic views greatly influenced Pound's attitude toward modern capitalism.

Stylistically Pound is dynamically brilliant, if not always coherent. He writes from tremendous conviction, a conviction ironical and sophisticated rather than naive. Unfortunately this power of enthusiasm all too readily degenerates into invective; Pound is probably the most irascible of modern poets. Not only does he despise the reading public, but he is belligerent toward critics, scornful of all authors who make money as well as the majority of his fellow poets; it is a rare craftsman who can win a word of praise from Pound. His early poetry more or less resembled the work of the other Imagists (Amy Lowell, H. D., John Gould Fletcher)—or the other way around. Around 1915 he became intrigued with Oriental poetry of various kinds; the verse of Li Po and Japanese forms such as the *hokku* (or *haiku*) undoubtedly had an influence on his subsequent work as well as on the Imagist movement as a whole. The later poems, especially the *Cantos,* lack the enamel-like simplicity of his Imagist period; after 1918 he variously referred to his own style as "Vorticism" or "the ideogrammic method" (a term suggesting the influence of Chinese poetry). In this period Pound resembles the Eliot of *The Waste Land,* although if there is a connection it is probably Pound who influenced Eliot.

Pound's ideas are emphatic but sometimes seem confused. In his early period he was much concerned with the theme of personal freedom, which he found in a variety of writers from Jefferson to Henry James and which he offered as the basis of his own ethic; yet by 1941 he had allied himself with Italian fascism so completely that he was making anti-American broadcasts on the Rome radio and serving as an adviser for the Italian government in its propaganda war against America. The link between these apparently incompatible extremes lies in Pound's concept of the term "usury." The Latin word *usura* and the term "usurious society" occur frequently in his later work, and the concept is woven deeply into the *Cantos*; it is simultaneously Pound's politics, his economics, his personal ethics, and even his criterion for the criticism of art. Briefly, Pound convinced himself that usury (i.e., capitalism, banks, the lending of money for interest, the whole money economy) was the basic evil in organized society and the first symptom of the degeneration and collapse of all civilizations throughout history. Athenian society before approximately 450 B.C. was tribal and aesthetic rather than usurious; thus the poetic achievements of Aeschylus and Sophocles. With the inception of a money economy Athens entered a decadent period, which was reflected in its epigonistic literature and its baroque art. Another example, one of Pound's favorites, is that of medieval Italy. The poetic triumph of Dante and Cavalcanti and the superb art and architecture of the Quattrocento occurred in an age when usury was a mortal sin; with the advent of modern commerce and capitalism around 1500 Italian society degenerated, and so did its art. It was because of this hatred of *usura* that Pound vented his spleen on modern capitalism, voiced paranoid warnings of "international Jewry," viewed Churchill and Roosevelt as sinister villains, and found a hero in Mussolini, whose syndicalist economics seemed to him to be a return to the usury-free middle ages. Such ideas, however, were subjective and emotional rather than rational in Pound. "As a political thinker," comments Untermeyer, "Pound was not only ineffectual but absurd;

as a person he was intermittently unbalanced." As a poet, it might be added, he is believed by many critics including Allen Tate and T. S. Eliot to be one of the greatest creative talents of the century.

Life: Ezra Pound was born in Hailey, Idaho in 1885; he half-satirically refers to himself in *Mauberley* as "born/ In a half savage country, out of date;/ Bent resolutely on wringing lilies from the acorn." His parents, however, soon moved to Pennsylvania; Pound entered the University of Pennsylvania at fifteen, and had commenced a private study of comparative literature by the time he was sixteen. Traditional college courses annoyed him, however, and he changed to the status of special student to avoid the requirements of a fixed curriculum; he later took a bachelor's degree at Hamilton College. In 1905 he returned to the University of Pennsylvania and was granted an M.A. the following year; meanwhile he served briefly as an instructor on the Pennsylvania staff. After a brief excursion to Europe he returned to what he thought was a career as a college teacher, but the experiment lasted only four months; he was dismissed from the staff of Wabash College for a long list of reasons, "all accusations," he later asserted, "having been ultimately refuted save that of being 'the Latin Quarter type.' " Returning to Europe in 1907, he spent some time in Italy; his first volume of poems, *A lume spento,* was printed in Venice in 1908. The following year he established himself in London, where he remained until 1920. He met W. B. Yeats and soon gained acceptance into the Yeatsian circle; before long, however, he had acquired a coterie of his own. *Personae,* a second volume of verse published in London in 1909, was favorably greeted by critics; thenceforth his reputation, at least in avant-garde circles, increased constantly.

In 1914 Pound collected and published an anthology of poetry under the title *Des imagistes,* a book which played an important part in launching the Imagist movement both in England and in America. When the group was taken over by Amy Lowell, however, he gradually drifted away from it; the poems of *Lustra* (1916) anticipate his later and more mature style. Shortly after this Pound began to apply the term "Vorticism" to his poetry; the label, which he shared with Wyndam Lewis, was intended to signify a highly "centered" or unified poetic effect, as in Imagism, but swirling, like a vortex, with a dynamic energy in contrast to the static quality of Imagist poetry. Meanwhile Pound had produced a number of important translations and adaptations, including lyrics of the thirteenth-century Italian poet Guido Cavalcanti (1912) and a set of adaptations of Chinese poetry (*Cathay*, 1915). In 1920 appeared the first major work of his new period: *Hugh Selwyn Mauberley*, a somewhat esoteric and highly allusive cycle of poems (actually a single poem divided into sections) which influenced such later works as Eliot's *The Waste Land* and *Gerontion* and Hart Crane's *The Bridge*. The same year he moved to Paris, where he remained until 1924, an intimate of the Left-Bank expatriate circle which included Hemingway and James Joyce. It was through Pound's influence that Joyce's *Portrait of the Artist* was accepted by the Egoist Press, and Pound also played a large part in bringing the work of Eliot to the attention of publishers and editors. In 1924 he moved again, this time to Rapallo, on the Italian Riviera, where he remained more or less permanently for the next two decades. The first of his *Cantos* appeared in 1925 as *Cantos I–XV;* he continued to publish sections of this major work through 1955 and is still publishing it. Meanwhile his economic and political views led him to sympathize increasingly with the fascist regime in Italy; as early as 1935 he had published *Jefferson and/or Mussolini*, and by 1941 he was openly broadcasting anti-American propaganda on the Italian radio. In 1942 he was indicted for treason *in absentia* in the American courts, and in April of 1945 he surrendered himself to advance units of the conquering American army. Imprisoned in a stockade near Pisa, he sketched out amid great hardships and discomfort the poems of the *Pisan Cantos*, which were published in 1948. After his return to America for trial he was examined by a committee of psychiatrists and found insane; the indictment was therefore set aside, and he was committed to St. Elizabeth's Hospital in Washington, D.C., as an incurable psychotic. The next year a violent controversy broke out over his work; in February of 1949 he was announced as winner of the newly-established Bollingen Award, sponsored by the Library of Congress. The award committee, which included T. S.

Eliot, W. H. Auden, Allen Tate, Robert Penn Warren, and Katherine Anne Porter, defended their choice of a poet who had been indicted as a traitor and was presently confined in an insane asylum by stating, "To permit other considerations than that of poetic achievement to sway the decision would destroy the significance of the award . . ." The award was attacked by the poet Robert Hillyer in a celebrated *Saturday Review* article, and the controversy continued for several months. The prize was eventually granted as announced, although as a result of the dispute the sponsorship for the Bollingen Award was transferred from the Library of Congress to Yale University. Another volume of the *Cantos,* entitled *Rock-Drill,* appeared in 1955; *Thrones: 96–109 de los cantares,* in 1959; *Drafts and Fragments of Cantos cx–cxvii,* in 1968.

Long a thorn in the flesh for the United States government (he was obviously different from Tokyo Rose and Lord Haw Haw—after all, Yale University had published his work) Pound was finally released from St. Elizabeth's where he had been "crazy like a fox" through the concentrated efforts of friends in April 1958. His wife Dorothy Shakespear Pound, the daughter of Yeats' lifelong friend Olivia Shakespear, had stood faithfully by him; they left as soon as possible and understandably for Italy. There is a story, and it may be true, that a reporter had the temerity to knock on his door, "And how are you, Mr. Pound?" The answer was "Senile!" as the door slammed. Pound did go to England for the T. S. Eliot memorial service on February 4, 1965, and returned to Italy almost at once.

The death of Ezra Pound on November 1, 1972 in Venice at the age of eighty-seven became the center point for reevaluations of his work, still a matter of controversy—all the way from the Harvey Gross assessment that the *Cantos* are "an unfinished, totally flawed, almost totally destroyed poem" to the most complete adulation. Hugh Kenner's early 1972 book, *The Pound Era,* speaks of the "innovative genius of its most famous exponent." It is generally conceded that he is one of the most (if not the most) significant poetic influences of the twentieth century. In failing health in recent years, estranged from wife and son, he lived finally in Venice with his companion (and the mother of his illegitimate daughter, born the year before his son), Olga Rudge. Pound was buried on the island of San Michele in the Venetian Lagoon, where also rest Igor Stravinsky and Sergei Diaghilev.

Chief Works: The most important poems of Pound's early period are contained in *Personae* (1909) and *Exultations* (1909); poems from both volumes are reprinted in the 1926 edition of *Personae*. The word *personae* signifies "masks," here used in the sense of personalities which the poet assumes in order to create a dramatic monologue or characterization. Not all the poems of the 1926 volume, however, come under this heading; some are simple Imagist impressions in the style adopted by H. D. or Amy Lowell. Of the true *personae* in the volume, the best known is "Sestina: Altaforte," a dramatic monologue spoken by the medieval Bertrand de Born, put in Hell by Dante "for that he was a stirrer up of strife." (See *Inferno*, Canto XXVIII.) In contradiction to Dante, Pound portrays Bertrand, a thirteenth-century troubadour and knight, as a lusty and energetic warrior who cries that "The man who fears war . . . is fit only to rot in womanish peace." The form of the poem loosely imitates troubadour verse-forms like the ballade which Bertrand is known to have written.

"A Girl," an often-anthologized favorite from Pound's early period, is an Imagistic impression of a young girl and at the same time a subtly symbolic network of metaphors: on the immediate level the girl is compared with a tree, yet the underlying sub-metaphor treats the tree as the girl's lover, permeating her very essence through his intense sympathy.

Even briefer is "In a Station of the Metro," in form an English-language version of the two-line Japanese *hokku*, which, after the suggestive word "apparition," concludes with a single metaphor comparing the faces in the crowd to "petals on a wet, black bough."

Hugh Selwyn Mauberley (1920) is the first major long poem of Pound's work as well as the first poem to demonstrate his mature technique and attitude. The Mauberley of the title is an imaginary poet of the pre-1914 era, invented by Pound partly as a tongue-in-cheek analysis of himself in his early period and partly as a satire on the poetic temper of the fin-de-siècle. Mauberley, however, does not appear until the latter part of the poem, the first half of which is devoted to various poetic excursions in Pound's own voice. The work in its entirety consists of eighteen separate poems which form an integrated whole, although their connection is not immediately apparent upon first reading. The first of these sections, "E. P. Ode Pour L'Election de Son Sepulchre," is a parody of Ronsard's famous self-written epitaph; Pound, writing as though he were a superior, pompous, and slightly hostile critic of his own work, describes himself as "out of key with his own time" and concludes wryly in the last stanza that he passed from men's memory in the thirtieth year of his age, i.e., 1915, approximately the end of his Imagist period. The second section is also well known; it characterizes the age in which the poem was written, especially English literary circles of the prewar era, which demanded a "mould in plaster" (stylized nineteenth-century verse) rather than the "alabaster" of true classic poetry. Section III continues the theme, revealing the age as dominated by "A tawdry cheapness." Other interesting sections are the seventh, titled "Siena mi fe'; disfecemi Maremma" (a quotation from Dante), which characterizes Pound's friend Victor Gustave Plarr under the pseudonym Monsieur Verog and thereby sums up the literary temper of the Nineties; "Mr. Nixon," the ninth section, a satire on the modern successful novelist of the type of Arnold Bennett; and "Mauberley," the opening section of the second part, in which the title-figure of the poem is characterized as a minor artist of limited creativity but retaining a pride and self-respect which he derives from a long literary tradition. This theme is continued through the remaining four sections of the work.

The *Cantos* (1925–55—and continuing) are the major work of Pound's career, a gigantic unfinished poetry cycle which in its final form was to contain one hundred cantos or chapters but which passed that number sometime before 1960. The various sections of the work which have so far appeared are *Cantos I–XVI* (1925), *XVII–XXVII* (1928), *A Draft of XXX Cantos* (1930), *Eleven Cantos: XXXI to XLI* (1934), *The Fifth Decade of Cantos* (1937), *Cantos LII–LXXI* (1940), *The Pisan Cantos* (1948), *Rock-Drill* (1955), *Thrones* (1959), and *Drafts and Fragments of Cantos cx–cxvii* (1968). Although the *Cantos* are confused and seemingly disconnected upon first reading, critics have discerned in them a highly involved formal structure, comparable in some ways to the plan of the *Divine Comedy*. The two dominant themes are said to be 1) the idea of the Descent into Hell, derived from Vergil and Dante, and 2) the motif of metamorphosis, the divine transformation of one thing into another, as found in Ovid and as treated by modern mythologists such as Ranke and Frazer. The theme of the *Odyssey,* an extended sea-voyage replete with adventures many of which are erotic in nature, also recurs periodically. At least two cantos of the voluminous work should receive individual mention. Canto I, one of the best-known as well as the most straightforward and explicit sections yet published, is actually a loose translation or paraphrase of Book XI of the *Odyssey* via the Renaissance Latin version of Andreas Divus, who is mentioned in the final lines of the canto. The passage in which the ghost of the sailor Elpenor describes the manner of his death ("Ill fate and abundant wine" through ". . . that I swung mid fellows") has been cited as a splendid example of Pound's elliptical style, which skips over trivial details to achieve a classic Greek simplicity. Canto XLV, often anthologized, is a kind of ode or dissertation on *usura,* including Pound's theory of the relation between the usurious society and the decline of the arts. The style, in sharp contrast to the discursive quality of most of the *Cantos,* is Biblical, containing extensive parallelism and utilizing a consciously archaic English to establish a dignified and prophetic mood. Much history, transcribed almost literally but in Pound's highly individual and condensed style, is included; Cantos LII through LXI list in detail the succession of Chinese dynasties and their accomplishments, and Cantos LXII through LXXI include a fairly complete history of nineteenth-century America. Also interesting is Canto LXXIV of the *Pisan Cantos,* which includes an ironic picture of Pound's imprisonment by the U.S. Army in Pisa: ". . . and they digged a ditch round about me/ lest the damp gnaw thru my bones."

It is likely that future criticism will view the *Cantos* as more important for their influence on other poets than as works of intrinsic quality in their own right. Among the poems in which a definite influence of the *Cantos* has been noted, or is thought to have been noted, are Eliot's *The Wasteland* (published three years before the first *Cantos,* but worked over by Pound himself at a time when he must have been writing them), Hart Crane's *The Bridge,* and MacLeish's *Conquistador.* American poets of the Sixties seem quite familiar with the *Cantos* and make casual reference to them frequently.

T. S. Eliot (*American-British, 1888–1965*)

Beginning around 1909 as an avant-garde poet whose esoteric work was read only by a small circle of cognoscenti, Eliot has through the years acquired popular prestige until a 1954 *Life* article could describe him as "the world's most distinguished living poet." His acceptance parallels the gradual acceptance of modern poetry by the public, at least that lettered and educated portion of the public which reads something more than its daily newspaper. Meanwhile Eliot as a poet has not remained static. His poetry, beginning with *Prufrock and Other Observations* (1917) and continuing through the dramas of the post-1945 era, shows a definite progression in content as well as in technique. Four periods may be roughly distinguished in this long poetic career. Eliot's first published poems (1909–17), while not lacking in originality, were strongly derivative; they were influenced in technique by Imagism, by the dramatic monologues of Browning, by Elizabethan drama, and by the work of the French impressionist poet Jules Laforgue (1860–87) as well as the Symbolists. Several of the poems of this period (e.g., "Dans le restaurant") were actually written in French; the two most important of them, "The Love Song of J. Alfred Prufrock" and "Portrait of a Lady," are monologues or miniature dramas (really dramatic lyrics or soliloquies—the "you and I" of Prufrock being one split personality) partaking of the rhythm of Elizabethan verse. With *The Waste Land* (1922) a new period begins; Eliot, still influenced by Pound in technique, now began to develop a more personal religious and ethical system, marked by an increasing interest in the English metaphysical poets (Donne *et al.*) and Oriental religions (Buddhism, Vedanta) and a fascination with anthropological mythology inspired by reading Sir James Frazer's *The Golden Bough* and Jessie L. Weston's *From Ritual to Romance.* The trend from dramatic to philosophical poetry continues in the third period (1930–40), which is dominated by the serious and theological *Ash Wednesday;* and it finds its climax in the fourth period, beginning with

Four Quartets in 1943 and continuing through the dramas *The Cocktail Party, The Confidential Clerk,* and *The Elder Statesman.* The difficult *Quartets,* abstruse and lacking strong imagery, are dominated by the religious principles Eliot had first publicly professed in 1927; the same ideas are also latent in the plays. By 1950 Eliot had arrived at a philosophical position comparable to that of his contemporaries Huxley and Waugh: rejection of Western materialism combined with an eclectic spiritualism including elements of Oriental and Occidental religions. Eliot himself, in an unpublished lecture, has distinguished three periods of "metaphysical poetry" in world literature which have produced work of superlative quality: the Medieval (school of Dante and Cavalcanti); the Renaissance (school of Donne); and the Modern (school of Baudelaire and Laforgue). To these might be added the Contemporary: the school of Eliot and the younger poets who have taken him as their model.

Although Eliot has passed through several periods or stages in his long poetic career, his style and content follow a consistent pattern of development throughout his work. The elements in his poetry which rose to predominance during his later years are detectable in embryonic form even in his earliest work, and nothing he acquired along the line of his literary evolution was ever totally abandoned. Thus, examining his poetic work as a whole, a number of dominant characteristics or tendencies may be described:

(1) Eliot has a strong feeling for the PAST, especially for the literary and religious traditions of the past. It is probably this attitude which led him to abandon the relatively new American culture for the more traditional society of Britain. In his poetry the tendency takes the form of an interest in myths and ancient religions, as well as a preoccupation with obscure and difficult literary allusions. To Eliot the past is not something dead which is studied in books, but a memory vigorously manifested in present events; in his view mythology transcends time. He is fond of introducing figures from ancient Greece, such as Tiresias, into modern settings, or of drawing parallels between contemporary and archetypical situations. His interest in the work of Jung and Frazer (see below) is connected to this tendency.

(2) Eliot is fascinated with SYMBOLS, especially the mental symbols the psychiatrist and anthropologist Carl Jung calls archetypes. Archetypes or primordial images are symbolic concepts common to all mankind which relate to problems of man's natural or social environment; they are frequently concerned with fertility fetishes or with man's erotic nature. Much of Eliot's poetry presupposes a knowledge of these theories, and is therefore fully meaningful only after reading Jung, Frazer, and other authors.

(3) A political conservative, Eliot is anti-democratic on intellectual grounds; i.e., he feels little kinship with the unlettered masses and believes the important forces of society to lie in the educated, the talented, and the aristocratic. His apotheosis of heroism in *Coriolan* has led his critics to accuse him of a sort of proto-fascism, but this is unfair. A more judicious statement is Eliot's own in the 1928 introduction to *For Lancelot Andrewes,* where he describes himself as "an Anglo-Catholic in religion, a classicist in literature, and a royalist in politics."

(4) Eliot, especially in his earlier poems (before 1930), often portrays inadequate characters who feel a sense of their own impotence and the banality of their lives, who seek to rebel in an heroic fashion against their situations, but who generally fail through half-measures. This recurring theme is sometimes called the PRUFROCK motif, after the character in "The Love Song of J. Alfred Prufrock," but it occurs frequently elsewhere. Eliot finds this personality symptomatic of the plight of modern man in the broader sense; in *The Waste Land* the concept is depersonalized and pervades the entire poem.

(5) In his poetic technique Eliot takes his departure from the Imagists and from Ezra Pound, although from this starting point he evolved constantly toward a more personal and more original style. His use of free verse, his snatches of conversation, and the generally disjointed appearance of his verse resemble Imagism, while his copious allusions, his juxtaposition of ancient and modern, and the fact that he writes consciously for a small group of erudite readers show his kinship to Pound. Eliot specifically acknowledged his admiration of, and debt to, Pound in the dedication of *The Waste Land.* A *Times Literary Supplement* review well summarized the

character of his earlier poetry when it described it as having "two marks of 'modernist' work, the liveliness that comes from topicality and the difficulty that comes from intellectual abstruseness."

Life: Thomas Stearns Eliot was born in St. Louis, Missouri in 1888. His ancestry was distinguished; his family included President Charles W. Eliot of Harvard as well as a number of earlier writers, educators, and divines. He took his undergraduate degree at Harvard, where he was exposed to Santayana and Irving Babbitt; he then went to Paris to study at the Sorbonne (1910–11). Returning, he resumed his studies at Harvard, but made another trip to Europe immediately after the outbreak of the war. In 1915 he married an Englishwoman, Miss Vivienne Haigh-Wood, and took up his residence in London. He returned to America periodically, sometimes for considerable visits, but his loyalties leaned more and more to Britain during the early Twenties. From 1915 to 1922 he earned his living as a teacher, free-lance writer, and editor; in 1922 *The Waste Land* won the Dial Award and brought him both fame and a certain amount of economic security. The same year he founded a review, *The Criterion,* which he continued to publish for seventeen years. Neither his poetry nor his editorial ventures, however, brought him total economic independence, and he retained during most of his career a part-time position as literary editor for a British publisher, Faber and Faber.

In 1927 Eliot became a British subject, and the following year, in the introduction to *For Lancelot Andrewes,* he made the statement of literary, religious, and political conservatism quoted above. Since then he has become increasingly concerned with religion in his poetry and drama, and has in fact become one of the major metaphysical poets of the century. At the same time his style has diverged from that of the Imagists, becoming constantly more abstract as his content becomes more metaphysical. This tendency reached its climax in *Four Quartets* (1943); a concise statement of his final politico-religious position is contained in the essay *The Idea of a Christian Society* (1940). In recent years Eliot's interest turned increasingly to the drama; he wrote four major plays between 1935 and 1953, and at least two of them (*Murder in the Cathedral* and *The Cocktail Party*) were successful in theatre productions. In

1948 Eliot was awarded the Nobel Prize for Literature "for his work as a trail-blazing pioneer of modern poetry"; the same year he visited America to reside briefly at the Institute for Advanced Study at Princeton. He returned to America in 1950 for another visit, this time lecturing at Harvard and at the University of Chicago.

Back in England Eliot wrote two more verse plays, *The Confidential Clerk* (1953) and *The Elder Statesman* (1959), interesting in development if not successful in the theatre. On January 4, 1965 in London T. S. Eliot died, and on February 4 memorial services were held at Westminster Abbey, attended by a large number of important people and poets.

Chief Works: "The Love Song of J. Alfred Prufrock" (1915) is the major poem of Eliot's first collection, *Prufrock and Other Observations* (1917). The style is free verse broken by occasional rhymes, the medium of most of Eliot's early poems. The epigraph from Dante, translated, reads, "If I thought my answer were to one who could ever return to the world, this flame should shake no more; but since none ever did return alive from this abyss [Inferno], if what I hear be true, without fear of infamy I answer you." In a parallel manner Prufrock, the "I" of the poem, speaks his thoughts within the abyss of his own soul; he lacks the courage to rebel, and his love song is one he never voices aloud.

Prufrock (his name suggests a dull and slightly pretentious respectability) is an ineffectual gentleman, no longer young, who is growing weary of the artificial London society in which he monotonously passes his days. He yearns for a more vital and adventurous existence, but lacks the courage to embark upon it. Since he is living in a puritanical Anglo-Saxon society, his rebellious thoughts turn first to erotic adventure. The first section (ll. 1–12) is an invitation to an unknown and perhaps as yet unchosen partner, or more likely to his own alter ego, to embark upon such an adventure: an expedition into the less savory quarters of the city is implied. The refrain (ll. 13–14, 35–36) ironically typifies the shallow aestheticism of tea-party society, the life Prufrock wishes to escape. Lines 15–34 extend the image of urban squalor, suggesting a clandestine adventure, and end with a temporizing compromise. Afraid of ridicule, from line 36 onward Prufrock seems to grow increasingly uncertain;

he asks, "Do I dare disturb the universe?" In 1. 82 and again in 11. 110ff he confesses his own inadequacy, admitting that he is after all no prophet or tragic hero. In the closing lines (119–130) his abortive revolt against convention is symbolized in several sea-images; the mermaids who sing "each to each" are uninhibited creatures luxuriating in their natural setting and producing exquisite unpremeditated song. Prufrock overhears the beckoning song of the mermaids, but realizes this invitation to adventure is not meant for him. The final three lines reveal the reason: although escape into the nirvana of sensualism, both physical and intellectual, is temporarily successful, "human voices wake us, and we drown"—mundane affairs press in upon us and we are recalled to conventional life. This closing passage, like the previous descriptions of fog and slums, is typical of the Imagist technique and if taken out of context might well be treated as a short Imagist poem complete in itself.

Prufrock is a type of character that Eliot knew well from first-hand acquaintance: the cultured, sensitive, but bored gentleman of Cambridge or London society, the literary man or professor, whose sense of decorum and fear of ridicule prevent him from seizing life and savoring it in a more virile manner. In the wider context the poem describes the human conflict between sensual desires and longings and the restrictions of civilization. Each human being longs for a nirvana where social censure will be forgotten in a passionate enjoyment of the senses; but most people, unheroic like Prufrock ("No! I am not Prince Hamlet, nor was meant to be."), are deterred by fear of ridicule and feelings of inadequacy.

"Portrait of a Lady" (poem, 1917) is laid in a similar setting. The speaker is a young man remembering; his companion is a lady, somewhat older who wishes to hold him although she realizes their affair cannot hope to be permanent. For his part the young man is torn between sympathy and a longing for freedom. Perhaps a little too refined and sensitive, the lady leads a highly artificial life among her flowers, her Chopin recitals, and her "few friends." In the penultimate stanza (11. 102–108) the lady, in spite of her sophisticated manner, scarcely conceals her anguish at the parting; yet the young man realizes this last separation is to be a permanent one.

The poem symbolically covers a cycle of time from winter to winter. Section I takes place in December; in Section II it is April and the lilacs are in bloom. In the final section October completes the circle and accentuates the young man's restlessness, nostalgia, and boredom. The last stanza in Section II (ll. 71–83) is the chief expression of the young man's attitude toward the lady, an attitude dominated by sympathy but lacking real passion. Like "Prufrock," this poem is a character study intended to communicate the mood of a certain social environment.

"Sweeney Among the Nightingales" (poem, 1918) is one of several Eliot poems involving the character of Sweeney, an "ape-necked" symbol of unthinking modern materialism. The epigraph from Aeschylus ("Alas, I have been smitten deep with a mortal blow") suggests the tragedy of Agamemnon's death and establishes the motif of archetypical murder and lust. Sweeney is observed in a bawdyhouse; all the persons present are vulgar and sensual, concerned only with their immediate physical desires. They are unaware of the wider and more sublime existence around them, mentioned in sections 2, 3, 9, and 10. Sweeney himself "guards the horned gate"—i.e., blocks the messages from the dead (traditions of the past) which might help him and his companions to escape from their plight. The rhythms of nature (the stars, etc.), the ecstatic experience of religion (the nearby convent), and the ever-present tragedy of Agamemnon are close at hand, even in our modern life; but Sweeney and his kind are insensible toward them. Eliot here pleads for a renewed contact with tradition and with the spiritual forces of human experience, the means by which mankind can rise again to sublimity.

A variant interpretation of the poem compares Agamemnon's death with a sordid and evil plot prepared against Sweeney by Rachel, the lady in the Spanish cape, and "someone indistinct" with whom the host converses. In either case the basic contrast is that between tradition and sublimity on one hand and contemporary banality on the other.

In "Burbank with a Baedeker: Bleistein with a Cigar" (poem, 1919) the same theme is repeated in the setting of Venice. Eliot views the city, the traditional home of the arts and of aristocratic luxury, as today vulgarized by the commercialism which was present from the inception of the city and which has finally conquered it. Burbank with his guidebook denotes intellectual curiosity, love of culture, and respect for tradition; he arrives to find Venice (symbolized by Princess Volupine, whose name suggests both the Latin root for "fox" and the word "voluptuous") in a state of decadent decline. Burbank "falls" for the Princess, but she is more receptive to the attentions of Bleistein, the vulgar embodiment of avarice, and Sir Frederick Klein, representative of a new commercial order. Bleistein's blatant commercialism is that of the mongrel cosmopolite who strikes crudely toward his goal, whereas Sir Frederick, perhaps British, assumes a veneer of culture and is accordingly more effective.

The imagery of the poem continually contrasts the glory of Renaissance Venice with the rats and slime of the modern city. In a wider context Venice stands for Western culture as a whole. From the creative magnificence of the middle ages and Renaissance it has degenerated into a sordid commercialism; fortune turns from the Burbanks of the world to the opportunistic Bleisteins.

"Gerontion" (poem, 1920) begins with an epigraph from *Measure for Measure* (III:1) suggesting that neither youth nor age has any importance, since life is essentially illusion. The title signifies "a little old man." Again the contrast is that between human life in a framework of tradition and spiritual kinship with the past and a bestial existence governed solely by the needs of the moment. The old man is a prisoner in contemporary society, a world obsessed with gain, ignorantly atheistic, and rotten from within. One of its chief qualities is instability, symbolized by the "rented house" in which the old man lives. Heroism is dead; the old man admits that he did not fight at Thermopylae (the "hot gates") or at any of the other battles of the ancient world against barbarism. He is "waiting for rain" (the refreshing and lifegiving spiritual vitality that comes like rain from above) but instead is continually tormented by winds, symbol of modern restlessness and uncertainty. Beginning with line 17 Christianity is introduced in contrast to contemporary avarice and vulgarity. In 11. 54ff, beginning "I that was near your heart," Gerontion refers to the estrangement of modern man from the religion which sustained him up to the time of the Renaissance. The penultimate section (11. 60ff) concludes that commercialism (the spider symbolizes the intricacy of modern finance) is likely to triumph permanently. Modern man, alienated from the spiritual forces which previously nourished him, is condemned to live in the "rotting house" of his cosmopolitan and rootless society.

The Waste Land (poem, 1922) is the most important work of Eliot's earlier period. The theme is again the banality and barrenness of the contemporary world contrasted with the richness of traditional spiritual and mythological forces. There are two chief sources for the structure and symbolism of the poem: Jessie L. Weston's *From Ritual to Romance* and Sir James Frazer's *The Golden Bough.* Some knowledge of both these books is essential to an appreciation of the poem. Miss Weston's book is a psychological and anthropological study of the Holy Grail legend. The story of the Grail appears in slightly different forms in many cultures, but it always concerns a dry, sterile, and cursed land (the "waste land") ruled over by a Fisher King whose sexual impotence is connected with the plight of his realm. The wanderer or knight who arrives to voice the ritual demand for the Holy Grail is the talisman through which king and land are restored to virility. Frazer's work begins in an attempt to explain another widespread racial myth: the priest of the sacred wood who is killed each year by a candidate who thereby becomes the new king and priest. According to Frazer and Miss Weston, both myths can be traced to primitive fertility rites; and students of comparative mythology believe that the element of sacrifice common to both has eventually found its way into Christianity as the ritual of the Eucharist. Miss Weston explains that secrets of these mystery religions were transmitted into Western Europe in pre-medieval times by Syrian and Phoenician merchants, and eventually emerged in the middle ages as the legend of the Grail.

In writing *The Waste Land* Eliot also utilized Carl Jung's theory of primordial images or archetypes (see above).

With these materials Eliot constructs a poem of which the dominant theme is the contrast between human universals and modern materialism and banality. The epigraph is from the *Satyricon* of Petronius: "With my own eyes I saw the Sibyl suspended in a jar at Cumae, and when her followers said to her, Sibyl, what do you want? she replied, I want to die." Thus two motifs of the poem are suggested: universal mythology and the death-wish deriving from boredom.

The poem itself is divided into five sections. The first, "The Burial of the Dead," introduces the motif of the recurrence of life out of death and corruption, but depicts April as "the cruellest month," since it destroys the serene oblivion of winter (death) in order to create new life. A snatch of banal conversation is interposed; the thematic contrast between sublimity and banality is established. The concept of "rootlessness" or lack of stabilizing tradition is suggested in the conversation and in the subsequent soliloquy (ll. 19–30). An exhilarating snatch of Wagner's *Tristan und Isolde* is quoted (31–35), but is followed by a bleaker line from the same opera: "Empty and bare the sea" (l. 42). In line 44 appears Madame Sosostris, a vulgarized clairvoyant who is the only descendant of the wise necromancers (or Sibyls) of the ancient world. She tells fortunes through the Tarot pack of cards, each of which bears a symbolic image. The Phoenician sailor is to reappear in the poem, and the man with three staves is identified by Eliot in a note as the Fisher King himself. The section ends with an allusion to the superstition of planting corpses with crops to insure fertility; the "Dog" connects the incident with the Egyptian Osiris myth, which also concerns the resurrection of life.

In Section II, "A Game of Chess," the motif is the absence of mythical meaning in contemporary marriage. Philomel, in an ancient myth violated by a king and transformed into a nightingale, can now produce only discordant sounds for the modern ear (ll. 99–110). Irony is achieved through reference to the sublime passions of Cleopatra and Dido. Snatches of neurotic modern conversation are introduced (ll. 120ff) and at line 139 begins a vulgar cockney dialogue concerned with abortion and other unsavory aspects of modern conjugal relations. The refrain "HURRY UP PLEASE IT'S TIME" is the call of the English pub-keeper at closing time. The idiotic farewells of the patrons then fade into the poignant song of Ophelia from *Hamlet* (ll. 169ff). Again sublimity is present, but the vulgar generation is too distracted to notice it.

The title of Section III, "The Fire Sermon," recalls a famous Buddhistic discourse on lust and fornication. Opening with a pastiche of Spenser's wedding song, the section soon contrasts this idyllic picture with the squalor of modern love ("Sweeney to Mrs. Porter in the spring"), heralded by motor horns and associated with the horror of rats. Mr. Eugenides (line 209) recalls the Syrian merchants who, according to Miss Weston, brought the mysteries to Europe; now they bring only sordid merchandise. Toward line 227 the narrator becomes Tiresias, the blind seer of Greek mythology who was the wisest of humans because he had been both woman and man; thus he embodies the sexual tension which is the motif of the section. Tiresias, present in modern London, views the sordid tryst of a typist and a clerk in a tenement bedroom. Modern love, promiscuous and perfunctory, has lost its mystery and has become no more significant than the playing of a phonograph record. The section ends with the song of the three Thames Daughters (inspired by the Rhine Maidens of *Die Götterdämmerung*), who relate the manner of their dishonoring, and with a final echo of the Buddhistic sermon.

The short fourth section, "Death by Water," parallels the drowning of the Phoenician sailor of "The Burial of the Dead" with the previously established archetype of death and subsequent resurrection.

The final section, "What the Thunder Said," begins on a note of hopelessness: "he who was living" (Adonis, Osiris, Christ, symbol of the incarnation of Divinity) is now dead, and contemporary man is dying spiritually. The rock (spiritual sterility) is contrasted to water, universal symbol of the beginning of life. The "falling towers" of the cities of the Near East and Europe are mentioned (ll. 373–376); the civilization which began in Greece and the Holy Land is toppling. The cock-crow (line 391), heard as Christ was seized by the soldiers, recalls the story of the Passion; rain (symbol of recurring life) shortly results. But this image is abandoned, and the poem turns to the Hindu myth of the thunder from the Upanishads. The protagonist has now become the Fisher King himself; he wonders what action he can take against the ruin of his land. Three quotations follow. The first is from Dante: "Then sprang he back into the fire that refines them." The sinner Arnaut Daniel, viewed by Dante in Purgatory, gladly accepts his suffering since he knows it will bring redemption. The second is from the anonymous *Vigil of Venus:* "When shall I become as the swallow?" Eliot's note connects this with Procne, in the Greek myth changed to a swallow to escape her suffering. The third, "The Prince of Acquitaine at the fallen tower," is from a sonnet of Gerard de Nerval; it refers to the poet whose life is ruined but who proposes to begin anew. The childish jingle of London Bridge stresses the theme of decay and collapse. The poem then ends with a Sanscrit benediction; the word *shantih* is equivalent to "the Peace that passes all understanding." But this consolatory note is almost ironic in the context of the previous pessimistic passage. Thus the poem's theme is that the mythical death and rebirth of Osiris, Adonis, or Christ, the ritual which has nourished mankind for centuries, is no longer possible, since our age has lost its contact with the past and has become spiritually sterile. *The Waste Land* is not, as is sometimes thought, a mere portrait of the generation of the Twenties; it is an analysis of the predicament of modern man in his relation to the universal spiritual forces of nature.

"The Hollow Men" (poem, 1925) is similar in tone and content but much less extensive in treatment. The double epigraph is from Conrad's *The Heart of Darkness,* which depicts the contrast between the artificiality of civilization and the elemental but savage power of primitive superstition, and from Guy Fawkes tradition: "A penny for the Old Guy." The Hollow Men are the citizens of modern Western culture, synthetically stuffed with opinions, ideas, and faiths they cannot feel. The senselessness of the modern man's daily routine is indicated in the childish nursery rhyme which begins Section V. The fourth stanza of this section ("Between the desire . . .") suggests the impotence of the Prufrock-Gerontion type of figure who is reduced to inaction through the "Shadow" of thought. The chief feature of modern culture is its banality and pettiness; the world ends "not with a bang but a whimper."

Ash Wednesday (poem, 1930) is a poetic contemplation expressing the religious ideas which Eliot had worked out in 1927–28. The major theme is the neo-Platonic love of Dante, Cavalcanti, and other medieval Italian poets; the Lady who dominates the poem is a symbol of perfection or beauty through which man may be drawn to God. There are many echoes of the Bible and of Church litanies.

Four Quartets (poetry, 1943) is a volume consisting of four symmetrical meditations on philosophical and religious subjects. The images of the poems are intended to communicate the subjective experience of religious faith. Each quartet is named for a geographical location and identified with one of the four humors of medieval medicine. "Burnt Norton" takes its name from a manor-house in Gloucestershire; its element is fire. "East Coker" is a small village in Somersetshire; the element of the poem is earth. The "Dry Salvages" are rocks off the New England coast; the element is water. "Little Gidding" is the site of a religious community of the seventeenth century; the dominant element is air. The quartets follow a quasi-musical structure, and each poem is identified with an aspect of Christian religious experience.

Dramas: *Murder in the Cathedral* (1935) is the most important of Eliot's early plays. In form a verse tragedy, it takes for its subject the historical incident of the murder of the Archbishop Thomas à Becket by followers of Henry II in Canterbury cathedral in 1170 A.D. The form is rigidly classical, and a chorus is included in the manner of the Greek tragedy. There is little action except for the murder itself; the play consists largely of a set of philosophical dialogues in which Thomas converses with his murderers and with others. The central scene is the debate with four Tempters who symbolize the inner conflict in Thomas' mind: his youthful love of pleasure, his later ambition for power, the threat of the feudal barons, and his own egotistical desire for martyrdom. Rejecting all four temptations, Thomas goes on to deliver a masterful sermon in which he defines his own attitude toward the tragedy which is approaching him: "The martyr no longer desires anything for himself, not even the glory of martyrdom." When the king's knights arrive later to murder him he offers no resistance. After the deed the knights present a foolish and unconsciously ironic defense of their crime, and the drama ends as Thomas' priests thank God "who has given us another Saint in Canterbury."

The Cocktail Party (drama, 1949), laid in a modern setting and written in an informal and vernacular free-verse style, has proved the most successful of Eliot's plays in the theatre. As the action opens four of the chief characters have become involved in a banal sexual impasse: Edward Chamberlayne, a successful solicitor, is having a clandestine affair with Celia Coplestone; his wife Lavinia is in love with Peter Quilpe, and Peter himself is courting Celia. Edward and Lavinia plan a cocktail party, but on the day it is to take place Lavinia leaves her husband, and he is forced to entertain the guests himself and make lame excuses for her absence. The most important guests at the party are Julia Shuttlethwaite, outwardly a silly woman dominated by her affected mannerisms, and an "Unidentified Guest" to whom Edward impulsively reveals his domestic troubles. The "Unidentified Guest" is actually Sir Henry Harcourt-Reilly, a kind of psychiatrist who is as much a spiritual practitioner as a medical one. The action gradually reveals that he has been called in on the case by Julia, who underneath her giddy silliness is actually a wise and intuitive woman. Dr. Reilly persuades Edward and Lavinia that they must break out of the shells of egotism which have isolated them from each other; realizing the seriousness of the situation, they do so, and their marriage continues on a new and firmer basis. As for Celia, who suffers from the sense of isolation from her fellow beings as well as from a "consciousness of sin," Reilly recognizes in her a true saintly personality; he sends her to a sanatorium, and then advises her to follow her own destiny as her heart guides her. She becomes a member of a religious order, goes off as a nurse to a remote tropical island, and there is martyred by the natives in a particularly horrible manner. Peter, also following his destiny, becomes a screenwriter, thus finding contentment at his own level of ability; Reilly tells him, "You understand your *métier*, Mr. Quilpe—which is the most that any of us can ask for."

Underneath this comedy-of-manners plot, which might have been written by a Sidney Howard or a Philip Barry, is a metaphysical undercurrent which is wholly Eliot's. Reilly, Julia, and her playboy friend Alex are beneath their superficial appearances deeply religious persons; the toast (actually an incantation) which they recite at the end of Act II clearly shows them to be members of some kind of spiritual cult—or perhaps they are Divinities masquerading under human form. Although Reilly at first appears to dominate the plot, it is Julia who is the real power behind him; she is evidently a kind of priestess or an earth-mother figure who knows all and who controls the latent instincts and impulses of her friends. Unlike *Murder in the Cathedral,* however, the play does not arrive at a neat theological conclusion; its philosophical meaning is latent and suggested rather than specific.

Other Eliot dramas are *The Family Reunion* (1939), similar to *The Cocktail Party* and set in an English country house, and *The Confidential Clerk* (1953), a poetic allegory of man's search for a father and a belonging-place. *The Elder Statesman* (1959) rounds out Eliot's verse dramas, utilizing the story line of the Sophocles' *Oedipus at Colonus* in a modern situation with modern characters in England. He had similarly used the Aeschylean *Oresteia* in *Family Reunion* and two plays by Euripides, the *Alcestis* as a background framework for *The Cocktail Party* and the *Ion* to give unity and point to *The Confidential Clerk.*

William Carlos Williams (1883–1963)

Beginning before the First World War in frank imitation of Ezra Pound whom he had known at the University of Pennsylvania in the early years of the century and the other Imagists of their group, William Carlos Williams gradually evolved a highly original and effective variety of free verse. He has become in the Sixties, along with Pound and E. E. Cummings, a major creative influence on young poets. Many of his subjects are taken from nature, and most of his images are visual ones, but he is by no means an ordinary "nature poet." His verse is never effusive or emotional; its main quality is a severe, almost naked starkness. Williams is basically romantic, but his scientific training and his masculine reserve lend him a control and hardness that preserve him from sentimentality. He is occasionally ironic, but never facetious; his whole work, even in his earliest Imagist period, is consistently mature in attitude and technique. Anti-sentimental and anti-Victorian, Williams is one of the most "masculine" of modern poets.

In style and diction particularly Williams rejects the sentimental literary heritage of the Victorians; he strives constantly to achieve the "brusque nervous tension, the vigor and rhetoric" of vernacular American speech. Although he avoids slang, his language is thoroughly idiomatic; he seldom uses a word which is beyond the vocabulary of the ordinary reader, and the rhythm, the intonation of his language, is that of common speech. He has been accused of metrical inconsistency; actually his metric is that of idiomatic conversation. A careful study of his typography and punctuation will show that they too are intended to reproduce the rhythm, the pauses and emphases, of ordinary speech; in spite of the visual quality of his images he has a keen ear for linguistic nuances.

In content Williams tends toward "pure poetry"; he seldom

moralizes or indulges in philosophical sermonizing, and if he has any religious principles they are not prominent in his poetry. Politically he is liberal, with a tendency to the left; criticism of bourgeois capitalism is sometimes found in his fiction (e.g., the story "Jean Beicke") but almost never in his poetry. The same thing is true of his medical background; he uses his scientific training and his experience as a doctor frequently in his fiction, but it seldom appears in his poetry except in an occasional term or phrase borrowed from medicine. As a writer of fiction—he has published four novels and a number of first-rate short stories—Williams is conventional in style but cuttingly ironic, sometimes even apparently callous, in attitude; his medical stories contain some of the most powerful descriptions of disease and suffering in modern fiction. In his fiction as in his poetry, however, Williams is objective rather than indifferent; he shows the sympathetic detachment of a man who has combined the writing of literature with a full-time career as a practicing physician.

Life: William Carlos Williams was born in 1883 in Rutherford, New Jersey, a small town where he remained to live and practice medicine all his life. His ancestry was polyglot: his father's family was English, and from his Puerto Rican mother he inherited a mixture of Basque, Dutch, Spanish, and Jewish blood. His religious background was likewise diverse; his mother, born a Catholic, and his Episcopalian father both later turned to Unitarianism. Williams, the eldest child of the family, attended a private school in Switzerland and went on to the University of Pennsylvania, where he received a medical degree in 1906; he thereupon returned to Europe to do graduate work in pediatrics at the University of Leipzig. Upon his return to America he married (1912) and settled down to medical practice in Rutherford. Meanwhile he had turned to writing poetry as an avocation; his first book, a tentative and rather imitative volume entitled *Poems*, appeared in 1909. *The Tempers* (1916) demonstrated a more mature command of style, although it was strongly influenced by Pound and the American Imagists. Gradually poetry assumed a place in his life at least equal in importance to his medical career. He found no handicap in conducting two careers simultaneously; "One feeds the other, in a manner of speaking," he explained. In 1926 he won the coveted Dial Award for "services to American literature"; from that time on he produced poetry at a steady but modest rate and continued to retain his reputation as a major American poet. Among the many other awards and distinctions which came to him during his career were a National Book Award (1950) and a Bollingen Prize, which he shared with Archibald MacLeish in 1952. In the same year he was appointed Consultant in Poetry to the Library of Congress, but because of political opposition to his alleged left-wing principles he never actually served in the office. From 1942 to 1951 he devoted himself chiefly to a long narrative poem entitled *Paterson,* based on the history and social background of the New Jersey industrial city, which he intended as a kind of epic of the American racial and cultural heritage. His autobiography which appeared in 1951 is a fascinating account of his relationships with some of the major literary figures of our time.

Williams tried his hand at most forms of literature at one time or another, including the drama. One play, *A Dream of Love,* was published in 1948, but at that time before *Hair* and *Oh Calcutta* it was not considered suitable for production. In 1961 *Many Loves, and Other Plays* appeared, in the same year with *The Farmers' Daughters,* his collected stories. Three of his novels form a trilogy: *White Mule* (1937), *In the Money* (1940), and *The Build-Up* (1952). In 1958 he published an additional book of *Paterson,* Book Five.

On March 4, 1963, William Carlos Williams died in his sleep at Rutherford, New Jersey, having delivered 2,000 babies mostly in Rutherford between 1910 and 1952, when he retired from practice. He was survived by his wife Florence and two sons, Paul Herman and Dr. William Eric Williams of Rutherford. It has been said that he wrote poetry like a doctor and practiced medicine with the sensitivity of a poet. In any event he joined the select company of Rabelais and Chekhov who were able to balance two such demanding and apparently diverse disciplines as art and medicine.

Typical Poems: "Metric Figure" (1917) is a characteristic example of Williams' vivid and succinct studies of nature subjects.

The short poem consists entirely of a description of the rising sun shining through poplars; the final effect depends on the striking metaphors (the leaves as "little yellow fish") and on the climax of the last three lines, in which the gleam of the sunrise "Outshines the noise/ Of leaves clashing in the wind." This confusion of the impressions of sight and sound suggests the influence of Pound, who in turn derived the device from the French Symbolists.

"Tract" (1917) is an exercise in extended irony, consisting of a set of instructions for a funeral addressed to a set of conventionally pompous townspeople. The effect of the poem is achieved through contrast between the conventional gestures of grief (the polished black hearse etc.) and the manifestations of genuine feeling (the weathered farm wagon "with gilt wheels," a brave and sad little touch which the poet feels is appropriate to the personality of the deceased).

"Poem" (the short lyric beginning "By the road to the contagious hospital," from *Spring and All,* 1923) is a poem of only twenty-seven lines which echoes some of the imagery as well as the concepts of Eliot's *Waste Land.* Beginning with a description of a bleak winter scene on a road through muddy fields, the poem turns (stanza five) to the tentative awakening of spring and the "naked,/ cold, uncertain" leaves of grass which are the first evidence of the return of life to the world. At first unconscious, the spring plants gradually acquire awareness as they come to life: "rooted, they/ grip down and begin to awaken." Thus the poem depicts the cyclical rebirth of life, which is here, through the allusion to the "awakening" and awareness of plants, connected to intelligence and thus to humanity. An adroit touch is the transition from winter images to images of spring, achieved in a mere seven words in the fifth stanza; the two lines of the stanza are connected organically to the preceding passage by the word "lifeless," which echoes "leafless" in the fourth stanza. The simple and understated ending is typical of Williams' pared-down style.

"The Red Wheelbarrow" (1923) is one of the shortest serious poems ever published by an American poet. The structure is rigidly formal; the poem consists of four miniature stanzas of four words each. Three images are involved: the wheelbarrow, described simply as "red," the qualifying adjectival phrase "glazed with rain," which relieves the excessive severity of the second stanza, and the contrasting white chickens of the final stanza. This poem suggests the cameo-like technique of the Japanese *hokku,* which influenced Pound and the other Imagists.

"The Yachts" (1935) is a medium-length descriptive piece inspired by a yacht race, one of the best-known poems of Williams' later period. The construction involves a paradox or shift in attitude; the yachts are first described as fragile compared to the boundless power of the sea (stanzas 1 and 2), then, toward the end, as triumphing over the sea's fruitless efforts to crush them. Meanwhile the sea, which has been personified in the first stanza, becomes virtually humanized before the poem ends; in stanza 9 it consists of "bodies" which reach out frantic arms to halt the yachts. The frenzied images of the angry sea continue up to the last stanza, and the poem ends with the calm triumph of human craftsmanship over nature: ". . . the skillful yachts pass over." From a technical point of view the poem is interesting as an exercise in sustained personification; aesthetically its chief merit lies in its powerful imagery ("Mothlike in mists, scintillant in the minute/ brilliance of cloudless days . . .").

Paterson (Book One, 1946; Book Two, 1948; Book Three, 1949; Book Four, 1951; Book Five, 1958) represents a major effort on Williams' part to write a major poem, an American epic (in which capacity it will invite comparison with Stephen Vincent Benet's *John Brown's Body* and Hart Crane's *The Bridge*). It is one of the longest of modern poems and we are probably going to have to live with it for a time until it emerges from some of its obscurities. In a sense Williams had to invent a body of myth, a cast of characters, and a religious sanction. Certain things are clear. The setting is a city, a realistic American city, not a romantic one, Paterson, New Jersey, and its topography is as imporant as its history. With the shadow of James Joyce's *Finnegans Wake* hanging over it (as it does in another sense with Wilder's *The Skin of Our Teeth*), Williams remembers that the body of the giant Finn MacCool lay spread out over Dublin, head on the Hill of Howth and upturned feet in Phoenix Park. Paterson will be similarly blessed. Not only is the city like a man, but a man is like a city. Williams searched to find his city, one that had a history, an important colonial history, and a river, the Passaic, and a Falls, and fell in love with it (as Joyce had with the Liffey) and wrote, "I began to write the beginning, about the stream above the Falls. I read everything I could gather, finding fascinating documentary evidence in a volume published by the Historical Society of Paterson. Here were all the facts I could ask for, details exploited by no one. This was my river and I was going to use it. I had grown up on its banks, seen the filth that polluted it, even dead horses . . . ; all I had to do was follow it and I had a poem." His Man-City became Dr. Noah Faitoute Paterson, who is Williams and also the giant. John Malcolm Brinnin has pointed out analogies to the method and matter of Eliot's *The Wasteland.* Indeed *Paterson* becomes a vastly comprehensive poem. Williams begins it with a question, "But how will you find beauty when it is locked in the mind past all remonstrance?" At the end he writes, "We know nothing and can know nothing but the dance, to dance to a measure contrapuntally, Satyrically, the tragic foot." And that is not far removed from Yeats' question, "Who can tell the dancer from the dance?" *Paterson,* Pound's *Cantos,* and Crane's *The Bridge* have become for America's new poets probably the most important long poems in the language.

Wallace Stevens (1879–1955)

Wallace Stevens is an extraordinary literary phenomenon, a successful insurance executive who became simultaneously one of America's most important modern poets. Even more remarkable, there is nothing of the Babbitt or the businessman mentality about his poetry; in fact criticism of it is more often directed toward its alleged obscurity, the highly specialized intricacy of its aesthetic. Stevens is a highly modern, even esoteric type of poet whose work, never popular with the general public, is appreciated chiefly by a small band of scholars, critics, and fellow poets. In these circles he is as highly regarded as any other poet of the century. "*Sunday Morning,*" writes Ivor Winters, a critic who is by no means always favorable to Stevens, "is probably the greatest American poem of the twentieth century and is certainly one of the greatest contemplative poems in English . . ."

A Harvard graduate and a wide reader, Stevens writes from a consciously aristocratic and educated point of view; his poetry is solidly erudite as well as thoroughly mature and sophisticated. The chief influences in his work are the aesthetic theories of Plato and Coleridge (both of which, however, he rejects in certain particulars) and the poetic techniques of the French Symbolists. Like Mallarmé, Verlaine, and the other members of the Symbolist school, Stevens is fond of brilliant visual effects, strong impressionistic images, and evocative but logically diffuse lines. One particular device he borrowed from the Symbolists is the intricate interchanging of sensual impressions, intermingling sight and sound, odor and texture. Following along the lines suggested by Rimbaud's famous sonnet "Voyelles" and by the critical theories of Mallarmé, he attributes definite and fixed values to various colors; for instance the color blue to Stevens invariably connotes poetry, the romantic, the life of the sensibilities, especially the world of the imagination (e.g., in "The Man with the Blue Guitar"). On this theoretical basis Stevens builds a poetry that is simultaneously vivid, erudite, and technically competent. In content it is often epicurean or hedonistic. "The world of *Harmonium* is rich, almost effete," says O'Connor in a remark which might be applied as well to the rest of Stevens' work. "It is a world of comfortable living, *objets d'art,* voyages in the Caribbean, French phrases, sophisticated knowledge and wit."

Moreover, this world is all there is for Stevens; although he has a considerable interest in metaphysics he rejects all Platonic or Christian concepts of immortality. The spirit exists for Stevens, but only as a substance that infuses matter in its mundane state. He has a tendency, in fact, to equate spirit with imagination, a term which has great importance in his aesthetic system. It is imagination (whether of a poet or of an ordinary concept-forming individual) which lends order to the confused diversity of the universe which would otherwise be mere chaos. And Stevens believes above all in order, in an orderly universe and in an orderly approach to the imaginative realm of poetry. Order is, in fact, his *summum bonum,* serving for him in the way the concept of virtue serves for the ordinary Christian. Yet this idea of order is not a political one; he is not, for instance, a religio-political conservative in the way that T. S. Eliot is. To Stevens order is the pattern, the sense, which the human imagination imposes upon experience. The higher the civilization the more sensitive and complex the imagination, and therefore the more refined the order which the imagination evokes. Stevens' concept is most clearly expressed in a poem which is otherwise not very important, "The Idea of Order at Key West" (1935), but it is implied throughout his work.

Another remarkable thing about Stevens' poetic career is that he turned seriously to writing only in his maturity and published his first volume, *Harmonium,* at the age of forty-three; thus he sprang full-blown onto the literary scene without the usual period of tentative and immature searching for an individual style. His poetry, written over the long period of time from *ca.* 1913 to the time of his death in 1955, is remarkably homogeneous in quality; the main development in it is that his later work (after 1936) tends to be more technically intricate and difficult.

Life: Wallace Stevens was born in Reading, Pennsylvania in 1879; his ancestry was Dutch. He attended Harvard (1897–1900) and went on to the New York Law School; he was admitted to the bar in 1904. After practicing law for a short time in New York City he transferred to the insurance business; in 1916 he joined the legal department of the Hartford Accident and Indemnity Co., and in 1934 he became a vice-president of the firm. He thus lived for the major part of his career in Hartford, Connecticut, where the home office of the company was located. Meanwhile he had entered upon a second, almost secret career as a poet. He had published verse while still a Harvard undergraduate, and during his period of law practice in New York he had associated with the modernist cénacle including W. C. Williams, Marianne Moore, and Alfred Kreymborg. Between 1914 and 1923 he published about one hundred poems in magazines, from *Poetry* and *The Little Review* to *The New Republic.* In 1914 and again the following year his work won prizes from *Poetry.* His first volume, *Harmonium,* was published by Knopf in 1923 chiefly through the influence of Carl Van Vechten; the book was not a commercial success, selling fewer than a hundred copies, although it received high praise from some critics. In his early period Stevens also wrote several verse dramas; his *Three Travellers Watch a Sunrise* was produced in

1920 by the Provincetown Players with Edna Millay in the leading rôle. In 1920 *Poetry* awarded him the coveted Levinson Prize, and in 1922 *The Dial* presented him as a distinguished contributor. His volumes continued to appear at a steady rate: *Ideas of Order* in 1935, *Owl's Clover* in 1936, *The Man with the Blue Guitar and Other Poems* in 1937. Meanwhile Stevens continued to live in relative obscurity, shunning literary publicity and conscientiously performing his duties as an insurance executive. Many honors came to him in his later years: election to the National Academy of Arts and Letters in 1946, a Bollingen Prize in 1950, a National Book Award in 1950 and another in 1955, and a Pulitzer Prize (for his *Collected Poems*) in 1955. He died in Hartford in August, 1955.

Important Poems: "Anecdote of the Jar" (1916) is on the surface a simple allegory of a jar placed on a hill in Tennessee and somehow transforming the wilderness. Critics, however, have widely disagreed as to its interpretation. Stanley P. Chase wrote, ". . . the little poem is meant to suggest nothing more than the superiority . . . of the simplest bit of handicraft over any extent of unregulated nature," and O'Connor speaks of the jar "imposing its order" on the wilderness. But Ivor Winters argues that, although the jar does dominate the wilderness, "it does not give order to the wilderness—it is vulgar and sterile, and it transforms the wilderness into the semblance of a deserted picnic ground." This latter interpretation has come to be the accepted one; it is not until the jar is placed in the middle of it that the wilderness becomes "slovenly." Man's works blight the naturalness of the countryside and make it shabby and synthetic; the poem is an objective picture of the slovenly borderline between civilization and wilderness.

"Peter Quince at the Clavier" (1923) is a soliloquy built around the idea that human emotions are equivalent to music and that music itself is "feeling then, not sound." The Biblical legend of Susanna and the elders is used as a skeleton; each emotion of Susanna and her watchers is interpreted in musical terms. Though these emotions die away with the passing of man (Stanza IV), abstract beauty lives on in successive individuals; Susanna's memory stirs music (emotions) in moderns like a "clear viol."

"Sunday Morning" (1923) is Stevens' best-known poem, and has been called one of the most important American poems of the century. It consists of eight stanzas of exactly fifteen lines each. In Stanza I we are introduced to the protagonist, a lady arising on a Sunday morning and taking her breakfast on a terrace. The Sunlight intensifies the pungence of the orange she is eating and the bright green wings of her cockatoo. These images do not seem quite real to the lady, however, since she is meditating on the meaning of death. Stanza II introduces the theme of the poem: what divinity does the lady possess, and what is the meaning of this divinity in the light of the obvious reality of death? The poet answers provisionally that delights of the senses are more valuable than any ephemeral hope of life after death.

But in V the lady refuses to accept this hedonistic solution; the human desire for immortality is too strong even in the midst of sensual pleasure. But, the poet answers, death is necessary in order to set life into relief; our appreciation of life is heightened by the ever-present consciousness of death. In VII a new religion is predicated; the poet describes a ritual in praise of the generative principle of life. Men will find comfort and strength in their "heavenly fellowship of men that perish." In the final stanza the immortality of Jesus is rejected, and by implication the hope of human resurrection is also abandoned. Man is inescapably destined to live on the earth, a whirling ball in "an old chaos of the sun." Yet nature, life, and the generative principle are all about us; in the final lines the doctrine of hedonism and life-worship is reiterated.

In "Le Monocle de Mon Oncle" (poem, 1923) the style is more intricate and Stevens' hedonism tempered by a more thoughtful examination of the meaning of life. The images of the poem constantly contrast sensual experience (the red bird, the apple, the skull, the pool of pink, and the lilacs) with thought and contemplation (the Chinese philosophers, the poet himself as a "rose rabbi"). The poem, however, does not treat of human nature in the wider sense as much as it does the nature of the poetic personality. Stanzas VI–X trace the evolution of the poetic temperament through youth and maturity to old age. In the final stanza (XII) the poet confesses to some difficulty in comprehending love; he now sees nuances where all seemed simple in his youth. The reference to "fluttering things" in the last line also suggests an interest in the realm of idea and spirit as opposed to the world of the flesh. Thus this poem comprises a statement of Stevens' more mature poetic and philosophic principles which may be contrasted with the ideas of his earlier work.

"The Emperor of Ice Cream" is reputedly one of Stevens' most obscure poems. The dominant theme is that of death, symbolized through a funeral which is evidently that of a poverty-stricken old lady; the obsequies are prepared by "the roller of big cigars," a personification of strong and lusty vitality, who is ordered in what is perhaps Stevens' most famous single line, to whip "In kitchen cups concupiscent curds," i.e., apparently to prepare funeral libations which are aphrodisiac in nature. For life must struggle with death; even as the funeral guests bring "flowers in last month's newspapers" we are reminded that "The only emperor is the emperor of ice-cream," i.e., that the only reality or truth, the ruling force in our lives, is necessarily the pleasure of the senses. Thus it is implied that man, believing in and serving "the emperor of ice-cream," gives to the enjoyment of the senses a validity, even a transcendental significance, which Christians previously gave to the idea of immortality through their faith in it.

"The Comedian as the Letter C" (1921–23) is a relatively long poem for Stevens, quasi-narrative and quasi-autobiographical. Stevens was always a Francophile (as the titles of half a dozen poems show) and he apparently knew the French Larousse dictionary with its marvelous drawings of things that begin with each letter of the alphabet. The hero of the poem is Crispin, a Feste-like clown, supercilious in his choice of words, poet and traveler, who takes a voyage from Bordeaux to Yucatan and apparently by way of Havana to Carolina, where he settles down, has a family of four daughters (Stevens had one in Hartford, Connecticut—but then Carolina was soul country and some critics see the four daughters as the four seasons). There is always the poet as ironist playing with the poet as comedian. Up to the point of leaving Bordeaux he considers his poetry frivolous, "musician of pears," but the sea teaches him about elemental life which he can't control by his intellect. It is a symbol of the imagination (Stevens was quite Coleridgean in this—fulfilling Coleridge as Frost and Hart

Crane fulfilled Wordsworth) like "blue," moonlight, and winter. Yucatan, of course, plunges Crispin into the violent world of the senses, of facts, of brilliant colors, of the "green" of reality, the sun, the lush summer. After this saturation he must move north to Carolina, "America was always north to him . . ./ And thereby polar." He tries to achieve control in his adjustment of reality and imagination, "How many poems he denied himself": "A fluctuating between sun and moon." He gives up the idea of a colony to settle in a cabin, Crispin as hermit thinking of himself as Candide, but wakes up to find in his dooryard four daughters with curls and accepts as fatalist his destiny, "Glozing his life with after-shining flicks"; "So may the relation of each man be clipped."

"The Man with the Blue Guitar" (1936–37) from the volume by the same name explores the same "blue-green" relationships but more abstractly and without the pseudo-narrative. The images are based on Picasso's clear, clean pictures of the old guitar player in his blue period (reminiscent of the way Rilke uses Picasso's *Les Saltimbanques* for the Fifth of his *Duino Elegies*—see Volume I). "Things as they are/ Are changed upon the blue guitar."

Archibald MacLeish (born 1892)

In marked contrast to the popular "ivory tower" concept of the poet, MacLeish is a highly social being, intimately in contact with his environment and sensitive to the atmosphere of ideas—intellectual, political, and economic—in the world around him. His long career has led him through a number of literary periods, each of which was conditioned by the changing social environment. In his early period, when he first began to write seriously as a poet (1923–30), he was considerably influenced in technique by Ezra Pound, T. S. Eliot, and the technical innovators of the age. His work of this period is introverted and subjective, concerned with aesthetic and personal problems; in style it is imagistic, highly polished and subtle, but lacking in strongly original content. With the end of the art-for-art's-sake epoch of the Twenties, MacLeish abandoned his pure aestheticism and became increasingly conscious of his social and cultural heritage as an American; the poems of this period (1930–33), e.g., *Frescoes for*

Mr. Rockefeller's Center, are broad in scope, thoughtful, often dominated by a strong consciousness of the American historical tradition. His tendency toward political engagement increased during the New Deal era; in his third period (approx. 1933–48) he is frankly collectivist, left-wing, internationalist, and anti-fascist. Much of his work in this period wavers between literature and propaganda; and during most of the period he held public office under the Roosevelt administration. Finally, in 1949, with his acceptance of a teaching position at Harvard, he shifted his interests once more to pure poetry and to a philosophical rather than political attitude toward the world around him. His later poems (e.g., *Songs for Eve,* 1954) are personal in theme and refined, subtle, and lyrical in technique.

Yet it is probably the work of the second and third periods (1930–48) which will insure MacLeish a permanent place in American literature. It is here that he is most original, most strikingly American and vernacular. Many critics object to the political bias of his work in this period, arguing that poetry must not be confused with propaganda. MacLeish's attitude, however, was a sincere one; he was personally convinced that poetry must be made to serve higher ends than the mere communication of subjective impressions. More than any other writer he helped to convince the American intellectual public of the need of opposing fascism with organized force. Even more important, he succeeded in this period in coming to grips with two problems which most poets prefer to ignore: the antagonism between the political order and the artist class in modern society, and the increasing power of the mass media (radio, newspapers, motion pictures) over the public mind. His answer to the first problem was political engagement; until the artist himself takes an active part in the political life of his society he will continue to be misunderstood and persecuted. (MacLeish himself, seeking confirmation in a political office, was once subjected to the ordeal of being grilled publicly by a congressman about the "meaning" of his poetry.) As for the second problem, his answer was similar: the artist, whether poet, composer, or painter, must contribute actively to the mass media and must develop new and more subtle artistic techniques to rescue them from banality. If poets object to the kind of motion pictures turned out by hack writers, they must write motion pictures themselves. Thus, in addition to working frequently as a screen-writer, MacLeish experimented with the ballet (*Union Pacific*), the drama (*Panic*), the radio play (*The Fall of the City*), and the documentary news-magazine (*Land of the Free*). Yet none of these undertakings has destroyed his integrity as a poet. He has achieved distinction in both realms, as poet and as propagandist; at one extreme his "You, Andrew Marvell" has been called the finest American short poem of the century, and at the other *The Fall of the City* seems assured of permanent fame as one of the great radio plays of our time.

Life: Archibald MacLeish was born in Glencoe, Illinois in 1892. His family was well-to-do, and he was educated at Hotchkiss School and at Yale (B.A. 1915). Married while still a student, he nevertheless served in the First World War as a volunteer member of an ambulance unit and later as a Field Artillery officer; his brother, an aviator, was killed in Belgium. After the war he entered the Harvard Law School, which awarded him an LL.B. in 1919. After teaching for a year at Harvard he practiced law for three years in Boston. Meanwhile he had begun writing poetry. His first book of poems was published in 1917, and in 1923 he took the decisive step in his life by abandoning his law career and going with his wife and two children to France to write. The family stayed in Europe until 1928; from 1924 onward MacLeish published approximately one volume of poetry a year through the period of the Thirties. Returning to America, he settled on a Connecticut farm; in 1932 a trip to Mexico provided the inspiration for the long narrative poem *Conquistador,* which won a Pulitzer Prize for that year. For a brief period during the Thirties he served on the staff of *Fortune* magazine; meanwhile his political activities on behalf of the Roosevelt administration increased. In 1939, in recognition of this active political attitude and of his poetic attainments, he was appointed Librarian of Congress; the appointment was strongly opposed in some circles, but MacLeish proved to be a capable and popular public administrator. In 1940 he published a highly controversial essay of political belief under the title *The Irresponsibles,* particularly attacking the generation of writers of the Twenties whose sentimental pacifism, as he considered it, had helped to turn public opinion away from an active participation in European affairs. During the Second World War he held another important public office: Director of the Office of Facts and Figures, the agency which later developed into the U. S. Information Service. In the period immediately after the war he was active in United Nations affairs, serving as chairman of the American delegation to the first UNESCO conference in Paris in 1946. In 1949 he accepted a teaching position at Harvard, the Boylston Chair of Rhetoric and Oratory, one of the most venerable professorships offered by an American university. His poetry output continued; in 1952 his *Collected Poems* were simultaneously awarded a Pulitzer Prize, the Bollingen Prize, and the National Book Award as the best volume of poetry published that year.

In 1956 MacLeish startled a number of people with a play in verse, *J. B.*, a redoing of the Job story (compare Frost's *Masque of Reason*, see Volume III) which also made good theatre, winning a Pulitzer Prize, with Raymond Massey as Mr. Zuss, a somewhat corrupted God figure, and Christopher Plummer as Nickles, an equally "corrupted" (if one may use that term) Satan or Old Nick. The play, staged in a run-down circus tent (compare MacLeish's sonnet, "The End of the World"), features J. B., his wife Sarah ("all New England"), and their children, running through again the sufferings of Job. Two of the comforters are modernized: Bildad offers an explanation through History—guilt a sociological accident; Eliphaz is a Freudian psychiatrist—guilt a disease. Zophar is still a religionist. Nickles is plain nasty. MacLeish did another play in verse, *Herakles*, in 1967, much admired in reading, and in 1968 a new volume of poetry, *The Wild Old Wicked Man*. In 1971 MacLeish celebrated his seventy-ninth birthday with the opening of his second play to make Broadway, *Scratch*, based on Stephen Vincent Benet's story, "The Devil and Daniel Webster." Reviews were not kind, suggesting that the poet's energy and "literary powers" were too much in evidence. This may indicate that the play reads better than it acts. *J. B.* did both and added measurably to his total reputation.

Important Poems: "Ars Poetica" (1926) is a short free-verse statement of MacLeish's youthful poetic principles. At this time

MacLeish's attitude stands squarely for art-for-art's-sake and against political commitment. The key line in the poem is the final one: "A poem should not mean but be." Poetry has no other significance than its own existence, its own illumination of statement, and its own beauty.

"Immortal Autumn" (1930) presents a novel thought on the autumn season. It is eminently the "human season," the poem argues, because in it nature retreats and becomes invisible; the birds and the leaves disappear, leaving man alone on his planet. The final line calls for love and understanding between men in a world where humanity is bereft of nature.

"You, Andrew Marvell" (1930) is the best-known of MacLeish's early lyrics. The title alludes to Andrew Marvell's "To His Coy Mistress," which contains the couplet, "But at my back I always hear/ Time's winged chariot hurrying near." The chariot of Marvell's poem suggests death, and in MacLeish's poem the gradual encroachment of the shadow of night over the globe of the earth achieves a similar impression. The shadow of dusk is seen falling, first over Babylon and the Near East, then through the classic lands to the Atlantic; at last it reaches the poet, lying "face downward in the sun" somewhere in America. The path of the dusk-line from east to west parallels the march of civilization, which began in the Euphrates valley, passed to Greece and Rome, thence to Europe, and came finally to America. In technique the poem is interesting for its sustained grammatic suspense; it consists of a single long sentence of parallel clauses connected by "and."

"Memorial Rain" (1930) is a tribute to the war dead in a form suggested by the classic English elegy. The reflections of the poet alternate with the conventionally patriotic remarks (". . . these happy, happy dead") of a diplomat making a memorial speech; thus the mood of the poem is one of irony mixed with sorrow. The setting, an American military cemetery in Belgium, reminds the poet of "one" (evidently MacLeish's aviator brother) who lies under foreign earth remembering his Illinois home and troubled by the constant and monotonous wind (symbol of unrest). The ambassador's speech is at last interrupted by the coming of rain, which drives away his audience; and with the moisture "seeping/ Between cracked boards" (symbol of the cycle of life, of the merging of the body with earth) peace comes again to the dead soldier. In addition to its content the poem is interesting from a technical point of view; its concrete, even blunt images (e.g., the rain seeping in to the corpse) are relieved by the subtle originality of diction (the "thin grating" of ants, the "spurts of water that ravel in the dry sand") and by its use of half-rhymes and other prosodic innovations (*thin/continues, lake/like,* the slight variations in the "o" vowels in lines 3–4). This poem, which owes something to Ezra Pound, nevertheless marks the transition in MacLeish's work to the more mature and politically conscious style of the Thirties.

"Burying Ground by the Ties" (1933) is the best-known piece from *Frescoes for Mr. Rockefeller's City.* The speakers are the thousands of foreign-born workmen who helped to build the Union Pacific line through the Rockies, and by extension all of America's foreign-born proletariat. Deprived of status as "true" Americans, they are nevertheless the foundation of the wealth which the rich enjoy. Yet their only satisfaction lies in knowing that they "laid the steel to the stone stock of these mountains." This is one of the first of MacLeish's poems to show a definitive political attitude.

The Fall of the City ("verse play for radio," 1937) was the first radio script to be written by an established poet. The plot, laid in a mythical city, is an allegory of fascism. The play opens as an announcer, viewing the crowd milling about in the central plaza of the city, relates the situation: a woman recently dead has come back to life and is about to speak to the people. As the crowd listens she tells them in oracular accents that the city of masterless men is to take a master, and there will be "blood after." Confusion sweeps over the crowd; then a messenger arrives to warn of a conqueror who has taken all countries "east over sea-cross." Faced with the menace, the people are terrified. An orator speaks to them, exhorting them to pacifism; only with "freedom" (i.e., passiveness), he tells them, can freedom be preserved. His motto is "weakness conquers." After the orator (personification of the pacifists and isolationists of the nineteen-thirties), another messenger arrives to report that the conqueror has now landed and is marching on the city. The people become frantic with fear and begin to accuse their leaders of treason. Then the priests (symbols of organized religion) speak to them; they argue that salvation will be found only if the population turns back to its traditional gods. Next comes a general, a personification of the spirit of preparedness; he calls the politicians and priests "foolish old men" and warns that freedom can be preserved only if men unite to fight against it. But the people do not listen; they are hypnotized by the imminent arrival of the conqueror. When he appears, clad in armor, they fall on their faces before him; in their supine attitude they do not notice that when the conqueror opens his visor his armor is empty. The shell of armor might easily be toppled, but the people cannot see this; they have fallen down before a nonentity because they are afraid of the responsibility of their freedom. Fascism does not conquer free and courageous men; it triumphs only over the morally weak who are tired of "the long labor of liberty" and too cowardly to fight against their enemies.

E. E. Cummings (1894–1962)

Opinion is about equally divided as to whether Cummings is a poet of genius or merely a facetious exhibitionist. In either case he is one of the most highly individual literary figures of his generation, as strikingly original in technique as he is eccentric and irrepressible in personality. Above all he is the enemy of complacent middle-class respectability: "the godless are the dull and the dull are the damned," he stated in a 1941 poem. His spontaneous individualism has led him as well to revolt against traditional poetic technique; not only does he abandon conventional structure and content, but he rejects even the usual techniques of conveying information and emotion through the printed word. His experiments in typography have become his trademark; the mere appearance of his poetry on the page instantly identifies its author. Comparable idiosyncracies are present in his syntax, punctuation, and diction.

Cummings is primarily concerned with the auditory impact of language; his verse is meant to strike the ear and not the eye. This is instantly apparent when Cummings is heard reading his own poetry on phonograph records; the curious innovations in typography which give his verse such an odd appearance on the page are then seen merely as aids to oral reading, as guides to timing, accentuation, syllable stresses, and even to pitch. He breaks lines to indicate stress; he sometimes capitalizes key words for the same reason, and he uses punctuation to indicate the rises and climaxes in tone. In his more radical poems he avoids capitalization for any purpose, even spelling his name "e. e. cummings." These eccentricities have been widely imitated, but it requires a poet of Cummings' skill to make them vivid and meaningful.

In content Cummings is (a) a total individualist, virtually a philosophical anarchist, and (b) a kind of Dionysian hedonist. These two attitudes serve as his politics and ethics respectively, although they are hardly systematic enough to be considered under these terms. His aversion to social groups, to right wings and left wings, to organizations, clubs, parties, institutions, and committees of all kinds approaches the pathological; Cummings is the individualist *par excellence*. In spite of their alleged respect for "rugged individualism," Americans are a nation of joiners, a highly gregarious people; thus Cummings, the absolute individualist, often finds himself at odds with "the American Way of Life." His personality is essentially satirical; he lacks that quality so necessary in the Good Citizen, an awe in the presence of venerable institutions. Basically a serious person, he refuses to be caught in the attitude of seeming to take anything seriously, even his own poetry; he is one of the few modern poets of the modernist school who has enough sense of humor to combine poetry with genuine comedy. Horace Gregory has compared his bawdy humor to that of the Italian Commedia dell'arte; a comparison with Rabelais is also apt.

As for his ethics of hedonism: Cummings is enthusiastically on the side of love, poetry, springtime, freedom, and sensual pleasure. The Dionysian quality in his poetry ("o sweet spontaneous earth") is connected to his antagonism toward puritanism and Anglo-Saxon propriety; much of his more serious poetry is concerned with tributes to the earth as a source of life, to female beauty as a symbol of the life force, and to vitality and sensory beauty in every form. Erotic themes play a large part in his work; more than any other American poet of his time he has revived the romantic love-poem, the lyrical tribute to the beauty of the beloved, which has tended to grow out of style since the eighteenth century when it was the chief subject of lyric poetry.

Cummings is a controversial figure, and opinions of his importance differ widely. Theodor Spencer has termed him "the most truly delightful lyric poet in America," and Lloyd Frankenburg in 1950 called him "one of the major lyric poets of our time." On the other hand Allen Tate has complained that "he replaces the old poetic conventions with equally limited conventions of his own," and Untermeyer concludes, "Robbed of typographical oddities, reduced to essential statements, most of [his] verse is not so spectacular as it first appears." In the future, as the startling quality of Cummings' typographical experiments wears off, he will probably be admired chiefly for his content as one of the important romantic lyricists of his generation.

In the nineteen-sixties Cummings has been big with the student protest generation. His sharp, easily understood, specific attacks on Establishment and commercialism have found attentive ears and responsive hearts. He is quoted in hip and rock services, church, baccalaureate, even weddings. It can be something of a shock to have Cummings thrown back at you in a new context. What seemed relatively conventional criticism in the Forties may be dynamite in the Sixties and Seventies. New American poets are getting as much from Cummings as from Pound and Williams.

Life: Edward Estlin Cummings was born in Cambridge, Massachusetts in 1894. His father was a well-known Congregationalist minister. Cummings attended Harvard, where he received a B.A. in 1915 and an M.A. in 1916; immediately thereafter he embarked for France, where he served as a volunteer ambulance driver. His radical and pacifist remarks, however, soon brought him under the suspicion of the French authorities, and he found himself confined for several months in an internment center for "subversive aliens." He related these experiences in a saucy and highly original novel, *The Enormous Room* (1922). After serving out the rest of the war in the American army, he returned to New York and set himself up as a poet. Two years of this brought little success; he returned to Paris, where he remained until 1924 studying painting. Meanwhile he continued to write poetry; when he returned to America he found that his novel and his first collection of verse had earned him a considerable reputation. In 1925 he won the *Dial* prize for poetry; he continued to produce verse at a prolific rate until 1930, when he returned for several years to Paris.

Married in 1928 to Ann Barton, Cummings was later divorced; since 1933 he has lived chiefly in New York. His interest in painting continued; he has exhibited several times with the Society of Independent Artists in Paris and has held several one-man shows in America including two (1944 and 1949) at the American-British Art Centre. In 1952 he was invited to give the annual series of Norton Lectures at Harvard University; his rather eccentric and highly informal talks were later published as *i: six nonlectures* (1953). In 1955 Cummings received a special citation from the National Book Awards committee for his definitive volume *Poems, 1923–1954*.

Two of his plays, highly experimental in their time, should be mentioned: *Him* (1927) and *Santa Claus, A Morality* (1946). They have been rediscovered by avant-garde theatre in the Sixties. E. E. Cummings died of a stroke in September of 1962 in Conway, New Hampshire. Obituaries referred to him as novelist and painter as well as poet and quoted one of his sayings: "I have no sentimental fear of sentimentality."

Typical Poems: "La Guerre" (from *Tulips and Chimneys,* 1923) consists of two antiphonal sections which contrast the evil of war with the changelessness of the "sweet spontaneous earth." The love-death conflict in the second section, which finally results in the rebirth of spring, suggests the Greek Persephone-Pluto myth; a semi-religious paganism is often implied in Cummings' "Dionysian" lyrics.

"Chanson Innocent," from the same collection, is similar. Beginning as a kind of child's song accompanied by the whistling "far and wee" of the balloon-man, it builds rhythmically to a climax in which the balloon-man (now "goat-footed" and thus recognized as a satyr or follower of Dionysus, a symbol of joyous Bacchic abandon) ends the poem with a final exultant note of his pipe. The two compound adjectives "puddle-wonderful" and "mud-luscious," which strikingly convey the child's delight in spring, are often-cited examples of Cummings' verbal experiments.

"Portrait VIII" (the poem beginning "Buffalo Bill's/ defunct," also from *Tulips and Chimneys,* is a whimsical but sincere tribute to the legend of the famous American cowboy. The running together of "break onetwothreefourfive pigeons justlikethat" is a typical instance of Cummings' effort to convey reading directions through typography.

"The Cambridge ladies who live in furnished souls" (also from *Tulips and Chimneys*) is a satirical "sonnet" characterizing the respectable ladies of Cambridge, Massachusetts, priggish, religious, superficially cultivated, gossip-mongering, who are too narrow and prim to be aware of the tremendous vitality of the world all about them; thus they do not notice that the moon "rattles like a fragment of angry candy."

"Poem, Or Beauty Hurts Mr. Vinal" (from *is* 5, 1926) is one of Cummings' best-known satires, a devastating portrait of the business-minded middle-class American citizen. The poem consists mainly of parodies of advertising slogans interspersed with bombastic Fourth-of-July oratory; the passage in the middle beginning "i do however protest" turns to a personal attack by the poet on the stereotyped banality of advertising, motion pictures, and other mass media. The poem ends with a ribald but masterful description of obsession with patent medicines and the cult of personal fastidiousness in America.

"Next to of course god" (Poem III of Section Two of *is* 5) is similar but shorter, consisting entirely of a parody of a banal patriotic oration. The speaker, after spouting unconvincingly about the "heroic happy dead" who "rushed to the slaughter," then pauses to drink "rapidly a glass of water"; the sudden and incongruous return to the prosaic turns his pretentious speech into a comic mockery.

"Since feeling is first" (Poem VII, Section Four, in *is* 5) is one of the best known of Cummings' love-lyrics. The traditional *carpe diem* theme is treated in half-serious, half-whimsical modern terms; the poet, insisting to his mistress that his intelligence is unimportant beside her beauty ("your eyelids' flutter"), implores her to love him, since life is short and death ("no parenthesis") is long.

Relatively conventional in form, this short poem is one of Cummings' most successful treatments of the theme of love, avoiding exhibitionistic eccentricity on one hand and sentimentality on the other.

"Space being (don't forget to remember) Curved" (Poem VII in *ViVa*, 1931) is a boisterous pastiche of the clichés of modern science and its inevitable result, the arrogant self-glorification of the human race; "god being Dead," man has become the Lord of Creation. His supremacy is illustrated through an incongruous and mocking example: at the least crooking of his trigger finger, "earth's most terrific/ quadruped" (the elephant) "swoons into billiard Balls!" Cummings, the total individualist, rejects even modern scientific humanism as a philosophical dogma. This theme, that of man's arrogance in assuming his superiority over the rest of the universe, is one frequently found in Cummings' later work; see also "pity this busy monster, manunkind" (1944).

Chief Play: *Him* (play, 1927) is "a drama whose loving nonhero and lovely heroine are called Him and Me"; as Cummings explains in nonlecture five, "whose possibly principal protagonist impersonates (on various occasions) nine other people; whose so-to-speak-chorus consists of a trio of Weird Sisters; and whose twenty-one scenes revolve the distinction between time and eternity, measurable when and illimitable now." It is basically the love story of Him and Me, married to each other. Him is an artist trying to write a play. And Me is probably having a baby. In the first scene the three fates or weirds are presiding mysteries: Miss Stop, Miss Look, and Miss Listen. In the three acts the room in which Him and Me live revolves with a different wall to the rear each time. In the last scene there is great surprise when they discover there is no fourth wall, only people—which gently mocks the fourth wall removed concept of realistic drama.

Him remembers odd scenes from his past, particularly in Paris, wonderfully comic scenes, one with drunks who wannaplay tennish, another of American tourists in a Paris café with two women ordering an *homme*, one stewed, the other boiled. There are also circus scenes which Him and Me have shared a fondness for and freak shows which Me never wanted to look at. Him says, "Damn everything but the circus! And here am I, patiently squeezing four-dimensional ideas into a two-dimensional stage, when all of me that's anyone or anything is in the top of a circustent." And Me responds, "I didn't imagine you were leading a double life—and right under my nose, too." Apparently the whole play can be thought of as the dreams under anaesthesia of Me during childbirth. And the nonhero Him certainly brings his play to birth by the end of the third act. There are difficulties of communication and understanding between Him and Me, as between any Man and Woman in such a relationship; but there is also much tenderness and love, even in a crass twentieth century world.

Marianne Moore (1887–1972)

Like Pound and Hart Crane, Marianne Moore is a poet's poet, read and appreciated chiefly by specialists; T. S. Eliot believes that "her poems form part of the small body of durable poetry written in our time." But unlike Pound and Crane she is not a "difficult" poet; her work is limited in popularity not because it is obscure but because it is highly specialized in content and attitude. She is not "socially conscious" in the political sense; she is not an embattled humanitarian, and she is not usually concerned with profound philosophical or religious problems. In her own words, her purpose is to create "imaginary gardens with real toads in them"; i.e., to describe an impressionistic world of the imagination, but to do so in images so concrete and vivid that they spring to life in the reader's mind. Her attitude is objective; she does not permit herself surface displays of emotion, and her poetry is almost devoid of any passionate warmth toward her fellow man. In a sense she is a nature poet; she has a fondness for small living things struggling valiantly to hold their own against a hostile universe. In all living things, even in vegetable organisms, she sees the operation of a wondrous life force; in one poem she marvels, "What sap/ went through that little thread/ to make the cherry red!"

Stylistically her poetry is chiefly remarkable for its vivid and highly original images: an elephant is described as "black earth preceded by a tendril." Structurally her work is fragmentary, virtually anarchistic; one critic objects that hers is "an outlook that has to break things into small pieces to see them," and another applies the term "mosaic" to her disconnected and apparently irrelevant series of images. Miss Moore's own term for this quality in her work is "elasticity," which she opposes to "logic"; in other words her sequence of ideas is intuitive rather than logically consecutive. The influence of the Imagist movement is apparent; the idea also has something in common with the method of Gertrude Stein in such books as *Tender Buttons,* where an irrational and wholly feminine intuition guides the selection of words with a rich associative content.

Life: Marianne Moore was born in St. Louis, Missouri in 1887. Her grandfather was a Presbyterian minister and her brother a clergyman and Navy chaplain; in her private life Miss Moore has remained a serious and rigidly moral church-goer. Educated at Bryn Mawr (B.A. 1909), she went on to study stenography at the Carlisle Commercial College in Pennsylvania and then to teach for four years at the Carlisle Indian School. She had begun writing while still a student; in 1915 *The Egoist,* a British review devoted chiefly to Imagist verse, published her first poem to appear in a major magazine. From 1918 she lived in New York City, first in a Greenwich Village apartment and later in a Brooklyn flat, which she and her chaplain brother first rented because it was conveniently near to the Navy Yard where he was stationed. Miss Moore remained in this apartment for the rest of her career, living frugally and working steadily at her poetry. In 1921, after a number of her poems had appeared in magazines, her friends including Hilda Doolittle published at their own expense a small volume of her work entitled simply *Poems. Observations* followed in 1924; between 1921 and 1951 she published seven volumes of verse, including a volume of *Selected Poems* (1935) with an introduction by T. S. Eliot and a *Collected Poems* (1951). From 1921 to 1925 she worked as a librarian in a Brooklyn branch library; in 1926 she became editor of the important literary review *Dial,* a position she held until the magazine ceased publication in 1929. Many awards and recognitions came to her during her long career; among them were the Dial Award in 1924, the Levinson Prize of *Poetry* magazine in 1932, the Hartsock Memorial Prize in 1935, the

Bollingen Prize (for her *Collected Poems*) in 1951, and a Pulitzer Prize in 1952. For nine years (1944–53) she labored at her painstaking translation of *The Fables of La Fontaine,* which finally appeared in 1954. A wide reader, Miss Moore interests herself in virtually every aspect of learning, from classic languages to zoology and botany; she is said to be an avid lecture-goer and a keen observer of the objects and persons around her. *Predilections,* her first volume of prose essays, appeared in 1955. Marianne Moore died in her sleep at the age of eighty-four on February 5, 1972 in New York. The *New York Times* carried many personal and critical tributes to her work as a poet and to her life as a person.

Typical Poems: "To a Steam Roller" (1924) is typical of the whimsical and slightly rococo style of her early work. The steam roller, which crushes down the "sparkling chips of rock" (perhaps equivalent to individual objects of beauty) and then walks back and forth on them, suggests a comparison with humans who must categorize everything according to a dogmatic system. Toward the end of the poem the stupid and ponderous machine is incongruously compared to a butterfly, an image suggesting a contrast between the steam-roller mentality of the dogmatist with the poet's own whimsical and intuitive changeability.

"Poetry" (1935) expresses Miss Moore's chief statement of her poetic philosophy and of her intent as a poet. She begins by confessing that she dislikes poetry: "there are things that are important beyond all this fiddle." Upon first approach poetry seems to everyone, even to a poet, a trivial exercise much less important than the more physical and concrete occupations in life. But if one reads it "with a perfect contempt," i.e., without expecting anything, much value may be found in it. The middle sections of the poem (stanzas 2–5) discuss the obscurity of some modern poetry, the importance of other forms of language like "business documents and school books," and the stupidity of the "immovable critic," who is depicted in the guise of an ill-tempered and flea-bitten horse. The final stanza presents the key phrase: poetry must present "imaginary gardens with real toads in them." The real lover of poetry likes it first of all because he likes its "raw material," i.e., the physical sensations of life; he then demands that its technique be "genuine," i.e., unaffected, free from deliberate obscurity, and motivated by true emotion on the part of the poet.

"In Distrust of Merits" (1944) is one of Miss Moore's rare statements on contemporary social issues, a thoughtful consideration of the implications of the Second World War. Beginning pessimistically in the mood of disillusioned pacifism which has inspired so many war poems, the poem gradually evolves into an analysis of the millions of personal hatreds which go to make up the national war psychology. If war is to have any point (stanza 5) we must promise never again to hate "black, white, red, yellow, Jew,/ Gentile, untouchable"; the only possible meaning in war is that "hearts must feel and not be numb." The final stanza, rising to a magnificent climax, turns to a searching analysis of the poet's own emotions toward the war: has she too felt hatred toward the official enemies? "There never was a war that was/ not inward"; this is the conclusion of the poem. Wars arise, not from conflicts of international interests, but from the sum of the hatreds of individuals; until hatred is replaced by love in the heart of each human being wars will continue. This idea is one which Miss Moore expressed frequently in the period after 1941; in her reply to a 1955 biographical questionnaire she stated, "I feel that the unselfish behavior of individual to individual is the basis for world peace."

Langston Hughes (1902–1967)

It is for his poetry (a dozen or two poems) out of a large publication that the future will probably remember Langston Hughes, for that and for the man himself. He has been given the unofficial designation of "Negro poet laureate" of our time. His ten books of poetry span forty years of the century from *The Weary Blues* (1926) to *The Panther and the Lash* (1967). But he has produced also short stories, plays, autobiography, novels, translations, and anthologies; and he has created one Harlem folk character, Jesse B. Semple, better known as "Simple," in newspaper columns and stories and a musical play, *Simply Heavenly* (1957), who with low-keyed irony and satire is likely to have a little immortality of his own. For many people it is Lorraine Hansberry's choice of her title *A Raisin in the Sun* from

Hughes' poem, perhaps his greatest, "Dream Deferred," that has recalled attention to his real poetic talent that was being obscured by the militancy and rhetoric of some of his declamatory verse of involvement. Being "right on" can sometimes turn off the thrust of poetic image and metaphor. From the beginning such volumes as *The Weary Blues, Fine Clothes to the Jew* (1927), *Fields of Wonder* (1947), and *Ask Your Mama* (1961) were placed in the tradition of Masters, Sandburg, and Vachel Lindsay, realistic, colloquial, stripping life to the buff but still poeticizing it, rhythmic with the insistence of jazz beat, but containing indignation and "wild comedy" which belong to Hughes distinctively.

Life: Born in Joplin, Missouri on February 1, 1902, and living his childhood variously in Buffalo, Cleveland, Lawrence (Kansas), Mexico City, Topeka, Colorado Springs, and Kansas City, James Langston Hughes found that in Lawrence, Kansas he could not go to the movies, could not buy an ice cream soda, could not swim at the Y.M.C.A., early experience with discrimination he would not forget. A separation between father and son began early in Mexico; Langston was often with grandparents. In the Twenties he began his extensive travels, working on shipboard, going to Africa, Holland, Paris, Genoa. In Washington, D.C. and later in Harlem which became his home base, he wrote and published his first poetry and began to give university readings with musical accompaniment. Awards and fellowships came his way, including a Guggenheim, as he worked on stories and plays as well as poetry. One story, "Father and Son," became the basis for the best of his plays, *Mulatto*. Work on *The Big Sea* (1940), a fascinating autobiographical account of his early years into the Thirties, carried him into even wider fields of interest, translating Federico Garcia Lorca and Gabriela Mistral, the "Simple" columns, anthologies of black literature, teaching and encouraging other writers, work with the NAACP, and in the Forties and Fifties a resurgence of poetry. His output was prodigious, and in general his protest was more amiable than that of writers who followed him. He liked to quote Bert Williams as saying: "It is not a disgrace to be a Negro, but it is very inconvenient." Langston Hughes died in 1967, having been along with Richard Wright both guide and inspiration to a new generation of black writers who could more easily approach the public on terms of equal opportunity than had been possible in the past. He was known as "A Wheel in Harlem."

Representative Poems: "Jazzonia" (1923) is one of the jazz poems that impressed Vachel Lindsay so favorably. It opens with "Oh, silver tree!/ Oh, shining rivers of the soul!/ In a Harlem cabaret/ Six long-headed jazzers play./ A dancing girl whose eyes are bold/ Lifts high a dress of silken gold." Its "Picasso-like image of the jazz men's six long heads massed and tilted" is followed by the sexuality of the dancing girl—an effective, almost imagistic, poem.

"Dream Boogie" (from the volume, *Montage of a Dream Deferred,* 1951) continues the syncopated jazz rhythm with a built-in message:

> "Good morning, daddy!
> Ain't you heard
> The boogie-woogie rumble
> Of a dream deferred? . . .
>
> *You think*
> *It's a happy beat?*
>
> Listen to it closely:
> Ain't you heard
> something underneath
> like a—
>
> *What did I say?* . . .
> Hey, pop!
> Re-bop!
> Mop!
> Y-e-a-h!"

"Dream Deferred" (1959) inspired Lorraine Hansberry to create her first play. It is brilliantly conceived in a series of five questions, one provisional questioning statement, and a final sixth question. "What happens to a dream deferred?" Perhaps it dries up like a raisin? Or does it "fester like a sore—/ And then run?/ Does it stink like rotten meat?/ Or crust and sugar over—/ like a syrupy sweet?" The incongruity of these images, three of them of food, although one decidedly inedible, and one of disease, is shocking (with heightened awareness) and precise in descriptive power and implication. The statement slows the pace: "Maybe it just sags/ like a heavy load." The final question with the third rhyme does what it suggests: "Or does it explode?" There is not one word too many or too few or in the wrong place.

"Mother in Wartime" (1967) seems to present the black protest to the Vietnam War. "As if it were some noble thing,/ She spoke of sons at war,/ . . . She thought that only/ One side won,/ Not that both/ Might lose." The quietness of the irony and implied protest makes the poetic statement none the less effective.

"Dinner Guest: Me" (1967) is a longer, more personal poem than many by Hughes which twists the stiletto brilliantly; it has the ring of truth: "I know I am/ The Negro Problem/ Being wined and dined" by those whites who "probe in polite way/ The why and wherewithal/ Of darkness U. S. A.—" The elegant hosts and other guests murmur "Over *fraises du bois*,/ 'I'm so ashamed of being white.' " With lobster and wine, and the center of attention, "To be a Problem on/ Park Avenue at eight/ Is not so bad./ Solutions to the Problem,/ Of course, wait." There is an astringency and good humor that go with the criticism.

As a candidate for best poem along with "Dream Deferred," "Merry-Go-Round" from *Shakespeare in Harlem* (1942) and reprinted in *The Panther and the Lash* (1967) should be mentioned. The colored child at the carnival asks "Where is the Jim Crow section/ On this merry-go-round,/ Mister, cause I want to ride?" Coming from the South he knows "White and colored/ Can't sit side by side." It's easy to see on a train or a bus, "But there ain't no back/ To a merry-go-round!/ Where's the horse/ For a kid that's black?" The merry-go-round as a metaphor for modern society, for our world, makes the poem apt and probing.

Theodore Roethke (1908–1963)

Among a sizable group of American poets who have made a name for themselves in the period since 1940, Theodore Roethke, Robert Lowell, Richard Wilbur, Richard Eberhart, Karl Shapiro, John Ciardi, Randall Jarrell, to mention a few, the name that seems best established to a number of critics (along with Lowell who paid him tribute) is that of Theodore Roethke. The poets who are following in the sixties seem to be legion, for the most part with something to say. Some colleges have as many as one a week to visit and give readings.

Theodore Roethke is not alone in having developed a unique and personal lyrical voice, although he has done that; his poetic lines carry his own signature. His forms include a return to more traditionally tight structures, ballad measure, even the villanelle, and song, with more rhyme and rhythm and perhaps reason than the loose freer verse that has been dominating the American scene, although he can do that too. If he develops new form, it must be seen in his very individual approach to "sequences" of related lyrics and to links between sequences. It is a kind of sonnet sequence, but they are not sonnets—something like Yeats' Crazy Jane poems. Roethke has been accused of writing like Auden or Yeats, to which he replied wittily and with insight in a lecture, "How to Write Like Somebody Else." Three of his best lyrical sequences are "The Lost Son," "The Dying Man" (an elegy for Yeats), and "Meditations of an Old Woman." His content seems also to be uniquely his own, a new dimension in human experience for poetic expression. He is a humanist in a world of nature (a touch of Wordsworth), without needing to lead us into either political activism or religious commitment. Other poets have looked into man's place among the animals (William Vaughn Moody's "The Menagerie," for instance). Kafka and O'Neill in other media looked at the ape, and the ape looked at man. But initially, fundamentally, Roethke goes further back, deeper into the evolutionary past—man as worm and fish is a late development. He has sympathies with plant life, and even with more elemental things like rock, mud, water, and wind. Roethke looks at the "lower" orders with microscopic eye, very intently focused, and only slightly distorted by Freudian and Jungian insights for effective human application. There is also a journey into himself, including his occasional periods of insanity, from which he learns and writes much, incorporating them into the total human experience of us all.

Roethke has written in his poetry his own spiritual autobiography or search for identity; the poems follow a manic-depressive alteration between joy and anxiety, which except for degree is our common fate. His own "best" friends among his contemporary poets were probably Dylan Thomas, W. H. Auden, Louise Bogan, Edith Sitwell, and Thomas Kinsella. Although in attempting to place Roethke among the poets, one cannot put him on a level with Yeats, Eliot, or Rilke, critics like Malkoff, Ransom, and Ralph Mills tend to place him in the company of Wallace Stevens, William Carlos Williams, and E. E. Cummings—which is a very good place to be.

Life: Born in Saginaw, Michigan in 1908, the son of Otto and Helen Roethke, of German immigrant families, whose pride was the greenhouse started by Grandfather Wilhelm (who changed his name to William) Roethke, moving from market gardening to the florist's business, Theodore grew up with the plants under glass that he was later to write about. He worked in the glass house he came to love, went regularly with his sister June to the Presbyterian Sunday School, read such books as *Birds of Michigan, Wild Flowers of Michigan,* and completed his studies at public school in spite of his father's agonized death, then went to Ann Arbor and the university, worked for a master's degree (which he finally received in 1936), and took a teaching job in English at Lafayette College in Easton, Pennsylvania in 1931. He devoted himself equally to teaching and writing poetry from then on, although manic-depressive seizures began to require periodic hospitalization and leaves of absence from such schools where he was teaching as Michigan State College, Pennsylvania State, Bennington College, and the University of Washington in Seattle.

Such attacks did not apparently materially interrupt his production of poetry. *Open House,* his first volume, was published in 1941, *The Lost Son* in 1948, and *Praise to the End!* in 1951. In 1953 Ted married Beatrice O'Connell, a former student at Bennington, and they honeymooned at W. H. Auden's villa on Ischia in Naples Bay. Auden had made the offer as best man; Louise Bogan was matron of honor. The newlyweds settled down to respective teaching jobs in Seattle. *The Waking* had been published in 1953; *Words for the Wind* appeared in 1958 and *I Am! Says the Lamb* in 1961. Robert Heilman as the chairman of the department where Roethke was teaching defended his leaves of absence, including sick leave, with vigor, pointing out his inestimable service to the University of Washington. Having made a film, *In a Dark Time* (which is available for showing), very sensitively done, poetry reading with interspersed scenes of the natural growths he loved, Ted Roethke had recorded himself for posterity. He died of a coronary, floating in a swimming pool on August 1, 1963.

Typical Poems: "The Minimal" is precisely what the title announces, not because it's only an eleven line poem, but because the poet proclaims his microscopic study of "the lives on a leaf": "little/ Sleepers, numb nudgers in cold dimensions," "bacterial creepers." The close fixed attention given to such a small world increases its dimensions. Something in the human soul not rational responds to these minute activities, sympathizes with these lower orders of life, and is disturbed by "Their wan mouths kissing the warm sutures,/ Cleaning and caressing,/ Creeping and healing." The poems "Root Cellar" and "Cuttings" do much the same kind of thing.

"The Lost Son" is one of Roethke's first lyric sequences, five numbered and separately titled poems, a kind of experimental monologue, pursuing correspondences in a kind of free associational, or stream of consciousness scheme, in this case the spiritual journey of a child protagonist but without logical sequence, a series of ordeals to be overcome from graveyard fears through a greenhouse world to a waiting for the return of light. The Flight of Part 1 is full of toads, leaves, snail, bird, worm, fly (and may be a kind of delirium tremens picture of the lost week-end of a son lost in hospital—the child become a man become a child again). Part 2, The Pit, asks, "Where do the roots go?" and "Who stunned the dirt into noise?" The mole knows about such beginnings, and the child-man-poet says, "I feel the slime of a wet nest./ Beware Mother Mildew." The death-wish is resisted with the last line, "Nibble again, fish nerves." Part 3, The Gibber, treats sexual fears and alienation darkly understood. Everything "Said to me: Die." But from this point on comes release. The last two parts of the poem, The Return and "It was beginning winter" take the boy home to the greenhouse of his father (as much of a double image for Roethke as for Kafka—"Ordnung! Papa is coming!") and a period of waiting. This is not quite "God's in his greenhouse, All's right with the world," but a relative affirmation with apprehension none the less.

"The Waking" is a villanelle, an odd restrictive form for a modern poet but used by Joyce in *A Portrait of the Artist as a Young Man* in Stephen's "Are you not weary of ardent ways" and by Dylan Thomas in "Do Not Go Gentle into that Good Night" as well as by Roethke (also in "The Right Thing"). "Going is knowing" and "We think by feeling" are favorite Roethke concepts and the simplicity of his ultimate line in "The Waking"—"I learn by going where I have to go," has a stoic ring of conviction. "Great Nature has another thing to do/ To you and me," which is of course death. We all "wake to sleep" and are equal with the worm climbing "up a winding stair."

Robert Lowell (born 1917)

In the Fifties Robert Lowell was one of the Younger Poets whose work led many critics to refer to him as a prodigy, perhaps because of the charisma of the name. In the past fifteen years he has developed further and produced poetry at a steady rate from *Life Studies* (1959) through *Imitations* (1961), *For the Union Dead* (1964), *Near the Ocean* (1967) to *Notebooks 1967–68* (1969) which assure him a place as a major American poet. He is literate and highly allusive (in the Pound, Eliot, Auden fashion) but his frame of reference is more likely to include his New England heritage, particularly Hawthorne and Melville, as well as the Latin classics even more than Dante and Homer. He struggles with his puritan heritage, ostensibly denies it in his conversion to Catholicism; but he can't get rid of it and it is precisely the combination of Catholic and puritan in a New England setting that gives his poetry its distinctive and original impact. Lowell's dominant theme is a search for faith in a modern world of materialism and skepticism; his contemporary Peter Viereck has termed him "the best qualified to restore to our literature its sense of the tragic and lofty." The conflict of opposites, on the one hand the closed: imperialism, militarism, capitalism, Calvinism, Authority, the rich, the Father—on the other hand, the open: change, accessibility to experience, freedom, Grace, is his subject matter, along with himself (the confessional poetry of *Life Studies*) and history (the parallels between present day America and the decline and fall of Rome in *Near the Ocean*). Lowell as a professional poet of great technical skill and variety discovers powerful, homely, grotesque images as objective correlatives for his ideas. Randall Jarrell wrote, "The poet's rather odd and imaginative Catholicism is thoroughly suitable to his mind, which is so traditional and dramatic." It's another frame of reference. "Such a Catholicism is thoroughly suited to literature, since it is essentially literary, anthropomorphic, emotional." Only occasionally does it seem offensive, inappropriate, poetically ineffective—like the parenthesis in "Waking in the Blue" from *Life Studies*: "(There are no Mayflower/ screwballs in the Catholic Church.)" A Proper Bostonian might be tempted to say, There were no Catholic screwballs on the Mayflower either. But the other parenthesis in the poem tells us "(This is the house for the 'mentally ill.')" Lowell's antagonism to his parents ("the anarchy of my adolescent war on my parents") and to his "puritan past" led him from the church to the psychiatrist's couch but gave him good material for his poetry. The tensions between Catholic and Protestant views in New England have been more fruitful for Lowell than those in Georgia for Flannery O'Connor, perhaps because they are never fully or finally resolved in his own mind.

Life: On March 1, 1917 Robert Lowell was born into a family and a heritage. As early as the adolescence of an only child he felt serious estrangement from his father, an undistinguished naval officer and subsequent failure in business positions ("By the time he graduated from Annapolis . . . he had reached, perhaps, his final mental possibilities. He was deep . . . with the dumb depth of one who trusted statistics and was dubious of personal experience.") and even more from his mother who had been a Winslow. The autobiographical Part Two of *Life Studies* gives us in prose a grim picture of his early years—particularly of attending a school primarily for girls and of endless Sunday entertainment of naval officers and their wives. His happiest days were apparently spent with his Grandfather Winslow. Two years at Harvard bored him, and at Allen Tate's suggestion he transferred to Kenyon College, and John Crowe Ransom who accepted two of his poems in spite of their being "forbidding and clotted" for the *Kenyon Review*. He graduated in 1940, was converted to Catholicism (*that* was a gesture for the Lowells), married Jean Stafford, and finally prepared his first volume, *Land of Unlikeness* (1944). During this time his war experiences were somewhat confused: he first tried to enlist (1943) in the Armed Forces but was rejected; when he was later drafted he refused as a Catholic conscientious objector to serve; upon being sentenced he served five months of a prison term—more material for poetry and resentment. The second volume, *Lord Weary's Castle* (1946), attracted more attention than the first and contains some of his most often anthologized poems. It received the Pulitzer Prize in 1947.

According to late poetry Lowell felt oppressed by both mother and first wife for some time; he needed to be free of them. In 1949 he went to teach at the Writers' Workshop of the University of Iowa with his second wife, Elizabeth Hardwick (who with his daughter Harriet born some years later seems to have had his full affection), published a third book of poetry, *The Mills of the Kavanaughs* (1951), and began to work on *Imitations,* a new approach to translation. Then there was a period of difficulty and growth. Settled in Boston in 1954, he became interested in psychoanalysis ("Freud seemed the only religious teacher."), and began his "confessional" poetry, letting it all hang out, loosening his forms and metrics, and moving to his most original and creative period from *Life Studies* (1959) to the present. More and more preoccupied with Harriet, "Don't hate your parents," he says with a new awareness of his own guilt and responsibilities for the generation gap which he had seen as an abyss, but for him largely a creative one. He seems to have made his peace with his New England past without condoning the injustices of the present. "Increasingly in the sixties, a sense of alienation and collective disaster darkened the American mind," and Lowell described it. "One side of me is a conventional liberal, concerned with causes, agitated about peace and justice and equality," he has said. "My other side is deeply conservative, . . . wanting to slow down the whole modern progress of mechanization and dehumanization, knowing that liberalism can be a form of death too." At his best he has related his private *angst* to the public anxieties of the shattering Sixties in meaningful ways.

Representative Poetry: In spite of the brilliance of the early volumes, they often seemed "musclebound." As Mr. Rosenthal says,

"The awkwardly contained violence of *Lord Weary's Castle* struggles against tight rhymes and a general formal rigidity, as well as against elaborate, stifling overlays of religious and social symbolism, themselves fairly derivative." A typical poem from this volume (1946) often admired is "The Holy Innocents," a short contemplative lyric in which the poet sees from his automobile (symbol of modern material civilization) a pair of oxen "blunder hugely up St. Peter's hill." The oxen, the "Holy innocents" of the title, are then developed as a symbol of human innocence, of the childlike faith which the world of the automobile has lost. In the last line the poet sadly remarks the absence of the spirit of Jesus from modern life: "Lamb of the shepherds, Child, how still you die."

Life Studies (1959) has been analyzed in great detail as a genunine breakthrough in "confessional" poetry by M. L. Rosenthal in *The New Poets* (1967). The new Lowell may best be represented for us in the penultimate poem of the volume, "Skunk Hour." This is the poem that was featured along with "Lady Lazarus" by Sylvia Plath (1932–1963), whose suicide gave the discussion of confessional poetry special suggestibility and agitation, in a special BBC Third Programme program on July 30, 1965. The speaker or persona in the poem is centered in such a way that "his psychological vulnerability and shame" become equated with those of his civilization. "At its lowest point of morale, Lowell's poem presents him as for the moment a *voyeur* suffering from a sickness of will and spirit that makes him, literally, lower than the skunks that take over the poem at the end." The image of self-loathing, the destructive, disgusting character of his psyche, has something to do with the poet's ability to survive and transcend it in recognition. The initial description is of a specific New England village in degeneration. The speaker whose "mind's not right" climbs the "hill's skull" (seen by some as Golgotha) but returns after peering at lovers in cars to his own back steps where he sees the skunks "under the chalk-dry and spar spire of the Trinitarian Church," looking for food. As he breathes the rich air he watches; "a mother skunk with her column of kittens swills the garbage pail./ She jabs her wedge-head in a cup/ of sour cream, drops her ostrich tail,/ and will not scare." But "dogged animal vitality" is that on which everything really depends.

Imitations (1961) is Lowell's attempt to do something different with translation or transposition of the verse of European poets from Homer through Boris Pasternak (even though he knows no Russian). What he reveals is himself, through his choices and through "one voice running through many personalities, contrasts, and repetitions, . . . the dark and against the grain." He tries for tone rather than literal meaning, "to do what my authors might have done if they were writing their poems now and in America." It often works surprisingly well. The opening line, "Sing for me, Muse, the mania of Achilles," is a brilliant choice of word *mania* for the Greek *Μηνιν*; if not a cognate it ought to be, revitalizing the more often used *wrath* or *anger*. The method points to the freedom of adaptation, the kind of thing that can be seen in Robinson Jeffers' *Medea* and Richard Wilbur's more recent *Misanthrope* of Molière.

Near the Ocean (1967) may be Lowell's most poetically satisfying volume, not an "afterbeat" as Rosenthal suggested. There are fewer excrescences here, a unity of impact that even the poet didn't fully realize apparently, writing "How one jumps from Rome to the America of my own poems is something of a mystery to me." It's a simple mystery, like all great ones; only the ocean (Atlantic, of course) and almost two thousand years keep them apart. The insights of Horace, Juvenal, Dante, Quevedo, and Gongora, in "imitations" rather than translations, tie in very tightly, almost inextricably, with those of Lowell near the ocean, "the greatness and horror" of empire and the cracks of decline and fall. The first five poems represent the present: "Waking Early Sunday Morning" has inevitable echoes of Wallace Stevens, but the despair is Lowell's, "O Bible chopped and crucified/ in hymns we hear but do not read. . . . No, put old clothes on, and explore/ the corners of the woodshed for/ its dregs and dreck. . . ." And then: "Pity the planet, all joy gone/ from this sweet volcanic cone;/ peace to our children when they fall/ in small war on the heels of small/ war—until the end of time to police the earth. . . ." On "Fourth of July in Maine" and listening to Joan Baez on the phonograph, "We watch the logs fall. Fire once gone,/ we're done for: . . . give us this day the warmth to live,/ and face the household fire. We turn/ our backs, and feel the whiskey burn." The elegy "For Theodore Roethke" has a place of honor as transition with "1958" to the poems from and about Rome. "Spring" from the Odes of Horace says, "Move quickly, the brief sum of life forbids/ our opening any long account with hope;/ night hems us in, and ghosts, and death's close clay . . ." Juvenal's tenth satire, "The Vanity of Human Wishes," is the most apt of all, "Devoured by peace, we seek devouring war,/ the orator is drowned by his torrential speech. . . ./ Wealth is worse; how many pile/ fortune on fortune—like the Atlantic whale,/ they bulk above the lesser fish and die." A mélange of Quevedo and Gongora, "The Ruins of Time," brings this unified, elegaic yet biting, book to its end: "Death only throws fixed dice, and yet we raise/ the ante, and stake our lives on every toss./ The hours will hardly pardon us their loss. . . ."

Notebook 1967–68 (1969) is a longer yet lesser volume than *Near the Ocean.* More than two hundred poems, all fourteen line unrhymed "sonnets"—except for casual, almost inadvertent rhymes, are included almost unweeded. Besides numerous responses to wife and daughter, the events to which the poet-persona responds are listed and include: The Vietnam War, 1967; The Black Riots in Newark and Elsewhere; Martin Luther King's Murder; The Columbia Student Demonstrations; Robert Kennedy's Murder; The Republican Convention in Miami; The Russian Occupation of Czechoslovakia; The Demonstrations and Democratic Convention in Chicago; The Vietnam War, 1968. Lowell remains sensitive to the turns and turmoil of our times.

Some Younger Poets

In addition to the poets discussed above, who in most cases had published the major body of their work before 1935, save for Roethke and Lowell, the work of a number of younger and other poets should be briefly mentioned. Born roughly around the time of the First World War, these poets constitute a second generation which underwent its literary formation under the influence of Eliot, Pound, Auden, and the other modernists of the Twenties. The group began publishing in the late Thirties, in some cases (e.g., Jarrell and Shapiro) not until the time of the Second World

War. Since they belong, so to speak, to the "second wave" of modern poets, their work is necessarily derivative; it utilizes the devices, styles, forms, even the attitudes of the older generation which revolutionized modern poetry during the Twenties. Yet their work, at least their better work, is not merely imitative; the web of influences in which they operate has become so intricate and diffuse that the influence of a single poet is seldom detectable in their work. In addition they share an experience which the older generation lacked: they grew to maturity in the atmosphere of European fascism, world tension, and the social upheaval of the Depression and New Deal, and most of them were young enough to participate directly in the Second World War. The war particularly left its mark on their work, not only in content but in attitude, in a pessimism, a certain mature cynicism which is evident in their common outlook. Some of our younger poets have died as young poets.

Richard Eberhart (born 1904), somewhat older than the others, began publishing poetry as early as 1930. A Master of Arts from Cambridge, he has held a position as a college teacher during most of his career, although his history includes a year as tutor to the King of Siam (1930) and service during the Second World War as a naval officer. His poetry is often concerned with nature-subjects or with the simple objects of daily existence; his first volume, *A Bravery of Earth*, came out of his experiences on a freighter trip around the world. A typical Eberhart poem is "The Fury of Aerial Bombardment," a consideration of the religious implications of war ending with a simple and moving reference to the young men, now dead, who "distinguished the belt feed lever from the belt holding pawl" in the Naval gunnery school where the poet was an instructor. He remembers when on the faculty at St. Mark's prep school that Robert Lowell brought him some sixty poems for reading. His recent publications have included *The Quarry* (1964), *Thirty-One Sonnets* (1967), and *Shifts of Being* (1968).

Kenneth Patchen (born 1911), raised in the Ohio steelmill country, briefly attended the University of Wisconsin and afterwards held a variety of odd jobs while he began to write his first poems. Awarded a Guggenheim Fellowship in 1936, he produced his first volume, *Before the Brave*, the same year. A radical modernist, Patchen is influenced by European surrealism in technique; his work has a genuine and striking originality, but its weakness is its total subjectivity and its disregard for the accepted values of language. Several of his books, including *The Journal of Albion Moonlight* (1941), *Memoirs of a Shy Pornographer* (1945), and *Sleepers Awake* (1946), are written in a heterogeneous style which combines poetry and prose with exercises in verbal experimentation resembling those in Joyce's *Finnegans Wake*. His best-known single poem is probably "Do the Dead Know What Time It Is?", a narrative vignette in a tavern in which the hero's conversation with a harlot is constantly interrupted by the harangue of a maudlin and philosophical old drunk. In 1966 he published *Hallelujah Anyway* and in 1968 *But Even So*. Kenneth Patchen died of a heart attack on January 8, 1972 at his home in Palo Alto, California.

Delmore Schwartz, born in Brooklyn in 1913 of Jewish extraction, was educated at Wisconsin, N.Y.U., and Harvard and has taught college English during most of his career; from 1940 to 1947 he held a position on the Harvard faculty. From 1943 to 1946 he served as editor of *The Partisan Review*, and he has since held several other important editorial positions. His first volume of poetry, *In Dreams Begin Responsibilities*, appeared in 1938. His work is rich in concrete imagery but built on a basis of thoughtful philosophical content; it often involves a metaphysical theme, e.g., the relation between spirit and flesh. A typical example is "In the Naked Bed, In Plato's Cave," in which the poet, lying in his bed in a room on a busy street, imagines for an instant that he is in the cave of shadows which Plato invented as an allegory of the relation between the Material and the Ideal (*Republic*, Book VII). "The Heavy Bear," another of Schwartz's best-known poems, symbolizes the poet's corporeal body as a heavy and somewhat stupid bear which he (the "real" he, his ego or spirit) must carry with him through the world. A gross and appetitive creature, the bear constantly drags his owner down to a lower level of existence, but he realizes he can never divest himself of its burdensome flesh; human beings are inexorably condemned to "the scrimmage of appetite." Delmore Schwartz was awarded a Bollingen Prize in 1959. He died of a heart attack alone in a hotel in New York City in July 1966. The body and effects were still unclaimed the next day.

Karl Shapiro, born in 1913 in Baltimore, was deeply marked as a poet and thinker by his experience as a soldier in the Second World War; his first two major books, *Person, Place, and Thing* (1942) and *V-Letter and Other Poems* (1944) appeared while he was still serving in the South Pacific. *V-Letter* won a Pulitzer Prize in 1945; Shapiro has since published several more volumes of verse and criticism. In 1947 he was appointed Consultant in Poetry to the Library of Congress; from 1948 he has held teaching positions in various universities, and beginning in 1950 he served as editor of *Poetry* magazine. As a poet Shapiro is original in form and content without being eccentric; Eliot and Auden are often cited as influences on his style. Although his work is thoughtful, it is neither pessimistic nor cynical; Babette Deutsch wrote in a review of his *Poems, 1940–1953,* "His interest in his immediate surroundings, together with his verbal facility, set him apart from those of his fellows who stand in the street damning a disjointed world . . ." A typical poem is "The Leg," in which a soldier who has lost a leg in combat at first feels as though part of his soul has been amputated with it, that he must "pray for the part that is missing," then comes to understand the body itself as "a sign/ To love the force that grows us," i.e., divinity, or the life force in the universe. As the poem ends the soldier realizes that this knowledge, "the substance of our understanding," is a kind of immortality that transcends the flesh. *The Bourgeois Poet* appeared in 1964 and a kind of older young poet's lyrics in *White-haired Lover* in 1968. Mr. Shapiro is an engaging reader of his verse on college campuses.

Randall Jarrell (1914–1965) is another poet who was strongly influenced by his experience in the war, during which he served as an instructor in the Air Corps. A Master of Arts from Vanderbilt, he has served on the faculties of various American colleges including Kenyon College (1937–39) during the years when Lowell was there as student (they became friends) and Princeton (1951–52). His poetry is highly condensed, compact, and unerringly precise;

a battle alarm on an aircraft carrier is described as a "jew's harp's sawing seesaw song" which "plucks at the starlight where the planes are folded." A student of psychology in college, he often utilizes the concepts and symbolism of the Freudian and other schools of modern psychology; at the same time he is one of the few poets of his generation to treat the theme of love with seriousness and dignity (e.g., in "Burning the Letters"). A typical poem is "Pilots, Man Your Planes," a vivid and objective description of air combat in the South Pacific. Another well-known Jarrell poem is "The Death of the Ball Turret Gunner," a short monologue of only five lines, spoken by the dead aircraft gunner, in which the round ball turret serves as a symbol of the womb to which the gunner subconsciously longs to return. The deliberately brutal last line of the poem provides a shocking return from the dream-world of the gunner's subconscious to the physical horror of modern war. Jarrell was struck by an automobile near Chapel Hill, North Carolina in October 1965; his death was ruled an accident. "His last and best book," according to Lowell, *The Lost World* had just appeared.

Peter Viereck (born 1916), holder of a Ph.D. in history from Harvard, is a well-known essayist as well as a poet. As a political writer he is one of the leading spokesmen of the "New Conservatism," which he defines as "a revolt against revolt," anti-Fascist and anti-Communist. He published four volumes of essays and three volumes of verse, in addition to single poems in magazines, between 1941 and 1955; his first volume of poems, *Terror and Decorum,* won a Pulitzer Prize in 1948. Stylistically Viereck is ingenious, vernacular, with a weakness for trick effects and eccentricities; one critic has objected to his "combined will to preach and to be pert." During the Second World War he served as a sergeant in the African and Italian campaigns, and like Jarrell and Shapiro has written some of his most important poems out of his war experience. Although he is a pacifist in principle, he differs sharply from most of his contemporaries in his romantic attitude toward the adventure of war. In "*Vale* From Carthage" he commemorates the death of a soldier friend in a philosophical mood recalling the *Frater ave atque vale* of Catullus; and in "Kilroy," a vernacular and sentimental lyric built around a bit of G.I. folklore, he compares the peripatetic

American soldier of 1944 to the wanderers and heroes of all history from Ulysses to Columbus. The concluding lines suggest that the young men who missed this great experience of their generation will regret it throughout their lives: *"And in the suburbs Can't sat down and cried." New and Selected Poems* was published in 1967.

Some Younger Younger Poets

In the past decade poets have flourished in America like dandelions on a suburban lawn. Every college has at least one, most of them two or three. The poet without an academic home base can go on tour and do the circuit. And a very large number are surprisingly competent. Publication may be in many forms, from books to professional journals like *College English* to mimeographed sheets. The younger younger poets were all born after World War I; the Twenties and Thirties gave birth to the largest group of poets in our history. We can choose only representatives of a number of tendencies for brief comment.

The "beat poets," although hirsute and colorful, are in many ways less impressive as poets (Lawrence Ferlinghetti, Allen Ginsberg, and their followers) than others. They lack compression. They are insufficiently precise, succinct, controlled, and authentically original. Logorrhea does not make for good poetry unless the genius of a Whitman puts patterns on it, including the rhythmic. Ferlinghetti's one poem about poetry, "Constantly risking absurdity/ and death/ whenever he performs/ above the heads/ of his audience/ the poet like an acrobat," Number 15 of *A Coney Island of the Mind* (1958) is fairly good but still wordy. The book's title comes from Henry Miller, and the "beats" congregate at Big Sur, California in the Miller aura. For the other poets, many academically oriented, many confessional, many satiric, the following may speak.

Howard Nemerov (born 1920), a native New Yorker, is urbane and Auden-like in his poetry, only very American in his diction, idiom, and imagery, rather than very British. He has published at least three books of poetry in the Sixties, of which one, *The Blue*

Swallows, received the first Theodore Roethke Memorial Prize in 1968. He has been a teacher at Brandeis University, and writes novels as well as poetry, "caught between the modes" as he describes it in *Journal of the Fictive Life.* "The Goose Fish" is an ironic, gently macabre poem about two lovers who have just made love on a moonlit beach, suddenly aware of being stared at by a grinning dead goose fish. "It was a wide and moony grin/ Together peaceful and obscene;/ He might mean failure or success. . . ." A poetic sequence, "The Scales of the Eyes," is brilliantly morbid in reaching back toward childhood, as in the opening of the fifth section entitled "A Can of Dutch Cleanser": "The blind maid shaking a stick,/ Chasing dirt endlessly around/ A yellow wall, was the very she/ To violate my oldest nights;/ I frighten of her still."

Richard Wilbur, another New Yorker, was born in 1921, has lived with wife and four children in Connecticut, Massachusetts, France, New Mexico, Texas, and Italy, has taught English literature at Harvard, Wellesley, and Wesleyan University. He wrote lyrics for the Lillian Hellman-Leonard Bernstein musical *Candide* and has translated Molière in iambic pentameter couplets for successful stage production. *The Misanthrope* as staged in October, 1968 received rave reviews; Wilbur, "supple, subtle, witty," has turned "one rare wine into another," giving us the complex pleasure of rhyme. Four volumes of poetry appeared between 1947 and 1959. His verse is crisp yet full-bodied (if cut, it bleeds—very Molièresque), more impersonal and less perturbed than Nemerov, "Mind" is a good example of his shorter reflective lyrics. The mind complete with radar is compared with a bat in a cavern, Plato's cave perhaps, and the simile is ironically pushed farther than it will go: "The mind is like a bat. Precisely. Save/ That in the very happiest intellection/ A graceful error may correct the cave."

W. D. Snodgrass (born 1926) from Pennsylvania lives with his second wife and two children in Syracuse, New York, where he teaches at the university. Graduate of the University of Iowa, he has taught at Cornell, Rochester, and Wayne. His first book, *Heart's Needle,* won a Pulitzer Prize for poetry in 1960. In it he extends his personal experience, the agonies of a father's relationship with a three-year-old daughter while he is being divorced and remarried, into new areas of poetic form and insights. (George Meredith had done a similar thing in 1862 with his sonnet sequence *Modern Love,* analyzing the break-up of a love relationship.) He leaves the child, Cynthia, in April, having made a little garden for her, "Child, we've done our best./ Someone will have to weed and spread/ The young sprouts. Sprinkle them in the hour/ When shadow falls across their bed." Bird and flower images are particularly effective. "Like nerves caught in a graph,/ the morning-glory vines/ frost has erased by half/ still crawl over their rigid twines./ Like broken lines/ of verses I can't make." The impossibility of verbal communication makes the attempt more pathetic, "Child, I have another wife,/ another child. We try to choose our life."

Donald Hall (born 1928) is Connecticut born and teaches at the University of Michigan. Perhaps his most impressive volume of poetry is *A Roof of Tiger Lilies* (1964). With Robert Pack and Louis Simpson he has edited an anthology, *The New Poets of England and America* (1957). He also reads on circuit. The poem "My Son, My Executioner," slightly reminiscent of Joyce's "Ecce Puer," deals with the realization of the parents, twenty-five and twenty-two, that now they start to die together with the birth of their son and "instrument of immortality." "Your cries and hungers document/ Our bodily decay." "The Snow" is an interesting combination of image, abstract argument, and implication: "Snow is what must/ come down, even if it struggles/ to stay in the air with strength/ of the wind. Like an old man,/ whatever I touch I turn/ to the story of death."

Denise Levertov (born 1923), the daughter of a Russian emigré who became an Anglican priest and a Welsh mother, came to the United States in 1948 and has become an American citizen and the wife of Mitchell Goodman, novelist and political activist. They live in New York City and Maine. She has been associated with the Black Mountain School of "Projectivist" poetry, but her recent volumes, *The Jacob's Ladder* (1961), *O Taste and See* (1964) and *The Sorrow Dance* (1966), seem to represent a new break-through to her own maturity. Traveling and reading she seems a "liberated" woman. Writing about married love with "confessional frankness and pyschological immediacy," she has produced one of her best poems in "Losing Track": "Long after you have swung back/ away from me/ I think you are still with me." Her husband nudges her awake as "a boat adrift nudges the pier."

Sylvia Plath (1932–1963) from Boston was married to English poet Ted Hughes and had two children when she committed suicide in London. The notoriety has brought particular attention to two of her books, a novel *The Bell Jar* originally published under a pseudonym in England (1963), a month before the suicide, and the posthumous second volume of poetry, *Ariel.* As Howard Moss said in a 1971 review in the *New Yorker* (July 10), she has become "someone who had faced horror and made something of it as well as someone who had been destroyed by it." Her poems were "Murderous experiences of the mind and body, stripped of all protection, . . . total exposures, and chilling." This gifted writer might be a genius, her work unlike anything seen before. She said that all her new poems were written at about four o'clock in the morning. "Lady Lazarus," her "Skunk Hour" confessional poem, promises suicide, by destroying herself she will be destroying the world she hates; but she promises to return from the grave, a witch who "eats" men. As Mr. Rosenthal says, "She sees herself as a skilled suicide-artist whose self-loathing the sadistic and voyeuristic audience, easily envisioned as the Nazi-tending aspects of the civilization, appreciates all too well." This "fusion of the private and the culturally symbolic" is difficult but can be devastating. Even an earlier poem like "The Applicant": "First are you our sort of person?/ Do you wear/ A glass eye, false teeth or a crutch,/ A brace or a hook/ Rubber breasts or a rubber crotch,/ . . . No, no? Then/ How can we give you a thing?" is brutal when all that can be offered is a marriage with death. Sylvia Plath gives us the "raw experience of nightmare."

V

MODERN LITERARY CRITICISM, CHIEFLY AMERICAN, AFTER 1930

In the nineteen-fifties and-sixties literary criticism and critics have proliferated at what might be considered in student circles an alarming rate. New Criticism has held its ground and expanded its holdings. In general it has built upon the insights of such critics as I. A. Richards, Ransom, Tate, and Winters to attempt a new organization of these perceptions or to apply them to specific writers or periods or genres. From what might be thought of as a primary emphasis of textualism (the work itself without consideration of historical, humanistic, philological, biographical, sociological, or psychological interpretations—above all no "intentional fallacies" in the Wimsatt-Beardsley frame of reference) this body of critics by 1950 were claiming contextualism and structuralism as an initial widening of the circle. Structuralism as a technique to focus on formal and comparative patterns became a viable critical term in the monumental work, *Theory of Literature* (1949) by René Wellek (born 1903) and Austin Warren (born 1899), both professors of literature at the University of Iowa in the early 1940's who moved on to Yale University and the University of Michigan respectively.

Contextualism became the subject of argument for Eliseo Vivas (born 1901) and his advocate Murray Krieger (born 1923) against the attacks of Walter Sutton. In fact the pathways and byways of recent criticism are often tangled and confused by contention and stridency. When Northrop Frye wrote a book in 1963 entitled *The Well-Tempered Critic,* he called attention to a need rather than a reality. And Hazard Adams in an excellent summary of recent critical trends, *The Interests of Criticism* (1969), views these tendencies in a final chapter called "System and Violence." Apart from name-calling, certain trends and modifications of New Criticism have emerged in major works, a revised nomenclature or jargon depending upon the involvement of your sympathies, and at least some redefined insights. The former discursive/imaginative uses of language by science and literature respectively (and still earlier denotative/connotative) become "referential" and "constitutive" in contextual terms.

Northrop Frye (born in the Quebec province of Canada in 1912), although he has been either ignored or touted as a leader in the field of literary criticism, now seems above and beyond the clamor clearly the most important critical voice of the past twenty years. The Reverend Herman Northrop Frye, educated at Toronto and Oxford, has been a university English professor at Toronto since 1939. His earliest publication was *Fearful Symmetry: A Study of William Blake* in 1947; this was followed ten years later by what is probably his most important single volume, *Anatomy of Criticism,* significantly an "anatomy" in the old Burton *Anatomy of Melancholy* sense, being a kind of organized compendium. Mr. Frye has been very productive in the Sixties; besides the volume on the well-tempered critic mentioned above, we have *The Educated Imagination* (1963), *T. S. Eliot* (1963), *A Natural Perspective* (1965), *The Return of Eden* (1965), *The Fools of Time* (1967), and *The Modern Century* (1967).

Anatomy of Criticism, parts of which appeared in the *Kenyon Review* in the early Fifties, examines potential bases of literary criticism as a science as well as an art, taking off from both I. A. Richards and Aristotle's *Poetics* in a search for order and new terminology. Among a number of new terms (and old ones with new meanings), Mr. Frye "invents" most interestingly "babble" and "doodle" to represent Aristotle's last two of six elements of a tragedy, melody and spectacle, as the constructions of poetry which have most to do with audible and visual patterns. He takes off equally from Freud and Jung, from James G. Frazer (1854–1941) and *The Golden Bough* and Ernst Cassirer (1874–1945) to examine the application of the Jungian racial unconscious in archetypal patterns in literature, which has been fruitful in studies of Milton and others. Frye's work in this area, when coupled with Eric Auerbach (1892–1957) in *Mimesis; the Representation of Reality in Western Literature*, reveals a new and potentially exciting dimension of criticism on a philosophical level.

Modes, symbols, myths, and genres are reexamined from new perspectives. Unlike most of the earlier new critics Frye is as interested in drama and fiction as he is in poetry. He makes an almost complete breakdown of the terms *tragic* and *comic* as dramatic modes, throwing them equally onto fiction, poetry, and literature in general. The hero is considered under five categories, which represent something of a Viconian cyclical movement and return: 1) a divine being superior in kind to men and environment whose story will be myth, 2) a hero of romance superior in degree but not in kind, 3) the hero of what Frye calls the "high mimetic mode," including epic and tragedy, superior to other men in degree but not to the natural and social environment, 4) the hero of the "low mimetic mode," really neither "heroic" nor superior to other men at all but one of us, both in comedy and realistic fiction, and 5) the "hero" of the ironic mode, inferior to ourselves in power or intelligence. The seasons are given mythic dimensions and control: Spring over Comedy, Summer over Romance, Autumn over Tragedy, Winter over Irony and Satire. Insights of a comparative nature into world literature are often unusual and perceptive, even evaluative although Mr. Frye earlier attacks this principle. The uses of Biblical typology in understanding literature are at least indicated and ways of study pointed to.

Among other critical trends of our times are the uses of Husserl and Heidegger as phenomenologists for the anti-novelists like Sarraute and Butor who turn to literary criticism to undergird their creative departures from tradition. José Ortega y Gasset (1883–1955) in *The Dehumanization of Art*, translated from the Spanish and first published in this country by Princeton University Press in 1948, presents a provocative overview of art and letters from the beginnings of romanticism through realism and naturalism (they are all realistic movements to him) into the reactions against them in the twentieth century, a brilliant defense of the artifices of art. Somewhat different approaches to similar reaches of literature from the eighteenth century into our own, modified by the groundwork of new criticism, are to be found in Meyer H. Abrams (born 1912) in *The Mirror and the Lamp* (1953) and Robert W. Langbaum's *The Poetry of Experience* (1957). George Wright in *The Poet in the Poem* (1960) and Wayne Booth in *The Rhetoric of Fiction* (1961) have looked carefully at persona and authorial voice in comparative studies. Much talked about recently is Susan Sontag (born 1933) with *The Experience of Literature* (1961) and *Against Interpretation* (1966). George Steiner (born 1929), an American born in Paris who travels back and forth between Cambridge, England and New York City, visiting professor at a number of universities, writes provocative criticism in a socially oriented key, *Language and Silence* (1967) as an example. He is, however, uneven in his evaluations (going way overboard for Hermann Broch) and uneven in his writing (some of his reviews in *The New Yorker* are not up to their usual standard). But he is young; a thinking man, he makes others think; and he has a view of the importance of comparative literature, breaking out of the national pattern, which is a worthy continuation of Edmund Wilson. Literary criticism seems likely to continue to flourish whether produced by the academically oriented or by the creative writer who backs up to look at things, often with clear vision, as Albert Camus did in his critical essays collected as *Resistance, Rebellion, and Death* in the year of his own death in 1960.

BIBLIOGRAPHY VI

This bibliography is compiled for the convenience of students of modern American literature who wish to make further study of the authors and literary movements treated. It does not pretend to be complete; in the case of some authors who published fifty or more separate items during their careers, a complete list of works would be both inconvenient and confusing. The bibliography therefore includes (a) the most significant or important works of each author, and (b) a selected list of critical or biographical materials for further reference.

Dates of publications of works in volume are in all cases those of the first edition. In the case of poems, short stories, or other works not originally published in volume form, the bibliography generally gives the date of first volume publication, since the magazines or reviews of original publication are not often available to the ordinary reader.

Especially significant or useful works are indicated with an asterisk (*).

American Literature: General

Van Wyck Brooks, *New England: Indian Summer*, N.Y., 1940, and *The Confident Years*, N.Y., 1952; James D. Hart, *The Oxford Companion to American Literature*, N.Y., 1956; Robert Van Gelder, *Writers and Writing*, N.Y., 1946; Harry R. Warfel, *American Novelists of Today*, N.Y., 1951; Edward Wagenknecht, *Cavalcade of the American Novel*, N.Y., 1952; Stanley J. Kunitz and Howard Harcraft, eds., *Twentieth Century Authors*, N.Y., 1942; Malcolm Cowley, *Exile's Return: a Literary Odyssey of the 1920's*, N. Y., 1934; Alfred Kazin, *On Native Grounds*, N.Y., 1942; Edmund Wilson, *The Shores of Light*, N.Y., 1952, *The Bit Between My Teeth*, 1965; Philip Rahv, *Image and Idea*, N.Y., 1949; Robert Spiller,

The Cycle of American Literature, N.Y., 1955, *A Time of Harvest, American Literature 1910–1960*, N.Y., 1962; John W. Aldridge, *After the Lost Generation*, N.Y., 1951; Jack Ludwig, *Recent American Novelists*, Minneapolis, 1962; Robert Bone, *The Negro Novel in America*, New Haven, 1965; Ihab Hassan, *Radical Innocence*, Princeton, 1961.

Gertrude Stein:

**Three Lives*, 1908; *Tender Buttons*, 1914; *The Making of Americans*, 1925; *Matisse, Picasso, and Gertrude Stein*, 1932; **The Autobiography of Alice B. Toklas*, 1933; *Four Saints in Three Acts*, 1934; *Everybody's Autobiography*, 1937; *Picasso*, 1938; *Paris France*, 1940; *Wars I Have Seen*, 1945; *Brewsie and Willie*, 1946.

ABOUT: *Donald Sutherland, *Gertrude Stein: a Biography of Her Work*, Yale U.P., 1951; *Elizabeth Sprigge, *Gertrude Stein, Her Life and Work*, N.Y., 1957; A. Stewart, *Gertrude Stein and the Present*, Cambridge, 1967; Richard Bridgman, *Gertrude Stein in Pieces*, N.Y., 1970.

Elliot Paul:

Indelible, 1922; *Impromptu*, 1923; *Imperturbe*, 1924; *Low Run Tide*, 1929; *Lava Rock*, 1929; *The Amazon*, 1930; *The Governor of Massachusetts*, 1930; **The Life and Death of a Spanish Town*, 1937; *Concert Pitch*, 1938; *Hugger-Mugger in the Louvre*, 1940; **The Last Time I Saw Paris*, 1942; *Linden on the Saugus Branch*, 1947; *A Ghost Town on the Yellowstone*, 1948; *My Old Kentucky Home*, 1949.

ABOUT: Robert Van Gelder, *Writers and Writing*, N.Y., 1946.

Henry Miller:

**Tropic of Cancer*, 1931; **Tropic of Capricorn*, 1939; *Black Spring*, 1939; *The Cosmological Eye*, 1939; *The Colossus of Maroussi*, 1941; *The Air-Conditioned Nightmare*, 1945; *Nights of Love and Laughter*, 1955; *A Devil in Paradise*, 1956; *The Rosy Crucifixion*, 1949–60.

ABOUT: Nicholas Moore, *Henry Miller*, 1943; Bernard H. Porter, ed., *The Happy Rock: A Book About Henry Miller*, Berkeley, 1945; *Kenneth Rexroth, introduction to *Nights of Love and Laughter*, N.Y., 1955; J. A. Nelson, *Form and Image in the Fiction of Henry Miller*, Detroit, 1970.

John P. Marquand:

The Unspeakable Gentleman, 1922; *Lord Timothy Dexter*, 1925; *Ming Yellow*, 1934; *No Hero*, 1935; *Thank You, Mr. Moto*, 1936; *The Late George Apley*, 1937; *Think Fast, Mr. Moto*, 1937; *Mr. Motto Is So Sorry*, 1938; *Wickford Point*, 1939; **H. M. Pulham, Esq.*, 1941; *So Little Time*,

1943; *Last Laugh, Mr. Moto,* 1942; *Repent in Haste,* 1945; *B. F.'s Daughter,* 1946; *Point of No Return,* 1949; *Melville Goodwin, U.S.A.,* 1951; *Sincerely, Willis Wayde,* 1955.

ABOUT: Edward Wagenknecht, *Cavalcade of the American Novel,* N.Y., 1952; Robert Van Gelder, *Writers and Writing,* N.Y., 1946; C. H. Holman, *John P. Marquand,* Minneapolis, 1965.

Ernest Hemingway:

STORY COLLECTIONS: *Three Stories and Ten Poems,* 1923; *In Our Time,* 1924; *Men Without Women,* 1927; *Winner Take Nothing,* 1933; *The Fifth Column and the First 49 Stories,* 1938.

NOVELS: *The Sun Also Rises,* 1926; *A Farewell to Arms,* 1929; *To Have and Have Not,* 1937; *For Whom the Bell Tolls,* 1940; *Across the River and Into the Trees,* 1950; *The Old Man and the Sea,* 1952; *Islands in the Stream* (posthumous), 1970.

NON-FICTION: *Death in the Afternoon,* 1932; *Green Hills of Africa,* 1935; *A Moveable Feast,* 1964.

ABOUT: Louis Henry Cohn, *A Bibliography of the Works of Ernest Hemingway,* N.Y., 1931; *Carlos Baker, *Hemingway: The Writer As Artist,* Princeton U.P., 1952; *Philip Young, *Ernest Hemingway,* N.Y., 1952; John A. Atkins, *The Art of Ernest Hemingway,* N.Y., 1952; Malcolm Cowley, *"Hemingway and the Hero," New Republic,* CXI (1944), pp. 755ff; Lillian Ross, *Portrait of Hemingway,* N.Y., 1961; E. Rovit, *Ernest Hemingway,* N.Y., 1963; Carlos Baker, *Ernest Hemingway, a Life Story,* N.Y., 1969; Philip Young, *Ernest Hemingway, a Reconsideration,* University Park, Penna., 1966.

Thomas Wolfe:

NOVELS: *Look Homeward, Angel,* 1929; *Of Time and the River,* 1935; *The Web and the Rock,* 1939; *You Can't Go Home Again,* 1940.

STORIES: *From Death to Morning,* 1935.

CRITICAL ESSAY: *"The Story of a Novel,"* in Maxwell Geismar, ed., *The Portable Thomas Wolfe,* N.Y., 1948.

ABOUT: *Herbert J. Muller, *Thomas Wolfe,* Norfolk, Conn., 1947; Pamela H. Johnson, *Hungry Gulliver* (in England *Thomas Wolfe*), N.Y., 1948; Bernard DeVoto, *"Genius Is Not Enough," Saturday Review of Literature,* April 25, 1936; C. H. Holman, *Thomas Wolfe,* Minneapolis, 1960; B. R. McElderry, *Thomas Wolfe,* N.Y., 1964.

Regionalism and Rural Naturalism: General

Louis D. Rubin, Jr. and Robert D. Jacobs, *Southern Renascence: The Literature of the Modern South,* Baltimore, 1953; Allen Tate, *et al.,* eds., *I'll Take My Stand,* N.Y., 1930.

Pearl Buck:

NOVELS: *East Wind: West Wind,* 1930; **The House of Earth* (*The Good Earth,* 1931; *Sons,* 1932; *A House Divided,* 1935); *The Mother,* 1934; *The Exile,* 1936; *Fighting Angel,* 1936; *This Proud Heart,* 1938; *The Patriot,* 1939; *Other Gods,* 1940; *Dragon Seed,* 1941; *The Promise,* 1943; *Portrait of a Marriage,* 1945; *Pavilion of Women,* 1946; *Kinfolk,* 1949; *God's Men,* 1951; *The Hidden Flower,* 1952; *Come My Beloved,* 1953; *The Living Reed,* 1963.

STORIES: *The First Wife,* 1933; *Today and Forever,* 1941; *Far and Near,* 1948.

AUTOBIOGRAPHY: *My Several Worlds,* 1954; *A Bridge for Passing,* 1962.

NON-FICTION: *China as I See It,* 1970.

ABOUT: Harry R. Warfel, *American Novelists of Today,* N.Y., 1951; *James Gray, *On Second Thought,* Univ. Minn. Press, 1946.

William Faulkner:

NOVELS: *Soldiers' Pay,* 1926; *Sartoris,* 1929; *The Sound and the Fury,* 1929; *As I Lay Dying,* 1930; *Sanctuary,* 1931; *Light in August,* 1932; *Pylon,* 1933; *Absalom, Absalom!,* 1936; *Intruder in the Dust,* 1948; *Requiem for a Nun,* 1950; *The Fable,* 1954; *The Hamlet,* 1940; *The Town,* 1957; *The Mansion,* 1959 (the last three making up the Snopes trilogy); *The Reivers,* 1962.

STORIES: *These Thirteen,* 1931; *Go Down, Moses,* 1942; *Knight's Gambit,* 1949.

MISCELLANEOUS: Malcolm Cowley, ed., *The Portable Faulkner,* N.Y., 1946; *The Faulkner Reader,* N.Y., 1954.

ABOUT: Irving Howe, *William Faulkner, a Critical Study,* N.Y., 1952; Frederick J. Hoffman and Olga W. Vickery, eds., *William Faulkner: Two Decades of Criticism,* Mich. State Coll. Press, 1951; *William Van O'Connor, *The Tangled Fire of William Faulkner,* Univ. Minn. Press, 1954; Robert Coughlan, "*The Private World of William Faulkner,*" *Life,* September 28–October 5, 1953; W. Beck, *Man in Motion; Faulkner's Trilogy,* Madison, Wisc., 1961; R. P. Adams, *Faulkner, Myth and Motion,* Princeton, N.J., 1968; M. Backman, *Faulkner the Major Years,* Bloomington, Ind., 1966; Cleanth Brooks, *William Faulkner, the Yoknapatawpha Country,** New Haven, 1963; W. Brylowski, *Faulkner's Olympian Laugh,* Detroit, 1968; J. B. Meriwether, *Lion in the Garden,* N.Y., 1968; M. Millgate, *The Achievement of William Faulkner,* N.Y., 1966; K. E. Richarson, *Force and Faith in the Novels of William Faulkner,* Paris, 1967; W. J. Slatoff, *Quest for Failure,* Ithaca, 1960; J. W. Webb, *William Faulkner of Oxford,* Baton Rouge, La., 1965.

John Steinbeck:

The Pastures of Heaven, 1932; *Tortilla Flat*, 1935; *In Dubious Battle*, 1936; **Of Mice and Men*, 1937; *The Long Valley*, 1938; **The Grapes of Wrath*, 1939; *The Moon Is Down*, 1942; *Cannery Row*, 1945; *The Wayward Bus*, 1947; *The Pearl*, 1948; *East of Eden*, 1953; *Sweet Thursday*, 1954. SEE ALSO Pascal Covici, ed., *The Portable Steinbeck*, N.Y., 1943; *The Winter of Our Discontent*, 1961; *Travels with Charley*, 1962.

ABOUT: *Harry T. Moore, *The Novels of John Steinbeck*, Chicago, 1939; Lewis Gannett, *John Steinbeck, Personal and Bibliographical Notes*, N.Y., 1939; Edmund Wilson, *The Boys in the Back Room*, San Francisco, 1941; Peter Lisca, *The Wide World of John Steinbeck*, New Brunswick, N.J., 1958; W. French, *John Steinbeck*, N.Y., 1961; J. E. Fontenrose, *John Steinbeck, an Introduction and Interpretation*, N.Y., 1963.

Erskine Caldwell:

STORIES: *American Earth*, 1931; *We Are the Living*, 1933; *Kneel to the Rising Sun*, 1935; *Southways*, 1938; **Jackpot*, 1940; *Georgia Boy*, 1943; *Stories by Erskine Caldwell*, 1944; *The Courting of Susie Brown*, 1952.

NOVELS: **Tobacco Road*, 1932; **God's Little Acre*, 1933; *Journeyman*, 1935; *Trouble in July*, 1940; *All Night Long*, 1942; *House in the Uplands*, 1946; *The Hand of God*, 1947; *This Very Earth*, 1948; *Episode in Palmetto*, 1950; *A Lamp for Nightfall*, 1952; *Love and Money*, 1954.

NON-FICTION: *You Have Seen Their Faces* (with M. Bourke-White), 1937; *All Out on the Road to Smolensk*, 1942; *Call It Experience*, 1951; *When You Think of Me*, 1959; *Wordsmanship*, 1961; *Close to Home*, 1962; *Deep South*, 1968; *Summertime Island*, 1968.

ABOUT: *Introduction by Henry Seidel Canby to *Stories by Erskine Caldwell*, N.Y., 1944; John D. Wade, "*Sweet Are the Uses of Degeneracy*," *Southern Review*, I (1936), pp. 449ff.; *Malcolm Cowley, "*The Two Erskine Caldwells*," *New Republic*, CXI (1941), pp. 599ff.; J. Korges, *Erskine Caldwell*, Minneapolis, 1969.

Robert Penn Warren:

BIOGRAPHY: *John Brown: The Making of a Martyr*, 1929.

VERSE: *XXXVI Poems*, 1936; *Eleven Poems on the Same Theme*, 1942; *Selected Poems*, 1944; *Promises*, 1957; *Audubon, a Vision*, 1969.

NOVELS: *Night Rider*, 1939; *At Heaven's Gate*, 1943; *All the King's Men*, 1946; *World Enough and Time*, 1950; *Band of Angels*, 1955; *The Cave*, 1959; *Flood*, 1964.

STORIES: *The Circus in the Attic*, 1949.

CRITICISM: *Understanding Poetry* (with Cleanth Brooks), 1939.

ABOUT: Harry R. Warfel, *American Novelists of Today,* N.Y., 1951; *Louis D. Rubin, Jr. and Robert D. Jacobs, eds., *Southern Renascence: The Literature of the Modern South,* Baltimore, 1953; C. H. Bohner, *Robert Penn Warren,* N.Y., 1964; P. West, *Robert Penn Warren,* Minneapolis, 1964.

William Saroyan:

FICTION: **The Daring Young Man on the Flying Trapeze,* 1934; *Inhale and Exhale,* 1936; *Three Times Three,* 1936; *Little Children,* 1937; *A Native American,* 1938; *The Trouble with Tigers,* 1938; *Love, Here Is My Hat,* 1938; *Peace, It's Wonderful,* 1939; **My Name Is Aram,* 1940; *Fables,* 1941; **The Human Comedy,* 1943; *Dear Baby,* 1944; *The Adventures of Wesley Jackson,* 1946; *The Assyrian and Other Stories,* 1950.

DRAMA: *The Time of Your Life,* 1939; *My Heart's in the Highlands,* 1939; *Love's Old Sweet Song,* 1940; *The Beautiful People,* 1941; *Razzle-Dazzle,* 1942; *Don't Go Away Mad,* 1949; *The Cave Dwellers,* 1958.

AUTOBIOGRAPHY: *The Bicycle Rider in Beverly Hills,* 1950; *Here Comes, There Goes, You Know Who,* 1961.

MISCELLANEOUS: *I Used to Believe I Had Forever, Now I'm Not So Sure,* 1968 (stories, plays, essays, poems); *Days of Life and Death and Escape to the Moon,* 1970.

ABOUT: James Gray, *On Second Thought,* N.Y., 1946; H. R. Floan, *William Saroyan,* N.Y., 1966.

Eudora Welty:

FICTION: *A Curtain of Green and Other Stories,* 1941; *The Robber Bridegroom,* 1942; *The Wide Net and Other Stories,* 1943; *Delta Wedding,* 1946; *The Golden Apples,* 1949; *The Ponder Heart,* 1954; *The Bride of the Innisfallen,* 1955; *The Shoe Bird,* 1964; *Losing Battles,* 1970; *The Optimist's Daughter,* 1972.

ABOUT: R. Vande Kieft, *Eudora Welty,* N.Y., 1962; A. Appel, *A Season of Dreams,* Baton Rouge, La., 1965; J. A. Bryant, Jr., *Eudora Welty,* Minneapolis, 1968.

Ernest Gaines:

FICTION: *Catherine Carmier,* 1964; *Of Love and Dust,* 1967; *Bloodline,* 1968; *The Autobiography of Miss Jane Pittman,* 1971.

John O'Hara:

NOVELS: *Appointment in Samarra,* 1934; *Butterfield 8,* 1935; *Hope of Heaven,* 1938; *A Rage to Live,* 1949; *The Farmer's Hotel,* 1951; *Ten North Frederick,* 1955; *The Big Laugh,* 1962.

STORIES: *The Doctor's Son,* 1935; *Files on Parade,* 1939; *Pipe Night,* 1945; *Here's O'Hara,* 1946; *Hell Box,* 1947; *Assembly,* 1961; *The Hat on the Bed,* 1963; *And Other Stories,* 1968.

NON-FICTION: *Sweet and Sour,* 1954.

ABOUT: Robert Van Gelder, *Writers and Writing,* N.Y., 1946; C. C. Walcutt, *John O'Hara,* Minneapolis, 1969.

Irwin Shaw:

DRAMA: *Bury the Dead,* 1936; *The Gentle People,* 1939.

STORIES: *Sailor Off the Bremen,* 1939; *Welcome to the City,* 1942; *Act of Faith and Other Stories,* 1946; *Mixed Company* (collection), 1950.

NOVELS: *The Young Lions,* 1948; *The Troubled Air,* 1951; *Lucy Crown,* 1956; *Voices of a Summer Day,* 1965; *Rich Man, Poor Man,* 1970.

NON-FICTION: *Report on Israel,* 1950.

ABOUT: *John W. Aldridge, *After the Lost Generation,* N.Y., 1951.

Herman Wouk:

NOVELS: *Aurora Dawn,* 1947; *The City Boy,* 1948; *The Caine Mutiny,* 1951; *Marjorie Morningstar,* 1955; *Youngblood Hawke,* 1962; *Don't Stop the Carnival,* 1965.

DRAMA: *The Traitor,* 1949; *The Caine Mutiny Court-Martial,* 1954.

ABOUT: "*The Wouk Mutiny,*" *Time,* 66:48–50 (September 5, 1955).

J. D. Salinger:

**The Catcher in the Rye,* 1951; *Nine Stories,* 1953; *Franny and Zooey,* 1961; *Raise High the Roof Beam, Carpenters; and Seymour: An Introduction,* 1963.

ABOUT: F. L. Gwynne and J. L. Blotner, *The Fiction of J. D. Salinger,* Pittsburgh, 1958; W. F. Belcher and J. W. Lee, *J. D. Salinger and the Critics,* Belmont, Calif., 1962; W. French, *J. D. Salinger,* N.Y., 1963; H. A. Grunwald, *Salinger: A Critical and Personal Portrait,* N.Y., 1962; J. Miller, Jr., *J. D. Salinger,* Minneapolis, 1965.

James Jones:

FICTION: **From Here to Eternity,* 1951; *Some Came Running,* 1957; *The Thin Red Line,* 1962; *The Ice-cream Headache, and Other Stories,* 1968.

ABOUT: A. B. C. Whipple, "*James Jones and His Angel,*" *Life,* 30:143 (May 7, 1951).

Norman Mailer:

"A Calculus at Heaven" (*in the anthology Cross Section*), 1944; **The Naked and the Dead,* 1948; *Barbary Shore,* 1951; *The Deer Park,* 1955; *An American Dream,* 1965; *Cannibals and Christians,* 1966; *The Armies of the Night,* 1968; *Why Are We in Vietnam?* (novel), 1967.

ABOUT: John W. Aldridge, *After the Lost Generation,* N.Y., 1951. Maxwell Geismar, *"Nightmare on Anopopei," Saturday Review of Literature,* 31:12 (May 8, 1948); R. J. Foster, *Norman Mailer,* Minneapolis, 1968; B. H. Leeds, *The Structured Vision of Norman Mailer,* N.Y., 1969.

Truman Capote:

FICTION: *Other Voices, Other Rooms,* 1948; *A Tree of Night,* 1949; *The Grass Harp,* 1951; *Breakfast at Tiffany's,* 1958; *Thanksgiving Visitor,* 1968.

NON-FICTION: *Local Color,* 1950; *The Muses Are Heard,* 1956; *In Cold Blood,* 1966.

ABOUT: L. Y. Gossett, "Violence in a Private World: Truman Capote" in *Violence in Recent Southern Fiction,* Durham, N.C., 1965; Mark Schorer, "McCullers and Capote," in *The Creative Present,* ed. by Balakian and Simmons, N.Y., 1963; P. Levine, "Truman Capote: The Revelation of the Broken Image" in *Recent American Fiction: Some Critical Views,* ed. by J. Waldmeir, Boston, 1963; I. Malin, ed., *Truman Capote's In Cold Blood: A Critical Handbook,* Belmont, Calif., 1968.

Regionalism and Naturalism in the City: General

Irving Howe, "The Culture of Modernism," *Commentary*, Nov. 1967; "The City in Literature," *Commentary,* May 1971.

James T. Farrell:

NOVELS: **Studs Lonigan* (*Young Lonigan,* 1932; *The Young Manhood of Studs Lonigan,* 1934; *Judgment Day,* 1935); *Gas House McGinty,* 1933; *A World I Never Made,* 1936; *No Star Is Lost,* 1938; *Father and Son,* 1940; *My Days of Anger,* 1943; *The Face of Time,* 1953; *Tommy Gallagher's Crusade,* 1939; *Ellen Rogers,* 1941; *Bernard Clare,* 1946; *The Road Between,* 1949; *This Man and This Woman,* 1951; *Yet Other Waters,* 1952; *The Silence of History,* 1962; *What Time Collects,* 1964; *When Time Was Born,* 1966; *A Brand New Life,* 1968.

CRITICISM: *A Note on Literary Criticism,* 1936; *The League of Frightened Philistines,* 1945; *Literature and Morality,* 1947.

ABOUT: W. M. Frohock, *The Novel of Violence in America,* Dallas, 1950; Joseph Warren Beach, *American Fiction, 1920–1940,* N.Y., 1941.

For Danny O'Neill series see *Time,* November 23, 1953; E. M. Branch, *James T. Farrell,* N.Y., 1963.

Richard Wright:

FICTION: *Uncle Tom's Children,* 1938; *Native Son,* 1940; *Black Boy* (autobiography), 1945; *The Long Dream,* 1958; *Eight Men,* 1961.

ABOUT: Ralph Ellison, "Richard Wright's Blues," in *Shadow and Act,* N.Y., 1964; Robert Bone, *Richard Wright,* Minneapolis, 1969.

James Baldwin:

FICTION: *Go Tell It on the Mountain,* 1953; *Giovanni's Room,* 1956; *Another Country,* 1962; *Tell Me How Long the Train's Been Gone,* 1968.

DRAMA: *The Amen Corner,* 1955; *Blues for Mr. Charlie,* 1964.

ESSAYS: *Notes of a Native Son,* 1955; *Nobody Knows My Name,* 1961; *The Fire Next Time,* 1963.

ABOUT: Robert Bone, *The Negro Novel in America,* rev. ed., 1965 (Yale Univ. Press); F. M. Eckman, *The Furious Passage of James Baldwin,* N.Y., 1966; Norman Podhoretz, "In Defense of a Maltreated Best Seller," in *On Contemporary Literature,* ed. by Richard Kostelanetz, N.Y., 1964, 69.

Ralph Ellison:

FICTION: *Invisible Man,* 1952.

ESSAYS: *Shadow and Act,* 1964.

ABOUT: Robert Bone, *The Negro Novelist in America,* rev. ed., 1965 (Yale Univ. Press); Ellin Horowitz, "The Rebirth of the Artist," in *On Contemporary Literature,* ed. by Richard Kostelanetz, N.Y., 1964, 69.

Saul Bellow:

FICTION: *Dangling Man,* 1944; *The Victim,* 1947; *The Adventures of Augie March,* 1953; *Seize the Day,* 1956; *Henderson the Rain King,* 1959; *Herzog,* 1964; *Mr. Sammler's Planet,* 1969.

DRAMA: *The Last Analysis,* 1965.

ABOUT: J. Baumbach, *The Landscape of Nightmare,* N.Y., 1965; D. Galloway, *The Absurd Hero in American Fiction,* Austin, Tex., 1966; P. M. Axthelm, *The Modern Confessional Novel,* New Haven, Conn., 1967; H. M. Harper, Jr., *Desperate Faith,* Chapel Hill, 1967; I. Malin, ed., *Saul Bellow and the Critics,* N.Y., 1967; Keith Opdahl, *The Novels of Saul Bellow,* University Park, Pa., 1967; E. Rovit, *Saul Bellow,* Minneapolis, 1967.

Bernard Malamud:

FICTION: *The Natural,* 1952; *The Assistant,* 1957; *The Magic Barrel,* 1958; *A New Life,* 1961; *Idiots First,* 1963; *The Fixer,* 1966; *Pictures of Fidelman, an Exhibition,* 1969.

ABOUT: L. Fiedler, *The Jew in the American Novel,* N.Y., 1959; L. Fiedler, *No! in Thunder,* Boston, 1960; I. Hassan, *Radical Innocence,* Princeton, N.J., 1961; M. Klein, *After Alienation: American Novels in Mid-Century,* Cleveland, O., 1964; S. Richman, *Bernard Malamud,* N.Y., 1966.

Thornton Wilder:

NOVELS: *The Cabala,* 1926; *The Bridge of San Luis Rey,* 1927; *The Woman of Andros,* 1930; *Heaven's My Destination,* 1935; *The Ides of March,* 1948; *The Eighth Day,* 1967.

DRAMA: **Our Town,* 1938; *The Skin of Our Teeth,* 1942; *The Matchmaker* (comedy), 1954.

ABOUT: Edmund Wilson, *Classics and Commercials,* N.Y., 1950, pp. 81ff.; W. T. Scott, "*Our Town and the Golden Veil,*" *Virginia Quarterly,* January, 1953; R. Burbank, *Thornton Wilder,* N.Y., 1961; B. D. Grebanier, *Thornton Wilder,* Minneapolis, 1964; M. Goldstein, *The Art of Thornton Wilder,* Lincoln, Neb., 1965; D. Haberman, *The Plays of Thornton Wilder,* Middleton, Conn., 1967.

Nathanael West:

FICTION: *The Dream Life of Balso Snell,* 1931; *Miss Lonelyhearts,* 1933; *A Cool Million,* 1934; *The Day of the Locust,* 1939.

ABOUT: J. F. Light, *Nathanael West, an Interpretative Study,* Evanston, Ill., 1961; V. Comerchero, *Nathanael West, the Ironic Prophet,* Syracuse, N.Y., 1964; J. Martin, *Nathanael West, the Art of His Life,* 1970.

Carson McCullers:

WORKS: *The Heart Is a Lonely Hunter,* 1940; *Reflections in a Golden Eye,* 1941; *The Ballad of the Sad Café,* 1943; *The Member of the Wedding,* 1946, 1951; *The Square Root of Wonderful,* 1958; *Clock Without Hands,* 1961.

ABOUT: I. Hassan, *Radical Innocence,* Princeton, 1961; Oliver Evans, *The Ballad of Carson McCullers,* N.Y., 1966; L. Graver, *Carson McCullers,* Minneapolis, 1969.

Flannery O'Connor:

FICTION: *Wise Blood,* 1952; *A Good Man Is Hard to Find,* 1955; *The Violent Bear It Away,* 1960; *Everything That Rises Must Converge* (posthumous, 1965).

NON-FICTION: *Mystery and Manners* (occasional prose, edited by Sally and Robert Fitzgerald), 1969.

ABOUT: Stanley E. Hyman, *Flannery O'Connor,* Minneapolis, 1966; Robert Drake, *Flannery O'Connor* (Contemporary Writers in Christian Perspective Series), 1966; F. J. Hoffman, *The Art of Southern Fiction,* Carbondale, Ill., 1967; Louise Y. Gossett, *Violence in Recent Southern Fiction,* Durham, N.C., 1965.

William Styron:

FICTION: *Lie Down in Darkness,* 1951; *The Long March,* 1955; *Set This House on Fire,* 1960; *The Confessions of Nat Turner,* 1967.

ABOUT: R. G. Davis, "The American Individualist Tradition: Bellow and Styron," in *The Creative Present,* ed. by Balakian and Simmons, N.Y., 1963; D. Stevenson, "William Styron and the Fiction of the Fifties," in *Recent American Fiction: Some Critical Views,* ed. by J. Waldmeir, Boston, 1963; L. Y. Gossett, "The Cost of Freedom: William Styron," in *Violence in Recent Southern Fiction,* Durham, N.C., 1965; R. H. Fossum, *William Styron: A Critical Essay,* 1968; J. H. Clarke, ed., *William Styron's Nat Turner, Ten Black Writers Respond,* Boston, 1968.

Modern American Drama: General

*Barrett H. Clark and George Freedley, eds., *A History of Modern Drama,* N.Y., 1947; John Gassner, *Masters of the Drama,* N.Y., 1954; Joseph Wood Krutch, *The American Drama Since 1918,* N.Y., 1939; *Frank H. O'Hara, *Today in American Drama,* Univ. Chicago Press, 1939; *Eric Bentley, *The Playwright as Thinker,* N.Y., 1946; Burns Mantle, *Contemporary American Playwrights,* N.Y., 1938; E. A. Wright and L. H. Downs, *A Primer for Playgoers,* 2nd ed., 1969; Martin Esslin, *The Theatre of the Absurd,* 1961; Martin Gottfried, *A Theatre Divided,* 1967.

Sidney Kingsley:

**Men in White,* 1933; **Dead End,* 1935; *Ten Million Ghosts,* 1936; *The World We Make,* 1939; *The Patriots,* 1942; *Detective Story,* 1949; *Darkness at Noon,* 1951; *Lunatics and Lovers,* 1955.

ABOUT: John Mason Brown, *Two on the Aisle,* N.Y., 1938.

Maxwell Anderson:

VERSE DRAMAS: *Elizabeth the Queen*, 1930; *Night Over Taos*, 1932; *The Sea Wife*, 1932; *Mary of Scotland*, 1933; *Valley Forge*, 1934; **Winterset*, 1935; *High Tor*, 1937; *The Masque of Kings*, 1937; *Knickerbocker Holiday*, 1938; *Key Largo*, 1939; *Candle in the Wind*, 1941; *Eve of St. Mark*, 1942; *Joan of Lorraine*, 1946; *Anne of the Thousand Days*, 1948.

REALISTIC PROSE DRAMAS: *What Price Glory?*, 1924; *Saturday's Children*, 1927; *Both Your Houses*, 1933; *Storm Operation*, 1944; *Truckline Café*, 1945; *The Bad Seed*, 1954.

ABOUT: Joseph Wood Krutch, *The American Drama Since 1918*, N.Y., 1939; M. D. Bailey, *Maxwell Anderson, the Playwright as Prophet*, N.Y., 1957.

Robert Sherwood:

DRAMA: *The Road to Rome*, 1927; *The Love Nest*, 1927; *The Queen's Husband*, 1928; *Waterloo Bridge*, 1930; *This Is New York*, 1930; *Reunion in Vienna*, 1931; *The Petrified Forest*, 1935; *Idiot's Delight*, 1936; *Tovarich*, 1936; *Abe Lincoln in Illinois*, 1938; *There Shall Be No Night*, 1940.

NOVEL: *The Virtuous Knight*, 1931.

HISTORY: *Roosevelt and Hopkins: An Intimate History*, 1938.

ABOUT: John Mason Brown, *Seeing Things*, N.Y., 1946; R. B. Shuman, *Robert E. Sherwood*, N.Y., 1964.

Clifford Odets:

**Waiting for Lefty*, 1935; **Awake and Sing*, 1935; *Till the Day I Die*, 1935; *Paradise Lost*, 1935; *Golden Boy*, 1937; *Rocket to the Moon*, 1938; *Night Music*, 1940; *Clash by Night*, 1941; *The Big Knife*, 1948; *The Country Girl*, 1950; *The Flowering Peach*, 1954.

ABOUT: Burns Mantle, *Contemporary American Playwrights*, N.Y., 1938; R. B. Shuman, *Clifford Odets*, N.Y., 1962.

S. N. Behrman:

ORIGINAL DRAMAS: *The Second Man*, 1927; *Meteor*, 1929; *Serena Blandish*, 1929; *Brief Moment*, 1929; *Biography*, 1932; *Rain from Heaven*, 1934; *End of Summer*, 1936; *Wine of Choice*, 1938; *No Time for Comedy*, 1939; *The Talley Method*, 1941; *The Cold Wind and the Warm*, 1959; *Lord Pengo*, 1963.

ADAPTATIONS: *Amphitryon 38*, 1937; *The Pirate*, 1942; *Jacobowsky and the Colonel*, 1944; *Jane*, 1952; *Fanny*, 1954.

NON-FICTION: *Duveen*, 1952; *The Worcester Account*, 1954; *Portrait of Max* (biography of Beerbohm), 1960; *The Suspended Drawing Room,* (collection of pieces for *New Yorker*), 1965.

NOVEL: *The Burning Glass,* 1968.

ABOUT: E. M. Gagey, *Revolution in American Drama,* Columbia U.P., 1947.

Lillian Hellman:

The Children's Hour, 1934; *Days to Come,* 1936; *The Little Foxes,* 1939; *Watch on the Rhine,* 1941; *The Searching Wind,* 1944; *Another Part of the Forest,* 1946; *The Autumn Garden,* 1951; *Toys in the Attic,* 1960.

AUTOBIOGRAPHY: *An Unfinished Woman: A Memoir,* 1969.

ABOUT: Burns Mantle, *Contemporary American Playwrights,* N.Y., 1938; Harry Gilroy, *"The Bigger the Lie," New York Times,* December 14, 1952.

Arthur Miller:

DRAMA: *All My Sons,* 1947; *Death of a Salesman,* 1949; *The Crucible,* 1953; *A View from the Bridge,* 1955; *After the Fall,* 1964; *The Price,* 1968.

FICTION: *Focus,* 1945; *I Don't Need You Any More* (stories), 1967.

ABOUT: John Mason Brown, *Still Seeing Things,* N.Y., 1950; Brooks Atkinson, *Broadway Scrapbook,* N.Y., 1947; R. G. Hogan, *Arthur Miller,* Minneapolis, 1964; L. Moss, *Arthur Miller,* N.Y., 1967; B. Nelson, *Arthur Miller, Portrait of a Playwright,* N.Y., 1970.

Tennessee Williams:

PLAYS: *Battle of Angels,* 1940; *The Glass Menagerie,* 1944; *Twenty-Seven Wagons Full of Cotton,* 1945; *A Streetcar Named Desire,* 1947; *Summer and Smoke,* 1948; *The Rose Tattoo,* 1950; *Camino Real,* 1953; *Cat on a Hot Tin Roof,* 1955; *Orpheus Descending,* 1957; *Suddenly Last Summer,* 1957; *Sweet Bird of Youth,* 1959; *The Night of the Iguana,* 1962; *The Milk Train Doesn't Stop Here Anymore,* 1963; *Small Craft Warnings,* 1972.

FICTION: *The Roman Spring of Mrs. Stone,* 1950; *One Arm,* 1950; *Hard Candy,* 1954.

ABOUT: S. L. Falk, *Tennessee Williams,* N.Y., 1961; N. M. Tischler, *Tennessee Williams: Rebellious Puritan,* N.Y., 1961; Edwina Dakin Williams, *Remember Me to Tom,* N.Y., 1963; F. Donahue, *The Dramatic World of Tennessee Williams,* N.Y., 1964; E. M. Jackson, *The Broken World of Tennessee Williams,* Madison, Wisc., 1965.

Edward Albee:

PLAYS: *The Zoo Story,* 1958; *The Sandbox,* 1959; *The Death of Bessie Smith,* 1959; *The American Dream,* 1960; *Who's Afraid of Virginia Woolf?,* 1962; *Tiny Alice,* 1964; *A Delicate Balance,* 1966; *Everything in the Garden,* 1967; *The Box and Quotations from Chairman Mao Tse-tung,* 1968; *All Over,* 1971.

ABOUT: M. Esslin, *The Theatre of the Absurd,* N.Y., 1961; R. Cohn, *Edward Albee,* Minneapolis, 1969.

Lorraine Hansberry:

PLAYS: *A Raisin in the Sun,* 1959; *The Sign in Sidney Brustein's Window,* 1964.

ABOUT: Robert Nemiroff, "The 101 'Final' Performances of Sidney Brustein," and adapted by, *To Be Young, Gifted, and Black,* 1969.

Modern American Poetry: General

Henry W. Wells, *The American Way of Poetry,* Columbia U.P., 1943; Edward Davison, *Some Modern Poets,* N.Y., 1928; Rica Brenner, *Poets of Our Time,* N.Y., 1941; Margaret C. Anderson, *My Thirty Years' War,* N.Y., 1930; *Cleanth Brooks and R. P. Warren, *Understanding Poetry,* N.Y., 1938; Louis Untermeyer, ed., *Modern American Poetry,* Mid-Century Edition (anthology), N.Y., 1950; M. L. Rosenthal, *The New Poets* (American and British Poetry Since World War II), N.Y., 1967; J. M. Brinnin and B. Read, *The Modern Poets* (anthology), 2nd ed., N.Y., 1970.

Ezra Pound:

A Lume Spento, 1908; *Personae,* 1909; *Exultations,* 1909; *Provença,* 1910; *Canzoni,* 1911; *Ripostes,* 1912; *Lustra and Other Poems,* 1917; *Hugh Selwyn Mauberley,* 1920; *Personae,* 1926 (includes poems from the earlier *Personae* and from *Exultations*); *The Cantos of Ezra Pound,* 1948 (also published in several sections under other titles, 1925–1955). Add *Thrones: 96–109 de los cantares,* 1959; *Drafts and Fragments of Cantos cx–cxvii,* 1968.

ABOUT: *Hugh Kenner, *The Poetry of Ezra Pound,* Norfolk, Conn., 1950; John J. Espey, *Ezra Pound's Mauberley, a Study in Composition,* Univ. Calif. Press, 1955; Peter Russell, ed., *An Examination of Ezra Pound* (collection of essays by various critics), Norfolk, Conn., 1950; G. S. Fraser, *Ezra Pound,* N.Y., 1960; C. Norman, *Ezra Pound,* N.Y., 1960; E. C. Mullins, *This Different Individual,* N.Y., 1961; G. Dekker, *The Cantos of Ezra Pound,* N.Y., 1963; D. Davie, *Ezra Pound: Poet as*

Sculptor, N.Y., 1964; N. Stock, *Poet in Exile,* N.Y., 1964; R. Goodwin, *The Influence of Ezra Pound,* N.Y., 1966; D. Pearlman, *The Barb of Time,* N.Y., 1969; H. Witemeyer, *The Poetry of Ezra Pound: Forms, Renewal,* Berkeley, 1969.

T. S. Eliot:

POETRY COLLECTIONS: *Prufrock and Other Observations,* 1917; *Poems,* 1919; *The Waste Land,* 1922; *Poems, 1909–1925,* 1925; *Ash Wednesday,* 1930; *Four Quarters,* 1943.

ESSAYS: *The Sacred Wood,* 1920; *For Lancelot Andrewes,* 1928.

DRAMA: *Murder in the Cathedral,* 1935; *Family Reunion,* 1939; *The Cocktail Party,* 1949; *The Confidential Clerk,* 1953; *The Elder Statesman,* 1959.

ABOUT: *F. O. Matthiessen, *The Achievement of T. S. Eliot,* Oxford U.P., 1947; *Elizabeth Drew, *T. S. Eliot, the Design of His Poetry,* N.Y., 1949; *George Williamson, *A Reader's Guide to T. S. Eliot,* N.Y., 1957; B. Rajan, ed., *T. S. Eliot, a Study of His Writings by Several Hands,* London, 1947; S. Lucy, *T. S. Eliot and the Idea of Tradition,* N.Y., 1960; D. E. S. Maxwell, *The Poetry of T. S. Eliot,* N.Y., 1961; H. Howarth, *Notes on Some Figures Behind T. S. Eliot,* Boston, 1964; N. Frye, *T. S. Eliot,** N.Y., 1963; G. Jung, *Approach to the Purpose,* N.Y., 1964; L. Unger, *T. S. Eliot, Moments and Patterns,** Minneapolis, 1966; E. M. Browne, *The Making of T. S. Eliot's Plays,* London, 1969.

William Carlos Williams:

POETRY: *Poems,* 1909; *The Tempers,* 1913; *Al Que Quiere,* 1917; *Kora in Hell,* 1921; *Sour Grapes,* 1922; *Spring and All,* 1923; *Collected Poems,* 1934; *The Complete Collected Poems,* 1938; *The Wedge,* 1944; *Paterson* (Books I–IV), 1946–51; *The Desert Music and Other Poems,* 1954; *Journey to Love,* 1955; *Paterson, Book Five,* 1958; *Pictures from Breughel and Other Poems,* 1962.

NOVELS: *A Voyage to Pagany,* 1928; *White Mule,* 1937; *In the Money,* 1940; *The Build-Up,* 1952.

ESSAYS: *In the American Grain,* 1925.

STORIES: *The Knife of the Times and Other Stories,* 1932; *Make Light of It,* 1950; *The Farmers' Daughters,* collected stories, 1961.

DRAMA: *A Dream of Love,* 1948; *Many Loves, and Other Plays,* 1961.

AUTOBIOGRAPHY: *Autobiography,* 1951.

ABOUT: Lloyd Frankenberg, *Pleasure Dome,* N.Y., 1949; Vivienne Koch, *William Carlos Williams,* Norfolk, Conn., 1950; J. M. Brinnin, *William Carlos Williams,* Minneapolis, 1963; A. B. Ostrom, *The Poetic World of William Carlos Williams,* Carbondale, 1966; W. S. Peterson, *An Approach to Paterson,* New Haven, 1967; J. Guimond, *The Art of William Carlos Williams,* Urbana, 1968; S. Paul, *The Music of Survival,*

Urbana, 1968; T. R. Whitaker, *William Carlos Williams,* N.Y., 1968.

Wallace Stevens:

POETRY: *Harmonium,* 1923; *Ideas of Order,* 1935; *Owl's Clover,* 1936; *The Man with the Blue Guitar,* 1937; *Parts of a World,* 1942; *Esthétique Du Mal,* 1944; *A Primitive Like an Orb,* 1948; *The Auroras of Autumn,* 1950; *Opus Posthumous,* 1957; *Letters,* 1966.

ESSAY: *"The Noble Rider and the Sound of Words,"* in Allen Tate, ed., *The Language of Poetry,* Princeton U.P., 1942.

ABOUT: *William Van O'Connor, *The Shaping Spirit: A Study of Wallace Stevens,* Univ. Chicago Press, 1950; Ivor Winters, *The Anatomy of Nonsense,* Norfolk, Conn., 1943; A. Brown, *The Achievement of Wallace Stevens,* Philadelphia, 1962; D. Fuchs, *The Comic Spirit of Wallace Stevens,* Durham, N.C., 1963; R. H. Pearce, *The Act of the Mind,* Baltimore, 1963; J. M. Reddel, *The Clairvoyant Eye: the Poetry and Poetics of Wallace Stevens,* Baton Rouge, 1965; E. P. Nassau, *Wallace Stevens: an Anatomy of Figuration,* Philadelphia, 1965; F. A. Doggett, *Stevens' Poetry of Thought,* Baltimore, 1966; H. J. Stern, *Wallace Stevens: Art of Uncertainty,* Ann Arbor, 1966; W. Burney, *Wallace Stevens,* N.Y., 1968; F. Lentricchia, *The Gaiety of Language,* Berkeley, 1968; Merle E. Brown, *Wallace Stevens: The Poem as Act,** Detroit, 1970.

Archibald MacLeish:

POETRY: *Tower of Ivory,* 1917; *The Happy Marriage,* 1924; *The Pot of Earth,* 1925; *Nobodaddy,* 1925; *Streets in the Moon,* 1926; *New Found Land,* 1930; *Public Speech,* 1936; *Actfive,* 1948; *Songs for Eve,* 1954; *Collected Poems,* 1952; *J. B., a Play,* 1958; *Herakles: a Play in Verse,* 1967; *The Wild Old Wicked Man and Other Poems,* 1968.

NARRATIVE POEMS: *The Hamlet of A. MacLeish,* 1928; *Conquistador,* 1932.

RADIO SCRIPTS: *The Fall of the City,* 1937; *Air Raid,* 1938.

ESSAYS: *A Time to Speak,* 1941; *The Irresponsibles,* 1940; *The American Cause,* 1941.

ABOUT: Edmund Wilson, *"Aachibald MacLeish and the Word,"* in *Classics and Commercials,* N.Y., 1950; S. L. Falk, *Archibald MacLeish,* New Haven, 1965.

E. E. Cummings

POETRY: *Tulips and Chimneys,* 1923; *&,* 1925; *XLI Poems,* 1925; *is 5,* 1926; *ViVa,* 1931; *no thanks,* 1935; *Collected Poems,* 1938; *50 Poems,* 1940; *One Times One,* 1944; *Kaipe,* 1950; *Poems, 1923–1954,* 1955.

PLAYS: *Him,* 1927; *Santa Claus,* 1946.

PROSE: *The Enormous Room,* 1922; *Eimi,* 1933; *i: six nonlectures,* 1953.

ABOUT: M. L. Rosenthal, *"Mr. Joy and Mr. Gloom," New Republic,* September 18, 1950; *Life,* November 24, 1952 (biogr. sketch); M. N. S. Whitely, *"Savagely a Maker," Poetry,* July, 1947; W. Friedman, *E. E. Cummings, the Art of His Poetry,* Baltimore, 1960; W. Friedman, *E. E. Cummings, the Growth of a Writer,* Carbondale, 1964; B. A. Marks, *E. E. Cummings,* N.Y., 1964; C. Norman, *E. E. Cummings, the Magic Maker,* N.Y., 1964; R. E. Wegner, *The Poetry and Prose of E. E. Cummings,* N.Y., 1965.

Marianne Moore:

POETRY: *Poems,* 1921; *Observations,* 1924; *Selected Poems,* 1935; *The Pangolin and Other Verse,* 1936; *What Are Years?,* 1941; *Nevertheless,* 1944; *Collected Poems,* 1951; *Tell Me, Tell Me; Granite, Steel, and Other Topics* (Poems and Prose), 1966; *Complete Poems,* 1967.

TRANSLATION: *The Fables of La Fontaine,* 1954.

ESSAYS: *Predilections,* 1955.

ABOUT: Lloyd Frankenberg, *Pleasure Dome,* N.Y., 1949; T. S. Eliot, *"Introduction to Marianne Moore," in Selected Poems,* N.Y., 1935; Winthrop Sargeant, *"Humility, Concentration, and Gusto," New Yorker,* February 16, 1957; Charles Tomlinson, *"Abundance, Not Too Much: The Poetry of Marianne Moore," Sewanee Review,* LXV:4 (Autumn, 1957), pp. 677ff; B. F. Engle, *Marianne Moore,* N.Y., 1964; J. Garrigue, *Marianne Moore,* Minneapolis, 1965; G. W. Nitchie, *Marianne Moore; an Introduction to the Poetry,* N.Y., 1969.

Langston Hughes:

POETRY: *The Weary Blues,* 1926; *Fine Clothes to the Jew,* 1927; *The Dream-Keeper,* 1932; *Shakespeare in Harlem,* 1942; *Fields of Wonder,* 1947; *One-way Ticket,* 1949; *Montage of a Dream Deferred,* 1951; *Ask Your Mama,* 1961; *The Panther and the Lash,* 1967.

DRAMA: *Five Plays,* 1963.

SELECTED PROSE: *The Big Sea,* 1940; *The Best of Simple,* 1961.

ABOUT: James A. Emanuel, *Langston Hughes,* N.Y., 1967.

Theodore Roethke:

POETRY: *Open House,* 1941; *The Lost Son and Other Poems,* 1948; *Praise to the End,* 1951; *The Waking,* 1953; *Words for the Wind,* 1958; *I Am! Says the Lamb,* 1961; *The Far Field,* 1964; *Collected Poems,* 1966.

ABOUT: R. J. Mills, Jr., *Theodore Roethke,* Minneapolis, 1963; K. Malkoff, *Theodore Roethke: an Introduction to the Poetry,* N.Y., 1966; A. Seager, *The Glass House; the life of Theodore Roethke,* N.Y., 1968.

Robert Lowell:

POETRY: *Land of Unlikeness,* 1944; *Lord Weary's Castle,* 1946; *The Mills of the Kavanaughs,* 1951; *Life Studies,* 1959; *Imitations,* 1961;

For the Union Dead, 1964; *Near the Ocean,* 1967; *Notebook 1967–68,* 1969.

PLAYS: *The Old Glory,* 1965; *Prometheus Bound,* 1969.

ABOUT: J. Mazzaro, *The Poetic Themes of Robert Lowell,* Ann Arbor, 1965; W. J. Martz, *The Achievement of Robert Lowell,* N.Y., 1966; M. L. Rosenthal, *The New Poets: American and British Poetry Since World War II,* N.Y., 1967; Jay Martin, *Robert Lowell,* Minneapolis, 1970.

Some Younger Poets:

Richard Eberhart: *A Bravery of Heaven,* 1930; *Reading the Spirit,* 1936; *Song and Idea,* 1940; *Poems New and Selected,* 1944; *Poems 1946–1953,* 1953; *The Quarry,* 1964; *Thirty-one Sonnets,* 1967; *Shifts of Being,* 1968.

Kenneth Patchen: *Before the Brave,* 1936; *First Will & Testament,* 1939; *The Journal of Albion Moonlight,* 1941; *The Dark Kingdom,* 1942; *Memoirs of a Shy Pornographer,* 1945; *Sleepers Awake,* 1946; *Red Wine and Yellow Hair,* 1949; *Hallelujah Anyway,* 1966; *But Even So,* 1968.

Delmore Schwartz: *In Dreams Begin Responsibilities,* 1938; *Genesis,* 1943; *Vaudeville for a Princess and Other Poems,* 1950.

Karl Shapiro: *Person, Place, and Thing,* 1942; *V-Letter and Other Poems,* 1944; *Essay on Rime,* 1945; *Trial of a Poet and Other Poems,* 1947; *Poems, 1940–1953,* 1953; *The Bourgeois Poet,* 1964; *White-haired Lover,* 1968.

Randall, Jarrell: *Blood for a Stranger,* 1942; *Little Friend, Little Friend,* 1945; *Losses,* 1948; *Selected Poems,* 1955; *A Sad Heart at the Supermarket,* 1962; *The Lost World,* 1965.

Peter Viereck: *Terror and Decorum,* 1948; *Strike Through the Mask,* 1950; *The First Morning,* 1952; *Shame and Glory of the Intellectuals* (prose), 1953; *New and Selected Poems,* 1967.

Some Younger Younger Poets:

Howard Nemerov: *New and Selected Poems,* 1960; *The Next Room of the Dream,* 1962; *The Blue Swallows,* 1968. Richard Wilbur: *The Beautiful Changes and Other Poems,* 1947; *Ceremony and Other Poems,* 1950; *Things of This World,* 1956; *Advice to a Prophet and Other Poems,* 1959. W. D. Snodgrass: *Heart's Needle,* 1957. Donald Hall: *A Roof of Tiger Lilies,* 1964. Denise Levertov: *Overland to the Islands,* 1958; *With Eyes at the Back of Our Heads,* 1959; *The Jacob's Ladder,* 1961; *O Taste and See,* 1964; *The Sorrow Dance,* 1967. Sylvia Plath: *The Colossus and Other Poems,* 1960; *The Bell Jar* (novel), 1963; *Ariel,* 1965. Northrop Frye: *Fearful Symmetry: A Study of William Blake,* 1947; *Anatomy of Criticism**, 1957; *The Well-Tempered Critic,* 1963; *The Educated Imagination,* 1963; *T. S. Eliot,* 1963; *A Natural Perspective,* 1965; *The Return of Eden,* 1965; *The Fools of Time,* 1967; *The Modern Century,* 1967.

INDEX

CONTEMPORARY LITERATURE
OF THE WESTERN WORLD

VOLUM

RECENT AMERICAN LITERATURE

AFTER 1930 BY DONALD HEINEY AND LENTHIEL H. DOWI

Contemporary Literature of the Western World is a 4-volume series presenting topical survey of the main currents of modern literature. The works of all maj figures are analyzed; their accomplishments are set against a world backgrou The series is a handy 4-volume reference for students, scholars, editors, and general readers.

Volume 1: Continental European Literature
Volume 2: Contemporary British Literature
Volume 3: Recent American Literature—To 1930
Volume 4: Recent American Literature—After 1930

BARRON'S EDUCATIONAL SERIES, INC.